Embodied Resistance

Embodied Resistance

Challenging the Norms, Breaking the Rules

Edited by Chris Bobel and Samantha Kwan

Vanderbilt University Press
Nashville

© 2011 by Vanderbilt University Press
Nashville, Tennessee 37235
All rights reserved
First printing 2011

This book is printed on acid-free paper
derived from sustainable sources.
Manufactured in the United States of America

Library of Congress Cataloging-in-Publication Data

Embodied resistance : challenging the norms, breaking the rules /
edited by Chris Bobel and Samantha Kwan.
p. cm.
Includes bibliographical references and index.
ISBN 978-0-8265-1786-9 (cloth edition : alk. paper)
ISBN 978-0-8265-1787-6 (pbk. edition : alk. paper)
1. Human body—Social aspects. 2. Mind and body. 3. Manners
and customs. 4. Women—Psychology. I. Bobel, Chris, 1963–
II. Kwan, Samantha.
HM636.E423 2011
306.4—dc22
2011003007

For Gracie, no matter what
    —C.B.

For Scott and Thals, my support and my smile
    —S.K.

Contents

Foreword

Rose Weitz

In 1968, at the age of sixteen, I talked two of my girlfriends into wearing slacks rather than skirts to school one frigid winter day. At the time, I knew nothing of the nascent feminist movement—let alone of "embodied resistance"—but at a truly visceral level it seemed unfair that only girls should have to suffer the cold and seemed wrong not to protest that unfairness. Unfortunately, I also knew nothing about creating effective resistance: threatened with suspension, and with neither an ideological grounding nor supportive others to turn to, the three of us caved immediately.

That same year, I decided to lose my virginity. Frankly, pleasure had nothing to do with it. I was (and remain) a deeply logical person, and at some level, I just couldn't figure out why a natural physical act should be so freighted with meaning for my parents and other adults. Nor could I understand why adults' fears about my body (or, more specifically, my virginity) should justify constraining my life so much more than the lives of my male peers. Combined with the realization that boys really wanted sex and the (not quite accurate) belief that having sex would cost me little, I decided to get the issue off my personal table by choosing my own time, place, and partner. Which I did, though not particularly wisely. After that (and a bit more "after" than I'd care to admit), I sought out the one place that would give birth control pills to a minor and thus support my somewhat inchoate resistance. (Thank you, Planned Parenthood.)

Six months later, after experiencing a slew of side effects from the high-dosage pills then prescribed, I fought Planned Parenthood—whose central mission was controlling population growth, not protecting women's health—to get a (far-safer) diaphragm instead. By this time, I was a freshman at Lehman College in New York City. I became a feminist during my second semester, when, as a try-out for the school newspaper, I covered the first meeting of Lehman's Women's Liberation Group and discovered a way of looking at the world that helped explain my previous experiences of embodied constraint and resistance. Feminism also helped me articulate why some of my professors would not call on me even when mine was the only hand raised in the room, why my (former) mother-in-law brought me a broom and mop as a house-warming present, why I was so angry about her choice of "gifts," and why I swallowed that anger.

The next semester, I began taking the subway from the Bronx to Manhattan, where, every Monday night, thirty or so of us would discuss a (mimeographed) chapter in what eventually became the book *Our Bodies, Ourselves*. The next year, I rode the subway for two hours to the other side of the city to hear Carol Downer and Lorraine Rothman, two of the founders of the U.S. women's health movement, explain the health and political benefits of viewing one's own cervix and vagina and to watch them demonstrate—in front of four hundred women—how to do so. I returned with a sense of exhilaration and my own speculum, as well as a new awareness of how, with resources, commitment, and a coherent political perspective, individual embodied resistance could lead to broad social change. Around the same time, I first learned of female orgasms (of any sort, never mind "vaginal" versus "clitoral") in my consciousness-raising group. All these experiences led me to decide on a career as a sociologist focusing on women's health.

My interest in researching women's health has continued throughout my career. But by the late 1990s, like numerous other scholars, I found myself increasingly drawn to research that went beyond issues of health and illness and looked more broadly at women's experiences of the body. My subsequent reading and research eventually inspired me to publish a collection that would reflect this emerging area of study. In the proposal for my anthology, *The Politics of Women's Bodies: Sexuality, Appearance, and Behavior*, I argued that the book would find a wide audience in the emerging field of "body studies" and the growing number of courses in that field. I was bluffing. Although I hoped the field would grow, I certainly wasn't counting on it. My fears, however, quickly proved unfounded. *The Politics of Women's Bodies* is now in its third edition, and courses on women (or gender) and the body can now be found across fields and across the country.

As one of the first anthologies in the field, my book aimed to cover a wide range of topics and approaches. Thus among other things, I included articles on both the bodily constraints women face and on how women resist such constraints.

Since the book's initial publication, much of the most exciting research on the body has delved more deeply into bodily resistance among women and, most recently, among men and transpeople. Until now, however, this research has largely taken the form of individual studies, each focusing on one form of resistance in one (usually small) population. *Embodied Resistance: Challenging the Norms, Breaking the Rules* is the first book to pull the best new ethnographic research on body "rule breaking" together into a coherent whole.

For this book, Chris Bobel and Samantha Kwan have collected an exhilarating mix of scholarly articles and personal narratives that explore how people are challenging the gendered norms, medical definitions of health and illness, and other social structures that have long constrained individuals' bodies and lives. My younger self would have loved to meet the young women described here who foreswear shaving for a semester or the young roller derby athletes who flaunt their sexuality, athletic prowess, and bodies of all shapes and sizes, while my current middle-aged self is cheered by the Red Hat Society women in these pages who refuse to let age render them invisible and the menopausal women who refuse to hide their hot flashes.

All the articles in this anthology are engaging, thought-provoking, and generally spectacular. Individually, each offers a fascinating and nuanced example and discussion of resistance, in settings ranging from the dominatrix dungeon to a queer-friendly church to a vulvar specialty clinic, and in voices ranging from those of belly-dancing mothers to gay "bears" and transgender Koreans. Taken together, the articles provide readers for the first time with a full view of the nature, sources, and consequences of embodied resistance. Through so doing, the articles address the broad swatch of theoretically and practically important issues embedded in embodied resistance and clarify just how complex, contextual, and contingent such resistance really is. For all these reasons, scholars, students, and general readers should all find something to ponder and to enjoy in this book.

Acknowledgments

Assembling this collection has been a humbling experience that has made clear the necessity of intellectual community. If it weren't for the eager readers of e-mail lists, newsletters, and blogs, this book would not exist. While we are aware that interrogation of embodied resistance is limited and partial, we cannot deny the rich and vibrant scholarship that is emerging and that we had the privilege of engaging as we made the tough choices of selecting pieces. Thus, we want first to thank each person who submitted his or her work for our review; every piece taught us something valuable and enduring. We also extend special thanks to Claudia Malacrida, Michael Atkinson, and Salvador Vidal-Ortiz, who supported the project and went out of their way to help us connect with scholars and writers.

Our editor, Michael Ames, stunned us with his incisive critiques (and lightning-speed turnaround). He embraced the project almost immediately, which deepens our pride that we signed with Vanderbilt University Press. We thank the two external reviewers who helped identify gaps in the collection, reconsider some of our assumptions, and smooth out some of the "rough spots." We also acknowledge Susan Ostrander, Frinde Maher, Anna Sandoval, Sarah Sobieraj, and Julie Nelson for their spot-on feedback on our introduction. We are further indebted to Camille Nelson for her meticulous manuscript preparation, Keiisha Pillai for her invaluable research assistance with the pedagogical resources, and Marcia Underwood for suggesting the design for our cover.

We are delighted to frame this book with a foreword and an afterword by the feminist embodiment studies pioneers Rose Weitz and Barbara Katz Rothman. Having long admired their work, we are immeasurably grateful for their wise words.

Finally, we express our deep appreciation to the people at the center of this book—the many people, from many social locations, who take risks, offer analyses, and push us all to think critically and coherently about embodiment. This book is about them, after all, and we hope that reading it engenders respect and admiration for those who "challenge the norms and break the rules" and inspire us all to take the risks that make our world a safer and more livable place for every*body*, everyone.

Embodied Resistance

Introduction

Few classroom discussions generate as much enthusiasm as those about the body.

Circumcision. Childhood vaccinations. Preschool beauty pageants. Steroids and sports. Designer vaginas. Hair straightening. Drag queens and kings. Burkas. Eyelid surgery. Sexual dysfunction. End-of-life care.

Since nearly everyone has a passionate opinion, knows someone who ———, or both, these topics inspire dynamic discussions and spirited disagreements. But despite the widely varying views expressed about "the body," people tend to agree on this point: when it comes to the body, there's tremendous pressure to play by the rules.

After all, the empirical evidence is compelling that bodies (and the people who inhabit them) are vulnerable to social norms of looking and behaving. There is no shortage of rules dictating what we should or should not wear, inhale, and ingest; the size, shape, and overall appearance of our bodies; and even our gestures, gait, and posture (Bartky 1988).

Yet this abundance of norms in no way implies their universality in form, content, and potential embodiment. Norms are complex and varied: an employer's mandate that women employees wear makeup differs from the unspoken workplace belief that women employees who wear makeup come across as more competent (Dellinger and Williams 1997).[1] To be sure, norms vary in form, but they also are dynamic and contingent upon time and place. Norms about natural bodily processes—regulating how we should eat, blow our noses, or even sleep—have evolved throughout the civilizing process, requiring increasingly greater restraint (Elias 2000). Bodily forms deemed "physical capital" are also subject to ongoing re-evaluation in social spaces where groups vie to define which bodily configurations are superior (Bourdieu 1984, 1985). Ideologies and practices of age, class, gender, sexuality, and race and ethnicity embedded in these particular times and places inform these sets of expectations.

Despite these variations, norms still have the potential to exert control. To state the obvious, norms *normalize*; they exert a near-magnetic effect on people, compelling them, often unwittingly, to fit in or risk censure, condemnation, and in some instances, danger.

As norms press on us, many avenues of action surface. The typical female college student may not be fair skinned, light haired, and thin, but chances are she has observed how others and the media valorize these ideals. She might actively work to lose weight, perhaps even dye her hair or use skin lighteners, in an attempt to conform to this Western beauty imperative. She might also elect not to do such things and instead hide her hips and belly with "slimming" clothes. Then again, she might fully embrace, even flaunt, her body and encourage her friends to do the same.

Here's where it gets interesting.

Cultural theorists have long asserted that social relations of power produce bodies that are disciplined and resistant (see, e.g., Foucault 1995). Typically through a feminist lens, body studies scholars interrogate *embodiment*, or the sociocultural relations that act on individual bodies.[2] These scholars refer to the "somatic society," a sociocultural context in which we understand the political and the personal, as well as the passive and the agentic, in and through the body (Turner 1996). In other words, we know that humans can be at once rule-bound and wonderfully inventive agents of social change. We can enact the mandates—trudging along, submitting and rationalizing—but we can also assert ourselves and break away. To quote Arthur Frank (1991, 47), "the 'government of the body' is never fixed, but always contains oppositional spaces."

To date, much scholarly analysis has focused on the structural forces that constrain agency. That is, the field has favored the study of the production of *disciplined* bodies—how bodies are constructed through cultural ideologies and social structures. But what can we learn from the (relatively) undisciplined, the so-called body outlaws?[3] What happens when we scrutinize the body as a site of opposition?

A growing body of empirical work examines resistance and the role of agency or "the body reacting back and affecting discourse" (Shilling 1993, 81). For example, researchers of the body have explored the medical power relations between women and their physicians (Davis 1988), the psychological and social tensions of extreme body modification, such as body art and repeat plastic surgeries (Pitts 2003, 2007), the complex interplay of resistance and accommodation with women's body hair norms (Weitz 2001), and how aerobics classes, hair salons, and fat acceptance organizations reproduce body norms yet simultaneously provide conceptual spaces to challenge cultural imperatives (Gimlin 2002). Indeed, all of these studies have called attention to how self-reflective actors are not merely acted on; they also demonstrate the doings and the "not doings" (Mullaney 2006) of resistance.

While scholars often allude to the tension between compliance and self-determination through the structure-agency dichotomy, what we learn from this research is that resistance is not an either-or story. For example, women who undergo cosmetic surgery insist they are acting out of their own volition because they feel they are "worth it." At the same time, their surgeries collectively reify hegemonic beauty norms, even pushing the limits of unattainable cultural beauty ideals (Gagné and McGaughey 2002). Every action thus potentially contains elements of both resistance and accommodation. At times, resistance is a clever and complicated dance of negotiation, and it is rarely a zero-sum game (Weitz 2001).

Thus, like norms, resistance is multifaceted. Scholars have theorized at length the many faces of resistance, involving lesser and greater degrees of intentionality and recognition by the many actors involved, that are typically threaded together by the common theme of "oppositional action" (Hollander and Einwohner 2004). We define embodied resistance, then, as oppositional action or nonaction that defies contextual body norms, and it comes in many forms. In the Christian Science practice of physical healing through prayer, embodied resistance may be both intentional and recognized by agents, targets, and observers; whereas in veganism, it may also be intentional but sometimes go unrecognized. At times, resistance may not even be an initial choice, evident with, say, conjoined twins who are born with anatomies that do not comport with conventional medical understandings of "normal."

Embodied Resistance contributes new analyses of what has been deemed inappropriate, disgusting, private, or forbidden in particular social contexts. It focuses on the exceptions to the socializing conformity thesis of embodiment and on what resistance can reveal about concepts foundational to the interdisciplinary study of the body: agency, identity, conflict, privilege, reclamation, negotiation, performativity, and intentionality. It tries to get at these slippery constructs by accessing the lived and messy realities of people from various backgrounds, social locations, and political orientations.

Because we are invested in resistance from the perspective of the resisters, we choose to feature primarily original ethnographic research and personal essays that center attention on the experiences of the rebels themselves. Through field studies, in-depth interviews, and content analyses, we present a range of voices—never to be mistaken as the sole voice representing a given group of resistors or a type of resistance. In a similar vein, recognizing the broad spectrum of individuals who subvert cultural body scripts and conventions, *Embodied Resistance* acknowledges that it by no means captures all forms and accounts. Indeed, we lament our failure to include enough high-quality, sociologically informed, and original works on masculinities and queer sexualities, along with globally situated studies. The body, after all, is not an exclusively Western, feminine, or heteronormative preoccupation. How does heteronormativity, and increasingly homonormativity, shape doing and not doing resistance? What do studies on men and masculinities and, say, body work and medicalization tell us about embodied resistance? These absences in the collection force important questions about the politics of research—who gets studied, who gets neglected, and why. Indeed this is our less-than-tacit call to colleagues and inquisitive students to take up the investigations of resistance to body norms that more directly engage intersectional analyses that bring to the fore how race, ethnicity, sexual identity, and geographic location shape transgression.

Through the voices captured in this collection, however, we are able to address an array of questions about resistance; their answers insist that we reckon with a multitude of issues.

- Why do some resist while most of us comply, even if we do so grudgingly? What motivates the outliers?
- Who are the resisters? Are there certain conditions under which resistance is more possible? What role does privilege play? What particular structures, institutions, ideologies, and discourses influence who resists and when and where?
- And, we must ask, what is resistance, anyway? What isn't resistance? What kinds of negotiations, of both identities and meanings, constitute resistance? Is resistance necessarily intentional?
- We also ponder perhaps the most fundamental of concerns: How does resistance occur? In an increasingly connected and global world, how does technology facilitate or hinder resistance?
- Finally, what are the consequences of resistance to body norms, at the individual level of the resister and for the rest of us? How does resistance influence identity at the level of the individual and of the collective? How does rule breaking either build up or tear apart community? Does resistance

bend or even break the corporeal status quo? Or might resistance—
ironically—reinforce the very norms it seeks to weaken?

Four interrelated parts make up *Embodied Resistance*. Concepts central to the study of
resistance to the somatic norm anchor each part. We acknowledge the limits of such
an exercise, since many of the concepts are not confined to their tidy sections. Indeed,
we are well aware of the hazards (and ironies) of oversimplifying for the purposes of
categorization in a collection about the perils and promise of not fitting in.

Each of the sixteen research-based chapters is written with the student in mind—
accessible, theoretically and methodologically transparent, and rich with the voices of
the actors at the center of inquiry. Eight personal narratives capture their respective
parts' main themes and drive home the often very intimate issues this emergent literature probes. For this reason, we label these narratives "Living Resistance," in contrast
to the research chapters that focus on studying resistance.

Part I, "Rewriting Gender Scripts," opens the book by taking up a favorite preoccupation of body studies—social and cultural constructions of hegemonic femininities and masculinities. The pieces in this section consider the bending, twisting, and
even breaking of some gendered norms of embodiment and the reinforcing of others.

We begin in the classroom with a simple experiment: imagine growing out your
body hair for a semester. Breanne Fahs and Denise A. Delgado present the intimate,
often painful stories of female students of various racial backgrounds who took advantage of a unique extra-credit opportunity to grow out their leg and underarm hair and
journal about their experiences. Did women emerge from this experiment resolved to
keep their razors in service, or did their experiences nudge them to put down their
blades and defy the norms, calling into question the cultural meanings of "good,"
"clean," "respectable" womanhood? The differential effects of race on resistance are
especially salient here. As the experiment progressed, women of color grew acutely
aware of how negative reactions to their transgression were raced. Their experience
leads us to ask, How does privilege facilitate resistance? How does disadvantage compromise it?

Hegemonic femininity's undertow is made real in the dungeon of the dominatrix—a place where powerful women exert total control over men who pay for the
service of erotic dominance. In the piece by Danielle J. Lindemann, the gender play
she describes manifests a fluidity of roles and identities. But, we find, some notions of
gender prove more viscous than others. For example, while the dominatrices reverse
gender norms by taking charge and calling the shots, they do so while displaying conventional (even exaggerated) tropes of femininity, revealing a gendered tug-of-war.

Picture women of all sizes dressed in fishnet stockings and tiny shorts racing
around a flat track at breakneck speed. This is today's women's roller derby and the
subject of Natalie M. Peluso's research. Fast-paced, athletic, dangerous, sexy, and often
ironic, the women competitors in this growing sport at once challenge traditional notions of (gendered) athleticism (even to the point of invoking the "robot," an athlete
impervious to pain) while capitalizing on certain features of conventional femininity.
What are the implications when women adopt so-called male traits of physicality,
aggressiveness, and even valorization of the superhu/man? Furthermore, how can culturally debased body types (read: large women and fat women) be reclaimed through
sport?

Now travel with Tari Youngjung Na and Hae Yeon Choo to South Korea and into the lives of South Korean female-to-males (FTMs). At birth, all South Korean citizens receive a national identification card differentiated by sex. What happens when an FTM's appearance no longer matches the sex indicated on his ID? How do FTMs negotiate an employment interview? A hospital visit? Na and Choo's fieldwork exposes how the often taken-for-granted pursuit of livelihood, community, and citizenship involves both resistance and subjection in the lives of many FTMs.

Part I rounds out with a pair of first-person narratives. Samantha Binford, a young woman who shaved her head "just because," describes the searching stares, unrelenting questions, and harsh judgments that greet the hairless female head. Why would she take this step, we ask? And why wouldn't we?

Sara L. Crawley then asks us to think the unthinkable for women: standing up to pee. As an avid boater, Crawley must deal with nature's call in a way that avoids "baring her assets" to all aboard or entering waters inhabited by sharks. Her solution—a $1.29 oil funnel—demonstrates how absurdly arbitrary rules of embodiment sometimes are, and also how powerfully ingrained they can be.

Part II, "Challenging Marginalization," concerns how some body rebels use the public sphere to disturb entrenched definitions and advance new ones. The resistant acts explored here situate the body coded as abject, even grotesque, as material and symbolic sites of reclamation and resistance to oppression, particularly the limits imposed by ageism, ableism, and appearance ideals.

M. Elise Radina, Lydia K. Manning, Marybeth C. Stalp, and Annette Lynch's exploration of the women of the Red Hat Society brings us close to middle-aged and older women who are, in the wry words of one informant, "not dead yet." Refusing to occupy the expected roles of aging women and quietly fade into the background, these women deploy ritual dress and model a reinvigorated approach to aging: fun, free, and social. While the Red Hatters shake up our notions of little old ladies, they also make clear the power of performance-as-resistance and even command male attention and co-opt the male gaze to their advantage. When bodies relegated to the margins take a bold step into the center, what is revealed about the tactical repertoires of body outlaws?

This same question animates Nathaniel C. Pyle and Noa Logan Klein's study of bears, hirsute gay men of size. In a body-obsessed culture that prizes the "six-pack" and the smooth, hairless physique of the male adolescent as the idealized object of gay desire, bears reclaim the marginal body as sexy and desirable as a source of pride, not shame. Pyle and Klein show how, united in community and focused on the social, bears use their bodies as instruments of cultural change. But is this social change in action? Is "just having a good time" resistance?

The body on display is a site of contention, no doubt, and this point crystallizes with pregnancy. Consider, for example, tabloid journalism's sport of celebrity "bump watch." The reproducing body, full, round, and ripening, is variously celebrated and shunned. While pregnancy, under most circumstances, is accepted as a healthy and natural state, the actual expanding womb in the flesh causes many to shudder and reinscribe cultural prescriptions for good mothering. Angela M. Moe turns our attention to pregnant and postpartum belly dancers who "unmask" their bodies in the ancient dance form of belly dance. Moe asks, What are the consequences for the dancers themselves and for others more generally? And what can the belly-dancing mommas teach us about the conceptual links between motherhood and beauty ideals?

Marginalization sometimes occurs at the hands of a long-standing and powerful religious institution. The tacit or overt exclusion of lesbian, gay, bisexual, and transgender (LGBT) individuals from some Christian churches reflects staunchly heteronormative embodiment norms. How, then, do some LGBT Christians reconcile their sexual and religious identities? J. Edward Sumerau and Douglas P. Schrock's field research introduces us to members of Metropolitan Community Church and the many ways the church challenges the typical norms of embodiment found in Christian establishments—from redefining Sunday best to embracing plays on masculinity and femininity.

Hanne Blank admits she is an unlikely sexuality educator, but she was willing and that was enough. She simply spelled out what was obvious to her but was, because of rampant fat phobia, a surprise to many: fat people have rich and varied love and sex lives. When she published her book *Big Big Love: A Sourcebook on Sex for People of Size and Those Who Love Them*, Blank was unprepared for the intense responses of her readers, especially the heart-wrenching stories of abuse that being fat "justified." But she quickly realized her limits: she was not qualified to provide the kind of help some asked of her. Still, she felt some responsibility to her readers since, as she puts it, she "opened the can of worms." Blank's tale invites us to ponder the "What's next?" of resistance. What is an activist's—even an unwilling one's—responsibility once the silence is broken, the norms violated?

Catherine Bergart's autobiographical short story deepens our exploration of marginalization, visibility, and reclamation. Through her lens, we encounter the beginning of her intimate partnership with a quadriplegic man. Her narrative of forging a union built on reciprocity dares us to interrogate the assumptions about physically disabled people and those who love them. How do dominant constructions of desirability, agency, and autonomy obscure the rich and complex lives of the socially marginal?

Part III, "Defying Authoritative Knowledges and Conventional Wisdom," introduces new and alternative epistemologies. Here we encounter unlikely conduits of knowledge—young girls online, mothers of small children, self-injurers, and women mistreated by the medical establishment, each of them agents who assert their own criteria for establishing what is healthy, "normal," and in their own best interest.

Pro-anas are (mostly) young girls and women who redefine severely restrictive eating not as illness but as a chosen lifestyle. This is pro-anorexia, or pro-ana. Abigail Richardson and Elizabeth Cherry's study of the pro-ana presence online raises many questions, such as who gets to define disease? and who decides what is healthy and sustainable and what is not? Pro-ana rattles many, especially those acutely aware of the deleterious effects of self-starvation, but pro-anas talk back: they are in control of their lives, they assert, and they refuse to be pathologized by the medical establishment. Through the sharing of tips on how to burn calories (drink cold water; it takes calories to heat it up to body temperature) and trick the doctor at weigh-ins (hide rolls of quarters in your pockets), pro-anas support each other as they quest for their version of the ideal body and their own self-determination.

Jennifer A. Reich's study of breastfeeding mothers, too, revolves around agency and authority. Reich interviewed mothers whose breastfeeding practices fall outside the norm; they nurse their children into toddlerhood and sometimes beyond, and they proudly nurse in public. Mothers who nurse "their way" (which is, incidentally, *the* way around most of the globe) are grounded in dearly held beliefs of the naturalness of breastfeeding and the importance of persisting despite censure from seemingly all sides—family, friends, strangers, and even health care practitioners. Reich's research uncovers the discursive and practical strategies nursing mothers use to resist pressures to conform, ranging from "mother knows best" to avoidance. Interestingly, Reich's mothers occupy privileged social locations, leading us to ponder (again) the who of resistance. Who can "afford" to resist, anyway?

Christine Labuski leads us into the private hell of women who experience chronic vulvar pain. Because of normative body shame and silencing, these women often suffer undiagnosed conditions that preclude effective management. After all, how can pain be addressed if it cannot be discussed honestly, completely, and safely? Labuski asks, referring to the social discomfort with female genitalia (or "dis-ease") that effectively negates the personhood of the women facing a vexing disease. Labuski's work makes visible the suffering of women who deserve better and sheds light on how medical discourse and norms of "polite talk" constrain agency.

From the private hell of vulvar pain, we turn to the painful and intimate emotional work of self-injurers. Boldly challenging conventional wisdom, Margaret Leaf and Douglas P. Schrock's work helps us to rethink cutting not as pathology but rather as a way for young self-injurers to alleviate distress, evoke feelings of authenticity, and elevate self-efficacy, even if this cutting can simultaneously nourish the same emotional dilemmas they try to escape. Leaf and Schrock's work points to the importance of seeing resistance through the eyes of the resisters themselves. As with the pro-anas we meet earlier in the collection, we must commit to listening, really listening, to their stories, even when they violate our notions of what is safe, healthy, and "normal."

Part III benefits from two personal narratives, both written by women who set out to fix what they see broken in health care. The intersex-rights activist Esther Morris Leidolf calls to account those who wield the tools of medicine to "correct" anatomical difference. Her story, simultaneously a cautionary tale and a call to action, elicits the question, How can pressures to normalize actually cause physical and psychological harm? Leidolf shows us how humiliating exams, a dearth of information, countless invasive procedures, and heteronormative directives disabled her much, much more than did her "missing" vagina. This narrative powerfully makes the case for bodily autonomy not only for the intersexed but for everyone.

The author of the second narrative, Angela Horn, is a doula, a childbirth attendant who provides informational and emotional support to birthing mothers. Resisting the medicalized birth that places a process in the hands of care providers, doulas work to return control to the laboring woman, thereby weakening "the American Way of Birth" (Davis-Floyd and Sargent 1997; Mitford 1992)—an unpredictable horror that necessitates high-tech intervention. She asks us to imagine an expanded role of the "patient" and the erosion of the absolute power of the "professional." Can we? If yes, are doulas and the mothers they serve a suitable model for this power shift?

In Part IV, "Negotiating Boundaries and Meanings," we train our attention on the relational dimension of "doing" resistance. Social theorists recognize that power is always embedded in social relations and, while individuals cannot necessarily disentangle themselves from this reality, they can make choices about how to engage with others and their attendant institutional structures (see, e.g., Foucault 1995). Because relations of power are social, it follows that they are constantly under deliberation, a perpetual give-and-take. These processes of negotiation effectively draw and redraw the lines that separate or unite people and the symbolic meanings they ascribe to their material realities.

Much has been written about how transgender and genderqueer identities profoundly trouble the entrenched gender binary. But less is known about the day-to-day realities faced by those who cross the Rubicon of gendered relations. We welcome Catherine Connell's research, then, into "the bathroom question" because it helps us see the complex processes of negotiation that trans- and gender-nonconforming people must engage in, in the name of daily survival. When faced with discrimination that compromises a most fundamental right and one that most of us take for granted, how do trans- and gender-nonconforming people adapt? And how do these potential adaptations impinge on an authentic sense of self? Furthermore, recognizing that resistance is not always an option, Connell leads us to ponder the conditions that facilitate and impede confrontation. What is the role of social class, for example?

Co-editor Samantha Kwan and Louise Marie Roth probe the political and personal bases of vegetarianism. Their in-depth interviews with women who choose a plant-based diet reveal provocative connections between vegetarianism and the rejection of industrialism, hierarchy, and patriarchy, thus leading the authors to designate vegetarianism as a form of counter-hegemonic embodiment. How is vegetarianism linked to other bodily practices, they ask, and how can deep critical reflection on the norms of "doing" negotiate identities of "not doing"?

When our bodies rupture the illusion that we are (or should be) the same, what happens next? And how are the outcomes reflective of raced and classed realities? The menopausal women Heather E. Dillaway interviewed did not set out to transgress norms, but their "misbehaving" bodies forced them into often uncomfortable and sometimes illuminating moments of negotiation. Menopause, like menstruation, is a natural body process women are expected to keep "under wraps," but nonetheless, hot flashes "just happen." When they do, menopausal women find themselves breaching the heavily guarded private/public divide. Dillaway's piece puts us in the room when red-faced, perspiring women unbutton their jackets and throw open the conference room windows as their colleagues shift uncomfortably in their seats. Dillaway shows us how these accidental resisters negotiate such tense moments and leads us to wonder about resistance that happens when we least expect it.

In contrast to these women who respond visibly to hot flashes, Lynn Davidman's religious defectors show how resistance can occur on a much subtler level. Haredi (Ultra-Orthodox) Jews practice numerous rituals and laws involving bodily practices that are central to the display and construction of a religious identity. What happens, then, when one departs from this highly disciplined and structured practice? Davidman's interviews with men and women living in Israel and the United States who leave Orthodoxy show how the process of fitting into mainstream culture now takes on heightened significance. Seemingly mundane acts such as wearing a pair of pants, consuming a bacon, lettuce, and tomato sandwich, or shaving one's *peyos* (curly sidelocks) become cosmic acts of rebellion and the basis of a new *un*orthodox identity.

David Linton, too, offers fresh thinking about the poignantly mundane. As a scholar of the cultural story of menstruation, he dwells in an assumed women's world.

Every time Linton responds to the oft-repeated "You study WHAT?" he troubles the too-easy divide between genders and their segregated preoccupations. His personal narrative raises a series of questions. Does a man's interest in menstruation have a legitimizing effect on this traditionally taboo topic? If so, what is unique to the "menstrual transaction" (as Linton calls it) when men are involved? And, finally, when the line that separates "lady talk" from "guy talk" is crossed, what do we discover about the gendered constructions of shame, secrecy, and risk?

Beverly Yuen Thompson expresses her love of the tattoo art form in our closing narrative. While her heavily tattooed body turned few eyes in tattoo-friendly Spokane, Washington, it brought heavy social sanctions from her father, the local Chinese community in her adopted home of Manhattan, and her elders. Her story reveals the precarious balance between self-expression and the preservation of cherished intergenerational familial relations.

We invite every reader to listen carefully to the nuances and complexities of risk-taking in context. The stories of resistance told here, through the lenses of both researcher and subject, invite us to enter the lives of these norm challengers and rule breakers. Here, we engage the many questions that resistance manifests—and interrogate the concepts and issues they force to the surface. We hope that *Embodied Resistance* takes our readers to a deeper understanding of bodies that refuse to fit into too-small spaces and a richer appreciation of the social meanings of all bodies.

NOTES

1. An employer's grooming policy requiring women employees to wear makeup was upheld in the case of *Jespersen v. Harrah's Operating Co., Inc.,* 444 F.3d 1104 (9th Cir. 2006).
2. For a feminist critique of sociologies of the body, see Witz 2000.
3. Here we borrow the title of the groundbreaking anthology edited by Ophira Edut (2004), *Body Outlaws: Rewriting the Rules of Beauty and Body Image.*

REFERENCES

Bartky, Sandra Lee. 1988. "Foucault, Femininity, and the Modernization of Patriarchal Power." In *Feminism and Foucault: Reflections on Resistance*, ed. Irene Diamond and Lee Quinby, 61–86. Boston: Northeastern University Press.

Bourdieu, Pierre. 1984. *Distinction: A Social Critique of the Judgement of Taste.* Trans. Robert Nice. Cambridge, MA: Harvard University Press.

———. 1985. "The Social Space and the Genesis of Groups." *Theory and Society* 14 (6): 723–44.

Davis, Kathy. 1988. *Power under the Microscope: Toward a Grounded Theory of Gender Relations in Medical Encounters.* Dordrecht, Holland: Foris.

Davis-Floyd, Robbie, and Carolyn F. Sargent, eds. 1997. *Childbirth and Authoritative Knowledge: Cross-Cultural Perspectives.* Berkeley: University of California Press.

Dellinger, Kirsten, and Christine L. Williams. 1997. "Makeup at Work: Negotiating Appearance Rules in the Workplace." *Gender and Society* 11:151–77.

Edut, Ophira. 2004. *Body Outlaws: Rewriting the Rules of Beauty and Body Image.* 3rd ed. Berkeley, CA: Seal Press.

Elias, Norbert. 2000. *The Civilizing Process.* Oxford: Blackwell.

Foucault, Michel. 1995. *Discipline and Punish: The Birth of the Prison.* New York: Vintage Books.

Frank, Arthur. 1991. "For a Sociology of the Body: An Analytical Review." In *The Body: Social Processes and Cultural Theory*, ed. Mike Featherstone, Mike Hepworth, and Bryan S. Turner, 36–102. London: Sage.

Gagné, Patricia, and Deanna McGaughey. 2002. "Designing Women: Cultural Hegemony and the Exercise of Power among Women Who Have Undergone Elective Mammoplasty." *Gender and Society* 16 (6): 814–38.

Gimlin, Debra L. 2002. *Body Work: Beauty and Self-Image in American Culture.* Berkeley: University of California Press.

Hollander, Jocelyn A., and Rachel L. Einwohner. 2004. "Conceptualizing Resistance." *Sociological Forum* 19 (4): 533–54.

Mitford, Jessica. 1992. *The American Way of Birth.* New York: Plume.

Mullaney, Jamie. 2006. *Everyone Is Not Doing It: Abstinence and Personal Identity.* Chicago: University of Chicago Press.

Pitts, Victoria. 2003. *In the Flesh: The Cultural Politics of Body Modification.* New York: Palgrave.

———. 2007. *Surgery Junkies: Wellness and Pathology in Cosmetic Culture.* New Brunswick, NJ: Rutgers University Press.

Shilling, Chris. 1993. *The Body and Social Theory.* 2nd ed. Thousand Oaks, CA: Sage.

Turner, Bryan S. 1996. *The Body and Society.* 2nd ed. Thousand Oaks, CA: Sage.

Weitz, Rose. 2001. "Women and Their Hair: Seeking Power through Resistance and Accommodation." *Gender and Society* 15 (5): 667–86.

Witz, Anne. 2000. "Whose Body Matters? Feminist Sociology and the Corporeal Turn." *Body and Society* 6 (2): 1–24.

PART I

Rewriting Gender Scripts

1

The Specter of Excess

Race, Class, and Gender
in Women's Body Hair Narratives

Breanne Fahs and Denise A. Delgado

Hairy.
Manly.
Dirty.
Animal-like.
Women face these accusations when they choose not to shave, because traditional gender roles have made the body a source of political contention. One recent study states, "Far from being the inevitable outcome of a biological imperative, femininity is produced through a range of practices, including normative body-altering work such as routine hair removal. The very normativity of such practices obscures their constructive role" (Toerien and Wilkinson 2003, 334). Thus, body hair removal is one way women obey social norms dictated by patriarchal expectations. Though over 99 percent of women in the United States reported removing body hair at some point in their lives, few studies have addressed this phenomenon in detail, particularly in light of social identity categories such as race, class, and gender. The few studies conducted on body hair have found that women overwhelmingly construct body hair removal as a normative and taken-for-granted practice that produces an "acceptable" femininity (Toerien, Wilkinson, and Choi 2005). Shaving and plucking—labor women invest in their bodies—constitute practices adopted by most women in the United States, with women typically removing hair from underarms, legs, pubic area, eyebrows, and face. Departure from these norms often elicits negative affect and appraisal for those who rebel; women who do not shave or remove hair report feeling judged and negatively evaluated as "dirty," "gross," and "repulsive" (Toerien and Wilkinson 2004). Further, women rate other women who do not shave as less attractive, intelligent, sociable, happy, and positive compared with hairless women (Basow and Braman 1998).

Research on Body Hair Norms

Historically men's hair has been linked to virility and power, while women's body hair has been associated with "female wantonness" and the denial of women's sexuality (Toerien and Wilkinson 2003). Some accounts, however, eroticize hairy women as desirable, powerful, and highly sexed; for example, some tribal cultures in central Africa embrace women's body hair as a source of power. Typically, female body hair has been linked to insanity, witchcraft, and the devil, while male body hair (particularly facial hair) has been linked to power, strength, fertility, leadership, lustfulness, and masculinity. Feminist scholars have noted that women pluck and shave in order to appear more sexless and infantile and that, in cultures that feel threatened by female power, hairlessness norms have become more pervasive. Lack of pubic hair, for example, may represent the eroticization of girlhood rather than womanhood, a fact that concerns those interested in full gender equality (Toerien and Wilkinson 2003). Some prominent feminists, such as the folk singer Ani DiFranco, have resisted shaving norms publicly and defiantly.

Body hair removal is normative in a variety of cultures, including England, Australia, Egypt, Greece, Italy, Uganda, and Turkey (Cooper 1971; Tiggemann and Kenyon 1998). Within these cultures, over 80 percent of women consistently comply with hair removal, typically beginning at puberty. Before the 1920s, however, few Western women ever removed body hair. Historians suggest that U.S. advertising campaigns in the 1930s ushered in body hair removal, with advice by "beauty experts" and changes in typical fashion (e.g., outfits revealing more skin, celebration of prepubescent female bodies), helping to establish hair removal as a new social convention (Hope 1982). Body hair removal, though relatively recent as a historical development, has spanned the globe: recent studies of Australian women found that nearly 97 percent of women shave their underarms and legs (Tiggemann and Lewis 2004). Research on American women has shown that 92 percent removed their leg hair and 93 percent removed underarm hair, indicating that women comply with body hair norms at rates much higher than those for other dominant body practices (e.g., thinness, long hair, makeup, manicured nails) (Tiggemann and Kenyon 1998).

Not all women are equally eager to remove body hair. For many decades, women in Europe shaved less often than U.S. women, yet this divide is narrowing. There is some evidence that feminist identity, lesbian identity, and older age may predict decreased likelihood of hair removal (Basow 1991; Toerien, Wilkinson, and Choi 2005). The 1960s and 1970s saw women growing underarm hair as a political statement attached to bohemian identity and leftist politics, suggesting that hair may also signify political, regional, and national attachment.

Still, researchers have found "strong evidence of a widespread symbolic association between body hair—or its absence—and ideal gender: to have a hairy body is a sign of masculinity, to have a hairless one a sign of femininity" (Basow 1991, 84). Emphasis on women's hairlessness emphasizes women's differentness from men and highlights that, unlike men's bodies, women's bodies are unacceptable in their natural state (Basow 1991). Women learn to associate their hairlessness with ideal femininity, in part because of mass media and marketing campaigns (Whelehan 2000). In particular, women shave their legs and underarms to achieve femininity and overall attractiveness, and they shave pubic hair to achieve sexual attractiveness and self-enhancement. In addition, women with partners—male or female—reported more frequent pubic hair removal (Tiggemann and Hodgson 2008).

Hair removal practices also correlate with other body modification practices; women who shave more often report unhealthy dieting, cosmetic surgeries, and general body dissatisfaction (Tiggemann and Hodgson 2008). That hair removal seems

The folk singer and feminist Ani DiFranco has frequently challenged gender stereotypes that women should be hairless, polite, and reverent to a music industry controlled by men. She runs her own music label, rebels against body norms, and is shown here with fully grown underarm hair at one of her shows. (Reproduced by permission from Matt Hagen.)

trivial and relatively unnoticed makes it all the more potent as a means of social control, because women adopt ideas about idealized femininity without considering the ramifications of those ideologies and accompanying practices. Hairlessness norms mark femininity as clearly different from masculinity; femininity becomes associated with "tameness," docility, and immaturity, while masculinity is associated with power and dominance (Toerien and Wilkinson 2003). Women with negative attitudes toward body hair more often felt disgusted with their bodies in general (Toerien and Wilkinson 2004). Also, women who shaved described feeling that their bodies were unacceptable and unattractive in their natural state (Chapkis 1986). Paradoxically, women recognize the normative pressures placed on them to shave but generally cannot accept these as a rationale for changing their specific behaviors around shaving (Tiggemann and Kenyon 1998). Though few studies have asked women why they remove body hair, some studies have indirectly and unsystematically included women's rationale for hair removal. Women said they removed body hair to feel cleaner, more feminine, more confident about themselves, and more attractive. Some women liked the "soft, silky feeling" of shaved legs, while others enjoyed feeling sexually attractive to men (Tiggemann and Hodgson 2008).

To date, no studies have directly and systematically addressed the race, class, and sexual identity implications of body hair practices, even though some research has identified female subjects by these categories (Tiggemann and Hodgson 2008; Weitz 2004). Feminist scholars have argued that femininity is a white, middle-classed signifier against which women of color and working-class women have been defined as deviant, thus requiring that they meet the standards of white, middle-class femininity "to avoid being positioned as vulgar, pathological, tasteless, and sexual" (Skeggs 1997, 100). Nonetheless, most body hair studies ignore race and class. One study found that whites, on average, have more body hair than most other "races" (Cooper 1971). Though no systematic studies exist about body hair and social class, some researchers have offered compelling theoretical links between these factors: "Given that the presence of hair on a woman's body may be taken to represent dirtiness, poor grooming, and laziness, by retaining her body hair, a woman may risk being negatively positioned by representations of the 'unruly,' 'out of control,' 'vulgar' working-class woman" (Toerien and Wilkinson 2003, 342). Still, direct analysis of how conformity to, or violation of, hair removal practices relate to social identities of race, class, and sexual identity remain relatively absent from the current literature.

Methods

The central research question of this chapter asks, How do women from different identity categories react when temporarily rejecting the social norm of shaving? In response, this chapter analyzes the role of body hair in the construction of women's raced, classed, and gendered identities. Our findings emerge from a content analysis of a class assignment undertaken by women enrolled in a course on women and health at a large southwestern university.

During a recent semester of Fahs's Women and Health course, students were invited to participate in an extra-credit assignment that asked them to grow out their body hair (underarm, leg, and pubic) for twelve weeks. Students kept weekly logs of their personal reactions to their body hair, others' reactions to it, any changes in behavior noted, and thoughts about how changes in body hair affected their health and sexuality. The twenty enrolled students included nineteen women and one man; as such, the man performed the opposite social norm by shaving for twelve weeks, though he did not turn in a paper and is excluded from this analysis because of the difficulty of generalizing from one person's experience.[1] The sample for this study included nineteen women (35 percent women of color, primarily Latina; 65 percent white women), nearly all of whom were under age thirty (only two students were over age thirty). Students turned in their weekly logs and a reflection paper based on the body hair experiment.

This chapter draws from those narratives to illustrate the compulsory qualities of body-hair-norm adherence and to illuminate the more specific elements of race, class, and gender norming related to depilation. The narratives discuss the following issues:

1. Misinformation that arises when women violate social norms (e.g., belief that hair is dirty, abnormal, and bacteria-laden)
2. The race, class, and gender implications of growing body hair (e.g., violation of raced and classed norms with their Latino/Latina family)

3. Confrontation of social responses to growing body hair (e.g., partner refusing sex; friends' teasing)
4. The relationship between social norms and social policing, particularly as it relates to postexperimental reflections (e.g., the difficulty of purposefully constructing one's body outside of "normal" body standards)

This chapter considers the perceived positive and negative outcomes of challenging body hair norms for these students, including the gendered, raced, and classed impact of social rejection as it affects different women. Additionally, the social psychological dynamics of reproducing social conformity and obedience to authority in the classroom is a secondary subject of inquiry. Despite the assignment's being extra credit and worth a mere two points, women who initially resisted participating eventually gave in to social pressures to grow their body hair as a way to join group dynamics. Finally, we consider two abstract themes: how challenging body hair norms forges new communities at the margins of pervasive social norms, and how women use their bodies as mechanisms for resistance and rebellion.

"Hiding in the House": Mythologies and Disgust about Body Hair

As expected because of the literatures on body hair removal for women, many women described strongly negative feelings about the process of growing out their body hair, noting, most prominently, several "facts" that indicated widespread misinformation and distortion about body hair. Women reported initial feelings—internally driven and communicated by friends and family—that not shaving would lead to razor rash, extreme bacterial growth, and excessive amounts of sweating, and that body hair was fundamentally unsanitary. Repeated discussions of cleanliness and hair as "dirty and gross" appeared in women's narratives of their body hair.

Also permeating women's narratives were internalized beliefs about hair as disgusting and inherently unhealthy. Participants claimed that body hair caused germs to multiply on their bodies, and that it posed a serious health risk. Esperanza, a woman of color, wrote, "My sister said it was absolutely gross and out of this world. My biggest problem I had was not shaving my pubic hair. I hated my body during my period. Hygiene wise, it was the worst experience I ever had. I would not stop shaving my pubic hair unless I had a medical impediment that forced me to do it."[2]

Often women described others as reacting in a negative or even overtly hostile manner, such as Latina-identified Ana: "My mom said it was unsanitary and disgusting and that I needed to stay away from her because the look of it grossed her out, and if my leg or underarm hair touched her, she'd have to take a shower."

Consequently, women altered their behaviors to avoid negative social penalties. The substantial list of behavior changes women made included refusing to wear certain kinds of clothes (e.g., dresses, shorts, Capri pants, tank tops, and bathing suits), hiding in their houses rather than going out with friends, avoiding exercise or the gym, having sex with their partners less often or not at all, not going on job interviews, taking more showers, putting on more lotion, wearing excessive amounts of deodorant, and avoiding the sensation of the "wind blowing through the hair." Women also reported emotional reactions to the exercise: developing fear that strangers (e.g., mailmen, servers, gynecologists) would ridicule them, having nervous reactions when visiting family members, and feeling general unease.

In addition to these behavioral changes, women reported that others accused them of not being womanly enough or of conforming to stereotypes of women's studies students as hairy and manly. Cecilia, a woman of color, described this heteronormative patrolling:

> My sister called me a women's studies lesbian and said I needed to change my major because it was messing with my mind and turning me into a man. My male relatives were name-calling me lesbian, he-she, ape, mud flaps, and they were laughing. My partner explained that I had been doing it for a school experiment. They could not understand why I would even do something like this for school or why my partner would allow it.

Mariah, a white woman, said, "My family and my mom said I looked like a feminist dyke and I looked disgusting," and Samantha, a white woman, said, "My boyfriend made a joke about how I might as well go as a werewolf for Halloween because I already have a costume. I feel like a man."

Dreaded Otherness: Race, Class, and Gender Narratives about Body Hair

Many reactions to women's body hair carried raced and classed dimensions. Women of color and working-class women reported more familial regulation about body hair and far more social penalties for growing out their hair than did the white middle- or upper-class women. Women of color and working-class women, particularly working-class women of color, struggled with body hair because it exacerbated their sense of "differentness" from the white middle- or upper-class women in class. While the assignment was a useful tool for self-analysis, it also, unexpectedly, encouraged students to reflect about otherness. For example, Ana said,

> When I compared my hair to the hair of the other girls in class, there was an obvious difference. My hair grew in thick and coarse. The other Latina women in the class understood that the white girls had it easier because their hair was thinner. I felt like people would think I was a "dirty Mexican" because of the hair, that I was doing something nasty, and people would connect my body hair to my being lesbian or Mexican.

The patrolling of gender norms also appeared more strongly for women of color, among whom being a "good woman" appeared frequently in their discussions of family reactions. Ana wrote about her family reactions, "My mom told my uncles and grandparents so next time I went over to have dinner with the family, there was a lot of talking about my body hair and everyone wanted to see. My grandpa said, '*Mija*, no one wants a girl that doesn't shave and looks like a man.'"

Several other Latina women described their parents as engaging in similar heteronormative patrolling of their bodies. This behavior could reveal their preoccupation with not adding further stigma to already stigmatized bodies, as Patricia Hill Collins

(2006) discussed in her work about stigmatized black identities. For example, Cecilia said, "My mother was so upset that she scolded me and asked if I needed money to purchase razors or if something was wrong. She thought she did not teach me the proper way to clean myself. My mom could not look at me and asked that I cover up. She called me a lesbian and wanted me to stop my women's studies classes because they were corrupting my mind, my beliefs, and my identity." Lupe, a woman of color, admitted that race and class affected her reactions to body hair; she discussed the fear of dreaded Otherness, that is, not wanting to confirm stereotypes of women of color or poor women as unkempt or dirty. She said, "I come from a family that didn't have much money, and to let yourself go is going against everything I have been taught. I'm always careful about coming across as respectable and clean, just so I don't confirm all of those stereotypes people have of me as dirty and low class."

Many women of color noticed that their hair grew in thicker and darker than white women's hair. This theme emerged directly and indirectly in their reflection papers, and it also appeared, combined with fear of further stigma, in their narratives. Esperanza wrote, "Just looking at my armpits in the mirror doesn't scare me, but knowing that somebody else might see them and look at me like a dirty and unhygienic person can be disturbing." Sharon, who could not finish the assignment because she found it intolerable for her self-image, also wrote about her fear of being perceived as dirty, saying, "As a black woman, I know what it's like to be looked down upon by white people. I don't need to be made aware of that any more than I already am."

Some students of color felt a need to enhance their outward appearance of femininity to compensate for their hairiness (though this need also occurred, to a lesser degree, for white women). A few students of color dressed in more typically "feminine" dress. Ana wrote:

> I found myself wearing makeup more often, at first unconsciously. Before I'd stopped shaving, I hardly ever wore makeup. I started because I didn't want anyone to think that I didn't "take care of myself" and I'm always aware of the fact that as a Mexican, I have to go that extra mile. I'm not a college professor and I don't live and work with other feminists like some of my girlfriends do. I'm a waitress, and my coworkers would think I was a freak.

Again, this example reveals the way that violating one social norm may enforce other social norms more intensely, such that women of color and working-class women may adopt more traditional norms of femininity even as they violate norms of hairlessness.

Discourses of race and class also appeared in the white women's narratives about their body hair, as white women expressed awareness of their difference from women of color in class. Lauren, a white woman, wrote: "It has become not a big deal to me, but still a shock to my friends and family. Most say I could quit and no one would know. I replied, 'I like to show and tell in class.' It is fun for me because I have much less hair compared to the girls in the class of Mexican descent." Lana, another white student, noted: "There's such a clear difference between the light-skinned women and the women of color. I notice that I'm totally privileged in that no one really even notices if I grow my leg hair out, whereas for them, it's dark and noticeable right away."

Thus, race and class narratives appeared specifically when women described their fear of others' reactions, particularly within the family. This observation aligns with Beverly Skeggs's (1997) claim that women of color and working-class women face comparisons with "idealized femininity" represented by white, middle-class women. Women of color battle not only against patriarchal standards but also against white middle-class femininity as "superior" (Collins 2006; Lovejoy 2001). The additional stigma of body hair for women of color and working-class women may feel intolerable because of the bodily, social, and psychological stigma they already regularly encounter in their lives.

"Looking Like a Bear": Confronting Social Responses to Body Hair

Some of the most interesting findings from this experiment included women's confrontations of others' responses to their growing body hair. While women described concerns about going on job interviews and confronting their parents' disapproval or worrying about siblings' reactions, women's feelings about the reactions of their romantic partners and friends were particularly intense. Specifically, women reported heightened awareness of seeking approval from their partners, particularly their boyfriends, as they overrelied on male approval when assessing their self-worth and personal identity (notably, women who had female partners expressed fewer such concerns). Eva, a woman of color, wrote: "My boyfriend's opinion is the person whose opinion I tend to value the most. He never said anything hurtful. He did, however, dismiss it as another one of my crazy feminist approaches to dealing with the world. Ouch. Being called crazy is perhaps more painful than being laughed at or called gross."

Several women said their male partners initially offered support but then changed their minds and felt threatened later on during the semester. Nadia, a white woman, wrote:

> On our way to bed he said, "I love you but I have something to say to you. Your leg hair is poking me." I was like, "Do you want me to shave it off?" and he was quiet and said no. Later, he said, "I didn't want to tell you but your hair is as long as mine and I really didn't think it would grow that long in such a short amount of time. I miss the smoothness of your skin." Then later, my boyfriend called to make sure that I didn't start *liking* that manly hair and that I didn't continue with the experiment.

This reaction may represent common homophobic reactions, because other women reported that their boyfriends feared, at least implicitly, that they would turn into lesbians. Samantha reported:

> I was fine with the whole idea of not shaving until my partner started making comments. He was very supportive at first but he had a hard time with it later. He joked a lot about it being gross. I felt gross during sex. I would get distracted and I could not reach orgasm. My boyfriend would ask me every day to shave my pubic hair and say that the teacher would never know anyways. I think it might be because he thinks he has some control over my sex organs.

That some women's boyfriends who worried about women turning into lesbians also sensed a loss of control over their girlfriends sheds light on some dangerous implications for heterosexual relationships.

Some women described intense hostility from their male partners. Kim, a white student, said, "My partner said, 'I'm not going to wipe my ass until you shave,' as if that was the same thing!" Cecilia wrote:

> My partner noticed for the first time and was appalled by the sight of my pit hair being so long. He requested that I shave and would laugh at me. He boycotted sex with me, saying it was too hairy or a jungle down there. He asked that I not put my arms up while sleeping because it troubled him just the sight of it. He stopped rubbing my legs or showing me any affection. He made a decision not to be in the same room while I changed clothes or when I got out of the shower. He would compare me to an ape or a man.

She later reflected that his resistance to her body hair made her question her relationship with him.

Women also confronted social regulation through their friends, who were often hostile, disapproving, and disgusted by their hair. At the same time, other women had friends who happily joined them in not shaving just to see what it felt like. Perhaps not shaving had some degree of "hipness," particularly if women had a formal excuse to do so (e.g., "It's for a class assignment!"). Ana wrote, "A friend at work stopped shaving with me after she heard, as did another friend of mine. Most of my friends were very supportive and weren't nasty about it—a much better reaction than my family. . . . I liked comparing hair length and thickness with the other women in the class each day." Negative reactions, however, dominated women's response papers. Lauren wrote, "My friend took one look at my hair and said he would kick his wife out of bed if she decided to stop shaving. He said it was disgusting and unattractive." Mariah said, "My friend freaked out and said, 'Daaaang.' People just don't seem to understand the reasoning for it even if I explain that I'm going against a social norm to see how people react." Eva also experienced negative reactions from her friends: "My best friend said I looked like a bear. She said I was lucky I had a boyfriend and wasn't in the 'singles scene.' She said I better shave for her party next weekend or wear something to cover it up because she didn't want me to scare guests."

"Painful and Freeing": Postexperimental Reflections

Women's postexperiment reflections provided textured and relevant comments about body hair norms and their experiences resisting them. Their responses indicate that even temporary and purposeful breaks from social norms can powerfully socialize women into an altered understanding of how much they "choose" to do things such as shave, wear makeup, or conform to standard presentations of femininity. Even the few women who felt lukewarm about the assignment described more awareness of how their bodies circulated in public space.

Some women described genuinely positive reactions to not shaving for a set period. Zoe, a white student, wrote:

> I have noticed I have become more comfortable in my own body. My hair
> isn't some foreign object that routinely must be removed for fear of not being
> feminine enough. I have come to realize that shaving as a whole is a patriarchal,
> consumerist-driven chore that society has required and frequently reprimanded
> women for if they don't do it enough. I'm sick of being criticized for my natural
> bodily hair. This is my body. . . . This assignment has helped me to feel more
> confident and more comfortable about who I am as a person. I won't be pushed
> around or bullied into what others feel is right, clean, or sanitary.

Stories of personal empowerment appeared regularly in women's reactions to this
experiment.

Women also expressed a heightened awareness of gender norms and expectations
in general. Lauren, for example, wrote:

> This makes me think, when will it end? Are women worse off or better off now?
> We don't have to stay at home and wear pearls while vacuuming and cooking
> all day for our husbands. We have more rights and choices, but in a way we
> have only added to the expectations of women rather than fully changed them.
> Now we wear pearls, heels, shave, wear makeup, have styled hair, are thin—the
> look of today's most desired women. Combined with this, we're supposed to
> have an education, a successful career, a social life, and a happy (traditional)
> family life. I feel like now that I know these things I have a responsibility to
> myself as well as others. I am not at all a radical, not the kind of person to
> speak or act out, but I can keep myself informed, think more critically, and
> change my actions if need be.

Similarly, Mariah expressed outrage about gender norms, noting that this assignment
flagged many gendered behaviors she had not previously acknowledged: "I thought
it was interesting and fun because we were being unique and not conforming to the
rest of society. I'm upset with how we instill in women to look a certain way to be accepted. There's not only one way to look. I wish that society could change their view
of women's bodies so it's more healthy."

Some women were acutely aware of the limitations of their feminist politics after
participating in this exercise. For example, Parker, a white student, wrote: "It was
a hard experiment for me because I can honestly say that I conform to what society expects of me as a female—high heels, Victoria's Secret, looking good in public,
makeup. I have been happy but I do see that I need to sometimes take a step back and
look at the reasons I do things." Eva indicated even more ambivalence, wondering
whether her feminist politics had advanced enough to support such an assignment.
She wrote:

> This experience was more painful than freeing because it made me realize that I
> have a lot of soul searching to do. Although I am always the first to reject many
> of our society's norms, they never quite affect me as directly as this assignment
> did. I can't yet deal with the backlash of others when resisting social norms about
> looking good. This assignment did help me to get one step closer to who I aspire
> to be. I want to accept myself.

Still, women described consciousness-raising around gender as a result of the body hair experiment, particularly when considering implicit societal norms and the value women receive from "feminine" bodies. Cecilia wrote:

> Going through this opened up a new world for me. When other women would make fun of me or call me names, it made me realize that they were very ignorant to the social construction of body norms. It upset me that we're in the twenty-first century and women still don't get it. My partner's rejection was the most painful, and it made it apparent to me that it's not what's inside of me that matters, but rather, the outside of me. I have learned that hair is powerful.

Several women from that semester contacted us many months later to report some of the long-term changes they had made. Most said that they shave less often now, though a few said that after feeling deprived of shaving for several months, they started shaving more often. Cecilia reported that she broke up with her partner. Ana wrote, "Whether I want to give up shaving altogether is something I don't know, but I know it made me more accepting of body hair in general." Mariah said, "I'm not as self-conscious about it and I don't shave everyday anymore. I think this task is interesting and life altering. It may not change my life completely but it did make me think about social constructions long after the class ended." Some women continued not shaving. Cecilia, for example, said, "I enjoyed letting my body hair grow free and not have a care in the world about what others think. I have learned to respect and appreciate my body since this experience. I'm still a real woman with hairy pits, hairy legs, and an overgrown female bush." Generally, the experiment proved to have significance in their lives well after that semester and into the following year. The social justice implications for the experiment, however, had limitations.

Classroom Social Psychology of Body Hair Norms

Although the original intent of the experiment was to challenge social norms and subvert compulsory shaving demands, the assignment ultimately created a new social norm within the classroom—a point we think is worthy of further consideration for future semesters and, more generally, in pedagogical experiments of this sort. Originally, five women in the class decided not to participate in the assignment but eventually gave in and participated because they felt left out of the social conversations that occurred informally between students at the start of class. Creating a new social norm that demanded that women not shave in some ways defeated or at least minimized the original purpose of the assignment. This outcome again shows the fluidity of what constitutes a norm in any particular context and the powerful pressures women face when conforming to social norms about their bodies, whatever they may be in any given circumstance. Throughout the semester, the context of norm transgression itself became normative.

For Fahs, as instructor, it was puzzling to witness how the students relied on "authority" to resist shaving norms. Indeed, the optional assignment earned them a mere two points, yet students (and sometimes students' friends) seemed to enjoy having an excuse not to shave that was based on someone else's "telling them" not to. Interestingly, the following semester, students in Fahs's courses asked whether they, too, could participate in the body hair experiment, indicating that they wanted to try not shaving but apparently did not feel entitled to resist shaving without an authority figure demanding or endorsing it.[3] Seemingly, individuals perceived the subversion of social norms as a smaller offense if done for a reason other than subversion itself, particularly if it involved an authority figure. These dynamics point to the complexities of challenging social norms while simultaneously recreating those same norms, a problem that speaks to the fascinating and unsettling qualities of groupthink within resistance communities.

Conclusion

Women formed a community of resistance around rebelling against shaving norms, even while that community imposed its own set of norms on the straggling students who wanted to continue shaving. While the specter of excess—that persistent norm communicated to women that they must conform to hairless femininity and not be "too much" through the disciplining of their bodies—made itself apparent in their lives, their lack of shaving was a key form of embodied resistance. Notably, our sample included young undergraduate women, so we cannot in any way account for generational differences, gender differences, geographic (and weather) differences, or educational differences, nor can we broaden our findings to larger populations. We also remain uncertain about whether this pedagogical experiment would translate in other contexts or universities, though Fahs has found similar, yet more gender-specific, results after successfully completing the experiment in a larger class of sixty-five students.

Collectively, these results suggest that women of color and working-class women were most negatively affected by the process of not shaving, because not shaving added a layer of bodily oppression to the stigma they already experienced as lower-status women and because, for women of color, their hair was darker, coarser, and more pronounced than white women's hair. Further, women of color encountered more negative reactions from family members, indicating that the regulation of body norms within family environments may be more salient for women of color than for white women.

Still, all women encountered at least some negative reactions from others, friends or partners and even strangers. Feelings of disgust, self-loathing, lack of cleanliness, and lack of sexual desirability permeated women's narratives, indicating that shaving-engendered social penalties resulted for those who refused to comply with mandated female hairlessness. Yet, in resisting these body norms even temporarily, women made visible the processes by which they conformed while also challenging and resisting power imbalances between men and women, particularly the assumption that women are unattractive in their natural state. Their makeshift community around challenging body hair norms bolstered their courage, fostered communication, and opened dialogue around the junctures between feminist politics, race, class, and the subversion of body norms even as it generated a new, though temporary social norm in the classroom.

NOTES

1. The male student expressed surprise about the time and effort shaving took. Though he experienced less social penalty than female students, he felt physically uncomfortable and "itchy" throughout the experiment.
2. All participants were assigned pseudonyms to ensure anonymity.
3. Fahs recently conducted the experiment again in a larger class of sixty-five students. In the first week of the experiment, a group of men banded together to blog about their experiences, complaining online that shaving required effort, time, and carefulness and that they experienced homophobic reactions from other men when they shaved their bodies. These experiences are documented in forthcoming articles in *Feminism and Psychology* and *Women's Studies: An Interdisciplinary Journal.*

REFERENCES

Basow, Susan A. 1991. "The Hairless Ideal: Women and Their Body Hair." *Psychology of Women Quarterly* 15 (1): 83–96.

Basow, Susan A., and Amie C. Braman. 1998. "Women and Body Hair: Social Perceptions and Attitudes." *Psychology of Women Quarterly* 22 (4): 637–45.

Chapkis, Wendy. 1986. *Beauty Secrets: Women and the Politics of Appearance.* Boston: South End Press.

Collins, Patricia Hill. 2006. *From Black Power to Hip Hop: Racism, Nationalism, and Feminism.* Philadelphia: Temple University Press.

Cooper, Wendy. 1971. *Hair: Sex, Society, Symbolism.* London: Aldus Books.

Hope, Christine. 1982. "Caucasian Female Body Hair and American Culture." *Journal of American Culture* 5 (1): 93–99.

Lovejoy, Meg. 2001. "Disturbances in the Social Body: Differences in Body Image and Eating Problems among African American and White Women." *Gender and Society* 15 (2): 239–61.

Skeggs, Beverly. 1997. *Formations of Class and Gender.* London: Sage.

Tiggemann, Marika, and Suzanna Hodgson. 2008. "The Hairless Norm Extended: Reasons for and Predictors of Women's Body Hair Removal at Different Body Sites." *Sex Roles* 59 (11/12): 889–97.

Tiggemann, Marika, and Sarah J. Kenyon. 1998. "The Hairlessness Norm: The Removal of Body Hair in Women." *Sex Roles* 39 (11/12): 873–85.

Tiggemann, Marika, and Christine Lewis. 2004. "Attitudes toward Women's Body Hair: Relationship with Disgust Sensitivity." *Psychology of Women Quarterly* 28 (4): 381–87.

Toerien, Merran, and Sue Wilkinson. 2003. "Gender and Body Hair: Constructing the Feminine Woman." *Women's Studies International Forum* 26 (4): 333–44.

———. 2004. "Exploring the Depilation Norm: A Qualitative Questionnaire Study of Women's Body Hair Removal." *Qualitative Research in Psychology* 1 (1): 69–92.

Toerien, Merran, Sue Wilkinson, and Precilla Y. L. Choi. 2005. "Body Hair Removal: The 'Mundane' Production of Normative Femininity." *Sex Roles* 52 (5/6): 399–406.

Weitz, Rose. 2004. *Rapunzel's Daughters: What Women's Hair Tells Us about Women's Lives.* New York: Farrar, Straus, and Giroux.

Whelehan, Imelda. 2000. *Overloaded: Popular Culture and the Future of Feminism.* London: Women's Press.

2

"Is That Any Way to Treat a Lady?"

The Dominatrix's Dungeon

Danielle J. Lindemann

Sitting inside a café in downtown Manhattan, a woman in her early forties describes what she calls her "dungeon protocol": "In my sessions, I insist that I be called 'Mistress' or 'Ma'am,'" she explains, dipping her fork into her vegetarian entrée.[1] "But it's not just about protocol; it's about manners. It's about respect. If they don't follow the rules for my dungeon, I will ask them, 'Is that any way to treat a lady?'"

This chapter explores the production of gender during encounters between women like her—professional dominatrices (*pro-dommes*)—and their clients (also called *submissives* or *subs*). Clients pay pro-dommes money to physically and verbally dominate them through spanking, flogging, verbal humiliation, bondage, and "forced" cross-dressing and enacting a variety of other sadomasochistic and fetishistic "scenes." Though their work is erotic, pro-dommes are distinct from prostitutes; few of them provide "extras"—intercourse, oral sex, or hand jobs—to their clients.

By taking on the role of the powerful female in the D/S (dominance/submission) dyad, pro-dommes symbolically defy gendered norms, challenging traditional conceptions of female passivity in erotic encounters as well as in everyday life. But, like the woman in the café, they accomplish this by relying on traditional gender scripts. Further, their sessions invoke feminine archetypes, even in cross-dressing scenarios in which the client plays the part of the female participant. Looking at the way gender "works" in these encounters sheds light on the ways in which non-mainstream modes of erotic expression challenge traditional gender roles and, in contrast, on the persistence of normative gender paradigms within transgressive forms of erotic behavior.

Background

Prior research on erotic labor has focused largely on prostitutes, and sociological studies of BDSM (bondage, discipline, sadism, and masochism) have included professional dominatrices among all sadomasochistic (SM) participants, without fully examining the unique dynamics of these commercial encounters (Weinberg 1983 provides an excellent summary of relevant literature; see also Kamel and Weinberg 1983; Lee

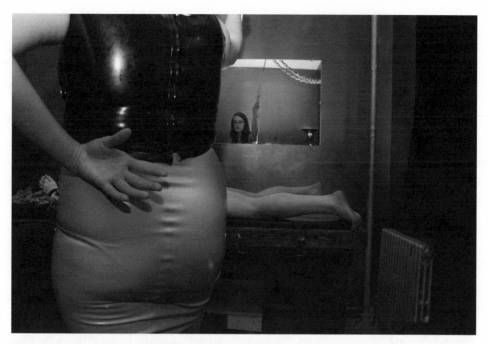

A New York City dominatrix performs a session with a female client.
(Photograph courtesy of Mae Ryan.)

1983; Patrias 1978; Weinberg, Williams, and Moser 1984).[2] Further, these earlier studies under-theorize the element of gender. None explores the ways in which dominants and submissives "do" their genders in such encounters, leaving open the question of how masculinity and femininity get produced or reproduced in the contexts of these erotic exchanges.

While a discussion of the production of gender on a micro level has been absent from the social scientific literature on sadomasochistic sexuality, the symbolic interactionist literature on "doing" gender within face-to-face encounters has enjoyed a long history (e.g., Riviere 1966, 213). Judith Butler (1999) is perhaps best known for developing the concept, by arguing that, while gender is performed, it cannot be put on and taken off at will because there is no "essential" femininity under the mask—femininity is itself a performance. Drag, for instance, is not a parody of "real" femininity; "indeed," she says, "the parody is *of* the very notion of an original" (175). For Candace West and Don Zimmerman (1987), too, gender is not something that one can put on and take off but rather an "ongoing activity embedded in everyday interaction" (130).

Other scholars, taking a more situational approach, have described the production of gender within specific interactions rather than as a whole (e.g., Salzinger 2003, 7–8). Even West and Zimmerman (1987) note that, although one cannot change one's gender in different contexts, "it is plausible to contend that gender displays—construed as conventionalized expressions—are optional" (130). When this chapter discusses the ways in which pro-dommes and their clients "do" gender, it describes the ways in which gender gets produced and maintained in a specific context; it conceptualizes gender in its "conventionalized expressions," not as a constant, routinized performance.

The one place in which the intersection of gender and BDSM has been a salient issue of concern is within some feminist communities. While many feminists, as Lynn Chancer (2000) summarizes, believe that sadomasochism is "a legitimate form of consensual sexual activity" in which women should be able to engage "without fear of discriminatory judgment by society or other feminists" (79), others, such as Catharine MacKinnon, have called for a ban on pornography that involves sadomasochistic acts, viewing it as reinforcing gender hierarchy. It is important to point out that it would be irrelevant for some feminist opponents of sadomasochism that women are ostensibly the "dominant" partners in dungeon interactions. Discussing a female sadist, for instance, MacKinnon (1989) argues that the "relational dynamics of sadomasochism do not even negate the paradigm of male dominance, but conform precisely to it" (142). For MacKinnon, even when the aggression emanates from women, sadomasochism echoes the connection between sexuality and violence, power, and contempt that creates and reinforces female oppression. Andrea Dworkin (1981) makes a related argument: the image of the female sadist perpetuates the "illusion" that women are acting freely when it comes to their own sexuality, not being controlled by men (136). This feminist conversation about BDSM as a theater for playing out larger gendered dynamics, however, has been largely theoretical. As a venue where the woman plays the dominant role in the BDSM interaction, the dungeon provides a laboratory in which to evaluate feminist claims about the connection between sadomasochism and gender display.

Methods and Sample

I conducted in-depth, semi-structured interviews with fifty-two female pro-dommes in New York City and fourteen female pro-dommes in the San Francisco Bay Area. I supplemented these with interviews with ten male clients of pro-dommes and three male professional dominants (*doms*). Every woman in this study advertised in a pro-domme Internet directory. While many of the women in this study are also "in the lifestyle"—that is, they engage in noncompensatory D/S within their personal erotic relationships—all of them have received money to participate in erotic dominance. I located respondents mainly through their Internet advertisements and snowball sampling. The sixty-six (female) dominatrices involved in this study ranged in age from 20 to 58, with a median age of 37 and a mean of 37.3. Forty-one (62 percent) self-identified as white, four (6 percent) as black, four (6 percent) as Latina, four (6 percent) as Asian, and one (2 percent) as Native American. The remaining twelve women (18 percent) classified themselves as biracial.

Pro-Dommes and the Challenge
to Female Passivity

In the dominatrix's dungeon, gender is produced subversively—that is, in contrast to the hegemonic standard of the male participant as the aggressor, erotically and otherwise. Scholars have well documented the normative, relational paradigm of the sexually aggressive male and passive female participants (Allen 2003; Bailey 1989; Cancian 1986; Flora 1971; Miles 1993). Pro-dommes present a challenge to this model by assuming the role of the aggressor (the "top" in the erotic exchange). As a particular domme takes up the whip or the paddle, as she places the client in restrictive ropes, as she gives him orders, as she humiliates and taunts him—she produces a femininity that is in direct contrast to conventional, submissive femininity.

Moreover, the industry of female dominance works because it relies on the inversion of the gender-power hierarchy—a point that even MacKinnon concedes. For MacKinnon (1994, 270), "The capacity of gender reversals (dominatrixes) and inversions (homosexuality) to stimulate sexual excitement is derived precisely from their mimicry or parody or negation or reversal of the standard arrangement." While, in MacKinnon's view, gender reversal in the dungeon reaffirms the conventional arrangement, her argument still rests on the recognition of female erotic dominance as a reversal. The cultural figure of the dominatrix is effective, in short, because it represents an alternative to the standard sex/gender arrangement.

Reliance on Conventional Gender Scripts

At the same time that pro-dommes transgress the boundaries of gender normativity within their sessions, however, they often do so by following traditional gendered scripts. Pro-dommes duplicate conventional models of feminine beauty, for instance, through a variety of mechanisms. First, they often wear lacy lingerie or fitted corsets that exaggerate their feminine curves, cinching their waists and pushing up their breasts. The industry also highly values other markers of the female body, such as long, flowing hair. One San Francisco–based domme described an ongoing internal conflict she had experienced over the length of her hair.

> I had my hair like this [very short] when I started this. And it grew as soon as I started this work. The Head Mistress was all about long hair. Long, goddess hair, right? I never cut it. I had it grow even down to here, and everyone said, "Oh, your beautiful mane!" And one of the things I've talked about with my partner is how I really want to get out of this. And he's like, "Will you please cut your hair for me? For us? You look so great with short hair." And I'm like, "Well, yeah, the subs—I know they like long hair."

She finally got a haircut—an act, she said, that "freed" her—but she is typical of pro-dommes who changed their looks to fit a more stereotypically feminine mold. As one woman put it, "You find yourself leaning more and more towards trying to look mainstream. 'Cause as kinky as [erotic dominance] is, most of the clients are quite vanilla in terms of what they think is attractive."

Respondents maintained complex and varied relationships to the standards of female attractiveness that pervaded the industry. While some condemned conventionally attractive "Disney dommes" ("Blonde. Fake boobs. Plastic."), others consciously embraced these stereotypes. Many within this latter group cited financial concerns and a desire to increase or maintain their popularity with clients as their chief motivations. Still others complexly rejected such standards while remaining hyperaware of their bodies and symbolically legitimating themselves within the industry by employing rhetoric about their own conventional attractiveness. Describing a dungeon where she had formerly worked, for instance, one woman, who had previously in the interview rebuked her "Disney" counterparts, explained, "I've got big tits, I'm pretty, I've got good legs, I've got a good body. I'm not like those fat bitches who are there now." Pro-dommes "wore" gender on their bodies for highly individualistic reasons, though women who were younger and newer in the industry tended to speak more often about being swayed by reviews of their appearances.

At the same time that it feeds into mainstream conceptions of the body that pervade the world of professional erotic dominance, the respondent's comment about "those fat bitches" also sheds light on the internal complexity of this industry when it comes to gender display. Despite the pressure to conform to conventional standards of feminine beauty, women who are overweight or otherwise do not fit the "Disney domme" mold can still become successful pro-dommes. Because pro-dommes' interactional scripts often rely on the clients' perceptions of their expertise, the ageism and physical conformity that exist within other forms of erotic labor (erotic dancing, for instance) are less pronounced here. Age, for instance, plays into the fantasy of female dominance, serving as a proxy for competence and authority. Similarly, some clients have fetishes for larger women, and a larger size can contribute to a more commanding presence.

Scenarios that are persona-based often stimulate the fetishes sustaining this industry. A client may call on a twenty-year-old to play the role of a schoolgirl, while "domestic discipline" scenarios—in which dommes act as authority figures meting out punishment—are more popular with dominatrices in their forties and fifties. One woman in her late fifties who specializes in performing enemas within such punishment scenarios explained, "Because of the niche I've created for myself, it doesn't matter if I'm a thousand pounds and I'm using a walker. I'll still be able to work." Even as this industry relies on the conventionally drawn image of the female body, there is still room for resistance to this paradigm.

Interestingly, however, the reason many dommes are able to deviate from the norm of feminine beauty is that they are role-playing as other female archetypes. The enema domme, for instance, invokes classic images of femininity—the mother, the babysitter, the school marm, the cruel governess—in her "punishment" scenes. Thus, a domme sometimes engages in a trade-off, fitting into one classical model of femininity in lieu of conforming to another. Further, in playing the roles of nurse, mother, and babysitter, pro-dommes often produce a nurturing femininity. In many punishment scenarios, a domme's solicitous acts of caring temper the "cruelty" she exhibits. One Bay Area woman explained, "I spend a certain amount of time petting people's arms or stroking their backs or things like that, because so many of my clients are so touch-starved. And, you know, it's the nurse who decided you needed an enema, and while she's being mean and making you hold it, she's also stroking your arm and it's for your own good. She has your best interests at heart." Although pro-dommes also get requests for role-playing sessions in which they take on more traditionally "masculine" roles (such as military commanders), more often they take on gender-normative characters whose nurturing gestures go hand in hand with their infliction of pain.

The dungeon also provides an arena for the production of scenarios to which the intersection of gender and race is crucial. One particularly salient theme that emerged during interviews with Asian dommes was that their sessions often played into clients' "Madame Butterfly" fantasies or other stereotypical images of helpless Asian women. An Asian American domme from California, for instance, described an experience in which comments she made about her real-life romantic partner disrupted the client's fantasy: "You get these guys who are interested in you 'cause you're Asian. And some of them have this Madame Butterfly complex, right? Which is that she's, like, the noble but fallen woman. She martyrs herself, you know?" She went on to describe this phenomenon in the context of a particular client who had stopped seeing her once he found out she had a romantic partner in real life. For him, the introduction of real-world data into the equation popped the fantasy bubble. The client's fantasy of a paternalistic relationship between himself and the domme was the fetish itself in this instance. The scenario played into stereotypical notions not just of gender but of a specifically racialized gender. It is another example of the ways in which both client and domme use the physical characteristics of pro-dommes to play out the various gendered fantasies that sustain dungeon interactions.

Pro-dommes of all races further do gender in a way that plays into conventional notions of femininity by maintaining their erotic value by withholding "extras" in their sessions. One form of power that women have held in some heterosexual relationships has been the power to deny sexual contact. This power dynamic feeds into the cultural stereotype of the male participant as the aggressor and the female participant as the resister. Beth Bailey (1989, 87), for instance, discusses the institutionalized and de facto systems of "sex control" underlying dating on college campuses in the 1950s that made women "the controllers of sex."

The imperative to enforce sexual limits to increase one's value to men, a convention of the 1950s, also appears in contemporary popular culture. In the 1995 best seller *The Rules* and its 1997 sequel, *The Rules II*, Ellen Fein and Sherrie Schneider advise women to wait to have sex in order to hold on to the men they are dating. In a chapter entitled "*Rule #15:* Don't Rush into Sex and Other Rules for Intimacy," they explain:

> You will just have to exercise a bit of self-restraint and character building here and trust that if you hold off for a few weeks or months, you won't be sorry. Why risk having him call you easy (and think of you that way) when he's talking to his buddies in the locker room the next day? Better that he be angry and strategizing ways of seducing you on the next date than moving on to the next girl. (Fein and Schneider 2007, 79)

This idea about the economic value of "holding off" also emerges in U.S. vernacular—for instance, the expression that women who have sex too early in a relationship are "cheap."

In their dungeons, some pro-dommes play on this trope of the resistant female to preserve their statuses as dominant. "The more sexual you get," one woman explained, "the harder it is to maintain dominance." Refraining from particular forms of sexual contact also emerges as a theme in some pro-dommes' "humiliation scenes," in which they tempt clients with the offer of sexual favors but ultimately deny them these experiences. "It's a dance," one respondent explained. "I make them think I'm gonna have sex with them. Then [I say], 'Are you kidding me? I'm a beautiful, glorious domme. Why would I have sex with a little troll like you?' . . . It's all part of the dance." It is important to point out that the clients know that they will never receive the sex that is offered. Such humiliation scenes would not work if they did receive it. In these scenarios, the body thus becomes a tool that can be used subversively to endow the female with sexual power, while at the same time crystallizing the connection between that power and the withholding of female sexual participation.

A third way pro-dommes invoke traditional gender scripts in their dungeon interactions is by requiring manners from their clients that draw on conventional notions about gendered conduct. As one woman from the Bay Area explained:

> When he shows up, I'm going to go out and meet him in the welcome room.
> There are two little curtained cubicles. . . . When I walk in, . . . if they don't
> stand up, I'm standing in the doorway of the cubicle and I tease them about it.
> "Your mother taught you better than that. What do you do when a lady enters
> the room?" And some of them have *no* clue. Some of them, their mothers did *not*
> teach them [*laughs*].

Requiring clients to stand when they enter the room, to not interrupt them when they are speaking, and to call them "Lady" or "Ma'am" are common gender-specific protocols pro-dommes employed in their sessions.

Many of these protocols hearken back to courtly eras when male and female roles were even more clearly defined than they are today. It is no social accident that the BDSM community intersects with other communities, such as the Renaissance Faire circuit, involved in the production of courtly, romantic fantasy. The members of these groups overlap and the communities sometimes cross-promote their events. Several respondents described incidents in which they had done gender atavistically within the theater of the dungeon. One woman, for instance, recounted:

> Some gentlemen get really annoyed if you go out of character. One time I
> answered the door, said, "Come in, come in," and this guy went right into
> *mode*—calling me "My Lady." For some reason people fall back into that kind
> of Renaissance, medieval kind of thing. He said something and "My Lady" and
> I was chewing on jelly beans because it was Easter and I had all these jelly beans
> in my mouth. And he's going, "Ugh, what are you doing?" And I said, "I'm
> eating my jelly beans." And he goes, "Oh. Oh. I'll come back." And he did.
> He *walked out* and he came back twenty minutes later. And I knew he wanted
> me to finish my jelly beans. Me eating jelly beans while he's trying to be Sir
> Galahad or court jester or I don't know what the hell—I learned a lesson on
> that one.

By not behaving like a proper "Renaissance, medieval" lady, she created a rip in the fabric of fantasy woven by this particular client. Underlying these types of encounters is a level of gallantry that sustains the woman's dominance (as she is put on a pedestal), while producing gender in accordance with anachronistic standards. This use of traditional etiquette and the production of courtly fantasy reveals something interesting about the persistence of historical gendered paradigms, as well as the way in which commercial BDSM scenarios play out. Even in an erotic context in which the female partner is ostensibly dominant not only do traditional notions about masculinity and femininity endure but both domme and sub consciously exploit them.

Cross-Dressing Sessions and the Reproduction of Gender

Another anachronistic female archetype that emerges in related fantasy-sustained organizations, such as Renaissance festivals, and in the dominatrix's dungeon is the "damsel in distress." In the world of commercial BDSM, this archetype can be seen most often in cross-dressing sessions, in which the client is feminized and treated like a helpless woman. While, in "damsel in distress" scenes, femininity is produced through the male body, it is still produced in accordance with the idea of womanly weakness that underlies traditional behavioral scripts.

Butler's (1999) characterization of the practice of drag is particularly relevant to these dungeon scenarios. For Butler, drag is a kind of theater in which gender, in being caricatured, is denaturalized: "Although the gender meanings taken up in these parodic styles are clearly part of hegemonic, misogynist culture, they are nevertheless denaturalized and mobilized through their parodic recontextualization" (176). While cross-dressing is distinct from drag—a caricatured form of cross-dressing for humorous or fantastical effect—their particular effect is the same in the dungeon. Cross-dressing in the dungeon produces an exaggerated form of femininity that plays on stereotypical "hegemonic, misogynist" meanings. At the same time, when she dresses the sub in women's clothing and outfits herself with a strap-on or arms herself with a dildo, the pro-domme exaggerates gender/power dynamics and divorces gender from the body. The "parodic recontextualization" of femininity in a cross-dressing session often relies on highly stylized representations of femininity, such as the "damsel in distress" or the "sissy maid," a scenario in which the client dresses in a maid's outfit and the pro-domme orders him to perform chores, such as dusting, that have traditionally been viewed as women's work.

At the same time that cross-dressing scenes draw on various gender meanings central to a hegemonic culture, however, the second part of Butler's characterization also applies: pro-dommes denaturalize femininity through this recontextualization, exposing gender as a performance. This ability to challenge the false naturalization of masculinity and femininity emerged as a theme in many respondents' descriptions of their work. When asked, "What do you like most about being a pro-domme?" one woman replied:

> It's the idea that I don't just accept the dominant paradigm of how men and women should interact with each other on a sexual basis or on a power basis. . . . It's that you screw up gender in general, in terms of who can be penetrated and who can be the penetrator, who can top and who can bottom. There can be a fluidity there. There doesn't have to be such a rigidity to our labels and our distinctions.

Another pro-domme asserted, similarly, "I hope I do a service for humanity. It's also for me, to impart empathy, because this is a male-dominated society. . . . I try to, you know, change the world positively." The women interviewed for this study commonly expressed this kind of desire to change the way the people think about masculinity and femininity as they relate to dominance and submission.

Although only three (male) doms were interviewed for this project, it is also useful to look at their sessions as examples of the ways in which participants in BDSM can simultaneously reproduce and resist gender norms. Two of these three men regularly engaged in sessions in which they dressed in drag, at once reproducing conventional femininity and recontextualizing it on their male bodies. Further, the male clients of doms—some of whom do not identify as gay or bisexual—at once reproduce their heterosexual eroticism and challenge it by going to the dungeon for these sessions. Many respondents emphasized the fact that BDSM sexuality tends to be more fluid than sexuality in other realms of life. For instance, one male bondage enthusiast explained that, although he considers himself straight, he regularly visits a dom because "men are better at [rope] tying." By engaging in erotic practices with male-bodied individuals dressed as hyperfeminized women, male clients thus both reinforce and complicate heterosexual norms.

The conventionalized displays of gender that take place in the dungeon are all the more striking when one considers this rhetorical emphasis on the fluidity of gender and sexuality within the commercial BDSM community. The majority of the pro-dommes interviewed for this study, forty-four women (67 percent), self-identified as bisexual. Ten (15 percent) identified as straight, four (6 percent) identified as lesbian, and the remainder either did not indicate an orientation or identified with other labels—for instance, "queer," "bi dyke," or "polymorphously perverse."

Despite BDSM participants' emphasis on sexual versatility, however, this chapter documents how the gender roles men and women play in the dungeon are often inflexible. In role-playing scenarios, pro-dommes "do" their gender in the forms of various feminine archetypes. At the same time, there is no question that the work these women do challenges the "standard arrangement" of gender. They defy a taken-for-granted gender/power hierarchy by assuming the role of the dominant female partner in the erotic dyad and by "playing" with gender, challenging the primacy of the body in gender displays through cross-dressing and dildo sessions.

Conclusion

The women and men who inhabit the social world of commercial BDSM demonstrate the ways in which conventional archetypes can be mobilized to subversive effect in an erotically charged, fantasy-sustained social context. Connections can be drawn to other areas of social life in which normative gendered paradigms can persist in the production of dominant and hegemonic as well as alternative sexualities, such as gay and lesbian relationships. Maureen Sullivan (1996), for instance, finds that a minority of lesbian coparents adopt a "Rozzie and Harriet" approach to family life, in which one partner is the primary breadwinner and one is the primary caretaker, and that this division of labor "mimics modern heterosexual expectations" (747). Dungeon interactions also shed light on the production of gender within other fantasy-based organizations, such as the Renaissance festival circuit, in which, even in the alternative, imaginative world of the community, gender is often "done" normatively. More generally, while earlier work on the micro-level gendered aspects of sadomasochistic interactions has been largely theoretical, looking specifically at pro-dommes demonstrates how gender actually works in a particular type of BDSM exchange. The examination of this exchange in a U.S. context could be the launch pad for a more global analysis. In fact, one interesting avenue for further research might be an exploration of BDSM activities within cultural contexts that have had different historical experiences with gender and power.

Pro-dommes do not role-play as feminine archetypes or cross-dress their clients in every session. However, many scenes involve these types of gender play and, in them, the domme's transgressive sexuality is produced and sustained through the use of these conventional tropes. It is revealing that one trans-female pro-domme who had undergone her sex change in her late forties indicated that this work has given her the opportunity she had lacked most of her life to "be a woman" in erotic situations. "That may have been my primary motivation for this," she explained. "It's kinda making up for missing out."

NOTES

1. I do not assign pseudonyms to the women interviewed for this project because doing so would imply a level of familiarity with the respondents that I did not have. I seldom knew these women's real names—only their "scene names," which they used for their professional sessions.
2. The term *erotic labor* is borrowed from Chapkis 1997.

REFERENCES

Allen, Louisa. 2003. "Girls Want Sex, Boys Want Love: Resisting Dominant Discourses of (Hetero)Sexuality." *Sexualities* 6 (2): 215–36.

Bailey, Beth L. 1989. *From Front Porch to Back Seat: Courtship in Twentieth-Century America.* Baltimore: Johns Hopkins University Press.

Butler, Judith. 1999. *Gender Trouble: Feminism and the Subversion of Identity.* New York: Routledge.

Cancian, Francesca M. 1986. "The Feminization of Love." *Signs* 11 (4): 692–709.

Chancer, Lynn S. 2000. "From Pornography to Sadomasochism: Reconciling Feminist Differences." *Annals of the American Academy of Political and Social Science* 571:77–88.

Chapkis, Wendy. 1997. *Live Sex Acts: Women Performing Erotic Labor.* New York: Routledge.

Dworkin, Andrea. 1981. *Pornography: Men Possessing Women.* New York: Perigee.

Fein, Ellen, and Sherrie Schneider. 2007. *All The Rules: Time-Tested Secrets for Capturing the Heart of Mr. Right.* New York: Grand Central.

Flora, Cornelia Butler. 1971. "The Passive Female: Her Comparative Image by Class and Culture in Women's Magazine Fiction." *Journal of Marriage and the Family* 33 (3): 435–44.

Kamel, G. W. Levi, and Thomas S. Weinberg. 1983. "Diversity in Sadomasochism: Four S and M Careers." In *S and M: Studies in Sadomasochism,* ed. Weinberg and Kamel, 113–28. Buffalo: Prometheus.

Lee, John Alan. 1983. "The Social Organization of Sexual Risk." In *S and M: Studies in Sadomasochism*, ed. Thomas S. Weinberg and G. W. Levi Kamel, 175–93. Buffalo: Prometheus.

MacKinnon, Catharine. 1989. *Toward a Feminist Theory of the State*. Cambridge, MA: Harvard University Press.

———. 1994. Sexuality. In *Theorizing Feminism*, ed. Anne C. Hermann and Abigail J. Stewart, 257–87. Boulder, CO: Westview.

Miles, Lesley. 1993. "Women, AIDS, and Power in Heterosexual Sex: A Discourse Analysis." *Women's Studies International Forum* 16 (5): 497–511.

Patrias, Dale. 1978. "The Sociology of Secret Deviance: The Case of Sexual Sado-Masochism." Ph.D. diss., New York University.

Riviere, Joan. 1966. "Womanliness as a Masquerade." In *Psychoanalysis and Female Sexuality*, ed. Hendrik M. Ruitenbeek, 209–19. New Haven, CT: College and University Press.

Salzinger, Leslie. 2003. *Genders in Production*. Berkeley: University of California Press.

Sullivan, Maureen. 1996. "Rozzie and Harriet? Gender and Family Patterns of Lesbian Co-parents." *Gender and Society* 10 (6): 747–67.

Weinberg, Martin S., Colin J. Williams, and Charles Moser. 1984. "The Social Constituents of Sadomasochism." *Social Problems* 31 (4): 379–89.

Weinberg, Thomas S. 1983. "Sadism and Masochism: Sociological Perspectives." In *S and M: Studies in Sadomasochism*, ed. Weinberg and G. W. Levi Kamel, 99–112. Buffalo: Prometheus.

West, Candace, and Don H. Zimmerman. 1987. "Doing Gender." *Gender and Society* 1 (2): 125–51.

3

"Cruising for a Bruisin' "

Women's Flat Track Roller Derby

Natalie M. Peluso

> Athleticism can be an activist tool for third wave feminists
> and can have important social consequences.
> —Leslie Heywood and Shari Dworkin

At a large indoor sports complex, an all-female flat track roller derby league prepares for the evening's game. Wearing shirts emblazoned with their derby names, the skaters rush around the complex hanging signs, testing electrical equipment, and taping down the track. As audience members pour into the stadium seating, the skaters pull on their protective gear and padding, scrawl their numbers on their arms with permanent marker, and lace up their roller skates. Pierced and tattooed, outfitted in booty shorts, fishnet stockings, and knee-high socks, the skaters take warm-up laps around the track and occasionally pose for pictures with adoring fans. The team bench is buzzing with adrenaline as skaters return to stretch their limbs and talk strategy. Even before the start of the game, these skaters are challenging conventional attire, appearance, and body norms.

Within the past six years, all-female flat track roller derby has caught the attention of the nation and media as thousands of women have flocked to the sport. By the end of 2010, according to the website of the Women's Flat Track Derby Association (WFTDA) ninety-eight leagues in the United States were full members of the association and another fifty-three leagues were under apprenticeship.[1] Embodying the "do-it-yourself" ethic, women around the country are starting up local leagues and taking on the roles of skaters, referees, coaches, business owners, managers, and spectators.

In this chapter I draw on my ethnographic research as a skater in an all-women's flat track roller derby league to show how roller derby creates performative and discursive opportunities for women to transgress cultural norms regarding the appearance and performance of the female body. My research shows, first, that flat track roller derby itself creates a safe space in sport for marginalized and transgressive bodies Second, skaters subvert attire and adornment norms by wearing sexualized clothing and sporting multiple piercings, tattoos, and unconventional hairstyles. Finally, roller derby participants reconceptualize corporeality by framing injuries as physical and subcultural capital, and by adopting narratives of the "cyborg" and "robot" when discussing bodily performances.

What Is Roller Derby?

Roller derby began in New York during the 1930s as a co-ed speed-skating competition. While roller derby began as an endurance sport, a points system and banked track were eventually adopted that transformed the game into a strategic and physical competition between two teams. Skaters were now encouraged to bump, block, hit, and fight on the track. Though the rules of the game gradually changed, roller derby remained a popular U.S. sport until the 1970s. Several revivals were attempted in the 1980s and 1990s, all with limited success. Their failures have been blamed on a combination of waning audiences, decreasing television ratings, concocted storylines, and absurd theatrical antics (Mabe 2007). Present-day roller derby differs in several ways from the televised roller derby of the past. It is now a form of recreation rather than an occupation; the vast majority of roller derby games now take place on flat tracks rather than banked tracks; and modern leagues have abandoned the staged theatrical fights typical of "old school" roller derby and penalize on-track fighting of any kind. Also, contemporary leagues pride themselves on being member owned and operated (Joulwan 2007).

Contemporary women's roller derby is an amateur, competitive, full-contact team sport played on traditional quad roller skates. The sport itself incorporates racing, hitting, positional strategy, and offensive and defensive blocking. During a game or "bout," two teams compete and attempt to score points on their opponent. A team lineup normally consists of one jammer, one pivot, and three blockers. After her initial pass through the pack, the jammer scores a point for every opposing player she passes legally. The pivot and three blockers escort their jammer through the pack while simultaneously blocking the opposing team's jammer. The team with the most points at the end of the bout wins.

Roller derby is a full-contact sport for which players are required to wear protective gear, including helmets, mouth guards, elbow pads, wrist guards, and kneepads. Roller skates and protective equipment, however, are costly, and most leagues expect skaters also to purchase some form of health insurance and to pay monthly dues. Thus, roller derby is an expensive sport to play, and because of class inequalities as well as racial and ethnic realities, not all women have equal access to roller derby as a form of leisure activity (Storms 2008).

Why Study Roller Derby?

The sporting female body has been overlooked empirically and theoretically. Hall (1996), for example, has called for grounded theories emerging directly from women's embodied experiences: "We need . . . concrete, material analyses of diverse women's 'body' experience in sport," she says, and "more studies in which women athletes are asked to reflect upon the significance of the body and physicality to their experience of sport. Work . . . done in a collective setting, linked to feminist body theory and ultimately to practice would be very powerful" (64). Extending Hall's recommendations, Hughson (2008, 58) says, "Non-conventional sport subcultures should be observed closely for their potential to challenge relations of gender and sexuality."

Teammates Nerdy Diana (*front row, second from left*) and Death Petal (*front row, fourth from left*) prepare to booty block two opposing team skaters as their jammer, Bon Bon Scott (*skater wearing a white helmet in the background*), approaches the pack. Distracting these opposing blockers, they hope, will guarantee Bon Bon a safe and point-accumulating passage through the pack. (Photograph courtesy of Michele Wilcox.)

Here, I argue that roller derby—as a full-contact, aggressive, "extreme" sport played overwhelmingly by women—is a nonconventional sport subculture that challenges gendered power relations. As such, it warrants increased academic attention.

Theorizing Women's (Bodily) Involvement in Sport

According to Messner (2007, 32), "the female athlete—and her body—has become a contested ideological terrain." Women's physical involvement in sports has been studied from a variety of disciplinary perspectives. Sports studies, feminist and gender studies, and subcultural studies have all generated theory pertaining to the female sporting body; and yet, these formulations tend to talk past one another. For example, theorists have argued that sport studies have marginalized feminist theory (Messner 2007), while feminist sport scholars have claimed that while "female bodies have been central to feminism, sporting bodies have not" (Hall 1996, 50).

Attempting to weave these conversations together, sport feminism, then, presents itself as a useful theoretical approach to the study of women's (embodied) experience in sport. Since there are multiple feminisms, there are also multiple sport feminisms informed by theory and practice. All forms of sport feminism, before the emergence of postmodernism, were focused on "expos[ing], challeng[ing], and eliminat[ing] gender-based dominant policies and practices" (Hargreaves 2004, 187). Taking a postmodern sport feminist perspective, I explore the ways in which women's potential empowerment through sport relates back to feminist politics and ask, How can women transgress gender and bodily norms through sport? And, how can sport be empowering for women?

Women, Contact Sports, and Gender Transgression

Eitzen (2009) highlights the ways in which sport operates as a social institution reinforcing the oppression of women within and outside the sporting world, She notes: "Boys are expected to participate in sports, to be aggressive, to be physically tough, to take risks, and to accept pain. Thus sport, especially aggressive physical contact sport, is expected for boys and men but not for girls and women. These expectations reproduce male domination in society" (313). Such cultural norms rely heavily on the binary construction of gender, which suggests that men and women are not just biologically distinct; they are complementary opposites. Hence, while men are associated with aggressiveness, physical strength, and risk taking, women are associated with passivity, weakness, and timidity (Hall 1996).

Infusing a gendered analysis into the respective works of Foucault (1979) and Bourdieu (1984), Bordo (1993) and Bartky (1997) acknowledge that behavioral expectations for men and women differ and argue that, in addition, women's physical bodies themselves have been "disciplined" or "trained" into slimness, smallness, passivity, and heteronormative beauty standards. The effect has been the production or creation of female bodies that seem "less suited" for physical activity on the whole and for contact sports in particular. "When women do participate," Deem (1986, 68) points out, "it is often in a sport which reinforces traditional ideas about femininity—yoga, keep fit, swimming—and which are hence compatible with stereotypes of beauty, grace and female attractiveness. What is much less rarely acceptable is women doing sports which involve physical contact, getting dirty or sweating profusely." Women who "pioneer new patterns" in sport or make inroads into those deemed "aggressive" or "extreme" risk severe stigmatization (Lenskyj 1986, 99).

Yet for some women, participating in sports deemed "inappropriate" or "off limits" is a way to challenge hegemonic gender norms. According to Howe (2003, 227), "confrontational contact within women's sport has long been considered taboo." In a discussion of women's rugby, he argues that players physically transgressed gender by engaging in aggressive physical contact with other sporting female bodies. In their study of adolescent female skateboarders, Kelly, Pomerantz, and Currie (2008, 118) assert that by "doing" skateboarding, the skaters "engaged in a transgressive bodily comportment." That is, "they were willing to stand with a wide gait on their boards, dangle their arms freely by their sides, and spread out for balance." Such "transgressive bodily comportment" allowed these female skaters to buck the tenets of conventional femininity and thereby experience embodiment in radically new ways. Another study of female skateboarders found that skaters consciously subverted traditional femininity through dress (e.g., wearing baggy clothing) and through the performance of "risky" physical feats (e.g., complex tricks, skateboarding in traffic) (Young and Dallaire 2008). Finally, in a study of bodybuilders, Wesely (2001) found that female participants negotiated gender identity by manipulating their bodies, increasing and decreasing their bulk. She asserts that since "muscles are *the* sign of male power . . . patriarchy, . . . and masculinity, . . . women who build muscle de-stabilize dominant concepts of gender identity" (166–67). To summarize, this body of research suggests that sportswomen accomplish embodied resistance through dress, muscularity, physical contact, bodily deportment, and the performance of physical risk. All of these forms of (gender) resistance are present in women's roller derby and contribute to the overall transgressive potential of the sport while presenting women with opportunities to trouble gender and body.

Researching Roller Derby

I entered the world of flat track roller derby four years ago when I accompanied a friend to observe an evening practice. What I saw during that two-hour practice amazed me. Not only did I want to study roller derby, I actually wanted to play it, so I joined a league and learned the game. I purchased the requisite gear, contacted the league in my area, and began attending two to four practices a week. I also attended numerous bouts, regional tournaments, social events, and league meetings. These gatherings became my primary field sites.

Through ethnographic field research, I gained key insights into how roller derby participants came to see, understand, and interact in their social settings. As a result of my immersion in the league, I experienced firsthand the bodily practices and interactional processes that constitute the world of roller derby. The amount of time we spent practicing, traveling, and hanging out together enabled me to develop friendships with many of the skaters—several of whom became my key informants. Additionally, I conducted formal interviews with twenty-one roller derby players. Interviews lasted between forty-five minutes and two hours. To ensure confidentiality, I created a pseudonym for each skater's derby name.

The twenty-one women I interviewed ranged in age from twenty-six to forty. Eighteen identified as white, one identified as "half-black, half-white," and two identified as Hispanic. The lack of skaters of color in my study reflects the overall demographics of the roller derby community. All of my informants completed at least some college and were employed in administrative (e.g., secretary), service sector (e.g., massage therapist), or professional (e.g., school teacher) positions. Eighteen skaters identified as straight, two as bisexual, and one as lesbian; five were married; and three had children.

The ability to physically experience the sport while researching it was rewarding and challenging. I found a community of similarly styled women who appreciated my numerous tattoos and piercings, "ironic" mullet, and quirky fashion sense, and they were as supportive of my five-feet-two-inch body at both its lowest (125 pounds) and highest (165 pounds) weight. Over the course of my fieldwork, I progressed from being barely able to stand on roller skates to being capable of sprily dodging, sprinting, jumping, hitting, and skating backward around the track. To my surprise, the sport itself was very enjoyable and provided a wonderful physical outlet.

I also took my fair share of abuse on the track. My list of injuries includes a broken finger, a black eye, a sprained wrist, a shoulder separation, knee tendinitis, countless scrapes and bruises, and several cases of mild whiplash. I left practice injured and aching, rendered unable to walk comfortably the next day. I felt disappointment and frustration when my skating was substandard. Yet, however rewarding or challenging, each of these embodied experiences allowed me to experience roller derby the same way my teammates did.

Findings

Creating Space for Transgressive Bodies

While sport offers women opportunities to challenge gender and body norms, it is important to keep in mind that it is a social institution informed by dominant cultural norms and values. As Cole (1993, 78) notes, we must recognize "'sport' as a discursive construct that organizes multiple practices that intersect with and produce multiple bodies embedded in normalizing technologies and consumer culture."

Sport therefore has the potential to normalize particular types of physical bodies, while marginalizing others. Dominant discourses of femininity have shifted to incorporate the slim but toned body into the feminine cultural norm. Consequently, "keep fit" sports such as aerobics have been said to encourage women's compliance to the ideals of femininity (Hall 1996). Further, Choi (2000, 76) argues, "in motivating women to exercise for beauty reasons, there is greater opportunity for disempowerment than empowerment and in such a predominantly beauty related exercise culture it is not always easy for women to find alternative exercise discourse."

Addressing Choi's concern, I contend that inherent in modern-day roller derby are seeds of resistance. As a grassroots sport organized by and for women, roller derby has the potential to pose challenges to many different cultural mandates. As Lenskyj (1986) found, female athletes encountered homophobia and heterosexism: "Some women formed lesbian-only outdoor clubs and sports leagues, while others developed organizations where lesbianism was accepted positively. . . . These developments demonstrate how sport and recreation organized by and for women at the grassroots level pose a significant challenge to the institution of compulsory heterosexuality" (107). Building on Lenskyj's claim, I argue that through roller derby, skaters are able to carve out safe spaces for transgressive bodies in sport. As Hughson (2008) notes, group membership in sports arises out of the attempt to "resist—or *win space* from—the 'dominant' sporting culture" (63). This is precisely how modern-day roller derby operates. As the skater Sour Applebottom notes, "We're creating this space where people who were 'the other' in sports could finally be 'the.'"

Specifically, in roller derby, fat bodies are accepted as readily as slim bodies, big as readily as small, old as readily as young. And, again, these transgressive female sporting bodies are welcomed into the sport. As the skater Robin Graves explains, roller derby "embrace[s] women of all shapes, sizes, [and] ages. It bring[s] all of these women in and say[s], 'You may not have any sort of athletic background or skill, *but you can be here.'*" Furthermore, Iron Maiven says, "to see other women my size do the same things I'm doing is really great because it was harder before in my [previous] sports to see that I was the only one at my weight. Being a part of a league where there were women that were larger than me . . . made me feel less out of the norm." Additionally, heavy skaters can play roller derby without fear of harassment, whereas women in other sports have reported being pressured to lose weight in order to play and being ridiculed by coaches and teammates if they could not (Heywood and Dworkin 2003). As Miss Demeanor, a league member who identifies as fat, explains, "I never thought of myself as an athlete or athletic because of my body. But in derby, I can be an athlete and still be the size that I am."

Derby provides women with a safe space to be transgressively embodied. It also broadens cultural definitions of the "sporting" body to include a wide range of corporealities. Thus, roller derby challenges hegemonic bodily norms that demand that women "discipline" themselves into slenderness.

The Props of Performance

Beyond challenging norms regarding body size, roller derby allows women to transgress attire and adornment norms. Skaters wear a variety of "sexualized" clothing items, including miniskirts, ripped fishnets, knee socks, and booty shorts—all reminiscent of a third wave feminist aesthetic. These items, however, are paired with "masculinized" elements of fashion (e.g., shaved heads) and sporting gear (e.g., mouth guards and protective padding). In a study of women's attire in music subcultures, Schippers (2002, 115) suggests that the pairing of "sexy" clothing with masculinized accoutrements disrupts the "seamless sexual objectification" that occurs when wearing "slut wear" alone. For derby skaters, the coupling of risqué attire with the bulky gear operates in a similar manner. Notably, women of all shapes and sizes, including those with bodies deemed culturally "undesirable," wear this derby apparel. Borrowing from Lloyd (1996), who suggests that "particular practices of femininity have the potential to operate transgressively" (250), when skaters of size don these sexualized uniforms, their doing so is both counter-hegemonic and subtly revolutionary.

In addition to wearing provocative apparel, many skaters sport multiple tattoos and piercings. To these skaters, part of the appeal of roller derby is that it attracts tattooed, pierced, and alternatively styled women. As Rumble Bunny notes, "It's like I come to practice and I look 'normal' because so many of the girls have tattoos." Sinead O'Rebellion, who has facial piercings and blue hair, adds that the roller derby community allowed her to meet "athletic girls with tattoos and piercings, and it was totally normal and they weren't [considered] freaks." For skaters like Sinead, the roller derby subculture, as Entwistle (2000, 139), points out, "employ[s] style, dress, body, posture and so on to create identity self-consciously, both to affirm group affiliation and difference to those on the outside and within." Skaters enjoy the subcultural niche (and the accompanying feelings of belonging and identity) that roller derby affords them (Hebdige 1979).

Moreover, as several league members observed, it is quite common for new members of the roller derby sporting subculture to begin getting tattooed when they join the league. Sour Applebottom, for example, said:

A lot of the derby girls have tattoos and things like that, and I know a lot of the girls didn't have tattoos going in. You'll see them start getting tattoos after they've been involved. I now have plans for a huge back piece and half a sleeve. While I always wanted tattoos and had one before I started, I don't think I would have made so many plans to continue getting more work if it wasn't for seeing all these other beautiful women. "Oh, wow! That looks really hot on them—I can do that too!"

Previous work on sport subcultures has found that new members "adopt mannerisms and attitudes, styles of dress, language and behavior" common among older members (Jones and Aitchison 2006, 58). Roller derby's acceptance of alternatively adorned bodies not only attracts modified women to the sport but also encourages and empowers previously unmodified women to begin seeking new ways to decorate their flesh.

The Bruised and the Broken: Reframing Corporeality

In my research, I found that skaters reconceptualized the physical body in radically new ways. First, bumps, lumps, bruises, and breaks were all considered forms of *physical capital* as expressed by Shilling (1993), who says, "When social fields (art, fashion, sport, etc.) bestow value directly on a specific bodily form, activity or performance, they are effectively creating a category of physical capital" (139). Physical capital can then be converted into other forms—such as economic, cultural, and social capital. In his ethnography of professional boxing, Wacquant (2007, 262) notes, "The fighter's body is simultaneously his means of production, the raw materials he and his handlers (trainer and manager) have to work with and on." "Properly managed," he adds, "this body is capable of producing more value than was 'sunk' in it." Applied to roller derby, the visible injuries of skaters testify to the amount of physical labor "sunk" into their bodies. While Waquant's informants attempted to convert their physical capital into economic capital (by becoming career athletes), skaters cannot do so because roller derby has not "professionalized" (i.e., no one is paid to play). Yet, while no economic gains are made, in many ways, the injuries themselves become the payoff for the skaters' hard work. For example, at practice one evening, Shenita Sling mentioned that she was angry because a hit she had taken in the face had never bruised.

NATALIE: Well, you're lucky because black eyes hurt a lot!
SHENITA: Oh no. This hurts too! I'm just mad because I figure if I'm going to go through this much pain, I might as well get something for it.

Further, skaters' bodily capital can be converted into subcultural capital—the "hip," "cool," or "in the know" within a particular subcultural context. Additionally, subcultural capital can be "embodied in . . . looking as if you were born to perform the latest dance styles" (Thornton 1997, 202) or skillfully play a particular sport (Hughson 2008). In the roller derby world, the accumulation of bruises and breaks conveys to fellow members one's knowledge of the game, one's skilled or "expert" status, and one's overall toughness; they may also be worn as badges of honor that distinguish skaters from women embodying traditional femininity (Kelly, Pomerantz, and Currie 2008). This attitude perhaps explains why at practice, skaters will go out of their way to show their fishnet-patterned patches of rink rash and black-and-blue marks to league mates, who "oooh" and "ahhh" over the truly spectacular ones.

Many leagues devote a section of their websites to displaying photographs of skaters' injuries, suggesting that skaters, while invested in showing their injuries to members of the roller derby community, are equally concerned about showcasing them to the outside world. Storms (2008), who also studied roller derby, writes, "It is . . . as if these women are saying, 'I played hard enough to get this.' It is a temporary inscription on their physical body as a testament to something women are not thought to be capable of by mainstream society" (82). Thus skaters may be seen as battling for cultural space for the (radical) sporting female body—an overtly political act.

Beyond conceptualizing the body as a form of physical and subcultural capital, skaters adopted narratives of the "robot" or "cyborg" when speaking about their own corporeality. The cyborg, according to Haraway (1991, 149), "is a matter of fiction and lived experience that changes what counts as women's experience in the late twentieth century." More specifically, the cyborg body can be understood as the pairing of organic matter with artificial machine (Balsamo 1996). For example, Sinead, who broke her collarbone, described the metal plate and screws implanted into her clavicle as her "robot parts." For roller derby practitioners, the cyborg body may offer an array of possibilities that surpass those offered by the human corpus alone.

The robot theme often reemerges in skaters' conversations about recovery. To underscore their bionic identities, recovering or recovered skaters modified their derby names by attaching either the prefix *robot* or the suffix *bot* to them. For example, after sustaining an injury that required several months of physical therapy, Skater Tot began referring to herself as "Robot Tot" or simply "Tot Bot." Even after a skater has healed from an injury, she may continue to use this language of hybridization. According to Cregan (2006, 149), "Women can take control of the logic of . . . biotechnologies to their own ends and 'rewrite' embodiment. In this narrative . . . the integration of medical technologies with the human form open[s] the way for women to use them to their own ends." Relatedly, derby skaters actively "rewrite" the narratives of their own embodiment in ways that are meaningful to them. For the derby skater, the cyborg body presents itself as another inhabitable position on the continuum of radical sporting bodies.

Thus, the grassroots sport of flat track roller derby offers women the physical and cultural space to be (through its acceptance of all sizes and shapes), to perform (through its embracing of sexualized clothing and alternative adornments), and to re-conceptualize (through its radical rethinking of embodiment) the transgressive (sporting) female body. In roller derby, women are enabled and encouraged to challenge traditional femininity through their bodies, and this—in itself—constitutes a feminist act of embodied resistance.

NOTES

The epigraph is from Heywood and Dworkin 2003, 45.

1. Women's Flat Track Derby Association, "Member Leagues," *Women's Flat Track Derby Association,* wftda.com/leagues.

REFERENCES

Balsamo, Anne. 1996. *Technologies of the Gendered Body: Reading Cyborg Women*. Durham, NC: Duke University Press.

Bartky, Sandra Lee. 1997. "Foucault, Femininity, and the Modernization of Patriarchal Power." In *Feminist Social Thought: A Reader*, ed. Diana Tietjens Meyers, 93–111. New York: Routledge.

Bordo, Susan. 1993. *Unbearable Weight: Feminism, Western Culture, and the Body*. Berkeley: University of California Press.

Bourdieu, Pierre. 1984. *Distinction: A Social Critique on the Judgement of Taste*. Trans. Robert Nice. Cambridge, MA: Harvard University Press.

Choi, Precilla Y. L. 2000. *Femininity and the Physically Active Woman*. Philadelphia: Taylor and Francis.

Cole, Cheryl L. 1993. "Resisting the Canon: Feminist Cultural Studies, Sport, and Technologies of the Body." *Journal of Sport and Social Issues* 17:77–97.

Cregan, Kate. 2006. *The Sociology of the Body*. London: Sage.

Deem, Rosemary. 1986. *All Work and No Play?* Milton Keynes, UK: Open University Press.

Eitzen, D. Stanley. 2009. "Sport and Gender." In *Sport in Contemporary Society: An Anthology*, 8th ed., ed. Eitzen, 313–18. Boulder, CO: Paradigm.

Entwistle, Joanne. 2000. *The Fashioned Body: Fashion, Dress, and Modern Social Theory*. Malden, MA: Blackwell.

Foucault, Michel. 1979. *Discipline and Punish: The Birth of the Prison*. New York: Vintage Books.

Hall, M. Ann. 1996. *Feminism and Sporting Bodies: Essays on Theory and Practice*. Champaign, IL: Human Kinetics.

Haraway, Donna. 1991. *Simians, Cyborgs, and Women: The Reinvention of Nature*. New York: Routledge.

Hargreaves, Jennifer. 2004. "Querying Sport Feminism: Personal or Political?" In *Sport and Modern Social Theorists*, ed. Richard Giulianotti, 187–205. New York: Palgrave Macmillan.

Hebdige, Dick. 1979. *Subculture: The Meaning of Style*. New York: Methuen.

Heywood, Leslie, and Shari Dworkin. 2003. *Built to Win: The Female Athlete as Cultural Icon*. Minneapolis: University of Minnesota Press.

Howe, P. David. 2003. "Kicking Stereotypes into Touch: An Ethnographic Account of Women's Rugby." In *Athletic Intruders: Ethnographic Research on Women, Culture, and Exercise*, ed. Anne Bolin and Jane Granskog, 227–46. New York: State University of New York Press.

Hughson, John. 2008. "'They Think It's All Over': Sport and the End of Subcultural Debate." In *Tribal Play: Subcultural Journeys through Sport*, ed. Michael Atkinson and Kevin Young, 49–66. Research in the Sociology of Sport 4. Bingley, UK: Emerald Group, JAI.

Jones, Amanda, and Cara Carmichael Aitchison. 2006. "Triathlon as a Space for Women's Technologies of the Self." In *Sport and Gender Identities: Masculinities, Femininities, and Sexualities*, ed. Cara Carmichael Aitchison, 53–73. Hoboken, NJ: Taylor and Francis.

Joulwan, Melissa. 2007. *Rollergirl: Totally True Tales from the Track*. New York: Touchstone.

Kelly, Deirdre M., Shauna Pomerantz, and Dawn H. Currie. 2008. "'You Can Break So Many More Rules': The Identity Work and Play of Becoming Skater Girls." In *Youth Culture and Sport: Identity, Power, and Politics*, ed. Michael D. Giardina and Michele K. Donnelly, 113–25. New York: Routledge.

Lenskyj, Helen. 1986. *Out of Bounds: Women, Sport, and Sexuality*. Toronto: Women's Press.

Lloyd, Moya. 1996. "A Feminist Mapping of Foucauldian Politics." In *Feminist Interpretations of Michel Foucault*, ed. Susan J. Hekman, 241–264. University Park: Pennsylvania State University Press.

Mabe, Catherine. 2007. *Roller Derby: The History and All-Girl Revival of the Greatest Sport on Wheels*. Denver: Speck.

Messner, Michael A. 2007. *Out of Play: Critical Essays on Gender and Sport*. New York: State University of New York Press.

Schippers, Mimi. 2002. *Rockin' out of the Box: Gender Maneuvering in Alternative Hard Rock*. New Brunswick, NJ: Rutgers University Press.

Shilling, Chris. 1993. *The Body and Social Theory*. Thousand Oaks, CA: Sage.

Storms, Carolyn E. 2008. "There's No Sorry in Roller Derby: A Feminist Examination of Identity of Women in the Full Contact Sport of Roller Derby." *New York Sociologist* 3 (October): 68–87. *newyorksociologist.org/08/Storms-08.pdf*.

Thorton, Sarah. 1997. "The Social Logic of Cultural Capital." In *The Subcultures Reader*, ed. Ken Gelder and Sarah Thorton, 200–209. London: Routledge.

Wacquant, Loïc. 2007. "Bodily Capital among Professional Boxers." In *The Sport Studies Reader*, ed. Alan Tomlinson, 261–66. New York: Routledge.

Wesely, Jennifer K. 2001. "Negotiating Gender: Bodybuilding and the Natural/Unnatural Continuum." *Sociology of Sport Journal* 18 (2): 162–80.

Young, Alana, and Christine Dallaire. 2008. "Beware*#! SK8 at Your Own Risk: The Discourses of Young Female Skateboarders." In *Tribal Play: Subcultural Journeys through Sport*, ed. Michael Atkinson and Kevin Young, 235–54. Research in the Sociology of Sport 4. Bingley, UK: Emerald Group, JAI.

4

Becoming a Female-to-Male Transgender (FTM) in South Korea

Tari Youngjung Na and Hae Yeon Choo

"Are you a man or a woman?" This question has followed Youn-Woo ever since he entered college in South Korea in 1998.[1] At five feet three inches, with a medium build and short hair, Youn-Woo could be seen as either a teenage boy or a masculine woman. Youn-Woo was always taken aback by this very personal question and was unable to provide an easy answer. At the time, Youn-Woo did not yet identify as a transgender individual—born female but wanting to live as a man.[2] But he was becoming increasingly aware that he was different from others, who did not hesitate for a second before identifying themselves as men or women.

Throughout his childhood, his friends and family called Youn-Woo a tomboy (*sonmosum*). As a child, he liked playing with boys more than girls and refused to wear a skirt. Because of the deep-seated Confucian culture of gender segregation, girls' schools were quite common in South Korea, and Youn-Woo attended all-girls schools for middle and high school. He flourished in this women-only environment—his tomboy personality attracted many classmates, and he routinely received love letters and gifts from admirers. His popularity is not surprising; in South Korea until the late 1990s, homoeroticism among girls was accepted as nonthreatening, a phase girls would grow out of as they became women and entered heterosexual relationships. In the 2000s, this subtle form of tolerance began to disappear. With the growing visibility of homosexuality, girls' schools in Korea became a target of moral surveillance, while *iban* girls faced increased regulation of their behavior and dress by school rules and became victims of bullying by their peers. By that time, however, Youn-Woo had already graduated from high school.

When Youn-Woo continued to act like a tomboy after entering college—resisting norms concerning the embodiment of the female gender—his behavior raised questions for himself and others. For the first time in his life, Youn-Woo began to wonder whether something was wrong with him. After years of confusion and searching for answers, in a critical moment of discovery, he considered the possibility that he might be transgender. "During an Internet search," he said,

> I stumbled upon a German guy's personal webpage. He identified himself as an FTM, and posted his photos showing his chest without the shirt. It looked

perfect! He posted a lot about surgery—how he felt after waking up after the surgery, what it was like to stand and pee. Only then did I realize that such surgery existed, and it was such an eye-opener. It was 2000, and knowing that the genital surgery is possible made me hopeful. Now I had a concrete future, a possibility I can be myself.

For Youn-Woo, this knowledge of FTM transgender identity and surgery as a means to achieve it offered a promising future, and he began to plan his life according to this new goal. He joined a South Korean FTM support group, made concrete plans for hormonal therapy, and began saving money for surgery. As Youn-Woo began the transition process in the company of others who identified as FTMs, he became a part of the nascent phenomenon of transgender community building in South Korea.

In this chapter, we examine the ways in which FTMs in South Korea like Youn-Woo resist norms concerning the embodiment of gender in the process of becoming FTM subjects, an identity that is not limited to a local subculture but is nationally organized and globally recognizable. The two ideas examined in this chapter, resistance and subjection, might seem to be opposing forces if power is understood only as a repressive external force that individuals either are subject to or resist. Yet, subjection encompasses a dual meaning. Based on a Foucauldian understanding of power, we complicate the unitary understanding of subjecthood. Foucault (1978, 95–96) argues, "Where there is power, there is resistance, and yet, or rather consequently, this resistance is never in a position of exteriority in relation to power." Power produces "subjects" (in the sense of an actor or agent), and these subjects, in turn, become "subjected to" the rules and regulations that accompany their identities in order to be recognized by others as such; the subjects, however, may also resist these regulations. Furthermore, the very act of resistance continues the cycle by creating new norms comprising identity and subjecthood. By highlighting this dual sense of subjection in our study, we examine how the development of resistance entails a process of subjection to a new set of rules that define who is entitled to claim this emerging FTM identity.

Methods and Setting

We use ethnographic research to explore resistance among FTMs who challenge the conventional gender binary in South Korea. Data was gathered by the first author through in-depth interviews conducted with eleven self-identified FTMs and three LGBT individuals involved in the FTM community from May to October 2006 in three South Korean cities (Seoul, Daejon, and Busan). Interviewees were identified through snowball sampling. Participants ranged from twenty-two to forty-six years old and all had participated in FTM support groups, online and off-line spaces where FTMs meet to exchange information about transition and support one another. The semi-structured interviews took place in a coffeehouse, lasted two to four hours, and at times involved one or two follow-up interview sessions. All interviews were conducted in Korean. Interview topics included how the interviewees experienced (trans) gender in childhood, school, and the workplace; how they sought and found support for transition; what their involvement was in LGBT activism and FTM support groups; and how they envisioned their future, including the pursuit of legal and medical sex reassignment. In addition, participant observation was conducted at FTM support group and the transgender rights activist group meetings.

In South Korea, the non-normative embodiment of gender existed before the collective mobilization of sexual identity groups in the 1990s. Documentation of sex reassignment surgery began in the 1950s, along with subcultures of masculine women in same-sex relationships. For example, a group of women in the 1970s called themselves *bajissi* (trousers), dressed in masculine outfits, and dated feminine women. Yet, such subcultures had limited visibility and involved and were known to only a small group of people. As political democratization progressed after 1987, cultural emphasis shifted from the Confucian notion institutionalized by authoritarian regimes of the patriarchal family as a central social unit to the notion of individual rights. In the context of globalization, inspired by gay activists in the Korean diaspora, LGBT activism in South Korea emerged in the mid-1990s, starting in 1994 with the founding of the gay men's organization Chingusai and the lesbian organization Kirikiri (Seo 2001). Organizing among gay and lesbian Koreans relied heavily on Internet communication. So too did organizing among transgender individuals, whose visibility in the early 2000s benefited from the 2001 rise of the cultural icon Harisu, a popular South Korean MTF singer who became a reference point for many South Korean transgenders. The ensuing formation of various transgender online support groups led to the foundation of Jirungi, the first transgender activist organization in South Korea, in 2006.

Resistance and Subjection
in the Lives of South Korean FTMs

In the following sections we explore the ways in which resistance and subjection manifest as South Korean FTMs become involved in power structures through their pursuit of three essential aspects of life: livelihood, community, and citizenship. Gender binary norms and segregation persist in South Korea, and FTMs continue to engage in everyday resistance and an organized legal struggle to demand collective rights. The contours of their resistance illustrate how FTMs are subject to new norms and rules enforced by medical-legal authorities and the FTM community.

The Pursuit of Livelihood: Everyday Resistance
in a Gender-Segregated Society

When FTMs begin a physical transition, they face societal sanctions, including discrimination and economic insecurity in their daily lives. All South Korean citizens receive a national ID card at birth, and the ID numbers differ by gender. When their appearance no longer matches the sex identified on their ID cards, FTMs are stripped of the ability to use the legal document in most realms of South Korean public life, including the labor market, medical institutions, and financial institutions (WIG 2008). Twenty-seven-year-old Jung-Won described an interview for a dispatch driver position that "totally crushed [his] spirit." His interview went well and the boss was ready to sign the contract. But, as Jung-Won explained, his ID proved problematic.

> The boss said, "Fine, start working tomorrow. Give me your driver's license. We need to keep a copy on file." I gave him mine and on his way to the copy machine, he looked at it and said, "What's wrong with this number?" I somehow felt guilty and meekly said, "because I was born a woman." Then, he said it was not going to work. "Why?" I asked. Do you know what he said? Because I would disgust their customers.

Such discrimination led many FTMs to employ passing as a strategy in daily life in order to sustain a livelihood, and to engage selectively in subtle, everyday forms of resistance. At their workplaces, many resorted to using a borrowed or forged male ID, found blue-collar jobs that did not require an ID, or fabricated their education history, listing boys' schools rather than the girls' schools they actually attended. The act of passing at work, however, required FTMs to face a new form of subjection: they were pressured to conform to the unfamiliar culture of male bonding. Interaction among Korean men often involves acts that downplay differences among them. As In-Tae, an FTM in his late forties, recalled: "When men become friends, they drink together and afterwards, they'd like to go to a public bathhouse, and to a brothel. Enjoying my woman, your woman, like that. But I don't feel comfortable going to those places, and I try avoiding it, but they are like, 'What's wrong with you, ruining our night!'" In-Tae felt uncomfortable because he was afraid to expose his body and because he was not familiar with men's culture and its objectification of women.

Some FTMs found interacting with other men unpleasant but viewed it as a necessity, because they were afraid people might suspect they were different from other men if they continued to resist taking part in these activities. For others, these situations proved to be exciting opportunities to learn about men's culture. Su-Han, a thirty-five-year-old factory worker who dropped out of college to begin transitioning, enjoyed smoking and eating ramen noodles with male coworkers during break times and taking part in "men's talk." He was surprised by how continually his coworkers talked about two things: military experience and women. In South Korea, male-only conscription makes the military an equalizing institution that overcomes age, class, and educational level, making it a common conversational topic for every man. At times Su-Han felt uncomfortable making up stories about his military days and putting down women as sexual objects, but he felt pressured to take part in these exchanges because he thought of his interaction "as part of the process of learning to become a man."

While passing as men in the workplace, FTMs cultivate resources for resistance. At age forty-five, In-Tae successfully secured a job—his first—as a motorbike delivery person. He had managed a small business over the years and thought getting a job would be impossible with a woman's ID, but at this job, he successfully passed as a man. Then one day In-Tae was hit by a car and he did something that he "would never have imagined possible": he reported the accident, entered the hospital, and used the health insurance provided by workers' compensation. Though seemingly mundane, this act was significant for In-Tae because all his life he had been afraid of any kind of situation in which his identity might be revealed. This time, however, having secured a job as a man gave him a confidence to claim his rights. He explained:

> When I was admitted to the hospital room [for women], nurses started laughing. I just watched how they would handle the situation. And they asked me to go back to the main office. "Why?" I asked. They said something is not right. When I went back to the office, the director said, "Sir, please don't take it personally. Your ID number begins with number two, which is woman, right? But we can't send you to a women's room. We can't send you to a men's either, because of the paperwork. So we will call the insurance and give you a private room." I said fine, so I had the whole room to myself!

For In-Tae, asserting himself at the gender-segregated hospital and being respectfully addressed as "Sir" were important accomplishments. He explained that the confidence he gained by passing as a man at work gave him the courage to face a situation in which his transgender identity was revealed. At the individual level, many FTMs like In-Tae engage in everyday acts of resistance, demanding respect and rights, while they employ a strategy of passing in other areas of their lives. Along with engaging in these daily acts of resistance, FTMs come together as a group with a collective transgender identity and engage in resistance as rights-demanding subjects under the law.

The Pursuit of Citizenship: Demanding Rights within the Institutions of Law

The legal sphere has been a critical area of resistance and subjection for South Korean FTMs. Transgender individuals have struggled to change their sex identification on legal documents. This resistance revealed and challenged the deep-seated gender binary in the state classification of citizens. Their demands have garnered social controversy since the first legal case in 1987, yet the decision was left to the discretion of individual judges until 2006. In one example, the Chongju Regional Court ruled to allow legal sex reassignment in 1989, arguing that "the person has achieved the opposite sex through surgery and is carrying on a social life as such, thus the legal change is necessary for the normal social activity of the person."[3] In contrast, the Seoul Regional Court ruled out legal change in 1990, arguing: "The surgery does not change sex genes, therefore a one's sex is something one is born with at birth; our Constitution demands that the state protect marriage and family based on the equality of two sexes, and two sexes signify male and female according to the sex genes. Thus, there is no need for the state to protect those who had a sex-change surgery."[4] As these decisions clearly demonstrate, transgender citizens' demands for legal sex reassignment raises the question whether the state has a responsibility to protect those who choose to live outside the normative gender order.

Our FTM interviewees were well aware of the significance of this legal matter. "What does it mean to be given the male ID?" Jong-Hwa, a twenty-seven-year-old FTM college student, answered his own question: "It is protecting a person's rights to happiness. A person makes a demand to the society, saying that he would live this way, asking the society to grant him rights. So the changed ID means that the society listens to this, a basic right to live as human beings." The discourses of human rights became prevalent in South Korean LGBT activism and informed the discussion of legal sex reassignment for transgender individuals.

The claims of transgender citizens, combined with growing LGBT activism in South Korea, culminated in a landmark decision of the Supreme Court. In June 2006, the Court authorized legal sex reassignment for transgender individuals and created guidelines for future cases, which include genital surgery as a prerequisite along with other requirements.[5] Many transgender individuals viewed the Supreme Court decision as a positive change. Others, however, disagreed; the Transgender Rights Activism Coalitions petitioned the National Human Rights Commission to revise the Supreme Court guidelines, arguing that because genital surgery is extremely expensive and results are unreliable, the surgery should not be a prerequisite. The coalition also claimed that without a changed ID, it is practically impossible for transgender citizens to find work and earn the money necessary for surgery. In November 2008, the Human Rights Commission accepted the petition; but the Supreme Court did not accept the recommendation.

This legal change engendered a series of debates about how the South Korean state should recognize trangender individuals. For example, Jung-Won, who successfully changed his legal sex identification in 2005, would have been denied legal sex reassignment if he had gone to court a year later, after the Supreme Court decision. Because his health did not allow him to have surgery, Jung-Won had just started the physical transition in 2005 by taking hormones. His FTM identity was not a result of his suffering from being "in the wrong body," in keeping with the medical diagnosis of gender identity disorder, but rather was a necessary choice under the circumstances. As he explained: "I heard other FTMs say that they would like to cut their breasts when they take a shower or see themselves in the mirror. But I don't feel that way about my body. It's just an inconvenience for me, like I can't take my shirt off when the weather is hot. My body is born as a woman, and I need a man's body, but I don't curse myself that I have a woman's body."

As Jung-Won's story illustrates, the meaning of surgery varies for FTMs. For some, genital surgery is integral to a life as a man, whereas for others, it is one among many important life choices. Young-Hyun, a thirty-five-year-old FTM, thinks about genital surgery in terms of relative benefits because of his limited resources: "If I can have the legal document changed, I don't think the surgery is that important. The cost is significant, and if my partner doesn't mind, I'd rather use that money for something else, like buying land for my partner and me." For FTMs like Young-Hyun, proof of manhood relies not on genital surgery but on their ability to provide for their family. Although the right to change legal documents was achieved only after a great deal of resistance, the surgery requirement in the Supreme Court guidelines created new rules of subjection for FTMs that exclude those who pursue their manhood outside medical institutions.

In a discussion of the Supreme Court decision, FTMs voiced the following opinions:

IN-TAE: Before, they didn't grant the legal change even after all the surgeries are done, but now they will. Don't we have to be grateful for that? And the surgery is, of course, something we have to do. What the activists say is that

> we should fight to have the sex change without the full surgery, but I don't think it's possible. If we were to fight, why not fight for the [public] health insurance coverage?
>
> KYU-WON: I agree. And with the insurance coverage, who wouldn't want the surgery?
>
> JAE-SUK: But the fight for the insurance is difficult because it is considered cosmetic surgery.
>
> IN-TAE: How dare compare it with cosmetic surgery! Without the genital surgery, you are not a man, and you can't adjust to the life as a man.

The use of "we" in the dialogue shows that these FTMs consider themselves a group, with the agency to make collective demands of the state. On the basis of their group identity, members debate what FTMs as a group should fight for. For example, under the South Korean public health insurance system, insurance coverage becomes a yardstick of what the state considers medically necessary. FTMs are engaging the question whether they should fight to expand the eligibility guidelines for legal sex reassignment—as a matter of civil rights—or demand that transition surgery be included in state-provided health care—as a matter of social rights. Despite its limitations, the Supreme Court's decision to recognize trangendered individuals as citizens who deserve the state's protection opened a space for the collective rights claims of FTMs in South Korea.

The Pursuit of Community: Searching for Belonging in FTM Support Groups

The search for community is the third realm in which resistance and subjection emerge among FTMs in South Korea. FTM support groups are spaces in which those who identify as FTMs can meet one another and develop their collective voices of resistance. According to the current legal guidelines in South Korea, doctors have the authority to decide who is a transgender person—who is classified as having gender identity disorder. FTMs resist this externally determined process by affirming FTM identity and the experience of transition within support groups. Initially created by FTMs as online groups with the benefit of the anonymity possible on the Internet, support groups were often the first and, for many, the only space in which they could affirm their identity as FTMs and attain mutual recognition.

When Jung-Min attended his first off-line FTM support group, he recalled, "Every problem I had disappeared like magic." He was astonished to see other members who had begun the physical transition before he had: "I was shocked. They looked perfect. Are they really transgender? So I can be like that? I'd be so happy. It will be a life worth living." Jung-Min felt a sense of community; meeting the senior members of the community gave him hope that all his troubles would disappear with the physical transition. After Jung-Min identified as an FTM through the support group, his life goal was to undergo surgery and legal sex reassignment.

Despite the potential for empowerment, support groups are also spaces that can further reinforce medical standards of transgenderism. The groups embrace explicit and implicit norms defining who is an FTM and members are subject to these norms. After a few years, Jung-Min observed that the degree of transition determined the internal hierarchy within the community. He lamented:

There are people who say, "I don't walk around with people who didn't have the top [chest] surgery because I don't want to be suspected." They say, when they are with normal men, they get less suspicion. Frankly, I admit that I feel that way sometimes. But you don't have to say that out loud, right? Don't we have to fight against it? We all have our past. I had the top surgery, but for years I struggled because I was not able to get the surgery. Why do we ostracize others when we went through the same thing?

Within support groups, senior members who have completed surgery and can pass as men have more authority to set community norms that determine who is or is not an FTM. To be admitted to a group, new members have to tell their life stories, and sometimes meet with senior members, to prove that they are in fact FTMs, rather than butch lesbians or cross-dressers; the boundary between these groups have only recently been recognized in South Korea (WIG 2008; for North American cases, see Halberstam 1998; Hale 1998; Prosser 1998).

The process of approval involves members surveilling their own narratives and appearances. Senior members often pressured others to follow certain masculine norms in the form of advice, for example, telling another member to cut his hair shorter. In addition, a typical narrative emerged within the communities, focusing on how members hated their bodies, how they suffered during middle school and high school because of the required uniform skirt, and how they dated women as heterosexual men. Members met those who diverged from this script with disapproval. For example, Tae-Yeon, a twenty-six-year-old graduate student, struggled with the uncertainty that he might not be truly transgender because he did not suffer from a sense of difference during childhood and did not mind having long hair in middle school. Despite the tacit acceptance of tomboys and homoeroticism before adulthood in South Korea, a narrative of suffering constituted the transgender script, reflecting the medico-legal standards of transgenderism in which suffering is central.

Further, the norm within the FTM community emphasizes heterosexual partnership; members suspect those who are sexually attracted to men of having a questionable FTM identity. Jae-Suk, a longtime support-group member recalled seeing members who liked men leave the community, because they and others in the community thought that homosexuality was not an acceptable part of FTM identity. Some members consider homosexuality a disgrace to the FTM community because they believe it is not masculine. In contrast, a stable relationship with a woman is evidence that the individual is recognized as a man and is a true FTM. In this cultural context, Jung-Min and Tae-Yeon had difficulty openly discussing their bisexual identity in support group meetings.

Some FTM group members challenged the norms embraced by support groups, and in doing so, created a spin-off group. Thirty-five-year-old Su-Han was tired of "pretending [to be] who I am not" in FTM support groups. He could not understand why he had to censor himself constantly when talking about his past as a woman. He explained:

I kept my diary from when I was twenty years old. I had all the records of how I lived in the past, but because it was not a life as a man, I got rid of all. But now I regret it. I think I have to acknowledge my past. Otherwise, it brings more pain.

I have to accept it and have confidence in myself. When Youn-Woo spoke about the times when he had long hair at a support group meeting, I was shocked. I was very moved by his courage. It made me think, how would an FTM not have a memory of those days? It was an a-ha moment.

Su-Han concluded that his life as an FTM must include his entire past, even the times when he did not have the language to explain his desire, when he led a life first as a woman and then as a gender-ambiguous person before he identified as an FTM. Jung-Min agreed: "I do not need to imitate other men. I am a transman." Su-Han, together with Jung-Min, found space to resist these norms in a small group for transgender human rights in which members employed the liberal language of being one's individual self and the language of queer—freer self-expression and subverting gender normativity. Tae-Yeon, another group member, dreamed of a future in which he could act "more queer." "After the surgery," he said, "when I feel more secure, I want to experiment with myself. I'd like to wear feminine clothing, like the one with laces, and have long hair." For Tae-Yeon and others, FTM identity was not a transient one adopted temporarily en route to a perfect manhood but rather one aspect of a queer identity that they embraced. Although these FTMs departed from the support group norms, without the support groups they would not have met one another. In this sense, the space created by FTM support groups, which offered a sense of collectivity to imagine their identity and subjecthood in different ways, enabled their mobilization and resistance.

Conclusion

This study of how FTMs in South Korea became a collective subject through their pursuit of livelihood, citizenship, and community examines the dynamics of resistance and subjection in the lives of FTMs. FTMs in South Korea continued to engage in actions of everyday resistance in the context of a persistent gender binary, while using the strategy of passing as nontransgender men and being subject to the conventions of a masculinist culture in a gender-segregated society. FTMs also engaged in the pursuit of citizenship by demanding sex reassignment in state-issued legal documents. While the 2006 Supreme Court decision constituted the FTMs as legal subjects who can demand rights from the state, the genital surgery requirement made them further subject to medical institutions for recognition as FTMs. Finally, FTMs' pursuit of community and belonging led to the formation of support groups, spaces in which collective identity building took place and a voice of resistance was cultivated. In these FTM communities, however, a certain script of being an FTM emerged—one that regulated members' life narratives, appearances, and sexuality if they wanted to be considered a true FTM.

The question Youn-Woo faced when he arrived on campus, "Are you a man or a woman?" continues to follow him; but it no longer renders him speechless. Now in his mid-twenties, Youn-Woo has multiple answers. When he attends FTM support group meetings, he is open about his FTM identity, chatting about the process of transition and the option of surgery. When he feels that the FTM community's rules are too rigid, he gets together with LGBT friends who are more flexible in their definition of manhood. Youn-Woo plans to publicly declare to the South Korean state that he is a man by demanding that his legal documents be changed. In constructing their subjecthood through the search for livelihood, citizenship, and belonging, contemporary South Korean FTMs like Youn-Woo engage in multiple forms of resistance and subjection.

NOTES

This chapter grew out of the first author's master's thesis (Na 2007), which we expanded through extensive dialogue to develop a focus on resistance and subjection. We thank the fourteen interviewees who participated in this research.

1. Youn-Woo is one of our interviewees for this study. All names used in this chapter are pseudonyms.
2. South Koreans commonly use the term *transgender* to refer to individuals who identify and live their lives as the gender different from the one designated at birth. A *transgender* identity signifies engaging in, or planning to engage in, a physical transition of the body; this definition encompasses transgender and transsexual identity in North America. South Koreans also use the English terms *MTF* (those who transition from male to female), *FTM* (female to male), *LGBT* (lesbian, gay, bisexual, and transgender), and *queer*, as well as the umbrella term *iban*, which refers primarily to gays and lesbians but can also include bisexual and transgender individuals.
3. No. 89Hopa299.
4. No. 90Hopa451.
5. The full seven prerequisites are: (1) the applicant is over twenty years old, never married, and childless; (2) the applicant has suffered from a difference between biological sex and self-conscious identity; (3) the applicant has completed genital surgery; (4) the applicant has lost reproductive ability because of the surgery and has little possibility of returning to the previous sex; (5) the applicant has completed or is exempt from military service; (6) the applicant has no intention of abusing the change for criminal or unlawful activity; and (7) the sex change does not affect the applicant's status and does not affect society negatively. (No. 2004Seu42.)

REFERENCES

Foucault, Michel. 1978. *The History of Sexuality*. Vol. 1, *An Introduction*. New York: Random House.

Halberstam, Judith. 1998. "Transgender Butch: Butch/FTM Border Wars and the Masculine Continuum." *GLQ: A Journal of Lesbian and Gay Studies* 4 (2): 287–310.

Hale, C. Jacob. 1998. "Consuming the Living, Dis(Re)membering the Dead in the Butch/FTM Borderlands." *GLQ: A Journal of Lesbian and Gay Studies* 4 (2): 311–48.

Na, Tari Youngjung. 2007. "Becoming a New Man? Emerging Subjectivities of FTM in Contemporary South Korea." Master's thesis, Ewha Women's University.

Prosser, Jay. 1998. *Second Skins: The Body Narratives of Transsexuality*. New York: Columbia University Press.

Seo, Dong-Jin. 2001. "Mapping the Vicissitudes of Homosexual Identities in South Korea." *Journal of Homosexuality* 40 (3/4): 65–79.

WIG, the Queer Cultural Theory Research Circle. 2008. *Spin the Channel of Gender*. Seoul, South Korea: Saramsaengak.

From Rapunzel to G.I. Jane

Samantha Binford

Rapunzel, Rapunzel, let down your hair . . .

Remember that fairy tale of a young maiden with long, beautiful hair who, when caught talking to a prince, is punished by a witch who holds her captive? The witch cuts off Rapunzel's silken locks and banishes her into the wilderness. One could say that the plot of this tale has been the story of my life over the past year.

It all began when I went bald. By choice. The story behind this action started when I was in the sixth grade. I decided then that one day I would shave off my hair and prove that I didn't care what people thought. I just wanted to do something a little out of the ordinary, something . . . different, but impermanent. So hair was ideal. It grows back.

In the eighth grade, I met my best friend, Shaelynn Enquist. Neither of us was very popular. We both danced to our own tune—bookworms who would rather make straight A's than work our way up the junior high food chain. After I told her about my plan, she wanted in. So we made a pact. Five years later, during my first year in college, I called Shaelynn and told her that I wanted to do the deed after the holidays. When I told Shaelynn that January 18 was the date, there was a long pause on the phone followed by, "Sammy—I don't think I'm going to do it." She explained that she liked the length of her hair and she didn't think her boyfriend or her family would be very happy about her shaving it off. I understood, but I was going ahead anyway. If I didn't, I would be disappointed in myself for not doing something truly different. I had vowed that I would and I would! As the date drew closer, I began to get nervous. What if my head was lumpy and oddly shaped? Did I have the right type of facial structure to support a shaved head? Would I be able to pull it off the way Demi Moore does in the film *G.I. Jane*, or would I just look like the little brother I never had?

I was nervous, but my boyfriend was freaked out. When we first met, I told him about my plan (which he didn't really believe). After we'd been together for several months, however, he realized that I wasn't joking and that his girlfriend would soon look like a boyfriend.

Finally, after years of thinking, months of planning, and days of worrying, the eighteenth was here. I went to a barbershop, sat in the chair, and asked the hairdresser to shave everything off. After about ten minutes of cutting, buzzing, and huge locks of hair dropping to the floor, it was done.

The author on January 18, 2009, before and after going G.I. Jane.
(Photos by Samantha Binford.)

I looked like a twelve-year-old boy.

My first move was to apply makeup; before I had always been too lazy to bother. Wearing makeup was just the beginning of many changes I began to notice. I also started to dress more femininely, as though I felt a need to prove that I was a woman.

People's reactions were even more surprising than my own. Strangers would gawk when I kissed my boyfriend or when we held hands. It was evident that people perceived two guys publicly displaying their affection (which triggered the usual homophobic responses)—not a guy with a girl with no hair. Once my roommate and I went to the campus recreation center to rock climb and a gym worker asked my roommate whether she had brought her little brother. I laughed off these incidences. I knew that there was a chance people would mistake me for a boy and I had accepted that before I cut my hair.

Many people would also ask me—in accusatory and judgmental tones—why I cut my hair. To this, I would reply, "Because I wanted to." This reaction rarely satisfied, I found. People seemed to believe that I must have been motivated by something beyond sheer will. Rebellion? Cancer? Queer identity? The truth was that I simply wanted to show that I didn't care what people thought and that I was secure enough with my appearance to do the (feminine) unthinkable. I have always thought that it takes a really strong person to do it. Correction. It takes a really strong woman. In a culture where shampoo ads and Hollywood images tell us that beautiful women have long flowing locks that can be flirtatiously flipped to get positive attention, it takes guts to break the norm.

It's almost been a year now and, I admit, I like having hair again. I've been called a lesbian, mistaken for a boy, and verbally attacked because of my decision to cut my hair. And I've noticed, despite my claim that I don't care what other people think, that I do care about people's perceptions of me. Rapunzel's knight in shining armor may not have had a problem with her haircut, but my life is not a fairy tale and the real world is harsh. I constantly wondered whether it was me people were whispering about when I entered a room. I grew weary of friends reassuring friends that no, I did not have cancer. After all, putting on more makeup or a tighter shirt and counting down the days to when I would have long hair again revealed my investment in how others see me. While I proved that I could take a risk, do something different, and challenge a norm, I also discovered that breaking the rules is hard and sometimes painful.

For all the raised eyebrows and hushed comments about me as I walked by, however, I'm glad I did it and I'd do it again. Besides, now, whenever people ask my boyfriend, "Hey, are you still dating that crazy chick that shaved off all of her hair?" I always get a good chuckle out of it.

LIVING RESISTANCE

Funnel as Phallus

Sara L. Crawley

I've been an avid boater since age sixteen. There is something mystical about skimming the water under power or sail while watching for fish, dolphins, sea birds, stingrays, manatees, and sea turtles. As a young transplant to South Florida, I was initially unaccustomed to subtropical waters, beaches, and sun, but after my teenage years spent around boats, I came to love anything that floats. Once you experience time on (or under) the water, it gets in you—the feeling of being at the mercy of the sea as your body rises and falls with the waves; the beauty of a sea turtle drifting just above the reef as you absently hear your own breathing through a scuba regulator; the synchronicity of boat and captain as the mainsail and genoa align perfectly on a close reach while you enjoy a cold, cheap beer. It's addictive. It becomes one of the highest priorities in a life well lived. It becomes a problem to figure out where to pee.

With all the beauty and communion with nature that is part of the salt life, an abiding problem is the dearth of public toilets. The subtropical heat requires constant rehydration, which translates quickly into the ever-present need to pee. Indeed, it feels like part of nature—its very calling, as it were. And it is no secret that my fair share of Bud Light intensifies the problem.

In summer 2005 after twenty years of patient waiting (for financial security, the end of grad school, you name it), I bought my first fishing boat—a twenty-two-foot open fisherman–style panga with a center steering console and an outboard motor, completely open to the elements—think large, open dinghy with 115 horsepower. With every necessity to get us out on the bay, it was missing only a head (i.e., a toilet, for you landlubbers). This lack is common for most boats under thirty feet, because an enclosed cabin only weighs down the boat, costing fuel and creating a kiln-worthy hotbox. As a result, any female-bodied person addicted to the water must fashion a solution to the problem of where and how to pee among friends.

Historically, there have been two solutions: drop your pants and bare your assets to everyone aboard while peeing over the side or in a bucket—which turns out to be fairly common—or jump over the side and warm up the water. But there were two obstacles to the usual tactics: I had purchased this boat to fish Tampa Bay, where six-hundred- to eight-hundred-pound sharks inhabit the channel, and I was expecting to spend a good bit of time around men on board. I needed a new option.

I was at the auto parts store one day buying oil for my next oil change when I found my solution—an oil funnel with an oblong-shaped aperture about three inches by four inches and an off-center spout about twelve inches long. It looked perfectly anatomically correct. It was. For $1.29, I had my solution—something just the right size to accommodate the task and just long enough to keep the outflow away from my pants. It seemed like a simple solution to a silly problem, and it worked like a charm.

Little did I know that I was challenging perhaps the single most significant gender boundary.

To explain, most male-bodied people simply walk to the stern (because you really want to pee astern, which is with—not against—the wind), lean one knee against the motor and one against the transom, and relieve themselves while the rest of the crew stares at the back of his head. Quick and simple. Apparently, nature's true advantage. My funnel would allow me the same advantage.

On the next boating excursion, I simply followed the same procedure. Chocking my knees in place, I leaned slightly against the motor and unzipped my pants, positioning the funnel under my crotch with the correct angle to allow physics to do the job, and just let go. It worked like a charm. My butt remained covered and my front parts fully private. Zipping my pants and dunking the funnel over the side, I then turned to see the incredulous stares of the men on board. That's when I realized I had traversed the most sacred boundary between females and males—a practice commonly assumed to be dictated by anatomy—I had dared to stand to pee. They had been staring at the back of my head. I felt triumphant. They were confused . . . infuriated . . . deflated.

Most of the guys who boat with me have more or less put up with my overt feminism. They even supported and encouraged my love of the water and willingness to overcome the propriety of femininity to be offshore for hours or days at a time. But now apparently, I had gone too far. I had actually usurped the male advantage. Indeed, I had taken the phallus. What I perceived as a simple tool for transferring fluid was regarded a contested, radical feminist act. The guys (and most women) considered me "crazy." This was, after all, men's "natural" domain, and I had spoiled it.

I became obsessed.

That year, I bought funnels for every female-bodied person that I knew spent time on boats. I encouraged everyone to use them. I placed them in my powerboat, in my sailboat, and in each of my trucks. (We all know bathrooms on interstates leave much to be desired.) My proselytizing began. I even bought them for my students. Seriously, they became the topic of my graduate seminar.

Two deeply theoretical issues about funnels emerged. First, when I pee with a funnel, I experience freedom in multiple ways. I am free to be in nature. I am free from public toilets. I am free from feminine propriety. Above all, I have usurped the freedom of the phallus. It is all mine—the bay, the interstate, the primacy of the functions of my body. I'm not kidding. I feel like a man—liberated to be and to do as I please. Tim Beneke writes that the threat of rape changes the meaning of nature for women.[1] Women are not free to visit a state park alone to commune with nature at six o'clock on a Sunday morning or to hike the Appalachian Trail solo, confident that they will not be sexual prey. Nature is made less available for women than for men. The propriety of peeing also shores up this divide. But I had taken that back. Maybe I have taken the phallus (at least in part) when I stand to pee without apology.

Second, most women cannot even imagine standing to pee. It just feels wrong. They too think I'm crazy. Why would they need a funnel anyway? Most of my female-bodied friends reject the funnel outright as a joke—until they are caught in a needy situation. Case in point: my old high school friend Debbie joined me on my boat on Tampa Bay with her two children, fourteen-year-old Paul and seven-year-old Savannah. Like each of the other adults, Debbie had had two beers, and she needed to pee. She did not want to drop her pants in front of her children. I offered the funnel, which she rejected. But as her bladder grew and the expanse of the bay loomed, she became desperate. Isn't there another option? Quickly I explained that the funnel doesn't have to be a feminist statement for everyone. It can be just a tool, like a toilet, to transfer liquid from point A to point B. "Oh," she said, "when you put it like that . . ." She used the funnel and was greatly relieved in many ways. Debbie, whom I love like a sister, turned to me and said, "Hey, that's a good idea."

NOTE

1. Timothy Beneke, *Men on Rape* (New York: St. Martin's Press, 1982).

PART II

Challenging Marginalization

5

"Give Me a Boa and Some Bling!"

Red Hat Society Members Commanding Visibility in the Public Sphere

M. Elise Radina, Lydia K. Manning,
Marybeth C. Stalp, and Annette Lynch

At seventy-four, Frances waits in her car in the parking lot outside the restaurant, feeling like a sixteen-year-old schoolgirl all over again. She sits looking around for her friends. With a new red pillbox hat on the seat beside her, she worries that no one else will show up in their signature Red Hat Society (RHS) dress—red hat, purple dress, sparkly jewelry, and feather boa. But slowly, the cars pull up and Frances spots her RHS friends. She sighs in relief as her first public outing with the "Red Hot Classy Ladies" is about to begin.

She is at once excited and nervous. Finally, knowing that she is not alone, Frances steps out, red hat in hand. She makes eye contact with her friend Patty and, nearly in unison, they plop their hats on their heads and begin to giggle. When they enter the restaurant, people stare and make comments. Were they captivated by the bold purple outfits and red hats? Were they taken aback by older women who were not "acting their age"? Inside the restaurant lobby, the group's numbers swell. As they wait to be seated, a few restaurant patrons approach the group and ask, "What's this about?" "What are you dressed up for?" "Is this a kind of club or something?" A woman in her fifties or sixties wants to know how she can join the group. A middle-aged man taps Frances on the shoulder and says, "I wish my wife would do this."

Some people, though, appear not to know what to make of Frances and her friends, especially when one of them wanders off from the group. Just before dessert, Frances excuses herself to use the restroom. On her way, she startles a young man of thirty-something. He looks at her and then immediately at his shoes. He seems embarrassed, but Frances keeps walking. When she turns back to look at him, she catches his eyes following her. He has a smirk across his face. Frances wonders what he is thinking. At the same time, she thinks, Being seventy-four means something different to me when I am with this group of women. With them, in my purple dress and red hat, I feel free to let myself go a little. Together, we are announcing to the world: *We may be old in your eyes, but we don't write us off yet. We aren't gone. We can still have fun.*

Frances's account of her experiences, thoughts, and feelings as a neophyte Red Hatter represents the collective experiences of Red Hatters that emerged during our qualitative investigation. The concluding sentence is a direct quotation from one of our informants. In this chapter, we present the RHS as one way older women resist stereotypes of "old ladies." In so doing, we weave together research on women, aging, dress, and appearance with the accounts of Red Hatters we gathered through interviews and observations.

A Brief History of the Red Hat Society

In 1998, the now Exalted Queen Mother, Sue Ellen Cooper (2004), began buying red hats for her friends who were turning fifty. Cooper was inspired by the poem "Warning" by Jenny Joseph (1974) that expresses how women's behavior can change and become less restricted as they age: "And I shall spend my pension on brandy and summer gloves; / And satin sandals, and say we've no money for butter." Cooper and her friends began meeting in public places wearing red hats and purple ("that doesn't go"). They decided to call themselves the Red Hat Society. Before long, women from across the country began sending e-mail messages to Cooper and she began the official "disorganization" of the RHS.

Through the Internet and word of mouth, the RHS has grown to include more than thirty thousand official, registered chapters in the United States, twenty-five foreign countries, and any number of regionally based unofficial chapters.[1] The total official membership of the RHS is over one million members (Son et al. 2007). Exalted Queen Mother Cooper encourages women to think positively about getting older and to have fun along the way by starting their own chapters. To wear a red hat one must be at least fifty years old. Those under fifty (i.e., "pink hats") can wear pink and lavender; they are red hats in training and will undergo a "red-uation" when they turn fifty (Cooper 2004). Thus, unlike mainstream society, which punishes women for aging (Calasanti 2001; Calasanti and Slevin 2001; Cooper 2004; Thompson 2001), in celebration, the RHS rewards its members with red hats.

Research on Women, Appearance, and Aging

In social science, the body as a topic has gained ground (e.g., Faircloth 2003). Twigg (2004, 59) claims, "Although bodies abound in sociology and the wider cultural milieus, their presence in social gerontology has been more or less muted and uncertain." Similarly, Cruikshank (2003, 147) notes the "almost unacceptable" judgment that women's aging bodies are unattractive. In other words, older women are rendered invisible and stigmatized because of their aging bodies. Twigg (2004) argues for a focus on the body that moves away from these approaches, which can be oppressive, to approaches that are reflexive, subjective, and empowering. She does this by underscoring that "age and aging are deeply social" and invoking feminist and humanistic gerontology, which argue that experiences of the body are socially and culturally constructed and negotiated (70).

While considering the social construction of the aging female body, one must take into account scientific studies of notions of older women's attractiveness, and, by extension, sexiness. Women's perceived attractiveness to men decreases significantly with age, while men's attractiveness to women is not affected significantly or similarly (Calasanti 2005; Mathes et al. 1985). Gender-role dichotomy, which establishes key differences in how men and women in the United States are socialized to measure accomplishment, explains in part these alternative perceptions (Kaiser 1985; Kaiser and Chandler 1984; Michelman and Kaiser 2000). Boys and men often gain power (and, by extension, attractiveness) as they age. In contrast, girls and women learn that physical attractiveness and dress are important to receiving positive feedback. This awareness leads to heavy reliance on youthfulness and beauty and a related loss of power with aging. Thus, not surprisingly, women experience higher degrees of negative stereotyping and stigma as they age than their male contemporaries (Deutsch, Zalenski, and Clark 1986).

Age plays a fundamental role in ratings of female attractiveness, with older models receiving lower ratings than younger models in image-based quantitative studies (e.g., Korthase and Trenholme 1982). In particular, studies show that aging is a fundamental component of how women evaluate themselves (e.g., Lennon 1997). Hurd (1999; Hurd Clarke 2001), however, notes how midlife and older women are beginning to challenge these definitions of aging, renegotiating their bodies and their selves as they age. Certainly the RHS is one example of how older women challenge these stereotypes.

Women and men alike alter dress and appearance regularly to influence audience response—whether to elicit a positive reaction or to challenge existing norms. In particular, women manage their appearance through dress (Lennon and Rudd 1994), hair (Weitz 2004), and cosmetics (Dellinger and Williams 1997) and by shaping their bodies (Dinnerstein and Weitz 1997) to meet cultural expectations of beauty. The wearer presents a dressed self to others; yet the meaning of this presentation is left to the individual wearer and the audience (Stone 1965). What does one's physical presentation (e.g., choice of shoes, makeup, clothing, or hairstyle) convey about who one is, where one fits into society, or what power (or lack of power) one has?

At the same time, society encourages women to participate in the consumption of clothing and beauty products designed to mask the aging process (Damhorst 1999). Women use cosmetics, undergarments, and custom-tailored garments to achieve this goal (Bartley and Warden 1962; Ebeling and Rosencrantz 1961; Jackson and O'Neal 1994). But this quest is fraught. Older women, when asked, often complain about clothing not fitting appropriately and the difficulties they encounter finding fashionable dress to accommodate their changing and aging body shapes (Richards 1981; Spuriell and Jernigan 1982).

Research on the RHS

Since the inception of the RHS, social scientists have been exploring this unique cultural phenomenon. Research has studied the importance of RHS clothing on image

Red Hat Society members of the "Mixed Age Fun Bunch" gather to meet with university students, October 2008. (Photo by M. Elise Radina.)

management in a society dominated by standards of beauty typically reserved for the young (Lynch, Radina, and Stalp 2007). Beyond this focus on appearance, studies also find that RHS participation provides older women the time, space, and freedom to engage in leisure activities that they may not experience elsewhere in their lives (Son et al. 2007; Stalp, Radina, and Lynch, 2008; Yarnal 2006; Yarnal, Chick, and Kerstetter 2008; Yarnal et al. 2009). Similarly, the RHS's dual emphasis on shopping as a group activity and dressing alike to secure a cohesive public image for members encourages the conspicuous consumption of goods (Stalp et al. 2009). Finally, the RHS has been found to play a role in promoting the positive health and well-being of its members by fostering connections among older women during a stage in life that is often linked to negative physical and psychological outcomes, such as social isolation and depression (Radina et al. 2008; Son et al. 2007; Yarnal 2006).

Feminist Gerontology

It seems logical to consider feminism and gerontology together because women tend to live longer than men and thus the rapidly increasing older population will be made up largely of women. Feminist gerontology has been described as one aspect of a larger movement in social science that focuses on giving voice to the marginalized and challenging dominate modes of thinking (Laws 1995). Feminist gerontological approaches to older women's lives have the potential to improve women's lives by providing the foundation for celebrating women's experiences of aging, making women a visible faction of society and culture. These approaches also place value on the reflexive and subjective and incorporate the voices of older women who live in a larger social and cultural context that oppresses them for being "old ladies" (Twigg 2004). A model of feminist gerontology also makes central the authenticity, potential, and opulence of aging for women (Browne 1998). It is our intention here to employ the tenets of this approach offered by feminist gerontology. In so doing, we consider how RHS participants use prescribed dress as symbols to convey a message to others that challenges stereotypes about female aging.

Methods

We conducted formal in-depth individual and focus-group interviews with seventy red hat members (i.e., women over the age of fifty), engaged in participant and non-participant observation at RHS events and meetings, attended an international convention, and employed content analysis of RHS publications. The majority of the women we interacted with were white and middle class; the other women represented the upper and the lower classes. Most of the women were between the ages of forty-five and eighty-five, with the majority between fifty-five and sixty-five. Most of these women worked at least part-time outside the home, either at the time of the interview or at some point in the past. A smaller number had no outside-work history. Our analysis was guided by feminist gerontology and focused broadly on how participation in the RHS enables members to resist the "old woman" stereotype.

Findings

Frances's story provides insight into new ways to conceive of the female aging body and how appearance and dress can be manipulated to challenge stereotypes. Frances recounts how she and her RHS sisters "decorate" themselves as a part of the performance of RHS membership. This collective embodied resistance of stereotypes of "old ladies" underscores the importance of exploring older women as subjects using the critical lens of feminism and focusing on female connectivity and visibility. Frances and others like her embed their experiences of aging within a specific ritualized, social framework (i.e., the RHS). This action enables them to combat ageism and reclaim their identity and visibility as older women.

Our analysis led to the identification of two themes related to aging and appearance that point to how RHS participation is a form of embodied resistance: combating stereotypes of the aging female body as unattractive and asexual, and undergoing personal transformation. Through this resistance RHS participation enhances self-concept and provides personal validation while affording a safe yet open place to be "unladylike."

The Aging Female Body: Demanding Visibility

RHS members respond to the social stigma associated with their bodies in unique, creative, and unapologetic ways and in doing so engage in embodied resistance. Specifically, these woman report having fun attracting public attention at a time in their lives when "old women" are typically expected to fade into the background. An example comes from Althea, who is a teacher:[2]

> If we're going to tea, we wear purple and the red hat. We had a hat day in school just last week. The four of us that are members in our school, we all wore our red hats. People stare at us and some people laugh at us, and then there are some people that come up and say, well we're just so glad you're doing this, what a good thing for people. Some people are, some people just look at us and say, Oh my goodness. My two daughters think I'm absolutely crazy.

Betsy also talks about the fun of being a member of the RHS.

> Fun. Fun. Fun. It feels good to get in a group with a bunch of women that have all different backgrounds. It is all just plain silliness too, lunches and dinners . . . when we get together at a house and have tea, just like we used to when we were younger. In our younger ages, ha! If we do go out, it is more fun to go out because everyone stares at you and laughs. See my son pokes fun at me, but that is . . . and it is fun to dress up, because we are from the era that wore gloves. And when we were younger, we went to meetings and we always wore hat and gloves. They don't do that anymore, it is kind of a shame. But when the Red Hats do it, it is kind of a throwback—it makes me go back to my youth.

When asked about how her husband reacts to her participation in the RHS, Hannah said, "I think he's secretly jealous. I bet the guys would just love to be able to put on pink pants and plaid golf hats and go out and have lunch with their buddies and have beer and just have a good afternoon, but you know, they can't. They have to go to work, poor things." These statements call to mind the carefree quality of RHS membership and activities as a reflection of the leisure these women embrace. At the same time, these statements suggest an almost deviant attitude about their behaviors; as if by participating in RHS activities, these women are "getting away with something." Statements that reflect this deviant attitude and related behaviors highlight the quality of RHS participation that encourages breaking with what is expected of "women of a certain age." Women, regardless of age, are expected to take care of others more so than themselves. By engaging in leisure for themselves and for the sake of leisure, these women resist social expectations and indulge themselves.

Combating the social stigma of the aging female body comes hand in hand with challenges to conventional notions of female attractiveness. Older women are beginning to challenge these negative definitions of aging that impose on them notions of unattractiveness or lack of sexual appeal (Hurd 1999; Hurd Clarke 2001). Certainly the choice of the color red—which carries with it meanings typically associated with youth and sexiness, such as power, heat, and sin—poses such challenges. RHS members, then, deploy red as a symbol of boldness. For example, Anne stated, "I think that it gives them [RHS members] a good outlook on life. Remember when we looked at our grandmas and they were OLD people! My kids and grandkids don't think of me as old! And it isn't like we are not at that age they were, but all they did was make cookies and stayed home." Anna's statement, while not directly related to sexiness, certainly reveals a mentality of seeing herself as youthful and shows that "old" does not reflect her self-concept as a grandmother. Among the stereotypes of older women that we present throughout this chapter (e.g., knitting, baking) is that older women (i.e., grandmothers) are asexual. Anna is saying that she does not see herself as this stereotype of "old" and others do not see her this way either. She sees herself as engaging in activities that are more typically associated with youthfulness, redefining "old" for herself in a way that is unlike the "old" she associates with her grandmother.

Appearance, Dress, and Ritual: A Transforming Arena

RHS members also use appearance management, prescribed standards of dress, and ritualized space (e.g., places and spaces where "ordinary reality is both suspended and heightened") as an arena that offers transformation and personal growth (Sween 2002). Older women are socialized to try to appear younger, rather than accepting and celebrating the aging process. In contrast, Thelma explains how the RHS has increased her range of color choice in clothes, which has contributed to a newfound sense of self.

> I never wore red [when I was younger] because I had red hair growing up. I NEVER wore red. This is the first red article [of clothing] that I have ever purchased, but I am over fifty and I am proud of it! I do wear red now and I don't care! The statement is . . . the whole red hat thing is . . . we were in essence controlled by society when we were younger. Taught how to look, how to act, but by the time you get to fifty you have self-actualized. In essence the statement that you are making is "I am not being 'controlled' by society's norms anymore!"

As Thelma points out, society encourages or "controls" women to participate in appearance management meant to dictate acceptable standards of behavior and appearance and to mask the aging process.

The clothing choices individuals make can contribute to part of a ritualized ceremony. Geertz (1973) argues that as individuals participate in ritual they dress to challenge or present alternatives to everyday normative identities. In other words, appearance within ritualized space is used to embody resistance. Ritual thus has the potential to create change as participants compare their everyday identities with those experimented with as a part of a ritualized event. As RHS members return to their everyday lives, they carry with them memories of RHS events where they expressed lively, alternative versions of being an older woman. These alternative identities thus begin to affect the daily lives of women even outside of the arena of the RHS. An example of this effect comes from our fieldwork during a multi-day RHS event held at a hotel.

> Elizabeth is in her seventies and is attending an RHS event with her friend's daughter. Elizabeth steals the show with her over-the-top costuming and behavior. When our group, who traveled to the event in the same shuttle, arrives at the event hotel, Elizabeth turns to me and quietly asks me where the bar is. The look on her face is one of slyness and readiness to kick back and have a crazy time. It is the kind of look one might expect when young people try to shock older people with their wild and daring behavior. Elizabeth has a secret. She has mentioned

to a few of us something about a tattoo. Toward the end of the event and a few drinks later, she reveals her tattoo. It is priceless. In her youth, Elizabeth got the tattoo on her left breast. At that time it was a rose. But, as time passed and gravity took its toll, the rose was no longer discernable. So, a few years ago, Elizabeth had it redone. What was once a rose in her youth is now a red hat about three inches wide with a purple plume emanating from the rim.

Elizabeth has thus embraced the RHS attitude of fun and frivolity that has extended beyond attending events and the ritualized dress of the RHS. This attitude has carried over into her everyday persona; she literally wears a symbol of RHS "hattitude" every day.

RHS members draw from a range of available dress options to create symbolic ensembles that function as visible embodiments of livelier, more rebellious versions of female aging. Lois described an RHS event that reflects how the symbolic dress encourages this behavior.

Nancy and I went up to the Funfest last April. We just had a ball. Nancy made us poodle skirts. There was a contest, so we decorated bras to wear. We had purple pajamas with red hats on them, *silk pajamas*! I mean, you just DO things . . . like we were going through this hotel, at eight in the morning, in our pajamas, some of the women had their bras on, and nothing else on top! Some had their bras over their pajamas. And we are tooting kazoos going all over this hotel. So people laugh and they just love it. I think it gives everybody this, "Isn't this great that we can still laugh and have fun" attitude.

Nancy and Lois's experience at the hotel was transformative for Lois in that she engaged in activities she would never have dreamed of (i.e., parading around the hotel in silk pajamas—something in her mind that should not be done in clothing ordinarily reserved for more private moments). The self-confidence gained from such activities that are outside one's comfort zone can be personally transformative. These ritualized expressions of dress have the power to affect the everyday lives of the women; they provide a visible and memorable point of comparison with the normative culture that surrounds them. While in everyday life older women are often ignored or dismissed as not important, within this ritualized space they get positive attention; they are in control. Their acts of resistance through dress indicate that they are not "past their prime," unattractive, or no longer sexy.

Conclusion

RHS members told us that the RHS enables them to embrace and celebrate their aging experience. They resist internalizing negative societal labels as invisible, aging women. RHS members create a subculture that re-creates what it means to be an old lady. This space allows members to cultivate a sense of purpose and personal validation that can contribute to personal well-being. Gullette (2002, 556) argues that, once women reach an age in which they are "postmaternal" (i.e., have launched their adult children), their social value plummets and any social or psychological benefit that these women might gain from being "empty nesters" is taboo. Similarly, Bolen (2001, x) explains that despite having a youth-oriented culture that promotes and upholds the notion of female social invisibility later in life, "it is possible for this third trimester to be a time of personal wholeness and integration; when what you do is an expression of who you deeply are." Participating in the RHS, for some women, is a way to challenge the labels often put on them because of their age and related social location and makes possible a newly discovered sense of self and self-worth.

Frances's story, our analysis, and the related discussions demonstrate that participation in the RHS is a form of resistance. By engaging in nonstereotypical dress and behavior, RHS members make a public statement about the state of societal attitudes. Red Hatters refuse to conform to the "little old lady" and quilting-bee normative standards prescribed for older women. In addition to being a model of "free and fun-filled" living and aging, these participants show us how older women live and practice a form of feminism that rejects stereotypes, explores new possibilities, challenges limitations, and insists on a redefining of what it means to be an older woman (Bolen 2001; Gullette 2002). The RHS offers denunciation and rejection of the invisible older woman and successfully imparts a way of aging that often is neglected at both the social and the scholarly level. By employing an approach guided by feminist gerontology, we have added to the ongoing and evolving dialogue about what it means to be an older woman in modern society. What the RHS has the potential to do for stereotypes about older women is significant. As we look to the future for older women, it seems that new attitudes and new ways of doing "old age" for women are not only possible but probable.

NOTES

1. "Fast Facts," Red Hat Society, *www.redhatsociety.com/press/facts.html*, accessed May 25, 2010.
2. All names are pseudonyms.

REFERENCES

Bartley, Lois, and Jessie Warden. 1962. "Clothing Preferences of Women Sixty-Five and Older." *Journal of Home Economics* 54 (8): 716–17.

Bolen, Jean Shinoda. 2001. *Goddess in Older Women: Archetypes in Women over Fifty*. New York: Quill.

Browne, Colette. 1998. *Women, Feminism, and Aging*. New York: Springer.

Calasanti, Toni M. 2001. "Retirement: Golden Years for Whom?" In *Gender Mosaics: Social Perspectives*, ed. Dana Vannoy, 300–310. Los Angeles: Roxbury.

———. 2005. "Ageism, Gravity, and Gender: Experiences of Aging Bodies." *Generations* 29 (3): 8–12.

Calasanti, Toni M., and Kathleen F. Slevin. 2001. *Gender, Social Inequality, and Aging*. Walnut Creek, CA: AltaMira.

Cooper, Sue Ellen. 2004. *The Red Hat Society: Fun and Friendship after Fifty*. New York: Warner.

Cruikshank, Margaret. 2003. *Learning to Be Old: Gender, Culture, and Aging.* Lanham, MD: Rowman and Littlefield.

Damhorst, Mary Lynn. 1999. "Dressing throughout Adulthood." In *The Meanings of Dress,* ed. Damhorst, Kimberly A. Miller, and Susan O. Michelman, 328–37. New York: Fairchild.

Dellinger, Kirsten, and Christine L. Williams. 1997. "Makeup at Work: Negotiating Appearance Rules in the Workplace." *Gender and Society* 11 (2): 151–77.

Deutsch, Francine M., Carla M. Zalenski, and Mary E. Clark. 1986. "Is There a Double Standard of Aging?" *Journal of Applied Social Psychology* 16 (9): 771–85.

Dinnerstein, Myra, and Rose Weitz. 1997. "Jane Fonda, Barbara Bush, and Other Aging Bodies: Femininity and the Limits of Resistance." *Gender Issues* 14 (2): 3–24.

Ebeling, Maloa, and Mary Lou Rosencrantz. 1961. "Social and Personal Aspects of Clothing for Older Women." *Journal of Home Economics* 53 (6): 464–65.

Faircloth, Christopher A., ed. 2003. *Aging Bodies: Images and Everyday Experiences.* Walnut Creek, CA: AltaMira.

Geertz, Clifford. 1973. *The Interpretation of Cultures.* New York: Basic Books.

Gullette, Margaret Morganroth. 2002. "Valuing 'Postmaternity' as a Revolutionary Feminist Concept." *Feminist Studies* 28 (3): 553–72.

Hurd, Laura. 1999. "We're Not Old!": Older Women's Negotiation of Aging and Oldness." *Journal of Aging Studies* 13 (4): 419–39.

Hurd Clarke, Laura. 2001. "Older Women's Bodies and the Self: The Construction of Identity in Later Life." *Canadian Review of Sociology and Anthropology* 38 (4): 441–64.

Jackson, Hazel O., and Gwendolyn S. O'Neal. 1994. "Dress and Appearance Responses to Perceptions of Aging." *Clothing and Textiles Research Journal* 12 (4): 8–15.

Joseph, Jenny. 1974. "Warning." In *Rose in the Afternoon.* London: J. M. Dent and Sons.

Kaiser, Susan B. 1985. *The Social Psychology of Clothing and Personal Adornment.* New York: Macmillan.

Kaiser, Susan B., and Joan L. Chandler. 1984. "Fashion Alienation: Older Adults and the Mass Media." *International Journal of Aging and Human Development* 19 (3): 199–217.

Korthase, Kathleen M., and Irene Trenholme. 1982. "Perceived Age and Perceived Physical Attractiveness." *Perceptual and Motor Skills* 54:1251–58.

Laws, Glenda. 1995. "Understanding Ageism: Lessons from Feminism and Postmodernism." *Gerontologist* 35 (1): 112–8.

Lennon, Sharron J. 1997. "Physical Attractiveness, Age, and Body Type: Further Evidence." *Clothing and Textiles Research Journal* 15 (1): 60–64.

Lennon, Sharron J., and Nancy A. Rudd. 1994. "Linkages between Attitudes toward Gender Roles, Body Satisfaction, Self-Esteem, and Appearance Management Behaviors in Women." *Family and Consumer Sciences Research Journal* 23 (2): 94–117.

Lynch, Annette, M. Elise Radina, and Marybeth C. Stalp. 2007. "Growing Old and Dressing (Dis)gracefully." In *Dress Sense: Emotional and Sensory Experiences of the Body and Clothes,* ed. Donald Clay Johnson and Helen Bradley Foster, 144–55. Gordansville, IL: Berg.

Mathes, Eugene W., Susan M. Brennan, Patricia M. Haugen, and Holly B. Rice. 1985. "Ratings of Physical Attractiveness as a Function of Age." *Journal of Social Psychology* 125 (2): 157–68.

Michelman, Susan O., and Susan B. Kaiser. 2000. "Feminist Issues in Textiles and Clothing Research: Working through/with the Contradictions." *Clothing and Textiles Research Journal* 18 (3): 121–27.

Radina, M. Elise, Annette Lynch, Marybeth C. Stalp, and Lydia K. Manning. 2008. "'When I Am an Old Woman, I Shall Wear Purple': Red Hatters Cope with Getting Old." *Journal of Women and Aging* 20 (1/2): 99–114.

Richards, Mary Lynn. 1981. "The Clothing Preferences and Problems of Elderly Female Consumers." *Gerontologist* 21 (3): 263–67.

Son, Julie S., Deborah L. Kerstetter, Careen M. Yarnal, and Birgitta L. Baker. 2007. "Promoting Older Women's Health and Well-Being through Social Leisure Environments: What We Have Learned from the Red Hat Society." *Journal of Women and Aging* 19 (3/4): 89–104.

Spuriell, Phyllis R., and Marian Jernigan. 1982. "Clothing Preferences of Older Women: Implications for Gerontology and the American Clothing Industry." *Educational Gerontology* 8 (5): 485–92.

Stalp, Marybeth C., M. Elise Radina, and Annette Lynch. 2008. "'We Do It 'Cuz It's Fun': Gendered Fun and Leisure for Midlife Women through Red Hat Society Membership." *Sociological Perspectives* 51 (2): 325–48.

Stalp, Marybeth C., Rachel Williams, Annette Lynch, and M. Elise Radina. 2009. "Conspicuously Consuming: The Red Hat Society and Midlife Women's Identity." *Journal of Contemporary Ethnography* 38 (2): 225–53.

Stone, Gregory P. 1965. "Appearance and the Self." In *Dress, Adornment, and the Social Order*, ed. Mary Ellen Roach and Joanne Bubolz Eicher, 216–45. New York: John Wiley and Sons.

Sween, Gretchen. 2002. "Rituals, Riots, Rules, and Rights: The Astor Place Theater Riot of 1849 and the Evolving Limits of Free Speech." *Texas Law Review* 81 (2): 679.

Thompson, Edward H. 2001. "Older Men as Invisible Men in Contemporary Society." In *Gender Mosaics: Social Perspectives*, ed. Dana Vannoy, 473–85. Los Angeles: Roxbury.

Twigg, Julia. 2004. "The Body, Gender, and Age: Feminist Insights in Social Gerontology." *Journal of Aging Studies* 18 (1): 59.

Weitz, Rose. 2004. *Rapunzel's Daughters: What Women's Hair Tells Us about Women's Lives.* New York: Farrar, Straus and Giroux.

Yarnal, Careen Mackay. 2006. "The Red Hat Society: Exploring the Role of Play, Liminality, and *Communitas* in Older Women's Lives." *Journal of Women and Aging* 18 (3): 51–73.

Yarnal, Careen Mackay, Garry Chick, and Deborah Kerstetter. 2008. "'I Did Not Have Time to Play Growing Up . . . So This Is My Play Time. It's the Best Thing I Have Ever Done for Myself': What Is Play to Older Women?" *Leisure Sciences* 30(3): 235–52.

Yarnal, Careen Mackay, Deborah Kerstetter, Garry Chick, and Susan Hutchinson. 2009. "The Red Hat Society: An Exploration of Play and Masking in Older Women's Lives." In *From Children to Red Hatters: Diverse Images and Issues of Play*, ed. David S. Kerschner, 144–62. Lanham, MD: University Press of America.

6

Fat. Hairy. Sexy

Contesting Standards of Beauty and Sexuality in the Gay Community

Nathaniel C. Pyle and Noa Logan Klein

Alex's jaw practically dropped into his lap when Dr. Nelson told him he was gay.

It's not that Alex is ignorant about homosexuality. In fact, he identifies as gay himself. He had come to Dr. Nelson's office hours to discuss a research project relating to sexual orientation and had casually sought information about another professor's sexual identity because he was looking for a gay mentor. Alex asked, "Is Professor Gardner gay?" Knowing that Dr. Gardner was open about his sexual orientation, Dr. Nelson answered, "Yes, he is. And so am I."

This revelation was shocking to Alex because Dr. Nelson weighs over three hundred pounds and sports a full gray beard. In other words, he does not fit the stereotype of a young, thin, and effeminate gay man. Alex walked out of Dr. Nelson's office with the realization that he had had this image subconsciously in mind and had assumed Dr. Nelson was heterosexual because of his body size and gender presentation.

Stereotypes and assumptions about gay men's bodies are prevalent within and outside the gay male community. Media images of young, thin, and hairless gay men marginalize those who do not fit this narrow ideal. In this chapter, we introduce a group of gay men who resist body image norms: fat gay men, bears, and their admirers.

Even within marginalized communities and social movements, there are institutionalized power relations. Men whom the gay male community considers beautiful (young, skinny, hairless) have an easier time navigating their social world (Levine 1998; Pyle and Loewy 2009). Men whose bodies do not conform to this narrow beauty ideal or whose sexual attractions are to men whose bodies do not conform to this type often feel ostracized in conventional gay spaces, such as bars, nightclubs, and community organizations (Hennen 2008; Pyle and Loewy 2009). As a result, these men have created alternative spaces in which they feel comfortable and, through gathering together, have begun to form identities as big men, bears, and their admirers (also known as chasers). Big men, or chubs, are large-bodied or fat gay men and bears are masculine, hirsute, and often large-bodied gay men. As spaces for big men, bears, and chasers grow and more men congregate, these individuals and groups begin to take on a more public presence at pride events and other queer community functions (Hennen 2008). Their public presence is an embodied contestation of queer power relations, legitimizing a broad range of body types that include fat and hairy male bodies and a multiplicity of sexual identities that includes attraction to these bodies. By applying Verta Taylor and Nella Van Dyke's (2004) definition of tactical repertoires to ethnographic, interview, and focus group data, we illustrate how big men, bears, and chasers use their bodies to challenge the institutionalized power relations that define sexiness within the gay male community.

The Gay Male Beauty Myth

As with other minority groups, the mainstream media often limit or narrowly stereotype representations of gay men. The one-dimensional image of the gay man in popular culture encompasses certain personality traits and physical characteristics: he is a young, white, thin, hairless, effeminate, shallow, flamboyant queen (Battles and Hilton-Morrow 2002). The mainstream gay media also promote a single body type as standard for gay men: young, hairless, and thin or muscular (Levine 1998; Locke 1997). The prevalence of these media representations creates an enormous pressure on gay men to conform to this narrow ideal body type (Locke 1997), much like the beauty standards that are imposed on women and have been thoroughly analyzed by feminists (Bordo 2003; Wolf 2002). Rates of eating disorders and other body image disturbances are high among gay men (Olivardia 2004), which may be taken as evidence that body image ideals exert pressures on gay men similar in strength to those faced by heterosexual women.

As gay community centers and support groups began addressing the needs of the gay community in urban centers around the country, small groups of gay men who did not conform to or were not attracted to the "gay ideal" body type also began to form. Just as not all bodies conform to the social ideal, sexual attraction does not always conform to mainstream notions of beauty. For example, some people are attracted to fat people even though fat bodies are strongly stigmatized in our society (Blank 2000). Some gay men are attracted to husky, hairy men (Hennen 2008; Pyle and Loewy 2009). These attractions are often seen as outside the norm and are referred to as fetishes (Gates 2000), rather than attractions that are simply different and that by their very existence, throw into relief the narrowness of the socially constructed beauty ideal and the exclusive attraction to those who approximate it. The equation of thinness with beauty in the contemporary United States is a historically and culturally specific construction, not a human universal, and should be understood as such (Bordo 2003; Stearns 2002).

A Brief History of Big Men's and Bear Clubs

Girth and Mirth (big men's) clubs, which attract gay men who value a different version of male beauty, were started in New York and San Francisco in the mid-1970s (Suresha 2002). Big men's clubs were havens for fat gay men and their admirers who felt ostracized in the gay bar scene, where many of them were made to feel inferior because of their larger or hairier bodies (Suresha 2002). The first bear clubs formed out of leather and big men's groups in San Francisco in the 1980s (Suresha 2002). Pe-

Finalists for Mr. Bear International 2010. International Bear Rendezvous, San Francisco, California, February 2010. (Photograph courtesy of Darwin Bebo.)

ter Hennen (2008, 176) describes the boundaries of bear identity as "loosely defined but nevertheless profoundly structured by gender." Though bears are physically bigger than the gay stereotype, the emphasis is generally on the hirsute and stereotypically masculine quality of the bear. This way, bears avoid the stigmatizing associations of being fat or chubby: laziness, self-indulgence, and femininity (Sedgwick and Moon 1994). Chubs or big men do not necessarily subscribe to the hypermasculinity of bear culture; bears' de-emphasis on body size and emphasis on masculinity could be the reason the bear community has since grown to a much larger size than the Girth and Mirth community that came before it. The two communities are distinct but have overlapping memberships. The intricate network of local, regional, and national gatherings of Girth and Mirth and bear clubs offers opportunities for big men, bears, and their admirers to come together publicly and celebrate their collective identity as a community.

Methods

The ethnographic and interview data about big men's and bear communities that empirically ground our argument were collected by the first author, Nat, who self-identifies as a chaser and has been a member of both communities since 1999. Between 2002 and 2007 Nat collected data as a participant-observer at three national, three regional, and sixteen local events sponsored by big men's and bear clubs around the country. Hundreds of men attend the annual national events—Girth and Mirth's Convergence and the International Bear Rendezvous (IBR)—which include bar parties, pool parties, dance parties, cocktail parties, sex and bathhouse parties, movie screenings, and (at IBR) the "Mr. Bear International" contest, where men perform and pose for an audience to see who is the "bearest of them all."

Local bar nights and bathhouse parties in various Southern California cities and in Minneapolis, Minnesota, drew between twenty and one hundred men. The majority of research participants were white men between the ages of twenty-five and sixty. Ongoing group communication occurs mainly on the Internet (implying access), and events cost hundreds of dollars to attend, so it is safe to assume that the majority of participants are middle class.

While attending these events, Nat observed the interactions between men and talked with them about their experiences in the big men's and bear clubs of which they were members. He took field notes after each event, focusing particularly on those observations relevant to the contentiousness members' embodied expression of fatness and sexuality (Brewer 2000). In addition, Nat organized a focus group at IBR 2007 where four bear- and fat-identified men talked with him about what the bear and big men's communities mean to them. The focus group was entitled "Are We Just Partying?" and was announced in the IBR program as part of the "community groups forum" on "ursology." We have used pseudonyms to identify our informants.

Being Fat and Sexy in Public as a Form of Protest

Social movement scholarship has recently begun to focus on collective action that targets public opinion or cultural norms rather than state apparatuses and that uses tactics that extend beyond marches and sit-ins to include new "cultural forms of political expression [such as] cross dressing, street performances, and gender transgression" (Taylor and Van Dyke 2004, 265). One important nonstate target of social movement activity is what Alberto Melucci (1996) calls "cultural codes," or the norms and identities of a given group or community. Dominant cultures and communities in society create and re-create cultural codes, while groups on the margins create alternative codes, which are still invested with normative power (Melucci 1996). The beauty standard within gay male communities is one example of such a cultural code, created and sustained through narrow media representation and discriminatory social interaction in gay male spaces (Locke 1997).

The public acts of big men, bears, and their admirers—such as flaunting and ogling fleshy bodies at a hotel pool party—contest gay male cultural codes of beauty and sexuality directly rather than indirectly, as do protest actions that target the state, such as holding signs in front of the Supreme Court Building. The everyday actions of big men, bears, and chasers can be defined as forms of protest within the definition of social movements' "tactical repertoires" put forth by Verta Taylor and her colleagues (Taylor, Rupp, and Gamson 2004; Taylor and Van Dyke 2004). This expanded interpretation of tactical repertoires, they point out, includes any incident where a group, bound by collective identity, intentionally contests cultural codes or authority. Thus, public theatrical displays, such as die-ins and kiss-ins (Van Dyke, Soule, and Taylor 2004) and huge artistic displays on skyscrapers (Gamson 1989) are recognized as social movement tactics. Tova Benski (2005) shows us that the very presence of particular bodies can be a form of protest. Because the Women in Black are in the streets at a time when the cultural code in Israel dictates that women should be at home, their mere presence in public is an embodied protest against the norms. Big men, bears, and chasers are similarly engaging in a type of embodied protest against aesthetic and sexual codes by holding large, visible public gatherings. Just as ordinary public displays of affection, such as hand holding, when performed by a recognizably same-sex couple, contest heteronormative cultural codes, the public enactment of sexual attraction among fat gay men and their admirers challenges the gay beauty ideal and its concomitant normative sexuality. Using the three-part definition of tactical repertoires laid out by Taylor and colleagues, we demonstrate that big men, bears, and chasers use their bodily presence and their embodied sexual or sexualized interaction to challenge cultural codes of beauty and sexuality, both within the gay community and in the larger heterosexual culture.

Collective Identity

Collective action by a group usually involves a certain degree of collective identity or solidarity and unity around a specific cause. The group must see how they are joined by something that is oppressing them and that acting together to change that structure gives them a certain amount of common ground (Melucci 1996; Taylor and Whittier 1992). United by a common goal of increased acceptance and decreased marginalization, actors foster a sense of collective identity around their cause. The process of coming to identify positively as a bear, fat person, or fat admirer is long and arduous for many gay men. One informant, Roberto, described his acceptance of his fat body as a direct result of involvement in big men's clubs.

> I never felt at home in the local gay scene in [outer suburb of Los Angeles]. I felt like nobody was interested in me sexually. As a result I tended to stay home a lot and didn't have a lot of sex. When I found *BiggerCity.com* I immediately started to find men who found me sexually attractive. Because of this I changed my own views about my body and began to see it as sexy to some. I am now much more

social and do not feel ashamed of my fat body because I know many find it sexy and attractive. When I go out to the bar with people who like me sexually, people still stare but it bothers me less because I know I'm sexy. (Pyle, field notes)

This statement illustrates a process of coming to identify with other big men and bears in which interacting with online communities nurtured a sense of confidence and belonging that led to public displays of fat-positive sexuality in off-line queer and nonqueer spaces. Roberto's relationship to his own body and sexuality was dramatically improved through the creation of a positive collective identity with other fat gay men and admirers. Such experiences were common among the bears and big men Nat interviewed. Many highlighted the need to congregate with other men who do not fit the image of the young, smooth, effeminate gay man prominent in gay communities. Similar processes of coming to identify with a larger group were apparent among fat admirers. Martin had this to say:

Before I found Girth and Mirth it was a constant struggle to find sexual partners. I lived in the suburbs [of Minneapolis] and didn't have easy access to the downtown gay clubs and so online communities were where I first heard of clubs for chubs and chasers. From there I heard about the national and regional events—many of the folks whom I met were from Los Angeles or San Diego. Girth and Mirth clubs were a major factor in my move from Minnesota to California. (Pyle, field notes)

Martin's identification with big men's clubs was a foundational reason for choosing where he lived. His experience fits with Melucci's (1995, 44) definition of collective identity as a "process of constructing an action system." For many informants, identifying with big men's and bear clubs is a central reason for their active and public expression of fat and fat-admirer sexuality.

Contestation

The second defining characteristic of tactical repertoires is the quality of actions in which "bodies, symbols, identities, practices, and discourses are used to pursue or prevent changes in institutionalized power relations" (Taylor and Van Dyke 2004, 268). Bears, big men, and their admirers seek to undermine the beauty norm that dominates mainstream gay culture and the resulting stigmatization of other body types and sexual attractions, and their bodies are the tools used to pursue this social change. By proudly embodying a counter-hegemonic gay male aesthetic, bears and big men are contesting and reformulating what a gay man looks like in the eyes of an outside observer. In effect, the self-presentation of big men and bears proclaims, "I'm fat and gay and I love it!" The dissemination of this message can have lasting effects on individuals, broadening ideas or perceptions of queer bodies for many whose previous perceptions of gay men were the result of the limited media representation described earlier. Similarly, the public sexualization of fat or hairy male bodies by chasers contests cultural codes of beauty and sexuality.

During national and regional events, the presence of bears, big men, and their admirers is palpable in the gay communities of the host cities and in the many bars and other businesses that sponsor activities. At pride festivals in cities across the United

States where the queer community as a whole converges, bear and big men's groups march in parades and operate festival booths. Many big men, bears, and their admirers proudly display their bodies and their sexualities in public every day, in the greater heterosexual world, as well as among other queer people. In addition, one can now turn on the television and find representations of both big men and bears, something that was unheard of even ten years ago. For example, in 2007 MTV produced a *True Life* episode about a fat gay man who is a member of *BiggerCity.com*. Bears have been represented in movies, such as John Waters's *Dirty Shame*. Donald had this to say about the increased visibility of bears and big men:

> It seems like just a little while back we were meeting at friends' houses for private parties. In the twenty years I have been an active member, I have seen the clubs balloon in size and public spaces open up for chubs and chasers. There was a time in my life when I had to work very hard to find activities that involved big men, but now I can find something to do almost every weekend in the Los Angeles area. It's really something how the community has grown and established itself. (Pyle, field notes)

Increased attendance by bears and big men at events has led to their getting together in public spaces and their more public presence has made their gatherings more noticeable to outside observers in their communities.

Prideful public self-presentation by bears, big men, and their admirers challenges the norms of dominant queer society by sexualizing fat and hairy bodies that are bothersome to some and revolting to others in the gay community. For example, the Los Angeles bathhouse that hosts the "Bears and Bellies Sex Party" is a popular spot for many members of the gay male community. When big men, bears, and their admirers gathered at the bathhouse and mixed with the usual patrons—young, thin, hairless gay men—interesting interactions resulted. Nat recorded his own experience.

> I was trolling the halls [looking for sex partners] when I bumped into two twinks [thin white twenty-somethings] who saw me and thought they'd found a comrade. "What's the deal tonight?" one of them asked, "Why are all these fat guys here?" "It's the Bears and Bellies Sex Party," I replied with a smirk. One of them actually said something to the effect of, "Eew that's gross!" The conversation ended with my telling them that they could expect to see the same crowd the first Wednesday of every month, to which they replied sarcastically, "Well, we know where we won't be then!" (Pyle, field notes)

These men asked Nat about the clientele in a flirtatious way, assuming because of his body size that he was not part of the group whose presence they questioned. Their response was typical of many interactions Nat has had with gay men who do not understand how someone could find attractive such "disgusting" body types.

By enacting their sexuality, big men, bears, and chasers challenge a socially constructed norm that dictates who is "attractive" and who is "disgusting." Socializing in public and semipublic gay and nongay spaces in which non–community members are confronted with their bodies and sexualities forces onlookers to notice their oppositional identities. In this way, they are contesting the cultural power of, as Mitchell put it, "the anorexic, gel in the hair, Prada-wearing, Beemer-driving . . . queens" (Pyle, field notes). For many participants, this contestation of the queen is intentional.

Intentionality

Intentionality is the notion that deliberate forethought informs the contestation of power structures. This intentionality cannot be accurately assessed if the assessment is based on appearance; intentionality is an element of the actors' staging a protest, not of the protest itself. Taylor and Van Dyke (2004) note that cultural performances can be "intentionally staged as part of a larger repertoire of contention of social movements" (269). Drawing on examples of street theater, drag performances, and art exhibits, they conclude, "We should not make *a priori* judgments about what constitutes a protest event" (270). The degree of intentionality behind the embodied protests of bear and big men's groups varies. This variation speaks to the different "levels of engagement" on the part of the participants (McCarthy and Zald 1977). Even if many bears and big men see the groups as places to find love, sex, and connection and are not intentional social-movement actors, the intentionality of the group leaders can guide the direction of less-involved members.

For many bears, big men, and their admirers, their public expression of positive body image and sexuality are an intentional strike against the dominant gay and heterosexual cultures that have made them feel like outsiders because of their body size or attraction to large bodies. Chris had this to say about his effect on people: "I love walking in public with my partner and kissing as we both turn to see who is looking. It gives me a feeling of satisfaction to know that I am making people think about my fat body and whether it can be sexy" (Pyle, field notes). The intention to expand the general public's understanding of what kind of body a gay man can have and what kind of gay male body can be sexy was reiterated by Julian, a contestant for Mr. Bear International 2007: "A Spanish contestant gave a very powerful speech as to the direction of bear communities and what Mr. Bear International should be a symbol of. He called for the bear community to move beyond the focus on circuit parties and orgies toward a more community-focused collective with power to influence perceptions inside and outside of the queer arena" (Pyle, field notes). The speech was quite provocative and elicited a supportive response from the community. After making this speech, Julian won. His coronation as Mr. Bear International is a clear sign that the community includes many members who are intentional in their efforts to expand perceptions of gay male beauty and sexuality.

Another example of intentional contestation are the public bodily displays at pool parties at various bear and big men's events. One pool event at Convergence 2002 in Minneapolis drew close to one hundred men. Here, Nat observed, "Big men and their admirers, all in and around the pool, were openly flaunting their proud fat sexuality under the public gaze of other hotel guests and staff who couldn't help but stop and stare" (Pyle, field notes). This display can be viewed as an intentional public performance of identity that contests cultural codes about what kinds of bodies are "allowed" to be scantily clad and what kinds of bodies can be sexy or sexualized. The reactions by the hotel patrons who were not members of Girth and Mirth were often shock and disgust, but onlookers may have been compelled to think about why fat sexuality seemed so out of place. Further research should include data collected from audiences targeted by such embodied protest actions (hotel staff, other guests), but there is reason to think that participants are having the intended effect on many on-lookers, some of whom may shift their preconceived notions about what it means to be sexually attractive (Rupp and Taylor 2003).

Conclusion

Big men, bears, and chasers proudly display their bodies and sexualities as a means to challenge narrow stereotypes of gay male beauty and sexuality. Applying the definition of tactical repertoires put forth by Taylor and her colleagues, we demonstrate how contestation, collective identity, and intentionality are present in the embodied public displays of big men, bears, and their admirers. Being fat and sexy in public and demonstrating one's sexual attraction to fat bodies are embodied forms of protest that challenge cultural codes. Bears, big men, and admirers configure their bodies in public spaces in ways that question and seek to undermine the socially constructed thin, hairless, young gay male beauty ideal. Through their protest actions, in which bodies are both literally and metaphorically central, they contest cultural codes that stigmatize and desexualize fat or hairy bodies, contributing to a redefinition of sexiness within and beyond gay male communities. Defining beauty and sexiness as excluding fat bodies diminishes fat people's moral value in the eyes of society and legitimizes discrimination. Thus, renegotiating the meanings of beauty and sexiness is an important goal in the body liberation movement as a whole. Unfortunately, U.S. cultural codes that define thinness as beauty and normative sexuality as exclusive attraction to thinness are being imposed worldwide at an increasing rate. Despite increasing media representation of fat gay men, a dangerously thin ideal is still being propagated in the United States and abroad.

REFERENCES

Battles, Kathleen, and Wendy Hilton-Morrow. 2002. "Gay Characters in Conventional Spaces: *Will and Grace* and the Situation Comedy Genre." *Critical Studies in Media Communication* 19 (1): 87–105.

Benski, Tova, 2005. "Breaching Events and the Emotional Reactions of the Public: Women in Black in Israel." In *Emotions and Social Movements*, ed. Helena Flam and Debra King, 57–79. New York: Routledge.

Blank, Hanne. 2000. *Big Big Love: A Sourcebook on Sex for People of Size and Those Who Love Them*. Eugene, OR: Greenery.

Bordo, Susan. 2003. *Unbearable Weight: Feminism, Western Culture, and the Body*. 10th anniversary ed. Berkeley: University of California Press.

Brewer, John D. 2000. *Ethnography*. Philadelphia: Open University Press.

Gamson, Josh. 1989. "Silence, Death, and the Invisible Enemy: AIDS Activism and Social Movement 'Newness.'" *Social Problems* 36 (4): 351–67.

Gates, Katharine. 2000. *Deviant Desires: Incredibly Strange Sex*. New York: Juno Books.

Hennen, Peter. 2008. *Faeries, Bears, and Leathermen: Men in Community Queering the Masculine*. Chicago: University of Chicago Press.

Levine, Martin P. 1998. *Gay Macho: The Life and Death of the Homosexual Clone*. New York: New York University Press.

Locke, Philip. 1997. "Male Images in the Gay Mass Media and Bear-Oriented Magazines: Analysis and Contrast." In *The Bear Book: Readings in the History and Evolution of a Gay Male Subculture*, ed. Les K. Wright, 103–40. Binghamton, NY: Haworth.

McCarthy, John D., and Mayer N. Zald. 1977. "Resource Mobilization and Social Movements: A Partial Theory." *American Journal of Sociology* 82 (6): 1212–41.

Melucci, Alberto. 1995. "The Process of Collective Identity." In *Social Movements and Culture*, ed. Hank Johnston and Bert Klandermans, 41–63. Minneapolis: University of Minnesota Press.

———. 1996. *Challenging Codes: Collective Action in the Information Age*. Cambridge: Cambridge University Press.

Olivardia, Roberto. 2004. "Body Image and Muscularity." In *Body Image: A Handbook of Theory, Research, and Clinical Practice*, ed. Thomas F. Cash and Thomas Pruzinsky, 210–18. New York: Guilford Press.

Pyle, Nathaniel C., and Michael I. Loewy. 2009. "Double Stigma: Fat Men and Their Male Admirers." In *The Fat Studies Reader*, ed. Esther Rothblum and Sondra Solovay, 143–50. New York: New York University Press.

Rupp, Leila J., and Verta Taylor. 2003. *Drag Queens at the 801 Cabaret*. Chicago: University of Chicago Press.

Sedgwick, Eve Kosofsky, and Michael Moon. 1994. "Divinity: A Dossier, a Performance Piece, a Little-Understood Emotion." In *Tendencies*, by Eve Kosofsky Sedgwick, 215–51. Durham, NC: Duke University Press.

Stearns, Peter N. 2002. *Fat History: Bodies and Beauty in the Modern West*. 2nd ed. New York: New York University Press.

Suresha, Ron Jackson. 2002. *Bears on Bears: Interviews and Discussions*. Los Angeles: Alyson.

Taylor, Verta A., Leila Rupp, and Joshua Gamson. 2004. "Performing Protest: Drag Shows as Tactical Repertoire of the Gay and Lesbian Movement." In *Authority in Contention*, ed. Daniel Myers and Daniel Cress, 105–37. Greenwich, CT: JAI.

Taylor, Verta A., and Nella Van Dyke. 2004. "'Get Up, Stand Up': Tactical Repertoires for Social Movements." In *The Blackwell Companion to Social Movements*, ed. David A. Snow, Sarah A. Soule, and Hanspeter Kriesi, 262–93. Malden, MA: Blackwell.

Taylor, Verta, and Nancy E. Whittier. 1992. "Collective Identity in Social Movement Communities." In *Frontiers in Social Movement Theory*, ed. Aldon D. Morris and Carol McClurg Mueller, 104–29. New Haven, CT: Yale University Press.

Van Dyke, Nella, Sara A. Soule, and Verta A. Taylor. 2004. "The Targets of Social Movements: Beyond a Focus on the State." In *Authority in Contention*, ed. Daniel Myers and Daniel Cress, 27–51. Greenwich, CT: JAI.

Wolf, Naomi. 2002. *The Beauty Myth: How Images of Beauty Are Used against Women*. New York: HarperCollins, Perennial. First published 1990 by Chatto and Windus.

7

Belly Dancing Mommas

Challenging Cultural Discourses of Maternity

Angela M. Moe

> I'm waiting backstage. The last minute checks—Shoes? I can't bend down far enough to reach them. Hip scarf? I can't reach far enough across myself to adjust it. Veil? If I turn around to ensure it's draped correctly, I'll bump into and move the stage curtains. Warm-up hip shimmy? No need. I'm always warm nowadays. My time is close, in more ways than one. The music, and the flutter in my belly, serve as reminders . . . I'm twenty-six weeks along and I'm still dancing. I'm proud of myself. I enter the stage feeling voluptuous and ripe. What an odd and unexpected empowerment. It takes just a few seconds for her to join in. "I can feel you, Baby!" She wiggles. "Are you dancing too?" This is our duet. Nothing else matters.

These were my thoughts during my last public performance before delivering my daughter. I had been belly dancing semiprofessionally for more than six years at the time I learned I was pregnant. It was the one form of exercise-recreation I maintained throughout my pregnancy, and it was the first such activity I resumed postpartum. While belly dance is a highly expressive and creative genre (Shay and Sellers-Young 2003, 2005), the public typically views it as a form of erotic entertainment, on par with striptease, burlesque, and cabaret (Carlton 1994; Dougherty 2005). It may thus seem inappropriate for a pregnant woman or new mother to be engaging in belly dance—an unsuitable display of the body and contrary to the asexualized, selfless qualities of maternity.

Indeed, pregnancy and early motherhood in the United States are subject to dominant cultural discourses that position them as central to normative femininity, a cultural rite of passage (Letherby 1994). As such, women face a host of gendered expectations about selfless devotion to (impending) motherhood. The pregnant and postpartum body becomes a subject of distinct patriarchal critique, with a range of activities and behaviors related to diet, exercise, and appearance deemed necessary for healthy pregnancy, birth, and postpartum recovery (Bailey 1999). In this chapter I examine the ways in which the act of belly dancing subverts dominant discourses surrounding pregnancy and motherhood.

Discourses of Maternity

A central premise of feminist theories is that women's bodies are perceived as a mystery, the Other, as de Beauvoir (1952) asserted several decades ago. Thus, they are abstract, unpredictable, suspect, and possibly threatening things that must be regulated and controlled. Through time and the evolution of various social, political, and religious institutions, women's bodies have become a "direct locus of social control" (Bordo 1990, 13). Activities associated with or performed on female bodies have become a "medium of culture" (Bordo 1990, 13), and the various means through which culture is displayed through and on women's bodies has been widely discussed by various feminist theorists (see Bartky 1988; Dimen 1989). As products and practitioners of culture, then, women are socialized throughout their lives to "do gender" (West and Zimmerman 1987).

Dominant discourses about what is and is not deemed appropriate regarding women's activities and displays of physicality arise from this rubric. These discourses place various and sometimes contradictory expectations on women's gendered performances (Bordo 1993; Butler 1990; Dyer 1992). Such paradoxical expectations become particularly salient during pregnancy and shortly after childbirth. For example, women may be expected to suspend certain normative practices related to their non-motherhood identities (e.g., being thin, acting sexually alluring) and prioritize, even if only temporarily, others (e.g., gaining weight, honing one's "maternal instinct," becoming asexual) (Bailey 1999; Dworkin and Wachs 2004; Marshall 1991). Thus, while the pregnant woman symbolizes maternal potential, she also becomes aesthetically problematic. She is both an admired subject and a physically unappealing object, according to contemporary standards of beauty. As such, the postpartum torso is to be modestly clothed or masked according to culturally appropriate standards. So while women may find pride and strength in their bodies during and after pregnancy, these same bodies may also become sources of discomfort and shame (Dworkin and Wachs 2004). Dancing in ways that emphasize and reveal the torso may provide a space for overt resistance and physical reclamation.

History and Social Context of Belly Dance

Belly dance, as it has come to be known in the West, is an eclectic genre with ancient origins throughout the Middle and Near East. To be more specific, it encompasses "a matrix of dances including those that originate in North Africa, the Middle East and Central Asia as well as related hybrid forms created in the United States and elsewhere that are currently part of private and public performances in villages, towns, suburbs, and urban communities across the globe in cafes, concert stages, community centers, and on the internet" (Shay and Sellers-Young 2005, 11). While examining the history of the dance can help one appreciate how and why contemporary women are drawn to it, its exact origin is difficult to determine because of the vast geographical area of the Middle and Near East and the lack of complete historical records throughout this region (Deagon 1998). The historical records and scholarly writings that do exist indicate, however, that belly dance is often considered a derivative of the oldest documented dances (Djoumahna 2000). Archaeological evidence dating to at least 3400

BCE (Knapp 1981) from lands on the southeastern edge of the Mediterranean Sea suggest that many of the movements associated with contemporary belly dance may have been incorporated into various rituals, celebrations, and community activities throughout the past several millennia (Stewart 2000).

The way in which belly dance has evolved to its contemporary, often misunderstood, state involves myriad social, economic, and political forces related to tourism, Orientalism (the portrayal, usually through negative or misleading stereotypes, of Eastern culture by outsiders, generally associated with the eighteenth and nineteenth centuries), and European colonialism over the past several hundred years. Such forces have formed a juxtaposition between the East, as it was originally perceived (hence references to the Orient), and the West. In the writings and paintings that emerged during the 1700s and 1800s, for example, women were often depicted as well-endowed, partially nude performers (MacMaster and Lewis 1998). Such images provided colorful sexual fodder about a seemingly exotic foreign land that was heightened by the strict propriety and social regulation often associated with that period (Carlton 1994; MacMaster and Lewis 1998).

Despite such negative portrayals, belly dance has become extremely popular in the past few decades, particularly among non–Middle Eastern women from various parts of the world (Wright and Dreyfus 1998). One negative effect of such widespread involvement is that dancers have been accused of appropriation (see, e.g., Maira 2008). While a full discussion of this issue would require more space than available here, it is worth noting two factors that complicate claims of appropriation. First, for an activity to be borrowed or stolen (as arguments of appropriation often claim), it must be possible to clearly determine a time and place from which the activity was taken. However, it is impossible to claim with any certainty that belly dance began at a specific place and at a specific time or even to reach agreement on what exactly constitutes belly dance. It has always been and remains a constantly evolving dance form with few universally accepted rules about technique (in contrast to more codified forms of dance, such as ballet, jazz, and tap) (Shay and Sellers-Young 2003).

Second, contemporary belly dancers, including those located in the United States, are not necessarily twenty-first-century Orientalists, knowingly adhering to and supporting exploitive and misinformed images of the dance and the Middle East. Quite the opposite, in fact; many struggle to improve understanding and appreciation of the art form and to enhance its legitimacy (Dox 2006). They do so knowing that their efforts may be in vain, because audiences are likely to retain their misconceptions about the dance despite a performer's efforts to correct them. Nonetheless, the constant challenge of altering stereotypes and improving public perceptions of the dance drive the efforts of these dancers. On the other end of the spectrum, however, are dancers who seem to purposefully play into stereotypes by incorporating elements of the Orientalist aesthetic into their performances (e.g., wearing "harem" outfits, veiling the lower face, working snakes and swords into choreography). To complicate matters, sometimes the same dancers draw from both ends of the spectrum, depending on the circumstances of their performances and the composition of audiences (e.g., a restaurant venue dictates a much different aesthetic than a stage production). Such is the reality of many professional belly dancers, past and present—negotiating the line between earning a living and correcting misconceptions.

Lynette Harris at seven and a half months pregnant in 1994.
(Reproduced by permission from Julie Faisst.)

Methods and Sample

This analysis is based on an ethnographic project on belly dance in the United States (Moe 2008) that aimed to understand contemporary women's reasons for and experiences with the dance. As a semiprofessional belly dancer, I have long been interested in why women participate in this genre of movement. As a new mother, I have also become intrigued with how this dance fits into the lives of pregnant and postpartum women. Thus, I conducted twenty-four semi-structured interviews with women who had belly danced or were belly dancing while pregnant or postpartum, focusing on (1) why pregnant and postpartum women belly dance; (2) the extent and ways belly dance affects women's views of their bodies; and (3) how the voices and experiences of pregnant and postpartum belly dancers might challenge the cultural discourse surrounding pregnancy and motherhood.

The interviewed women were between the ages of twenty-four and fifty-eight (average of thirty-six). Their belly dance experience ranged from one-and-a-half to thirty-five years, with 46 percent (eleven) identifying as amateur or hobbyists and 54 percent (thirteen) identifying as semiprofessionals, professionals, or retired professionals. All identified as heterosexual, with the majority currently married or partnered (79 percent, nineteen). The majority (88 percent, twenty-one) were also currently living in the midwestern states of Michigan, Indiana, Illinois, and Missouri, which likely contributed to the relatively homogeneous racial and ethnic composition of the sample, with 96 percent (twenty-three) identifying as white.[1] The sample was well educated as well, with 8 percent (two) having only a high school diploma, while 33 percent (eight) had completed some college or obtained college degrees, 46 percent (eleven) had completed some graduate work or obtained master's degrees, and 13 percent (three) had completed doctoral degrees. In addition to being busy mothers (averaging two children each), most retained paid employment (79 percent, nineteen). Five (21 percent) of the women were pregnant at the time of the interviews. They shared many thoughts, perceptions, and experiences that suggested their awareness of the dominant discourse surrounding pregnancy and motherhood. Indeed, they identified two elements of the discourse in particular, appearance and behavior, and then challenged each with regard to belly dance.

Appearance: Masking versus Revealing

As noted earlier, the pregnant and postpartum body, while socially admired for what it has accomplished by producing and sustaining a child, is also not typically seen as physically or sexually appealing in our society. Though this attitude is changing in some ways (e.g., the current trend among pregnant women to wear formfitting maternity clothes), pregnant and postpartum bodies continue to be subject to scrutiny. Indeed, a pregnant woman who remains proportionately thin throughout her pregnancy (e.g., being "all belly") or who is able to lose weight quickly after giving birth may escape some of this criticism and even receive praise for showing her body. The majority of women, however, whose bodies are not representative of societal beauty ideals about weight and firmness before pregnancy may face scrutiny. Such criticisms may intensify during and after pregnancy, when their bodies are even larger and less toned.

The women were well aware of the possibility that they would be judged negatively, recognizing that certain social expectations drive the ways in which they are to appear physically as pregnant women and as new mothers. These expectations were targeted at the torso, as a part of the body that ought to be covered in the name of modesty and social appropriateness. As Jaiye (belly dance hobbyist, mother of four) explained, "I think people want you to try to keep that belly covered. I think it embarrasses people who see your bare stomach when you are so long into your pregnancy as far as actually showing."[2] Echoing such sentiments, Jordana (professional belly dancer, mother of an infant) commented, "You should not dress provocatively. . . . You're pregnant! You're 'off the market.' Be very conservative." Julia (hobbyist, mother of two) indicated that this expectation to mask the torso extends into the postpartum period as well: "You have to stay covered. That's a big thing. It's forever. I wasn't wearing those little belly shirts or anything, but my clothes weren't to my knees either. I had shorter shirts and now it's like if my shirt slides up and my stomach shows, people are talking down to me. Even my son will go, 'Mom!'"

While aware of such expectations, the women were very frank about explaining how belly dancing provided them a direct means of subverting expectations of hiding their pregnant and postpartum torsos. In particular, there was a strong sense that exposing their bodies on their own terms in this way was liberating, regardless of the reactions by others. For example, Naia (semi-professional, mother of a toddler) described her experience of having maternity photos taken in a belly dance costume: "Somebody asked me, 'Did you show your belly?' Like that would be an awful thing to do! I was like, 'Oh yeah, I showed more than my belly!'"

Such emboldened resistance extended to the postpartum period as well. During this time the women dealt with social expectations to hide the physical consequences of pregnancy, particularly weight gain and stretch marks. Dana (hobbyist, pregnant with fifth child) asserted, "It's like you're supposed to be dissatisfied with your [postpartum] belly pooch. You're supposed to want to get rid of it. As a belly dancer you embrace that part of your body. You embrace all of it, however it is."

Indeed, embracing their bodies engendered a sense of greater self-acceptance for many women. This point is important, because during the postpartum period women face extreme social pressure to reconform to the social standards of beauty to which they were subjected before pregnancy. Thus, many struggled with losing their "baby weight" quickly, the connotation being that carrying any "extra" weight is unacceptable and unattractive. However, through belly dance the women were able to accept and appreciate their bodies just as they were. Bella (professional, mother of two) vividly recalled her experience of viewing her dancing body soon after birth:

> I went down to my studio by myself, I turned the music on and I stood there and looked at my body. I watched that movement and I watched that belly roll. It was one of the most beautiful things I have ever seen in my life, absolutely beautiful, and I was thirty to thirty-five pounds heavier. . . . I just stood there and I took it all in and I said, "This is what the female body is. This is what we should be praising."

The same held true for the women's handling of stretch marks, which are often a source of embarrassment and shame. With this issue, belly dancing again proved a means through which women could reclaim their physicality, in all of its manifestations, and resist social scripts that would have them mask their midsections. Sarah (professional, mother of two) recalled, "It was tough. I can't count the times that people have made comments about my stretch marks, especially photographers. It's just been obnoxious. . . . Occasionally there would be that self-consciousness that crept in, but for the most part I've been able to suppress that." In fact, such experiences actually prompted Sarah to take her dance business in a new direction, one that celebrated the totality of women's shapes, sizes, and markings. As she explained, "I decided to form my own troupe and all of my women were mothers and they all had stretch marks. . . . I will definitely challenge the status quo when it comes to the perception of what a beautiful female should be . . . should look like."

In short, the women's recognition of and resistance to social standards regarding the appearance of the pregnant and postpartum body informed their consciousness about how and why they belly danced. The ways in which this particular genre of movement challenged public perceptions of how women's bodies are supposed to be presented during and after pregnancy fueled their commitment to the dance and enhanced the benefits they derived from it. The contrast between the behavior deemed appropriate for pregnant and postpartum women and the behavior allowed under the guise of belly dancing had the same effect on the women's commitment and the benefits they derived.

Behavior: Modesty versus Reclamation

The women's recognition and subversion of the cultural discourse surrounding pregnancy and motherhood extended logically from discussions surrounding physical appearance to actual behavior. In this vein, belly dancing provided an avenue through which to balance their identities as both mothers who were dedicated to their families and autonomous women who yearned to reconnect to their individuality. For example, Jaiye commented, "Everyone wants you to be this sweet new mom, docile and temperate woman, not making any waves. They think you should just kind of waddle around with your hands at the small of your back and just sit down and take it easy until you have that baby." In explaining how such expectations continue well into motherhood, Geneveve (professional, mother of three) also highlighted the suspension of autonomy: "New moms are expected to do certain things, behave certain ways. . . . It seems like everything is censored. You're talking about the children most of the time, so there is this feeling of you disappearing."

As both Jaiye and Geneveve suggest, there is a strong gendered component to this discourse, in that pregnant and postpartum women are expected to epitomize subservience and vulnerability through their maternal status. Allie (hobbyist, mother of two) echoed these sentiments and hinted at an aspect of infantilization: "People treat you differently when you're pregnant. They'll act like you can't do things for yourself. Everyone thinks you're fragile." Finally, as suggested earlier, pregnant and postpartum women are often not thought of as being sensual or sexual beings. Naia candidly made this point: "Nobody ever wants to think about . . . pregnant women doing anything sexual."

The opportunity to do something sensually or sexually provocative, however, was often what the women found attractive about belly dance during and after pregnancy. That aspect elicited predictable responses by others. As Dana noted, "I had people who kind of gave me looks, like, 'Wow, that's a little risqué for you to be doing as a mommy. Do you want to expose your kids to that?' They really didn't have an idea of what it is besides the American mistaken idea of what belly dancing is—that it's just a step away from stripping. To be a mom of an infant and to be sensual and appreciate your body is not allowed." But unlike common stereotypes about the dance, which suggest that women are drawn to it for titillating and seductive purposes, the women in this study yearned for the opportunity to reconnect with their physicality through a form of movement that honors a woman's body and life course. Their experiences in this regard were tied more to their need to reconnect to their bodies in self-affirming ways, which encompassed empowering aspects of sensuality and sexuality, than to any desire to please or meet others' expectations. As Lynne (pregnant with first child) noted, "The freedom, just being able to go and just move. I really appreciate being able to do that. Recognizing that it's probably not as elegant or fluid as it could be, but I can still move. . . . It's not a prerequisite to look good per se. It's not the about the aesthetic. It's what feels good for you." Jeela (professional, mother of one) echoed these sentiments: "The body takes all sorts of different shapes and sizes throughout its lifetime. It functions in different ways for you, as an adolescent, as a young woman, as a pregnant woman, as an older woman. Pregnancy is just like a natural part of that whole timeline. . . . Belly dance gives you a beautiful vocabulary to express it."

In particular, women who viewed themselves as heavy before pregnancy, and who maintained such physiques after pregnancy, found a particular sense of physical acceptance through belly dance that remained salient throughout their pregnancies. As Jordana explained:

> Society tells you what beautiful is and what attractive is. . . . You try to tell yourself, "Maybe I'm an exception to the rule." . . . The community of belly dance says, "It doesn't matter how big or how small you are." . . . When I first started dancing and I was heavy. I used to wear fabric that would cover my belly. And then I started to dance more and become more confident with my body and then I completely took the cover away. The entire time I was pregnant I never wore a belly cover.

Belly dancing provided a way for the women in this study to challenge the status quo regarding the activities of expectant and new mothers. Indeed, for them, part of the draw of belly dance was that it uniquely subverted the social scripts that manage women's behavior during pregnancy and early motherhood, allowing them a means through which to reclaim and balance their public behavior in lieu of social standards that dictate otherwise. Janice (professional, pregnant with first child) defended her right to belly dance in light of others' expectations that she modify her behavior.

> The reactions I get when people find out I'm pregnant, they're like, "Oh my God! You're just out there dancing around and everything?" I just have the attitude of, "Screw it, I'll do what I want." . . . I went shopping with my in-laws this weekend and I bent down with a scanner to scan something and they're like, "Oh be careful!" I'm like, "I can squat! You know, I belly dance. You think this is bad? Don't come watch me at a show!"

Finally, the women also found that through the dance they were able to balance their old (prepregnant) and new (pregnant-motherhood) identities, an issue that was central to their reconnecting to their bodies. Julia commented on the responses she received for taking one night a week away from her family to belly dance. She, and the other women in this study, directly countered the social expectation that women suspend their pre-pregnancy activities in lieu of their family responsibilities: "Tuesday nights are 'mom's on strike' night. I get some horrified looks sometimes. 'You do what?' Maybe I'm a little nontraditional, but I have to do something for myself. People don't understand that. It's just, 'You actually leave them?' And I'm like, 'Yeah. I leave them with their father!'" While belly dancing is not unique in this way, as various activities may be used by women as an outlet for individual expression and exercise, the fact that the women in this study chose an activity that challenges the discourses surrounding their maternal-familial status was intriguing. As Gail (professional, mother of two) noted, "Seeing pregnant woman dance is a whole kind of a mind-altering thing. Oriental dance is sexy.[3] It's very sensual and very pretty and so the whole viewing a maternal body in a sensual way is really, really alien to the Western mind." In this way, belly dance allowed women to reclaim and balance their public behavior despite social standards that dictate otherwise.

Conclusion

Women who belly dance are subject to stereotyping and prejudice. Dancing during pregnancy and early motherhood challenges the dominant cultural discourses about what are and are not acceptable activities and displays of the female body. The women in this study were well aware of these discourses and referenced them when expressing their own embodied experiences. That they continue to engage in and defend belly dance, despite its contradictory positioning within socially acceptable behavior, speaks to the lure of this genre of movement. The findings here offer some insights about why belly dance is so appealing during pregnancy and early motherhood.

First, women may struggle with accepting their changing physical shape during and after pregnancy. Such struggles are complicated by the ways in which our culture enforces somewhat contradictory messages about the appearance and behavior of (expectant) mothers (Bailey 1999; Dworkin and Wachs 2004; Marshall 1991). For example, while it is acceptable for women to gain weight (to a certain extent) during pregnancy, it is incumbent on them to lose this baby weight as quickly as possible afterward. We often see this imperative presented under the guise of "getting your body back" (Dworkin and Wachs 2004, 610), as if one's true body is somewhere else, certainly not part of one's postpartum physique. Belly dance, as it was experienced by the women in this study, allows creative space for women of all shapes and sizes. Although individual women's reasons for belly dancing vary, and it would be inappropriate to assume that a purely aesthetic rationale (i.e., to prevent excessive weight gain during pregnancy and to more quickly lose weight after) is not at play, the point made by the women in this study is that the dance helps them to feel good about their bodies, in whatever shape or form they are in. While some of them were probably hoping to lose weight by belly dancing, this motive was not as salient in their rationales. What was salient were the means through which belly dance allowed them to view their fuller, maternal bodies as something powerful and admirable. Belly dancing seemed to provide a space in which to suspend social expectations of the body. As such, it offered women an avenue through which to appreciate, accept, and honor their bodies within different stages of their lives.

Second, women seem to be confronted with a disjuncture between identities during pregnancy and early motherhood that, again, is related to the dominant discourses surrounding these life events (Bailey 1999; Dworkin and Wachs 2004; Marshall 1991). As the women attested, being and acting sensual or sexual during and after pregnancy is not readily accepted by our culture. They reported ways in which belly dancing helped them to challenge, overcome, and otherwise disregard such social messages. Through belly dance, women may find a safe and creative outlet for exploring and reconnecting with their sensual and sexual selves. Such (re)discovery, and the (re)balancing of identity, can be central to a healthy personal state. It is indeed interesting that a dance so often dismissed as being overly and inappropriately erotic actually holds value to women on these same grounds. Part of the draw to the dance seems to be the permission it extends to women to claim a sense of sensuality and sexuality on their own terms. Rather than denying such elements of their identity, this dance seems to provide a safe space from which women may reexamine and redefine intrinsic aspects of themselves. It is thus worth examining how, why, and for whose interests certain activities are demonized, as well as why women's embodied experiences and opinions are so easily disregarded.

Overall, it seems belly dance may be too easily dismissed as an illegitimate form of movement and expression. This dismissal is largely due to the multifaceted history of the dance, which has supported long-standing misconceptions about it and the women who practice it (MacMaster and Lewis 1998). That women from the United States and various other non–Middle Eastern countries are engaging in this misunderstood art form (Wright and Dreyfus 1998) is suggestive of its salience within their lives. As is seen here, it is important to examine all aspects of appropriation, including the ways in which contemporary Western women are negotiating their own use of the dance in light of enduring Orientalist stereotyping. What is clear is that it is important to listen to the voices and learn from the experiences of contemporary belly dancers. Certainly when it comes to the strain, pressure, and adjustment required during pregnancy and early motherhood, an activity that helps women feel good about themselves and retain a sense of individuality by challenging social scripts and cultural discourses is worth exploring.

NOTES

1. The women did report a range of European and Mediterranean ancestries. Two also identified as part Native American and one identified exclusively as a Russian immigrant. One woman identified as black.
2. All names are pseudonyms.
3. Her use of the term *Oriental* was intentional, since some practitioners take issue with the disparaging connotations attached to the term *belly dance*, preferring labels more often used and accepted within the Middle and Near East (e.g., Arabic dance, Middle Eastern dance, Oriental dance). This seems especially common for those who see their particular style as more ethnically representative.

REFERENCES

Bailey, Lucy. 1999. "Refracted Selves: A Study of Changes in Self-Identity in the Transition to Motherhood." *Sociology* 33 (2): 335–52.

Bartky, Sandra L. 1988. "Foucault, Femininity, and the Modernization of Patriarchal Power." In *Feminism and Foucault*, ed. Irene Diamond and Lee Quinby, 61–86. Boston: Northeastern University Press.

Beauvoir, Simone de. 1952. *The Second Sex*. New York: Vintage Books.

Bordo, Susan R. 1990. "The Body and Reproduction of Femininity: A Feminist Appropriation of Foucault." In *Gender/Body/Knowledge*, ed. Alison M. Jaggar and Bordo, 13–33. New Brunswick, NJ: Rutgers University Press.

———. 1993. *Unbearable Weight: Feminism, Western Culture, and the Body*. Berkeley: University of California Press.

Butler, Judith. 1990. *Gender Trouble: Feminism and the Subversion of Identity*. New York: Routledge.

Carlton, Donna. 1994. *Looking for Little Egypt*. Bloomington, IN: IDD Books.

Deagon, Andrea. 1998. "In Search of the Origins of Dance: Real History or Fragments of Ourselves." *Habibi: A Journal for Lovers of Middle Eastern Dance and Arts* 17 (1): 20–21, 35–37.

Dimen, Muriel. 1989. "Power, Sexuality, and Intimacy." In *Gender/Body/Knowledge*, ed. Alison M. Jaggar and Susan Bordo, 34–51. New Brunswick, NJ: Rutgers University Press.

Djoumahna, Kajira. 2000. "Belly Dance: In Brief." In *The Belly Dance Book: Rediscovering the Oldest Dance*, ed. Tazz Richards, 10–13. Concord, CA: Backbeat Press.

Dougherty, Roberta L. 2005. "Dance and the Dancer in Egyptian Film." In *Belly Dance: Orientalism, Transnationalism, and Harem Fantasy*, ed. Anthony Shay and Barbara Sellers-Young, 145–71. Costa Mesa, CA: Mazda

Dox, Donnalee. 2006. "Dancing around Orientalism." *Drama Review* 50 (4): 52–71.

Dworkin, Shari L., and Faye Linda Wachs. 2004. "'Getting Your Body Back': Postindustrial Fit Motherhood in *Shape Fit Pregnancy* Magazine." *Gender and Society* 18 (5): 610–24.

Dyer, Richard. 1992. *Only Entertainment*. New York: Routledge.

Knapp, Bettina L. 1981. "Egyptian Feasts and Dances of Earliest Times." *Arabesque* 7 (1): 12–14, 22.

Letherby, Gayle. 1994. "Mother or Not, Mother or What? Problems of Definition and Identity." *Women's Studies International Forum* 17 (5): 525–32.

MacMaster, Neil, and Toni Lewis. 1998. "Orientalism: From Unveiling to Hyperveiling." *Journal of European Studies* 28 (1): 121–36.

Maira, Sunaina. 2008. "Belly Dancing: Arab-Face, Orientalist Feminism, and U.S. Empire." *American Quarterly* 60 (2): 317–45.

Marshall, Hariette. 1991. "The Social Construction of Motherhood: An Analysis of Childcare and Parenting Manuals." In *Motherhood: Meanings, Practices, and Ideologies*, ed. Ann Phoenix, Anne Woollett, and Eva Lloyd, 66–85. London: Sage.

Moe, Angela M. 2008. "Reclaiming the Feminine: Bellydancing as a Feminist Project." In *Dance Studies and Global Feminisms: 41st Annual Congress on Research in Dance Conference Proceedings, November 14–16, 2008, Hollins University, Roanoke, VA*, ed. Tresa Randall, 181–92. Chicago: University of Chicago Press.

Shay, Anthony, and Barbara Sellers-Young. 2003. "Belly Dance: Orientalism-Exoticism-Self-Exoticism." *Dance Research Journal* 35 (1): 13–37.

———. 2005. "Introduction." In *Belly Dance: Orientalism, Transnationalism, and Harem Fantasy*, ed. Shay and Young, 1–27. Costa Mesa, CA: Mazda.

Stewart, Iris J. 2000. *Sacred Woman, Sacred Dance: Awakening Spirituality through Movement and Ritual*. Rochester, VT: Inner Traditions.

West, Candace, and Donald Zimmerman. 1987. "Doing Gender." *Gender and Society* 1 (2): 125–51.

Wright, Jan, and Shoshona Dreyfus. 1998. "Belly Dancing: A Feminist Project?" *Women in Sport and Physical Activity Journal* 7 (2): 95–114.

8

"It's Important to Show Your Colors"

Counter-Heteronormativity in a Metropolitan Community Church

J. Edward Sumerau and Douglas P. Schrock

The regulation of human bodies is central to organized religion, though it has received little academic attention (Smith 2008). Religious traditions have rich histories of controlling, for example, what we eat, what we wear, how we move our bodies, how we sing, and with whom we have sex. Religious leaders seem to understand the importance the body has in marking one as a member of a religious culture. Because religious identities, like all identities, are humanly created fictions, religious cultures regulate bodies in order to socially mark who is an insider and who is an outsider. Thus, when worshipers adopt the embodiment codes of their faith and imbue them with meaning, they in turn feel more connected to their religious communities and traditions.

But what if your bodily practices contradict the religious tradition you grew up in? You could decide something is wrong with you and commit to changing your embodiment practices. If you decide changing is not possible or worth it, however, others may turn against you and make an example out of your bodily transgressions. While overtly challenging a church's culture might create change, it could also lead to further isolation and stigmatization. Under such conditions, you might decide the organization is not for you and leave. This is exactly what some lesbian, gay, bisexual, and transgender (LGBT) Christians have done.

The exclusion of LGBT people from some traditional Christian churches reflects these organizations' embodiment norms regarding what kind of bodies should be physically intimate and how people ought to embody gender. Christian churches often assert that God made men and women so different that they should not act or look like each other. Despite such differences, so goes the story, God approves of sexual unions only between men and women. These churches often have other bodily restrictions targeting heterosexuals: no sex before or outside of marriage and no birth control or abortion. Moreover, Christian authorities generally define the violation of these prescriptions as physical transgressions, sins of the flesh, or bodily threats to the sanctity of heterosexual marriage and the patriarchal family (Moon 2004).

Such rules of embodiment reflect what social theorists call "heteronormativity"

(Warner 1991). Heteronormativity refers to an ideology that assumes men and women are not just physically different but are designed to be socially different. According to this ideology, girls and women should act in ways culturally defined as "feminine," which includes being passive, nurturing, and concerned about appearance. Complementarily, boys and men should be assertive, emotionally reserved, and competitive. Also key to heteronormativity is a hierarchy of acceptable sexual behaviors: heteronormativity deems sex between men and women natural and normal, and sex between two men or two women unnatural and abnormal. Thus, for most traditional Christians, heterosexual marriage and the patriarchal family represent the primary expressions of God's will on earth (Bartkowski 2001).

Heteronormativity is a way of thinking that may promote and justify socially created inequality between women and men and between heterosexuals and sexual minorities. Having faith in this ideology, for example, may lead politicians to deny equal rights to LGBT individuals, men to believe women should attend to their emotional and physical needs (but not vice versa), and men and women to believe violence against women and sexual minorities is sometimes appropriate. True believers of heteronormativity can act in ways that cause others pain because the ideology itself provides an emotional shield. More specifically, because the ideology defines gender and sexual nonconformists as unnatural and immoral, adopting heteronormativity enables one to more easily ignore the suffering of those socially defined—and treated—as inferior.

Some Christian churches' tendency to promote a heteronormative worldview shapes how they respond to LGBT members. Church authorities often tell LGBT members that they must change their gendered and sexual desires or leave the church (Wolkomir 2006). Although 8.3 percent of Protestants and 8.4 percent of Roman Catholics report engaging in homosexual activity at some point in their lives (Turner et al. 2005), many still assume that one cannot identify as a Christian and a sexual minority. LGBT communities have responded by fighting to make some churches more tolerant and creating their own Christian organizations that define Christian and LGBT identities as compatible. These organizations represent a serious challenge to heteronormative assumptions permeating traditional Christianity (Moon 2004).

Research on LGBT Christians typically focuses on how they integrate their sexual and religious identities. Members of the gay Christian support group Wolkomir (2006) studied, for example, constructed gay-affirming interpretations of scripture, which offered its members relief from the shame and fear of living a life they previously defined as sinful (see also Thumma 1991). McQueeney (2009), however, found that many sexual minorities downplayed their sexual identities relative to their Christian identities and emphasized discourses of monogamy, manhood, and motherhood to normalize LGBT Christian identities. McQueeney noted that while these members subverted heteronormativity by making it acceptable to be sexual minorities and Christians, they simultaneously reinforced heteronormative family values and gender roles.

While these studies show how people use language to integrate sexual and religious identities, they neglect the importance of embodiment. In addition to language, we use our bodies to signify identities. By decorating our bodies with clothing and accessories, using nonverbal gestures, and managing interpersonal touching and personal space, we create images of who we believe ourselves to be (Goffman 1959; Stone

1981). Gimlin (2001) refers to how we use or mold our bodies to signify ourselves as social objects as "bodywork."

In this chapter, we examine how members of a southeastern Metropolitan Community Church (MCC) we refer to as Shepherd Church (all names hereafter are pseudonyms) employed their bodies to resist heteronormativity and integrate their sexual and religious identities. Composed of over three hundred congregations and forty-three thousand members, the MCC is an international LGBT Christian denomination that arose in response to traditionalists' marginalization of sexual minorities. Shepherd Church was in some ways unique during the period of observation because it did not possess a full-time pastor. After losing their former pastor to another organization, members collectively managed the everyday operations of their congregation. As such, members ran the church themselves by taking turns preaching sermons, organizing events, and maintaining the property. Although they felt like second-class citizens in other churches, members created a safe and affirming space to worship outside of the closet.

Methods

We learned how members of Shepherd Church embodied their identities through ethnographic methods. As part of a larger project (Sumerau 2010), the first author spent over eighteen months observing and participating in worship services, commemorative events, Bible studies, administrative meetings, choir practices, and a wide variety of social activities with members of the church. While in these situations, he jotted notes on what transpired, tape-recorded activities, and later used these resources to type up more complete field notes. He also conducted over 250 informal interviews with members before and after events. The vast majority of the eighty active members were white, middle class, and middle-aged. After spending fifteen years meeting in rental spaces and homes, they collectively purchased their first permanent church property just before fieldwork began. As the bisexual child of a gay man, the ethnographer was immediately welcomed into the church and treated as a friend and confidant.

We began our analysis by asking how members of the church embodied their sexual and religious identities in their social interactions. After comparing and contrasting our answers to these questions, three main embodiment processes emerged, which we term *queering fashion*, *embracing intimacy*, and *transgendering demeanor*. Gradually we came to see how members' embodied practices subverted traditional heteronormative Christian culture.

Counter-Heteronormative Embodiment

What follows is an analysis of how members of Shepherd Church embodied their sexual and religious identities in ways that symbolically resisted heteronormative conceptions of Christianity. First, we show how members queered fashion, which refers to how they used fashion to counter the traditional gender binary and signify pride as sexual minorities. Second, we examine how members embraced intimacy, by which we mean how members used their bodies to physically connect with one another in ways that repudiated heteronormative rules and more general embodiment norms restricting person-to-person contact. Third, we analyze how members transgendered demeanor, which involved men using their bodies in feminine ways and women using their bodies in masculine ways.

Queering Fashion

Traditional Christian churches, like all institutions, have informal rules about how one fashions the body. While there may be some regional variation, traditional Christians typically emphasize conformity and reservation in the decoration of the body, especially by gender. Church traditions dictate that members wear their "Sunday best" to show respect for their religious community. Members of Shepherd Church, however, fashioned their bodies in ways that expressed opposition to such traditions. We call such bodywork queering fashion because it subverted heteronormative assumptions about gender and sexuality.

While members did not talk about their dress as "resisting" heteronormativity, they did recognize that it contradicted what one generally finds in the "stuffy buildings" of traditional churches. Laney, for example, explained that coming to Shepherd Church "can be a bit of an adjustment" because "you grow up in stuffy buildings where everyone wears the same suit, dress, and 'Sunday best' each week, but it doesn't feel right. Then you come here and there may be men in dresses or women in baseball jerseys. It just shows there are different ways to be Christian and we don't all look the same. Rather than just trying to look the same, we just look for God." By defining wearing one's "Sunday best" as an exercise in conformity and emphasizing the freedom to wear clothes culturally associated with the opposite sex, Laney echoed others in valuing personal style. Statements like this also implied that subverting cultural expectations about gendered clothing was accepted, and focusing on God was more important than one's clothing. Ronald made a similar point before an evening service.

> You like my new gym shorts? [*He chuckles.*] My legs are going to look good when I'm up there reading the scripture. Man, I don't know. [*He chuckles and tugs on my sport coat.*] I went with my sister to her church, and everyone looked so uncomfortable in their pretty dress suits, I just don't get it. Look at Jesus, the man roamed around in sandals talking to the poor and the marginalized. You think he would really care what type of suit you wear to church? I think we have the right idea, just come out and express yourself—focus your energy on God rather than looking like you've done well.

By defining traditional Sunday fashion as "uncomfortable" and something Jesus would not care about, Ronald asserted that Christians should instead focus on their faith. As Martina told a visitor minutes after a service ended, "Dressing in more casual, comfortable clothes is a small way of making the church feel more like a place [where] we really belong; it's kind of like that old hymn about coming to God just as you are." As all of these comments imply, members defined their fashion choices as reflecting their Christian identities, as well as their personal preferences.

Members also fashioned their bodies to explicitly convey their identities as LGBT individuals. For example, as the ethnographer approached the church one evening, Michael, wearing a faded t-shirt proclaiming "I Slept with Your Boyfriend and He Loved It," opened the door to let him in. As he stepped inside, an African American woman named Margo, wearing a "Gay = OK" t-shirt, handed him some flyers for an upcoming drag show. Dan then walked over and asked for a sheet of paper as he flipped his feather boa in the ethnographer's face, saying, "Sometimes I just got to let my own little dream girl come out and play." As the members took their seats, a woman dressed in mud-stained work boots and a beat-up flannel shirt stepped to the front to start the service. Here we see how members used gender-discrepant clothing and messages on t-shirts to announce their sexual identities within the church.

Newcomers often learned it was acceptable to wear gender-discrepant clothing or clothing announcing one's sexual identity when observing or participating in special events. As the following illustration shows, these practices also affirm LGBT Christian identities.

> Walking to the back of the room, Carla says, "So we found these wooden crosses, and we thought it would be great for everyone to have one during the Easter season." As she began handing out crosses, she pointed to John who added, "Also, don't forget that it's important to show your colors, PRIDE [an annual festival celebrating LGBT and queer pride in the local community] is not that far off. And I think it's important, especially for those visiting the church, to understand and see that we are serious about creating a safe space for LGBT people. We are having t-shirts made with the church logo, and we will be handing out more of the rainbow pins so everyone can have the chance to show their PRIDE every day."

By making church t-shirts for gay pride events and handing out rainbow pins and wooden crosses, members encouraged each other to use fashion to blend religious and sexual identities in counter-heteronormative ways.

This type of subversive blending was particularly explicit when the church put on "Gospel Drag Cabarets," which helped raise money to support various causes and church programs. The following illustration provides a typical example of such an effort:

> The crowd begins to applaud vigorously as Jenny steps to the front of the stage in her top hat announcing, "And now we have, fresh from their latest world tour, the girls of God singing their hearts out in the way that only the truly devoted can do. So without further ado, here are the girls." Jenny steps to the piano and begins playing an upbeat number. Clapping, hooting, hollering, and laughter erupt as Tommy, Allan, and Mickey step on stage wearing fancy dresses, colorful wigs, and high heels. Each one has a Bible in one hand and a microphone in the other. As the music reaches a crescendo, and Allan hikes up his skirt, the "girls" begin singing, "Our God Is an Awesome God" to the delight of the hundred plus people assembled.

By combining the performance of hymns with unconventional gender displays, members embraced symbols of LGBT and Christian culture.

As the preceding analysis shows, Shepherd members used bodily decoration to

Three members (one in drag) of Shepherd Church pose in front of a large wooden cross after a special worship service. (Photograph courtesy of Winnie Miles.)

subvert heteronormativity while integrating Christian and LGBT cultural traditions. Although every church member did not queer fashion, all members affirmed those who did. Rather than subverting Christianity, however, members used Christian narratives to view their queering of fashion as evidence of Christian morality. Whereas Gray and Thumma's (1997) study of a special Christian night at a LGBT bar showed how LGBT evangelicals created a temporary safe zone to "express their Christian faith," Shepherd Church members created a more permanent sanctuary in which they used bodily decoration to signify both LGBT and Christian identities.

Embracing Intimacy

The embodiment culture of Christian churches reflects the larger culture in that there are implicit rules about person-to-person contact. As Goffman (1971) points out, there are norms regarding people's "territories of self," which include the body. These norms can be seen in the lessons taught to children, such as "Keep your hands to yourself." But person-to-person touch can also been seen as a "tie-sign" (Goffman 1971), that is, it indicates that people are connected to each other, as when parents and children or lovers hold hands in public.

Part of how heteronormativity works is through the regulation of person-to-person contact (Schilt and Westbrook 2009). In heteronormative settings, for example, it is generally acceptable for men and women in relationships to use touch to signify romantic involvement. And while some forms of touch, such as handshaking, are acceptable, full-body contact between acquaintances of the same or different sex is generally deemed inappropriate. An assumption underlying these rules is that such body contact should be interpreted as a sexual expression.

Shepherd Church members subverted heteronormative rules about person-to-person contact by embracing intimacy, which they accomplished primarily by hugging everyone they could get their hands on. Neither gender nor romantic involvement mattered. In opposition to the heteronormative culture of traditional churches, giving full-bodied hugs was the norm. The ethnographer encountered this practice during his first visit to the church.

> Michael grabs me by the arm and gives me a big hug saying, "We hope you come back and study some more. We'd like you to see a real caring community." Turning to Marcus, he hugs the big man and plants a kiss on his cheek. Marcus tells me, "Don't be alarmed, you'll be seeing a lot of kissing and touching in this place." Smiling, I survey the room finding members embracing all over the place. A group of lesbians are gathered in the corner giggling, talking, and hugging while looking at photographs from a recent trip. Beside them, two men are dancing together and posing with hymnals as a female-to-male transgender person takes photographs, and an older lesbian laughs saying, "Come on we have to get these hymnals put up before we go grab lunch." Heading toward the back, I am embraced by nine different people expressing their desire to see me return to the church.

Similar scenes repeated each week throughout the fieldwork. Such hugging did not include sexual innuendo or appear sexual; in fact, members described it as a way to express caring and build community. As Wiley explained one afternoon, "Sometimes everyone just needs to feel comfortable in the arms of another and in the heart of a community. Sometimes we all need a hug, and people here understand that." Thus, members were not only embracing bodies but also using their bodies to create deep connections and the foundation of their community. In doing so, they subverted the heteronormative assumption that close bodily contact should be interpreted as sexual.

During services church members also engaged in bodily contact in ways that signified they were in romantic relationships. For example, many couples spent each worship service holding hands, snuggling in chairs, occasionally sharing little kisses on the cheek or forehead, or rubbing each other's shoulders or knees. Often these couples spoke of, as one member put it, the "wondrous joy" of being able to worship without having to hide their relationships. Thus, such bodywork intertwined their religious and sexual selves.

Embracing intimacy also became an integral part of formal rituals, such as communion, for which people went to the front of the church to partake of wine and bread symbolizing the blood and body of Jesus Christ. Unlike the communion ritual in traditional churches, for which individuals typically walk to and from the altar in single file in a reserved manner, the ritual at Shepherd Church often involved body-to-body contact and intense emotional expression. As the lights went down each week to signal the beginning of the ritual, members walked to the front as individuals, couples, or groups. Often, couples signified their relationship by holding hands, sharing kisses, or walking arm-in-arm to the front. As they reached the altar, they were given a wafer and wine before embracing, praying, and often crying, with the person serving them and an accompanying partner or friend performing the ritual at the same time. Members often augmented the movements of the ritual by patting each other on the back, rubbing the shoulders of those overcome with tears, or swaying back and forth with other participants. As Whitney explained one morning while setting up the altar, "Communion is probably the most important thing we do. It allows people to come together openly, like really connect, heart, body, and soul, and it's a way to express ourselves in worship as Christians, as couples, as friends to show how we feel."

Whereas previous scholarship demonstrates how female rugby players (Ezzell 2009) and male-to-female transsexuals (Schrock, Reid, and Boyd 2005) use or mold their bodies to reinforce heteronormativity, here we see how people can use bodily contact to subvert heteronormativity. In the context of the church, body-to-body contact helped integrate Christian and LGBT identities, while fostering feelings of connection and powerfully evoking feelings that members defined as spiritual. Sometimes all one needs is a hug to feel valued and part of a larger religious community.

Transgendering Demeanor

As mentioned earlier, a crucial aspect of heteronormativity inside and outside of churches is maintaining clear boundaries between women and men. While clothing accomplishes much of this work, people are also generally expected to move and position their bodies in ways that are culturally coded as appropriate for their presumed sex category (Butler 1999; Henley 1986; West and Zimmerman 1987). Men tend to embody dominance by taking up more space, gesturing in assertive ways, and avoiding the expression of emotions (except anger). Women tend to embody subordination by taking up less space, gesturing in nonthreatening ways, and openly expressing emotions (except anger). In our daily lives, we often expect people we label men to maintain a culturally defined "masculine" demeanor, and people we label women to maintain a culturally defined "feminine" demeanor (Butler 1999; West and Zimmerman 1987). These expectations are a reflection of the larger heteronormative culture of embodiment.

Shepherd Church members, however, countered heteronormativity by creating a more inclusive embodiment culture. Specifically, members who moved or postured their bodies in ways that are culturally defined as more appropriate for members of the so-called opposite sex—what we term "transgendering demeanor"—were not only tolerated but affirmed as moral Christians. Whereas *transgender* is an umbrella term created by activists to refer to both transsexuals and cross-dressers (Schrock, Reid, and Boyd 2005)—that now also includes people who identify as "genderqueer" or "bigendered" or as a "third gender"—we use it here as a verb that refers to how people move and posture their bodies in ways that breech culturally defined rules of gendered demeanor.

Several members believed that they had constructed Shepherd Church as a safe space for individuals who regularly transgendered demeanor. Tonya, for example, said,

"Just because I like punching people out in the ring and working on my Mustang . . . doesn't make me any less of a woman or a Christian. It makes me a person capable of filling a whole lot of roles when I'm given a chance. And here [at the church] I think we try to give women and men that chance." Here Tonya suggested that the church was a place where worshipers could engage in gender-nonconforming demeanor without stigmatization. She later mentioned that the church provided members an opportunity to "express" themselves rather than trying to "fit into some kind of box."

Members also said it was acceptable to embody both masculinity and femininity. As Carla explained to the ethnographer one afternoon while repairing a church water pump, "Some of us just aren't into the whole role-playing thing, like Whitney and I are both somewhat masculine and somewhat feminine, and I think most people are that way. But in many churches you have to be one way. We have people who play roles here too, but the idea is that we want a place where fitting into a woman's role is not required. And that's what we're doing here." Constructing a culture where one did not have to embody gender "one way" subverted the assumption that one should act masculine or feminine, a key feature of heteronormativity. Members defined the freedom to embody gender any way one liked as part of a divine plan. As Dante explained to a transgender visitor one morning, "Don't worry about how you look or act here, Sugar. God made us in all kinds of ways, so just be your beautiful self."

Women also transgendered demeanor by engaging in masculine practices, such as taking up more physical space than is typical of women. For example, many women sat with their legs spread rather than close together during worship, opened their arms wide when talking with others or performing scripture readings, and moved around the sanctuary when preaching or performing musical numbers. Women also embodied assertiveness by sometimes playfully punching people in the arm, forcefully grabbing people for full-bodied bear hugs, smacking others on the butt, or physically reenacting moments of athletic triumph. For example:

> Jamie tells a group of women about a recent softball game. As she speaks, she
> pumps her fists in the air while running her hand through what's left of her hair
> (she had it shaved with the rest of her teammates for the big game). Spitting
> her gum out on the grass, she punches two of the other women in the arm in
> celebration and begins pounding on her chest saying, "It's good to be the toughest
> one on the field my friends, it's so good!"

By "pounding on her chest," spitting, pumping her fists, and punching friends in the arm to celebrate victory, Jamie engaged in stereotypically "masculine" behavior. Moreover, others accepted her transgendering of demeanor without hesitation.

Men also sometimes transgendered demeanor by using their bodies in ways culturally defined as "feminine," such as, taking up less space by sitting with their hands in their laps or crossed over their waists or walking with their hands close to their bodies. Several men minimized assertiveness by vocally announcing their presence before giving hugs, tentatively extending their hands to new members, or gesturing to their bodies as they spoke. Moreover, many cried openly during worship services, offered wide grins in response to the simplest statements, or giggled when talking about clothes and shopping trips.

Men's feminine gestures were observed regularly during informal interactions before and after services. For example, one morning Timmy skipped up to a group that included the ethnographer, snapping his fingers and singing softly, before announcing, "I think I have discovered the perfect boy. I'm going to cook for us tonight and—oh my God—he will hopefully be my king!" He then flipped his hair, snapped his fingers, and danced through the side door. At this point, Leon turned to the ethnographer, and said, "Don't write that down or I'll have no chance of winning queen of this week," before beginning to giggle and following Timmy and saying in a hyperfeminized tone, "No, no, Sugar, come back, you gotta tell me about this man of yours." Another man then chuckled and said, "All they need is some ice cream and a pillow fight and those two will be in heaven, don't you think?" Rather than displaying the reservation often required of men in traditional churches, Timmy enacted physical behaviors culturally coded as "feminine" by "skipping," "snapping his fingers," "singing softly," "flipping his hair," and giggling over the "perfect boy," while expressing his desire to "cook" for his "king."

While theoretical and empirical work often suggests that people "do gender" in ways that reinforce heteronormative codes of femininity and masculinity (see, e.g., Schilt and Westbrook 2009; West and Zimmerman 1987), members of Shepherd Church resisted heteronormativity by doing and affirming gender nonconformity. In doing so, they created a more inclusive embodiment culture. In this culture, they could openly use their bodies to signify integrated gendered, sexual, and religious identities without fear.

Conclusions

As our analysis reveals, people may strategically employ their bodies to signify their religious and sexual identities in ongoing social interactions. While studies of LGBT Christians typically emphasize their use of language to integrate their sexual and religious identities (McQueeney 2009; Thumma 1991; Wolkomir 2006), our findings suggest that the use of language may be only half the story. By dressing in ways that subverted the gender binary and signified pride in being members of sexual minorities, physically connecting with one another to signify sexual and nonsexual relationships, and breaking traditional norms of gendered demeanor, Shepherd Church members employed their bodies to signify LGBT Christian identities.

While researchers have shown how sexual (Rosenfeld 2009) and gendered (Ezzell 2009; Schrock, Reid, and Boyd 2005) minorities employ their bodies to conform to heteronormative ideals, we have shown how embodiment can resist heteronormativity. By queering fashion, embracing intimacy, and transgendering demeanor, Shepherd Church members created a group culture that countered heteronormative conceptions of gender, sexuality, and religion. Members of traditional churches may think that Shepherd members' embodiment practices were profaning the "sacredness" of Christianity, but the facts suggest otherwise. As shown in our analysis, members imbued their embodiment practices with religious meaning, often citing biblical stories about Jesus' nonjudgmental acceptance of outsiders. In doing so, they in effect constructed their counter-heteronormative embodiment as sacred.

It is important to point out that ways of using the body to integrate sexual and religious identities and subvert heteronormativity may vary widely among MCC churches. Within the United States, for example, the power structure of a church (e.g., whether hierarchically or horizontally organized) and the size, history, and political strength of the surrounding LGBT community may influence how MCC members locally embody their identities. Future researchers should consider comparing congregations in distinct geographical locations (e.g., San Francisco, California, and Alexandria, Ohio) to better analyze how historical, social, and political context affects embodiment. Cross-national comparative research would also help us move beyond the limitations of our case study. More specifically, because heteronormativity itself has culturally specific forms and the legal rights and stigmatization of LGBT people can vary widely from nation to nation (see, e.g., Collins 2009; Ward and Schneider 2009), counter-heteronormative embodiment in MCC churches would also likely take on culturally unique forms and be practiced more or less overtly.

Regardless of our particular social or historical context, we all act in ways that affirm or resist heteronormativity in our daily lives. However we define our sexuality, like Shepherd Church members, we may actively affirm or engage in counter-heteronormative practices. Doing so may help create safe spaces—whether at school or work, in families or social groups—to freely use our bodies as tools for self-expression. In contrast, we may act in ways, regardless of intentions, that pressure others to conform to heteronormative standards. We may also expend much energy trying to regulate our bodies to fit ideals created long ago by powerful others. Such regulating often comes from our fear of how others might react if we do not conform, ironically reproducing a fearful existence for nonconformists. Successfully resisting heteronormativity thus requires a bit of fearlessness from us all.

REFERENCES

Bartkowski, John. 2001. *Remaking the Godly Marriage: Gender Negotiation in Evangelical Families*. New Brunswick, NJ: Rutgers University Press.

Butler, Judith. 1999. *Gender Trouble: Feminism and the Subversion of Identity*. New York: Routledge.

Collins, Dana. 2009. "'We're There and Queer': Homonormative Mobility and Lived Experience among Gay Expatriates in Manila." *Gender and Society* 23 (4): 465–93.

Ezzell, Matthew B. 2009. "'Barbie Dolls' on the Pitch: Identity Work, Defensive Othering, and Inequality in Women's Rugby." *Social Problems* 56 (1): 111–31.

Gimlin, Debra L. 2001. *Body Work: Beauty and Self Image in American Culture*. Berkeley: University of California Press.

Goffman, Erving. 1959. *The Presentation of Self in Everyday Life*. New York: Doubleday.

———. 1971. *Relations in Public: Microstudies of the Public Order*. New York: Harper and Row.

Gray, Edward R., and Scott L. Thumma. 1997. "The Gospel Hour: Liminality, Identity, and Religion in a Gay Bar." In *Contemporary American Religion: An Ethnographic Reader*, ed. Penny Edgell Becker and Nancy L. Eiesland, 79–98. Walnut Creek, CA: AltaMira.

Henley, Nancy. 1986. *Body Politics: Power, Sex, and Nonverbal Communication*. New York: Simon and Schuster.

McQueeney, Krista. 2009. "'We Are God's Children, Y'All': Race, Gender, and Sexuality in Lesbian and Gay-Affirming Congregations." *Social Problems* 56 (1): 151–73.

Moon, Dawne. 2004. *God, Sex, and Politics: Homosexuality and Everyday Theologies*. Chicago: University of Chicago Press.

Rosenfeld, Dana. 2009. "Heteronormativity and Homonormativity as Practical and Moral Resources: The Case of Lesbian and Gay Elders." *Gender and Society* 23 (5): 617–38.

Schilt, Kristen, and Laurel Westbrook. 2009. "Doing Gender, Doing Heteronormativity: 'Gender Normals,' Transgender People, and the Social Maintenance of Heterosexuality." *Gender and Society* 23 (4): 440–64.

Schrock, Douglas, Lori Reid, and Emily M. Boyd. 2005. "Transsexuals' Embodiment of Womanhood." *Gender and Society* 19 (3): 317–35.

Smith, Christian. 2008. "Future Directions in the Sociology of Religion." *Social Forces* 86 (4): 1561–89.

Stone, Gregory P. 1981. "Appearance and the Self: A Slightly Revised Version." In *Social Psychology through Symbolic Interaction*, ed. Stone and Harvey A. Faberman, 187–202. New York: Macmillan.

Sumerau, J. Edward. 2010. "Constructing an Inclusive Congregational Identity in a Metropolitan Community Church." Master's thesis, Florida State University.

Thumma, Scott. 1991. "Negotiating a Religious Identity: The Case of the Gay Evangelical." *Sociological Analysis* 52 (4): 333–47.

Turner, Charles F., Maria A. Villarroel, James R. Chromy, Elizabeth Eggleston, and Susan M. Rogers. 2005. "Same-Gender Sex among U.S. Adults: Trends across the Twentieth Century and during the 1990s." *Public Opinion Quarterly* 69 (3): 439–62.

Ward, Jane, and Beth Schneider. 2009. "The Reaches of Heteronormativity: An Introduction." *Gender and Society* 23 (4): 433–39.

Warner, Michael. 1991. "Introduction: Fear of a Queer Planet." *Social Text* 29:3–17.

West, Candace, and Don H. Zimmerman. 1987. "Doing Gender." *Gender and Society* 1 (2): 125–51.

Wolkomir, Michelle. 2006. *Be Not Deceived: The Sacred and Sexual Struggles of Gay and Ex-Gay Christian Men*. New Brunswick, NJ: Rutgers University Press.

An Accidental Education

Hanne Blank

While pursuing a Ph.D. in a perfectly respectable humanities discipline at a perfectly respectable New England university, I chose to channel my activist energies into a perfectly disreputable side project, a fat-positive feminist 'zine about fat and sex. While the 'zine, *Zaftig!*, was well received, within the narrow band of folks who came into contact with such things, I certainly didn't set out with any plans to write the first (and so far only) book on the subject of fat people and sex, *Big Big Love: A Sourcebook on Sex for People of Size and Those Who Love Them* (Emeryville, CA: Greenery Press, 2000). I did not imagine I might end up being held up as a sexuality role model or find my work on fat and sexuality referenced in dissertations, among rather a lot of other things. But then *Big Big Love* turned out to be full of surprises, and to provide a rather intense education all its own.

My 'zine was, like most, an overgrown hobby, an excuse to talk a lot about sex. Interest in the 'zine led to invitations to give fat-sex workshops. I was pleased and flattered to be asked but also a bit surprised, because I knew dozens of people who could have led the same workshops—some of them probably better than I. But I had shown myself willing, and the willingness to step into a void is the only qualification anyone ever demands.

As if to prove the point, a publisher approached me out of the blue and asked whether I had ever considered writing a book on fat and sexuality. I hadn't. I wasn't a career sexuality educator and had no reason to suspect myself of writerly ambition. Nor was I any kind of anomaly in being fat and having a romantic and sexual life. I was nothing but a well-informed amateur with an activist streak. All that separated me from any of the other sex-positive fat people I knew was the intriguing offer of a book contract. I said yes.

As I wrote I began to realize that I have a knack for pointing out things that to me are glaringly obvious but that other people seem to have a hard time spotting—that I exist, that people like me exist, that there are millions and millions of fat people in the world, and despite all rumors to the contrary, most have love and sex lives. Perhaps naïvely, I did not—and still do not—consider this a particularly brilliant insight, merely one the general public is not encouraged to make.

And so I tried, in writing *Big Big Love*, to debunk as many myths about fat, love, and sexuality as I could, all in pursuit of getting readers to see what is right in front of their noses. The ideologies our culture teaches are often very different from what people actually do. My gospel, to the extent that I had one, was simply that size does not matter, that sexuality is an inalienable part of being human and not a rare reward bestowed on a magically deserving few by some mysterious, all-powerful Nookie Czar.

Or, as I had been known to say in workshops, "We're here, we're fat, we're sexy, get used to it."

It seemed simple enough to me. Perhaps that's why I was surprised by the range and intensity of reactions to the book. I gave many interviews to people who seemed to regard the whole project as a freak show. Those who heckled the fat lady quickly learned that she has a short fuse and a sharp tongue: I cut short one shock jock who started riffing about fat people having sex on top of a buffet table by interrupting that I was there to talk about my book, not his sexual fantasies. Other interviewers asked nigh-gynecological questions about my love life, as if the chronicles of my own personal genitals were the only legitimate proof that my book was valid. But these bothered me less than the self-consciously PC press. Just as uncomfortable with the idea of fat people being sexual as the shock jocks and voyeurs, they couldn't bring themselves to say so. I grew to hate the po-faced guilty liberal lip service. Fighting fire with fire makes a great show; milquetoast just lies there soggy.

Reader reactions were better, worse, and a thousand times harder to negotiate. Many responded with enthusiastic relief, finally feeling affirmed and seen as sexual people. Others delightedly took the book as permission to pursue the sexual interests they'd always had. I was privately tickled when certain readers wrote, in private e-mails and public reviews, that I had neglected to cover particular sexual techniques or activities of which they were especially fond: what better proof could one ask for that there were other fat people out there in the world leading active, engaged sex lives?

But there were also dozens who responded desperate for healing and help. Heartbreaking stories of physical abuse, sexual violence, and relentless humiliation, all with the victim's fatness as the excuse, came streaming in from people who, having read the book, saw me as the one person who might understand the specifically fat-shaped hell they'd been through. I'd had a lot of tough, emotional conversations in workshops and during book-tour events about people's histories and their processes of finding self-acceptance. But they were nothing compared with what came in over the electronic transom. The stories floored me and humbled my perceptions of what my work was worth, even though I understood from the outset that in such situations the putative reasons aren't, they're just nails to hang cruelties on.

I bore witness, recommended crisis centers, made referrals, and generally did what I could. Because resources that addressed fat issues were so rare, I felt a responsibility—having opened the can of worms—to at least respond to every contact, but the effort was fraught, to say the least. Some readers became distraught when I had to make it plain that I couldn't fix them or be their best friend or their therapist. (Others, in another category of unforeseen reader response, got snippy when I made it clear that I wasn't about to satisfy their unrequited hankerings for a hot-to-trot fat girl.) I felt ambushed, caught short, and I had to scramble to find and establish a whole lot of boundaries I hadn't known I'd need. I hadn't set out to be the poster child of fat sex, nor its Mother Teresa, and I hadn't really anticipated that anyone would act as though I should be. I had shown myself willing to talk about it, but I had severely underestimated the pent-up demand not just for that kind of conversation but for serious damage control, nursing, and therapy. Surprise!

What I learned from this experience is that I really have only one good trick in this world. I'm good at pointing out that the emperor is naked, at yanking back the curtain behind which Oz, the Great and Terrible, is revealed as a weedy old man with no chin. It's a pretty good trick, but like all tricks, limited. As grand and bold as it is to destroy false idols and debunk old lies, it doesn't do much to erase the badness that has been done in their names. That is very different work, and, alas, not where my talents lie. All I can do is to drag buried things out into the fresh air and sunlight and hope that the ancients were right, that such rudimentary medicine will help heal festering wounds.

The Pickup

Catherine Bergart

There wasn't any place to park, so Ed drove the van around the block while I ran in to get sushi at our favorite Japanese restaurant and a movie from the video place next door. Back at his house, I started the film—*Prelude to a Kiss*—and we ate in the living room: I on the sofa, he in his power wheelchair.

"I wish we could snuggle up together while we watch," I said, pressing the pause button.

"We can if we watch in the bedroom."

"Yeah, but how would you get into the bed? Viktor won't be home for hours," I said, referring to his live-in aide.

Ed is paralyzed from the chest down, although he still has some use of his arms. He was in a bus accident while traveling in South America twelve years before we met. I'd been seeing him for seven weeks, and one of the things that had surprised me most about dating a quad was how much attention we drew when we were out together. Normally shy, I found myself enjoying it, flattered by what I imagined people thinking: "Hey, look at that attractive, independent guy in the wheelchair out on a date with a cute, hip-looking woman who obviously harbors no bourgeois fear of people who are different."

Then one Saturday afternoon Ed drove into town to meet me, and we went for a stroll along the riverfront in lower Manhattan. Skaters zipped around on Rollerblades, and couples sat on benches eating ice cream, their dogs lollygagging at their feet. Sensing people watching us, I asked Ed whether he still noticed that kind of thing.

"Yeah, sometimes," he said. "They think you're my nurse."

"What?" I turned to him with a smile, but he wasn't joking. "You mean like I'm just taking you out of the institution for a little air?"

"Exactly," he said. "You're wearing a white shirt, and besides, who else could I be with?"

With our video still on pause, Ed said, "You could try transferring me to the bed—I mean, if you want to."

"There's no way I'm strong enough to pick you up!"

"Actually, it doesn't take strength—just technique. Beth, a young woman who fills in when Viktor's away, is smaller than you—she barely weighs ninety pounds—and she doesn't have any problem transferring me."

"Really?" I said, still skeptical.

We went into the bedroom, and Ed drove his wheelchair up along the side of the bed. "The first thing we have to do is take my shoes off," he said.

Kneeling on the floor in front of him, I undid his laces and pulled off his shoes.

I took one of his sock-covered feet in my hand. "This little piggy went to market, and this—"

"Let's try to stay focused," he said, fighting a smile. "The next thing you need to do," he continued, "is pull my hips forward a bit."

I followed his instructions to pull one leg forward, then the other.

"OK—now stand facing me, and press my feet together with your feet."

"Like this?" I asked.

"Yeah, that's perfect," he said. "Now bend your knees a little, press my knees between your knees, put your arms around my lower back—I'll put mine around your neck—and, as you straighten up, lift me by the waistband of my pants, swivel toward the bed, and sit me on it."

"Uuug!" I'd gotten him onto the very edge of the bed.

"Don't let go!" he barked.

"I'm not! I'm not!"

"OK—put your right arm under my knees, reach under my right armpit with your left arm, and rotate me on my ass so my feet are at the foot of the bed."

I managed to swivel his body lengthwise on the bed.

"Great!" he said, sounding relieved. "Now you just have to pull me up higher on the bed."

"How do I do that?"

"Reach your right arm over to my far hip and lift both hips while you pull me up."

"Uuuunh!" Nothing happened.

"OK, you're going to have to stand up over me and try to pull me up like that."

I climbed on the bed so that I was straddling Ed's legs, bent forward, lifted his hips, and shoved him up higher.

"Good! Can you do it once more?"

As I shoved him again, I lost my balance. He reached his arms out to me, and I flopped belly to belly on top of him.

"So is this how Beth does it?" I asked, giggling.

"Only when I pay her extra," he said with a wink. He began tracing a path of little kisses along my cheek toward my mouth.

(Graphic courtesy of Lindsay Olson.)

The following Monday, I was replaying our weekend in my mind during a boring meeting at work, when the subject turned to my project. I snapped out of my reverie and realized I'd left my notes in my cubicle. Excusing myself, I dashed out of the room, but instead of turning the sharp corner at the end of the hall, I accidentally ran straight into the edge of the wall. I found myself on the floor, dazed, embarrassed, and bleeding from a cut under my eyebrow. A work friend grabbed ice and a wad of paper towels and took me to the emergency room.

As the ER doc stitched me up, he said, "Just take it easy for the next couple days. Keep the wound dry, and stay cool—sweating will interfere with healing."

New York temperatures were averaging ninety, and my apartment wasn't air-conditioned. I wanted to call Ed at work, but I was conflicted. We hadn't known each other *that* long, and I didn't want to seem needy or dependent. I decided to risk it.

"What happened? Are you OK?"

"I ran into a wall at work and got a gash under my eyebrow."

"You're kidding!"

"No. I know it sounds ridiculous, but the problem is the doctor told me I'm supposed to stay cool and keep the wound dry—no sweating—and I don't have an air-conditioner."

"So come stay at my house," he said immediately. "I'll pick you up at the hospital and then we can stop by your place to get you some clothes. Let's see . . . it's three o'clock now. I can get there in about forty minutes."

For the first time since I'd hit the wall, tears welled. I'd been on my own for a long time, and having a guy take care of me was awfully touching.

"Are you going to be OK until then?" he asked.

"Yeah," I said. "I'll be fine. Carol's here with me."

Eighteen years have passed since those days when Ed and I first picked each other up. And we've been laughing, loving, and looking out for each other ever since.

PART III

Defying Authoritative Knowledges and Conventional Wisdom

9

Anorexia as a Choice

Constructing a New Community of Health and Beauty through Pro-Ana Websites

Abigail Richardson and Elizabeth Cherry

> "Pro-ana" [is] short for *proactive, volitional anorexia*. It refers to actively embracing the concept of anorexia as a lifestyle choice rather than an illness. By the word "choice" we indicate the active agency of volition, the seat of government in the human mind, the power of decision-making or of will. We are not "ED [eating disorder] sufferers" (though some of us at times may use the term "ED" in a self-referential fashion for convenience) but persons who have chosen anorectic praxis (practice) as a lifestyle of our own free wills.

The preceding quotation is from Ana's Sanctuary, one of the many "pro-ana," or pro-anorexia, websites that have proliferated in recent years. These websites portray the eating disorder anorexia in a positive light, as young women construct the sites in an attempt to create community around their redefinition of anorexia as a lifestyle rather than a disease. The mere existence of such websites alarms many people, including therapists and the general public. The media, for example, reports a fear that these sites might influence individuals to become anorexic, as indicated in news broadcasts and stories from the *Washington Post* (Payne 2004) and *BBC News* (Head 2007). Indeed, researchers have found that compared with nonviewers, women who view pro-ana websites engage in more image comparisons and experience lower self-esteem, lower appearance-related self-efficacy levels (Bardone-Cone and Cass 2007), higher levels of body dissatisfaction, and more eating disturbances (Harper, Sperry, and Thompson 2008). The majority of visitors read the sites quite frequently, with nearly 70 percent visiting once a week or more (Csipke and Horne 2007). Further, the mean rate of visitors to pro-ana sites is 25 percent higher than the rate of visitors to recovery sites (Chesley et al. 2003).

As feminist researchers who examine progressive food issues, health, and well-being, we are also concerned about the existence of these websites. But in this chapter we look beyond immediate, even visceral, reactions to these websites and attempt to disentangle the alternative discourses behind the pro-ana message—what are these young women saying, and why are they saying it? Do pro-ana websites constitute resistance, even if they reinforce problematic discourses and ideals of health and beauty?

In this chapter we examine agency in the creation of pro-ana websites. We argue that the creators of pro-ana websites resist two particular cultural structures. First, they resist the dominant ideal of beauty by idealizing extreme thinness. Second, they resist the authority of doctors by positioning themselves as experts on anorexia, and by redefining it as a lifestyle rather than an illness. We also recognize, however, that by exercising their agency in such a manner—by becoming anorexic—they reify and re-create the same structures they are attempting to resist.

Pro-Ana as Embodied Resistance

The idea of resisting by becoming anorexic and promoting anorexia seems contradictory. In addition, the young women who created these websites did not define their actions as resistance; they claimed their websites merely provided support for themselves and other anorexics. Thus, the first question we ask is, Must the website creators intend and claim to engage in resistance for these websites to be considered resistance? Theorists have addressed this question in three ways. While some claim conscious intent is key, and others argue that measuring intent is impossible, we favor an informed assessment of the third response—intentions are not central to understanding an action as resistance (Hollander and Einwohner 2004) when the targets of their resistance include cultural structures that are often hidden from practical consciousness but that inform people's actions. People are not always, or even often, fully conscious of such hegemonic aspects of culture: "because the liminal space between the hegemonic and the ideological, consciousness and unconsciousness, is also an area in which new relations are forged between form and content, it is likely to be the source of the poetic imagination, the creative, the innovative" (Comaroff and Comaroff 1991, 30). For example, pro-ana website creators clearly seek to fool their doctors by sharing tips and tricks on how to do so, but they do not call their actions resistance. Thus, their resistance entails strategies innovated in this liminal space, where actors may not be fully conscious of the constraints on their behavior or the implications of their actions. Following this perspective, actions may be termed resistance, even if the actors engaging in the supposedly resistant action do not call them resistance.

The second question we ask is, What type of resistance is enacted here? The contrast between "thick" and "thin" resistance (Raby 2005), or conventional political resistance and everyday resistance (Scott 1985), lies in its visibility. Pro-ana website creators could be seen as engaging in both; therefore we turn to Schilt's (2003) differentiation of covert, overt, and "c/overt" resistance. Schilt characterizes adolescent girls' zine writing as c/overt resistance—a combination of covert and overt resistance that "allows girls to overtly express their anger, confusion, and frustration publicly to like-minded peers but still remain covert and anonymous to authority figures" (81). The clear pro-ana message delivered through the relative anonymity of the Internet makes the pro-ana website creators' actions c/overt resistance.

Previous social theorists have generally neglected the possibility of resistance and agency of anorexics. Psychology provides an unsatisfying paradigm that locates the source of anorexia solely in failures of the individual or family unit (Hepworth 1999). In contrast, feminist authors present a compelling criticism of cultural structures, including the emphasis placed on appearance and thinness in femininity (Bordo 1993; Gimlin 1994). Bordo (1993) also recognizes the potential protest in feminized disorders such as anorexia but views it as an unconscious protest. In fact, she explicitly states that anorexia is "not embraced as a conscious politics—nor, indeed, does it reflect any social or political understanding at all" (159). Her theories thus cannot account for the conscious enactment of anorexia as a lifestyle evidenced by these websites. Turner (1984), a sociologist of the body, also argues that anorexia arises from competing cultural structures but similarly leaves little room for agency in the individual. Placing the focus on cultural ideals means these scholars cannot explain why some women become anorexic while others who receive the same cultural messages do not.

We do not wish to portray pro-ana website creators as cultural dupes, nor do we wish to ignore that they are embedded in a culture that promotes certain problematic notions of health and thinness as beauty. Shilling (2003) argues for a conception of what he calls the "body project" that includes the potential for agency but only within the frame of a rational choice model that hinges on accepting the advice of medical experts. Gremillion (2003) further points out how the primacy of self-management has become incorporated into treatment programs for anorexia, reinforcing the medicalization of the body through notions of appropriate weight and health statuses. Thus we turn to Giddens's (1984) duality of structures to understand how culture provides the tools for pro-ana website creators to exert a different form of agency by creating these websites.

Giddens characterizes structures as both constraining and enabling, and structure and agency as mutually interdependent. Individuals are agentic in that they are knowledgeable about their actions and they exert a relative power over the structures that constrain them. Thus we see the pro-ana website creators as exerting agency within the confines of the culture in which they live. Giddens also sees structures as changeable but utterly dependent on the choices made by individuals (26), and therefore we also show how pro-ana website creators simultaneously re-create the structures they attempt to resist.

Methods and Data

Our data came from thirty-nine pro-ana websites surveyed in the spring of 2004. We began with Ana's Secret Space, because its compendium of images, resources, links to other sites, and longevity made it the oldest and most comprehensive pro-ana website at the time. We used the links page from Ana's Secret Space as our source for other websites to analyze. This search yielded 137 sites for examination. Because many of the pages listed had been shut down when their webspace providers learned of their content (85, or 62 percent), 52 potential sites remained. Of those, a further 13 were eliminated because of content—the sites were not specifically pro-ana or were password-protected private pages. The final sample thus included 39 pro-ana websites for content analysis. We use pseudonyms for the website titles throughout this chapter to eliminate the possibility of readers' triggering eating disorder episodes by visiting one of the sites discussed.

Our decision about what to analyze came from an inductive grounded-theory perspective (Strauss and Corbin 1998). That is, we investigated many sites before choosing what seemed to be important aspects of these pro-ana sites. We first conducted a content analysis, which helped us find recurring patterns in multiple websites. We incorporate our findings from the content analysis to show the generalizability and importance of each area, though great variability existed between sites, and the sites did not necessarily agree on everything. A surprising amount of overlap between the sites, however, indicated that Ana's Secret Space could be said to represent an ideal-typical pro-ana website. We then conducted a semiotic analysis of Ana's Secret Space in which we sought to understand how the signs on the website (e.g., the words and symbols) carried and conveyed meaning in our culture. This sort of "instrumental case study" (Stake 2000) allowed us to analyze the types of images and texts found in most pro-ana websites in more detail than a simple content analysis would permit.

U.S. culture, and especially physicians, still view anorexia as experienced primarily by white, upper-middle-class, relatively well-educated, young women (Demarest and Allen 2000), despite the potential of increased eating disorders among men and minorities.[1] These sites confirm that view. In our sample, only a few sites were created by women of color or women outside the United States; the sites created by minority women were nearly indistinguishable from those created by white women; and we found no sites created by men.

The defining theme of the sites was the use of the term *ana* rather than *anorexia*. This term personified and familiarized the disorder, as in a site titled Ana's Friend. The individuals on these sites also referred to themselves as anas, implying a sisterhood—that only another ana can understand how they feel. To distinguish between young women with anorexia and these pro-anorexia website creators, which we compare throughout the chapter, we use the emic term *ana* as well as the etic term *pro-ana website creators* to denote the latter.

Resisting the Ideal of Beauty

The hegemonic ideal of beauty in U.S. society includes specific notions of thinness—be thin, but not too thin. This ideal is evidenced by the use of thin models in advertising, published alongside a consistent stream of articles on the dangers of eating disorders (Lager and McGee 2003), and the fact that tabloids and entertainment media criticize individuals who appear too thin, such as Mary-Kate Olsen, Nicole Richie, and many more. This hegemonic beauty ideal also includes ideals of facial structure, hair color and texture, being well groomed and made-up, and displaying grace in movements (Wolf 1991).

The pro-ana website creators revealed their resistance to mainstream beauty ideals and their recreation of a new hyperthin ideal through the use of "thinspiration" pictures. Overall, 70 percent of the sites included photographs of thin models and celebrities, many of which were accompanied by height and weight statistics. Site creators called these "trigger pictures" because they activated a renewed dedication to being thin. Ana's Secret Space stated the following at the top of its "thinspiration" page: "Everybody's ideal is different. Some of us like the chiseled look, some like the frail look, some just wanna see bones. Whatever your ana taste, hopefully you will find a picture here to trigger and motivate you."

As further evidence of this re-creation of beauty ideals, some of the sites included "bone pictures," portraying images of extremely emaciated women as the ultimate ana ideal. These images are revered as the holy grail of perfection—ironically, the sort of body they often described as being "to die for." But other sites called these images "scary," evidence of anorexia out of control.

Accepting the notion that beauty equals thinness also indicated accepting the corollary, that being overweight is ugly, gross, or unacceptable. We found this response to overweight in the final category of images, "reverse triggers," which depicted severely overweight women with captions that indicated disgust, a deep-seated fear of fat, and a skewed perception that only their anorexia saved these women from that fate. The website Ana's Song labeled a page of these images with the following: "You are what you eat, and you are fat. Obese. Wretched. Disgusting. A blob of disease rotting your pathetic life away, taking too much space on a planet only fit for thin."

As these young women resisted the hegemonic beauty ideal, they also reinscribed beauty norms. They did not challenge the idea of the body as a continual project, the notion of appearance as a sign of self-worth or the denigration of fat bodies. Following Williams and Reid (2007), our study identified similar values, including the notions that "a thinner body can symbolize perfection, beauty, strength, and control," as well as the experiences of self-control and a sense of achievement (150). These findings also support Bordo's (1993) cultural analysis identifying the cultural values promised by the extreme thinness of anorexia in a society that prizes thinness. Thus, anas could be viewed as enacting a hyperconformity to the beauty ideal.

Resisting Medical Authority

The medical model positions doctors as experts with control over the disease and the patient (Weitz 2009). Further, it views anorexia as a disease, implying an individual, natural cause and requiring treatment by medical and psychological experts. In a manner suggestive of embodied health movements (EHMs) (Brown et al. 2004), though with vastly different goals, pro-ana website creators challenge this construction by arguing that anorexia is a lifestyle rather than a disease, and by repositioning themselves as the experts on anorexia through their experiences.

In an example of the ana argument that anorexia is not a disease requiring medical attention but a choice they have freely undertaken and can maintain, Ana's Secret Space states, "This is a pro-ana website. That means this is a place where anorexia is regarded as a lifestyle and a choice, not an illness or disorder. *There are no victims here.*" The creators of these sites understood psychological labels of anorexia and included medical definitions of anorexia and other eating disorders on their sites. They insisted, however, that these definitions were insufficient for understanding their experiences.

As with other EHMs, anas challenged the scientific definition of anorexia with their own bodily experiences of the disease. Indeed, some research supports the notion that eating disorders exist on a spectrum such that many people experience subclinical symptoms of eating disorders yet do not qualify for treatment under the official criteria used to classify anorexia nervosa (Korndörfer et al. 2003). The anas argued one need not meet the medical criteria to be an ana. For example, very few of the pro-ana website creators would be officially classified as anorexic according to the medical definition. Of the thirty-nine websites, fourteen gave statistics about their creators. Their BMI (body mass index), a metric of body size used by the Centers for Disease Control and many of these sites, ranged from 17.1 (e.g., five feet three inches, 103 pounds) to 36.34 (e.g., five feet seven inches, 232 pounds). According to the BMI categories, only four of these fourteen young women would have been classified as underweight. Seven were at normal weight, two would be considered overweight, and one would even be classified as obese.

The pro-ana website creators also argued for an in-group orientation in which they actively rejected the stigmatizing standards that mark them as deviant and through which they proposed coping mechanisms. Rich (2006) sees these websites as important tools for combating this stigma, because young women can "construct more positive self-representations of anorexia and anorexic identities" (284). The following quotation from Flowers2Ana demonstrates this process: "These websites do not encourage people to have this disorder and is only used as inspiration and as an out from all the grief they get during the day for being so. It is an escape for them to be with people who understand their thoughts and feelings and will help them encourage their lifestyle and maintain it." We see support for Rich's argument in this passage, because the author of Flowers2Ana defends the right of individuals to take up the lifestyle of anorexia and demands the opportunity to gather online to share their experiences away from those who would stigmatize them. In this sense, anas differ from other EHMs in that anas did not seek scientific support and understanding of their illness claims. They also did not seek to create new anorexics through these websites. Rather, they sought to experience anorexia in their own private space away from medical authorities.

Rather than a disease or a stigma, anas saw anorexia as the epitome of controlling their bodies. As mentioned earlier, Bordo's (1993) cultural analysis centered on contradictory notions of bodily control among women who had little control over other aspects of their lives. But the pro-ana websites we examined extended control to the anorexia itself, maintaining a careful balance between extreme dieting and succumbing to nutritional deficiencies. As one young woman wrote, "We want to look thin girls, not like skeletons! No really! I quite enjoy my internal organs" (Angel4Ana). Further, the website creators encouraged each other to engage in practices designed to enhance their health and counteract their poor eating practices: "You must, I repeat MUST, take a daily multivitamin. You don't want your hair to fall out, your skin to break out, or the signs of malnutrition to show any more than they have to. What's the point of being thin when you look like shit anyway?" (Bone Perfection). These postings show that anas attempted to sustain themselves at the lowest possible weights without risking negative effects, including death. In this way, they enacted a redefinition of anorexia as an extreme diet, a lifestyle, and an eating practice they could control rather than an illness whose treatment lies outside the scope of the patient. Further, their recognition of nutritional needs challenges popular ideas about anorexia as concerned only with losing weight.

In addition to arguing that anorexia is not a disease, anas challenged the authority of the doctors by offering their own information about how to be ana with the express notion of fooling the doctors. In giving these tips, the pro-ana website creators exhibited purposeful and conscious resistance (Hollander and Einwohner 2004) to the medical model. They also differentiate themselves from other EHMs—rather than working with doctors so the medical establishment better understands anorexia, they used their experiences with doctors in therapy to devise ways of fooling doctors.

"Food Pyramid" showing the pro-ana redefinition of nutrition and eating habits.

Anas accomplished this by sharing two main types of information: eating tips and detection-avoidance tricks.

Twenty-seven of the thirty-nine sites had tips about eating or, more accurately, not eating. They included lists of "safe foods," those with few or no calories, such as diet soda, lettuce, and egg whites; reviews of diets and diet aids; and ways to distract from hunger, such as brushing one's teeth or cleaning house. They also gave tips on ways to fill up in order to eat less: "Drink tons of water, the colder the better—not only does it fill you up but your body also burns extra calories to bring it up to body temperature" (Fasting Fairy). These sections combined dieting tips with self-help advice to provide an encouraging and supportive environment. This supportive environment is reinforced by anecdotes and (slightly) humorous images, such as a remodeled ana food pyramid with the major food groups replaced with things like coffee, water, diet soda, and cigarettes. Through this process, the anas' practices are normalized and legitimated within the group (Fox, Ward, and O'Rourke 2005). And through this process, also, the anas superseded the culturally designated experts, replacing medical advice with advice based on their own experiences.

Embodied health movements blur the boundaries between lay and expert knowledge by allowing activists to gain knowledge of their illnesses (Brown et al. 2004). Some EHM activists gain knowledge by working with doctors, others by using the Internet and other resources. EHM activists then use this information to collaborate with or challenge medical providers to gain access to better health care. In a similar way, Anas used their knowledge from being in therapy to try to avoid medical detection, not cure their illness. They did so by sharing tips on avoiding detection: "When weighing in, make sure you wear the heaviest clothes you can get away with, possibly hide weights under your clothes, rolls of quarters in your underwear, change and cell phone in your pocket—anything you can get away with. But be careful not to get caught. Also, drink tons of water beforehand so you're full of added water weight" (Ana's Secret Space). Twelve sites included such tips. The website creators were therapy savvy—they knew what their parents and therapists were looking for as indicators of progress or regression in recovery. Thus, these tricks were designed to fool people into thinking the anas were eating healthily. In this perspective, the doctors were fallible and therefore not the experts they claimed to be. That anas could fool their doctors implied that they were actively challenging the doctors' competence and authority to make decisions about young women's health and treatment.

Conclusions

In this chapter, we analyze pro-anorexia websites in terms of their resistance and agency. By redefining contemporary cultural ideals of beauty, and by resisting medical authority, pro-ana websites and their creators may be seen as an embodied health movement (Brown et al. 2004), as well as a diffuse cultural or lifestyle movement. In contrast to traditional social movements that focus on changing laws or social institutions, diffuse cultural movements seek to change culture (Cherry 2006). The emergence of pro-ana websites could signify the beginning of a support movement similar to the movement formed to medicalize the illness and support the sufferers of postpartum depression (Taylor 1996). In contrast, however, the pro-ana website creators and users resist the medicalization of anorexia and do not attempt to encourage others to become anorexic, seeking, instead, only to change the cultural definition of anorexia as a means to renegotiate their own anorexia.

Of central importance to pro-ana as an embodied health movement is its ability to use the Internet to spread its oppositional message. While our data comes from the "first wave" of pro-ana websites, contemporary websites have emerged in many different languages and countries around the world. The Internet is seen as enabling a "global civil society" (Huey 2005). This "virtual public sphere" (Langman 2005) enabled the emergence of, for example, the Zapatistas and the transnational anti-globalization movement, as well as networks of local food activists protesting the globalization of food production (Huey 2005). But the Internet does not only bring together global forces for such progressive causes—the Internet works equally well for more distasteful groups, allowing, for example, the international spread of the white power movement (Eyerman 2002). The Internet base of the pro-ana movement has encouraged its global spread.

Anorexia can be characterized as expressing cultural contradictions of femininity, appearance, health, individualism, and self-management (Bordo 1993; Gremillion 2003). Ironically, these same contradictions are expressed in the clinical treatment of anorexia (Gremillion 2003). We similarly view pro-anorexia websites as an effort to resist the cultural ideals of beauty and the authority of doctors and parents over the self. But the form of resistance in which these individuals engage is conditioned by wider cultural structures that privilege appearance as a sign of the self and that promote the medicalization of contemporary society. These structures converge in the body as a site for self-work as in the "body project" (Shilling 2003).

Because the duality of structures means structures are both constraining and enabling and also are subject to change through human action (Giddens 1984), anas' resistance also re-creates other constraining structures. Thus, the outcome of pro-ana resistance is thoroughly bound to these same cultural contradictions of individualism, the importance of appearance, and medicalized understandings of anorexia. Despite arguing that ana is a lifestyle rather than an illness, pro-anas are inevitably bound to the same foci as those diagnosed with anorexia: an obsession with appearance and severe food restrictions that need to be hidden from parents and doctors. For example, within the reconceptualization of the ideal of beauty, these pro-ana website creators do not challenge the idea of the body as a continuing project. Nor do they challenge the prevailing assumption of appearance as a sign of self-worth and evidence of self-control. Rather, they uncritically accept these beliefs by implicitly incorporating them into their worldview. This fact is evidenced on the websites by the frequency of "trigger pictures" and discussions of the anas' own battles with their weight, as well as the tips and tricks to avoid detection of their anorexia and to keep their bodies functioning. Thus, in the end, the pro-ana website creators' resistance re-creates the cultural structures they sought to resist in the first place.

NOTES

The authors are listed in reverse alphabetical order. Both authors contributed equally to this chapter.
1. The lifetime prevalence rate of 0.3 percent for males compares with 0.9 percent for females (Hudson et al. 2007). The rate of anorexia among minorities, including African Americans, Latinos, and Asians, hovers in the vicinity of 1 percent of the group population (Alegria et al. 2007; Nicdao, Hong, and Takeuchi 2007).

REFERENCES

Alegria, Margarita, Meghan Woo, Zhun Cao, Maria Torres, Xiao-li Meng, and Ruth Striegel-Moore. 2007. "Prevalence and Correlates of Eating Disorders in Latinos in the U.S." *International Journal of Eating Disorders* 40 (Suppl. 3): S15–S21.

Bardone-Cone, Anna M., and Kamila M. Cass. 2007. "What Does Viewing a Pro-Anorexia Website Do? An Experimental Examination of Websites Exposure and Moderating Effects." *International Journal of Eating Disorders* 40 (6): 537–48.

Bordo, Susan. 1993. "Anorexia Nervosa: Psychopathology as Crystallization of Culture." In *Unbearable Weight: Feminism, Western Culture, and the Body*, ed. Bordo, 139–164. Berkeley: University of California Press.

Brown, Phil, Stephen Zavestoski, Sabrina McCormick, Brian Mayer, Rachel Morello-Frosch, and Rebecca Gasior Altman. 2004. "Embodied Health Movements: New Approaches to Social Movements in Health." *Sociology of Health and Illness* 26 (1): 50–80.

Cherry, Elizabeth. 2006. "Veganism as a Cultural Movement: A Relational Approach." *Social Movement Studies* 5 (2): 155–70.

Chesley, Eric B., J. D. Alberts, J. D. Klein, and R. E. Kreipe. 2003. "Pro or Con? Anorexia Nervosa and the Internet." *Journal of Adolescent Health* 32 (2): 123–24.

Comaroff, Jean, and John Comaroff. 1991. *Of Revelation and Revolution*. Vol. 1 of *Christianity, Colonialism, and Consciousness in South Africa*. Chicago: University of Chicago Press.

Csipke, Emese, and Outi Horne. 2007. "Pro-Eating Disorder Websites: Users' Opinions." *European Eating Disorders Review* 15:196–206.

Demarest, Jack, and Rita Allen. 2000. "Body Image: Gender, Ethnic, and Age Differences." *Journal of Social Psychology* 140 (4): 465–72.

Eyerman, Ron. 2002. "Music in Movement: Cultural Politics and Old and New Social Movements." *Qualitative Sociology* 25 (3): 443–58.

Fox, Nick, Katie Ward, and Alan O'Rourke. 2005. "Pro-Anorexia, Weight-Loss Drugs, and the Internet: An 'Anti-Recovery' Explanatory Model of Anorexia." *Sociology of Health and Illness* 27 (7): 944–71.

Giddens, Anthony. 1984. *The Constitution of Society: Outline of the Theory of Structuration.* Berkeley: University of California Press.

Gimlin, Debra. 1994. "The Anorexic as Overconformist: Toward a Reinterpretation of Eating Disorders." In *Ideals of Feminine Beauty: Philosophical, Social, and Cultural Dimensions,* ed. Karen Callaghan, 99–111. Westport, CT: Greenwood Press.

Gremillion, Helen. 2003. *Feeding Anorexia: Gender and Power at a Treatment Center.* Durham, NC: Duke University Press.

Harper, Kelley, Steffanie Sperry, and J. Kevin Thompson. 2008. "Viewership of Pro-Eating Disorder Websites: Association with Body Image and Eating Disturbances." *International Journal of Eating Disorders* 41 (1): 92–95.

Head, Jacqueline. 2007. "Seeking 'Thinspiration.'" *BBC News Service,* August 8. *news.bbc.co.uk/2/hi/6935768.stm.*

Hepworth, Julie. 1999. *The Social Construction of Anorexia Nervosa.* London: Sage.

Hollander, Jocelyn A., and Rachel L. Einwohner. 2004. "Conceptualizing Resistance." *Sociological Forum* 19 (4): 533–54.

Hudson, James I., Eva Hiripi, Harrison G. Pope, and Ronald C. Kessler. 2007. "The Prevalence and Correlates of Eating Disorders in the National Comorbidity Survey Replication." *Biological Psychiatry* 61 (3): 348–58.

Huey, Tina Andersen. 2005. "Thinking Globally, Eating Locally: Website Linking and the Performance of Solidarity in Global and Local Food Movements." *Social Movement Studies* 4 (2): 123–37.

Korndörfer, Sergio R., Alexander R. Lucas, Vera J. Suman, Cynthia S. Crowson, Lois E. Krahn, and L. Joseph Melton III. 2003. "Long-Term Survival of Patients with Anorexia Nervosa: A Population Based Study in Rochester, Minn." *Mayo Clinic Proceedings* 78: 278–84.

Lager, E. Grace, and Brian R. McGee. 2003. "Hiding the Anorectic: A Rhetorical Analysis of Popular Discourse concerning Anorexia." *Women's Studies in Communication* 26 (2): 266–95.

Langman, Lauren 2005. "From Virtual Public Spheres to Global Justice: A Critical Theory of Interworked Social Movements." *Sociological Theory* 23 (1): 42–74.

Nicdao, Ethel G., Seunghye Hong, and David Takeuchi. 2007. "Prevalence and Correlates of Eating Disorders among Asian Americans: Results from the National Latino and Asian American Study." *International Journal of Eating Disorders* 40 (Suppl. 3): S22–S26.

Payne, January W. 2004. "No, That's Sick: Pro-Anorexia Web Site Authors Claim the Condition Is a 'Lifestyle Choice.'" *Washington Post,* September 14.

Raby, Rebecca. 2005. "What Is Resistance?" *Journal of Youth Studies* 8 (2): 151–71.

Rich, Emma. 2006. "Anorexic Dis(connection): Managing Anorexia as an Illness and an Identity." *Sociology of Health and Illness* 28 (3): 284–305.

Schilt, Kristen. 2003. "'I'll Resist with Every Inch and Every Breath': Girls and Zine Making as a Form of Resistance." *Youth and Society* 35 (1): 71–97.

Scott, James C. 1985. *Weapons of the Weak: Everyday Forms of Peasant Resistance.* New Haven, CT: Yale University Press.

Shilling, Chris. 2003. *The Body and Social Theory.* 2nd ed. London: Sage.

Stake, Robert E. 2000. "Case Studies." In *The Handbook of Qualitative Research*, 2nd ed., ed. Norman K. Denzin and Yvonna S. Lincoln, 435–53. Thousand Oaks, CA: Sage.

Strauss, Anselm, and Juliet Corbin. 1998. *Basics of Qualitative Research: Techniques and for Developing Grounded Theory*. London: Sage.

Taylor, Verta. 1996. *Rock-a-by Baby: Feminism, Self-Help, and Postpartum Depression*. New York: Routledge.

Turner, Bryan S. 1984. *The Body and Society: Explorations in Social Theory*. Oxford: Basil Blackwell.

Weitz, Rose. 2009. *The Sociology of Health, Illness, and Health Care: A Critical Approach*. Boston: Wadsworth Cengage.

Williams, Sarah, and Marie Reid. 2007. "A Grounded Theory Approach to the Phenomenon of Pro-Anorexia." *Addiction Research and Theory* 15 (2): 141–52.

Wolf, Naomi. 1991. *The Beauty Myth: How Images of Beauty Are Used against Women*. New York: William Morrow.

10

Public Mothers
and Private Practices

Breastfeeding as Transgression

Jennifer A. Reich

Emily Gillette, a twenty-seven-year-old mother, was flying from Vermont to New York with her family. As the plane sat at the gate, Gillette sat in the window seat in the second-to-last row, discreetly breastfeeding her twenty-two-month-old daughter; her husband was seated next to her. According to Gillette, a flight attendant tried to hand her a blanket and told her to cover up, even though none of her breast was showing. Gillette declined, explaining she was within her legal rights. Moments later, a ticket agent approached and said the flight attendant had asked that the family be removed from the flight. Gillette said she didn't want to make a scene and complied (Associated Press 2006).

Gillette's story is not uncommon: elsewhere, a mall security guard told a woman she was being "indecent" while nursing in the food court; a woman was denied entrance to a public zoo because she intended to breastfeed and the attendant feared that "children might see"; another woman was asked to stop breastfeeding at a public pool because the staff claimed breastfeeding violated public health codes and constituted indecent exposure and nudity and, later, told her that they were afraid her breast milk "might infect the pool water" (Solomon 2002). "Exposed breasts. They are all over the media: in movies, magazines, even television," Solomon points out, summarizing the American cultural contradictions about breasts. "But put a nursing infant anywhere near those breasts and suddenly some people are offended."

In 1997 the American Academy of Pediatrics officially recommended that babies be exclusively breastfed (providing no other food or water) for the first six months of life. According to the Centers for Disease Control and Prevention, "Both babies and mothers gain many benefits from breastfeeding. Breast milk is easy to digest and contains antibodies that can protect infants from bacterial and viral infections. Research indicates that women who breastfeed may have lower rates of certain breast and ovarian cancers."[1] Similarly, the U.S. Surgeon General recommends employer support for nursing mothers (Galson 2008), and the U.S. Department of Health and Human Services lists the many benefits of breastfeeding for society as a whole, as well as for babies and mothers. Among the collective benefits, breastfeeding saves on health care costs, contributes to a more productive workforce, and is "better for our environment because there is less trash and plastic waste compared to that produced by formula cans and bottle supplies."[2] Although experts tout breastfeeding as ideal, breast milk is expected to be delivered in normative ways—from a birth mother to her biological child, discreetly, and for an expert-defined amount of time. While there is broad consensus that babies should be breastfed for up to a year, mothers who continue beyond that time face disapproval. And while women are expected to breastfeed young children, it is assumed they will do so without exposing their breasts in public. As Avishai (2007, 138–39) argues, "The lactating body simultaneously involves the feminine body, the maternal body, and the achievement of a standard of good mothering that happens to be measured in ounces produced per day." Breastfeeding defines the body, through personal interactions and the social meanings that are inscribed onto it. As the preceding examples indicate, it also can potentially mark suspect mothering. In short, breastfeeding represents the best of maternal care, as long as it is delivered according to narrowly defined norms.

This chapter analyzes interviews with twenty women who define themselves as participating in non-normative mothering practices, including extended breastfeeding, that is, breastfeeding past a baby's first birthday, and public breastfeeding. (Although some public breastfeeding occurs in spaces specially marked for maternal use, such as a mothers' lounge or a nursing room, public breastfeeding here means nursing babies and children in spaces not usually designated as appropriate for nursing.) Mothers described negative responses to non-normative breastfeeding from family members (particularly extended family members and in-laws), health providers, and the public.

Despite their awareness of others' condemnation, these mothers remain committed to nursing their children on their own terms. In the following sections, I show the criticism mothers face and some of the discursive strategies mothers use to manage those criticisms and justify their practices. In doing so, I suggest that mothers are not just defending themselves but also resisting pressures of normalization. Normalization, as defined by Foucault (1995), is an exercise of power through informal means, including condemnation, to hew behaviors to social norms. Foucault explains, "It is a normalizing gaze, a surveillance that makes it possible to qualify, to classify and to punish. It establishes over individuals a visibility through which one differentiates them and judges them" (184). Mothers who engage in extended and public breastfeeding perceive the gaze as one of disapproval and judgment, and an attempt to coerce them into conformity. By examining these mothers' stories and explanations, the subtle norms against which they are judged—the culturally appropriate meanings of femininity, motherhood, and embodiment—become visible, as does their commitment to maintaining practices they see as best for them and their children.

Methods and Description of Participants

The twenty mothers, all of whom are white and reside in Colorado, are between twenty-five and sixty years old. Six mothers have one child, six have two children, five have three children, two have four children, and one has eight children. Seven have bachelor-level degrees, seven have graduate degrees, and the remaining six have some or no college, but all are, at a minimum, high-school educated. Six women stay home full time, ten work in professions with great flexibility (e.g., artist, doula, freelance writer) or work part-time, and four work full-time at jobs with routine hours. These characteristics notably mark my participants as a fairly elite group of mothers who are best able to exercise individual choice, constrained by neither state supervision nor limited resources. The mothers report religious identifications ranging from conservative Christian to a self-identified pagan.

Participants were recruited to a larger study of parents' decision making in their children's health care, particularly in terms of vaccine decisions, using convenience sampling, through referral from others familiar with the research study, and from requests circulated on listserves and community boards. Interviews lasted between one and four hours and were recorded and transcribed verbatim. Transcripts were initially coded and analyzed thematically (Braun and Clarke 2006). I then built on those themes to reach what Charmaz (2002) has called constructivist grounded theory method where data are collected and analyzed "to learn participants' implicit meanings of their experiences to build a conceptual analysis of them" (678).

Breastfeeding as Embodied Resistance

Mothers in this study stated a clear intent, before their babies were born, to breastfeed, which they saw as consistent with the expectations of motherhood. Yet, they also knew continuing breastfeeding past their babies' first birthdays or in public were non-normative practices. The following sections explore some of the ways women articulated their choices, even in the face of the normalizing gaze. By looking at their responses and commitment to challenging others, we see how they deliberately use their bodies to resist social pressures and reiterate their commitment to their children, to show themselves as independent, freethinkers, to educate or empower others, or to more subtly resist pressures by avoiding confrontations. Each of these strategies also reveals broader meanings of embodiment and gender.

Breastfeeding as Commitment to the Mother-Child Relationship

Many women articulated their commitment to extended breastfeeding and nursing on demand, that is, when and where their children wanted, as an important part of the mother-child relationship. In describing their reaction to others' disapproval, they restated the importance of nursing to their mothering practice and their determination to decide what is best for their children. Solange explains her commitment to breastfeeding each of her three children for between three and five years:[3]

> Well, my kids adore it. I—I mean, it's traumatic when we stop . . . and I don't mind it. I do like it. I find it really easy to parent that way. No tantrums, when they're tired they fall asleep instantly. . . . I mean I'm a little more than "don't mind it," but I'm not doing it only for me, you know what I mean? I've been criticized—I mean there's some person who says that anyone who does it for over a year is doing it for their own selfish reasons rather than the children's needs. So I disagree with that and I'm not doing it because I think it's a blast. But it's a really nice thing.

Here Solange articulates the importance to her children and the way nursing comforts them. She also challenges a particular criticism. As she recalls, a mother at her children's preschool claimed that extended breastfeeding is "purely in the mother's selfish intentions if it's past a year because it does absolutely no good." She rebuts this criticism by explaining the benefits and pleasure her children gain from the experience. She reiterates that it is not for her own enjoyment; it is motivated primarily by her commitment to her daughters' comfort. As she came to feel confident in her own choice to continue breastfeeding, she remembers that she actively chose not to challenge the mother who criticized her.

> I remember deciding not to tell her why—all the great reasons that I breastfeed because she had had her three and she had weaned them all. Her oldest was—her youngest was eighteen months old and she had weaned at a year or before and I thought, "I don't want to break her heart if I'm persuasive enough." . . . Or that she feels, "Oh my god. I missed something and I—and it's too late to go back." . . . But I also wasn't confident enough at the time to really let her know, you know, why I felt she was wrong. Not to mention none of her business.

Although she recalls that she lacked confidence at the time, Solange came to view the benefits of extended nursing as so self-evident that expressing them might fill the critical mother with regret for having not engaged in it herself. In doing so, she positions herself as a keeper of insider knowledge and asserts the superiority of her nursing experience. She thus can feel validated in rejecting critics who would expect her to change her behavior, because she views them as ignorant or even deserving pity.

Gabriela, a mother of a two-year-old son, recognizes the controversy over extended and public nursing but views it as important and worthy of protecting. In describing her insistence on nursing, she cites the very naturalness of breastfeeding.

> It's not necessarily something that should be seen, but it should not be hidden. It shouldn't take place in a bathroom. It—I think it's a fine, beautiful thing and we're the only creature who feeds another creature's milk to our young. We're the only ones that, you know, don't do pretty extended nursing, or nursing until an appropriate time to switch over. . . . I won't do it purposefully out in the open as a statement. That's not where I'm coming from at all. But I won't hide it—if he wants to nurse, I'll nurse.

Gabriela's explanation challenges several aspects of the criticism of nursing mothers. First, she addresses cultural notions that breastfeeding should be private. She makes a point of explaining that she does not aim to nurse in public to force others to acknowledge it but also that she is unwilling to hide it either. She uses both the naturalness of breastfeeding and how she sees her son's needs as paramount to justify her own practices.

Describing breastfeeding as natural was common for women and was often invoked as justification. For example, Anna initially struggled with nursing but stuck with it and nursed her son until he was more than two years old. In recalling her challenges and commitment to continue, Anna too cites the naturalness of nursing but sees other women's failures to nurse as emerging from larger changes in family life.

> It's one of those secrets of—it's an unfortunate secret too because I feel like the way modern society is with the design of the nuclear family, we're missing out on, kind of our birthright. I mean I think that you know in thousands and thousands of years, humans have evolved to be social creatures and grow up in tribes or clans where you see women breastfeeding, you know what I mean? . . . we have to go to a class for that? Huh?

By asserting both the naturalness and historical tradition of breastfeeding, women claim a higher moral ground as they choose to breastfeed on their own terms. They romanticize women's bodies and their capability to nurse and link good mothering to history and biology (Bobel 2001). These claims also allow them to cast non-nursing mothers as missing out on a core mothering experience. In this way, they assert their commitment to mothering and to their children as a natural form that manifests in their use of their bodies' full potential (Bobel 2002).

Mothers also thought of breastfeeding as a time-limited experience that provides sustenance and affection. Katie, who nursed her son for over a year and was still nursing her two-year-old daughter at the time of our interview, knows that her mother-in-law disapproves of her extended breastfeeding and acknowledges that her mother-in-law's disapproval led her husband to challenge her as well. Katie notes, "She's very freaked out that I breastfed [my son], and I actually—like I'm still breastfeeding [my daughter] and it's like a big [deal]. My husband's kind of like, 'Why aren't you weaning her yet?' And I'm like, 'Well, 'cause she's my last one probably, you know.'" In contrast to Solange, who described her choice to continue nursing as a commitment to her children, Katie suggests that breastfeeding is also a mother-centered experience. While others view extended nursing as long, many mothers like Katie view it as a short chapter in the longer story of parenting and are loath to stop. By prioritizing her efforts to prolong a short period in a child's life, she rebuts the criticism from others and focuses on the significance of the experience to her.

Not all mothers were able to so fully buck others' disapproval. Many continued nursing, even as the criticism inspired ambivalence in them. Melissa, who was still nursing her toddler son when she was interviewed, focused her comments on how people's initial support of breastfeeding changes. She recalls interactions where others ask, "You're still breastfeeding that kid?" to which she replies matter-of-factly, "Yes. I am." She is aware of social pressures "definitely once the year marker [passed]" and acknowledges she is thinking about weaning her son because of it. She also lives in an apartment complex where there are few other mothers and, unlike Anna and Gabriela, she has little community support. For all these reasons, she feels ambivalent.

> I—and we've—we've been trying, like thinking about it and trying small things, but I think—I think I'm having a harder time with it because I'm gone all day and when I come home, if there's something that he—like if there's a way that I can nurture him and make him feel secure and supported, I want to do that for him. And it's hard for me to be like, "OK now I'm just gonna just go, you know,

Amy tandem nursing her newborn and two-and-a-half-year-old daughter.
(Photograph courtesy of Amy Swagman.)

separate ourselves so you can get over needing to, you know, nurse." And I think
that's what it's gonna take. . . . He loves to nurse.

Melissa's story of feeling intense ambivalence illustrates the way social critics force
women to question themselves, even as they struggle to find ways to balance their
desires to support their children with their perceptions of social disapproval.

Breastfeeding as Self-Determined Mothering

Some mothers articulated their decision to continue breastfeeding and to do so publicly as a manifestation of their independence and self-determination. Violating social
norms of breastfeeding was not simply about breastfeeding; it manifested their larger
self-image as independent freethinkers. For example, Marlene chose to breastfeed her
three children each for between three-and-a-half and four years. She was still nursing
her firstborn when her second child was born and for almost a year, she nursed them
both, a practice known as tandem feeding. Although she was committed to continuing nursing, she received little support from her family, explaining, "My in-laws . . .
frowned at a lot of things I did and they were doubtful about a lot of things I did.
You see this independent streak about not following the mainstream? I think it just
continued with a lot of things I did with the kids."

Tammy, a mother of a one-year-old girl, started a mothers' group in her community, with acceptance of nursing as an explicit component of the group. She describes

her experience with past mothers' groups as driving her desire to start her own. "A lot of moms' groups are just for moms and are not kid-friendly. And my daughter is attached to my hip. And I got tired of going to playgroups and have everybody whipping out bottles and then they look at me funny because I'm nursing." Rather than feel self-conscious or modify her own mothering practice, Tammy began her own group. Her online post for it insists that other mothers accept members' choices. "We have on our front page it says. 'Extended breastfeeding is common in our group,' so if people aren't comfortable around that, then they don't join." In describing conversations with some new members, Tammy cautions, "You're gonna see someone nursing an almost three-year-old at our group; don't freak out. You probably won't even be able to tell what they're doing. It'll look like they're giving their baby a hug. But know that it happens."

Both Tammy and Marlene felt confident in taking a proactive stance to assert their choices about nursing, even as they saw it challenged. In doing so, they take pride in their choices, while solidifying their self-image as impervious to disapproval or criticism. Thus, their resistance to social pressure defines them as individuals, as rebellious, independent, and committed to mothering in ways they see as natural and uniquely crafted.

Breastfeeding as Social Activism and Public Education

Rather than feeling pressure to change their practices, many mothers described their ability to push others around them generally and their family members specifically past their comfort levels. In doing so, they envisioned themselves as activists who improve the cultural landscape for others (Naples 1998). Tammy explains that her mother-in-law tried to convince her that extended nursing is inappropriate and to caution her that others would be critical. Tammy also remembers her response.

> I told this to my mother-in-law, which was funny. I go, "Well, the World Health Organization recommends breastfeeding for at least two years." And they go, "Yeah, in developing countries." I—and all I said was, "You know, I never used to think, but now I can't imagine not nursing her." So I'll be their first exposure to nursing that long. Well, I was their first exposure to Unitarian Universalists, I was my mother-in-law's first exposure to birth center and midwives and now home births.

In this story, Tammy describes her awareness of her mother-in-law's disapproval and her choice to push back. Her mother-in-law defines extended nursing as a practice of last resort, reserved for those without other options and with fewer resources. With almost 40 percent of infants in the developing world breastfed (UNICEF 2009), she quickly identifies breastfeeding as a practice among those in less economically developed countries. Rather than engage her rationalized beliefs on the inferiority of breastfeeding mothers, Tammy locates this strategy on a spectrum of other challenges she has made, including alternative birthing choices and liberal religious views. In doing so, she describes herself in terms akin to those of an activist who will challenge others to grow and accept difference.

Tammy also sees herself as a resource to other mothers—willing to advocate for them or validate their non-normative mothering choices. She explains, "A lot of my friends have had a hard time. You know, one of my friends, her doctor said at nine months she should be stopping breastfeeding. Her pediatrician told her this. I'm like, 'You need to find another doctor. That's not American Academy of Pediatrics. I mean that's crazy, you know. Find yourself another doctor.'"

In a similar way, Solange challenged her physician's views of extended breastfeeding. Solange recalls that her first baby's pediatrician was critical of her desire to nurse on demand and past age one. She remembers her discomfort but also her lack of confidence to challenge him. At the time she felt reverence for him as an expert, which made her doubt herself. Yet by the time she had her third child, she felt more secure in her ability to advocate for herself and her children. When Solange felt that her second pediatrician disapproved of her extended breastfeeding, she decided to act. She recalls:

> I had four friends who breastfed their kids at least as long as I did. . . . Two of us had the same pediatrician who on the two-year checkup was aghast that they were still nursing their child. And then that pediatrician said, "Oh my God. Does she eat any regular food?" So my first thought was to jump ship and get a different pediatrician. My second thought was, well, let's go and educate her. So I made an appointment as quick as I could and dropped little informative bits about—pieces here and there—about breastfeeding a two-year-old and everything. . . . I felt really good about it. And she didn't—she wasn't fazed at all, I think, because she'd heard one other person. Then when I came in it was like—it became common knowledge to her.

In aiming to educate her physician, Solange articulates a view of her as misinformed and herself as an expert who can indirectly help other nursing mothers. We do not actually know how the doctor reacted (only Solange's memory of feeling efficacious), but her story communicates her sense of transformation into someone empowered to challenge authority.

As mothers articulated their commitment to their children, which they saw as sometimes necessitating the violation of social norms, they often described that choice as an obligation to protecting other women who might face similar scorn. In doing so, they came to view their individual choices as having larger symbolic meaning. For some, like Solange, seeing this larger symbolic meaning helped to resolve ambivalence they might have felt and lent them new confidence. For example, Melissa recalled her experience of choosing to breastfeed in their small town:

> In society, there's more of the education that needs to happen and we lived in a small town, small-town Texas, so I think I had to get comfortable with it, especially the public part, and—and I think definitely there are people who are very uncomfortable being around it and I could tell that and it made me more uncomfortable, but I think people for the most part—like my family is very supportive and I think I'm a strong person and I'm really pretty assertive when people are like, "Why are you doing that?" or whatever. And people who have their, "Oh, it's so hard. It's such an inconvenience." I'm like, "Really? How is this

inconvenient? I'd rather get up and nurse him than have to like get a bottle ready when I'm half asleep and burn his mouth!" . . . I became a pretty big advocate.

By viewing themselves as able to challenge those who disapprove of them and educate them, these mothers see themselves as creating social change from which they may not directly benefit but that will help untold numbers of future mothers. This is not to suggest that asserting themselves was always comfortable. But as they identify the need to educate others or support other women, their choice to resist social pressure takes on greater meaning and allows them to redefine themselves.

Resistance as Management Strategy

Some mothers managed criticism by avoiding opportunities for confrontation. In this way, they remained committed to their mothering choices while moving around their critics. For example, Margaret, whose children are now adults, remembers her efforts to avoid challenges to her nursing in public, explaining, "You know, I was very discreet when I'd be out in public." She remembers getting reactions "every so often," though one incident stands out.

> One time, I was with a friend and we were at Neiman Marcus or another store like that, I forget, and I just sat in one of those comfortable chairs in the dressing room. And this lady came up to me and said, "You know, ma'am, you're gonna have to do that elsewhere." And I said, "Well, I'm not sure—you don't even know what I'm doing here," you know? And she said, "You'll have to take that outside." . . . I didn't want to make a scene—my daughter was about eight months, maybe, but I thought, "You don't know anything."

Margaret remembers this incident as frustrating but did choose to leave without making a scene. Because she was facing these dilemmas more than a decade before some of the other mothers in this study, she also had less social and legal support for nursing. In referencing how young her baby was, we see how her choice to leave was situated in her desire to be seen and to see herself as a good mother who made the best decision for her child. In describing this incident, she frames the store clerk as ignorant and intolerant and in doing so, reiterates the superiority of her mothering practice in contrast to the inferiority of the employee.

Mothers sometimes chose to strategically avoid situations in which their breastfeeding choices would be questioned. Most frequently, this decision, like Solange's, was cited in descriptions of interactions with physicians, whom the women saw as disapproving of their feeding strategies. This disapproval often came up not necessarily around breastfeeding specifically but around questions of co-sleeping, that is, sleeping in an adult bed with a baby. Breastfeeding mothers often choose to co-sleep, in part, because it makes nighttime feedings convenient. It also reflects a philosophy that children and parents are closely intertwined and will be happier by staying near each other. Touting the importance of co-sleeping, the anthropologist and natural parenting advocate James McKenna (1996, 14) explains, "Throughout human history, breastfeeding mothers sleeping alongside their infants constituted a marvelously adaptive system in which both the mothers' and infants' sleep physiology and health were connected in beneficial ways. By sleeping next to its mother, the infant receives protection, warmth, emotional reassurance, and breast milk—in just the forms and quantities that nature intended."

In contrast to this view is the official position of the American Academy of Pediatrics, which in 2005 posited that co-sleeping puts babies at greater risk for sudden infant death syndrome (SIDS).[4] Despite this position, many mothers believe co-sleeping is a key part of their ability to successfully nurse. As Heather, who nursed her two sons, explains, "Well, when they were breastfeeding at night, we always slept with them; otherwise I never got any sleep."

Because of the position of the American Academy of Pediatrics and other professional organizations, mothers like Heather are circumspect about what they disclose to their physicians. For example, despite how helpful Heather found co-sleeping in meeting both her sons' needs for nursing and her own for sleep, she shied away from discussing it with her children's doctor: "I kind of avoid that whole conversation with my doctor about co-sleeping. . . . I figure, this is my personal decision and nothing he's gonna say is gonna change my mind about that." She felt similarly about extended breastfeeding: "After a certain age, I stopped talking about it, because I just felt like there was really nothing . . . like, again, nothing they were gonna say was gonna change my mind. Like if they said, 'Well, it's probably time to stop,' it's not like I would say, 'OK.'"

Heather presumes her physician would disapprove and avoids opportunities in which he could express his opinion. She is confident in her choice and is unwilling to discuss the presumed risks. While Solange committed to persuading her doctor to accept extended nursing, Heather kept her objections to herself. In putting this choice into context, Heather explains the irrelevance of the information to her doctor's ability to care for her child. "I mean, it's not a medical question, really . . . unless they asked, 'Is he drinking milk?' and I'll say, 'No, he's breastfeeding.'" Thus, Heather accepts her pediatrician's views on issues she accepts are medical but refuses to engage those that she sees as, at core, mothering decisions.

Some mothers chose not to discuss their non-normative mothering practices in part because of their fear such discussions could lead to state intervention. As social workers attempt to evaluate children's safety and well-being, all aspects of children's lives are examined (Reich 2005). Marlene recalls an incident in which a friend was reported to social services because of her young son's injury but saw her other parenting choices—including extended breastfeeding—become subject to investigation. Although breastfeeding alone is not usually enough to generate a report to child welfare agencies, it becomes part of the subjective judgment of mothers (Reich 2010). Recent examples of children being taken from their homes on suspicion of child pornography after photo processors reported breastfeeding pictures to social services underscores the reasonableness of this fear (Korosec 2003). By managing information and avoiding confrontations with those who might bring them to the attention of the state, mothers attempt to limit the consequences of efforts to normalize them. While responses from strangers may be uncomfortable, intervention from child protective services holds the risk of losing custody of one's children.

Though often a threat, state power can also provide protection. In fact, many mothers were aware of legal protections for nursing mothers, as we saw when Emily Gillette insisted on her legal right to nurse on her flight from Vermont to New York (two states with laws protecting nursing mothers). Some mothers in this study touted the importance of these laws. As Tammy explains:

> I would be wary to be living in Idaho and nursing in public when they have no laws protecting the rights of women there for that at all . . . Colorado does. You have the right to nurse anywhere. . . . And that's in the current issue of *Mothering*, the lady who was kicked off Freedom Airlines is on the cover . . . they wrote an article—the case about the one lady who was who was arrested or had their children taken away for six months because of lewd, solicitous—lewd behavior with a minor because somebody at Eckerd or something, or Wal-Mart, somebody developed a picture of her nursing her baby. . . . Are you gonna arrest the lady when I can see her nipples through her bathing suit? 'Cuz I see a lot more of that.

Tammy points to other instances where breasts are revealed in a non-nursing context but do not receive social condemnation. In doing so, she points out the cultural ambivalence breastfeeding inspires and the hypocrisies of corporations who punish nursing mothers and state governments who fail to protect them. By referencing legal protection, she aims to challenge the negative view of breastfeeding and support change so that women can more freely exercise their own preferences for themselves and their children.

Conclusion: Embodied Resistance and Commitment to Transgress

Breastfeeding practices have become symbolic representations of the best and worst of mothering. While public health agencies and expert organizations promote breastfeeding, they do so with a limited view of how, when, and where breastfeeding should occur. Interpreting these views and societal norms of nudity, maternal bodies, and constructed categories between babies and children, those in mothers' closest communities express disapproval and attempt to control maternal bodies and practices through condemnation or confrontation.

It is important to reiterate that the group interviewed for this study comprises mothers who are fairly elite in their education and employment conditions. They also have more resources and experience less surveillance from government agencies than do poor women. And yet, even with a high degree of structural power, they nonetheless felt vulnerable to state intervention. As such, we can identify the normalizing gaze and how women experience and resist it. And as they experience it from their privileged positions, we can imagine how mothers without resources might feel.

These mothers' experiences of disapproval and challenges to their mothering practice are informative. Despite the public scrutiny, perceived risk to their families, and judgment from friends, family members, and health care providers, mothers articulated a commitment to continuing to breastfeed on their terms, and in support of what they see as best for their children. As Marlene reflects, "It always comes back to I'm willing—my husband and I are willing to take responsibility for the choices we've made because we believe in what we've learned about the bigger picture." As these mothers describe their choice to nurse their children for as long as they and their children choose, they identify both the cultural norms they violate and their commitment to resisting those pressures. Their stories should also encourage us to ask questions about the mothering practices other mothers might want to choose but do not feel able to because of disapproval, condemnation, and the risk of negative public response.

NOTES

1. "Breastfeeding," Centers for Disease Control and Prevention, *www.cdc.gov/breastfeeding/*, last modified October 18, 2010.
2. "Why Breastfeeding Is Important," in *Your Guide to Breastfeeding*, U.S. Department of Health and Human Services Office of Women's Health, available at *www.womenshealth .gov/pub/BF.General.pdf*, last modified June 2010.
3. All names in this chapter are pseudonyms.
4. The research on co-sleeping is controversial. While co-sleeping is widespread in non-Western countries, it appears evident that softer bedding, quilts, waterbeds, and elevated hard bed frames in the United States are more dangerous for babies. Additionally, parent alcohol or drug use and obesity appear to be associated with increased risk. Absent these risk factors, it is not clear that co-sleeping is potentially risky to babies.

REFERENCES

Associated Press. 2006. "Woman Kicked Off Plane for Breast-Feeding: Files Complaint Saying She Was Being Discreet, Airline Disagrees." *MSNBC*, November 16. *www.msnbc.msn.com/id/15720339/*.

Avishai, Orit. 2007. "Managing the Lactating Body: The Breast-Feeding Project and Privileged Motherhood." *Qualitative Sociology* 30 (2): 135–52.

Bobel, Christina G. 2001. "Bounded Liberation: A Focused Study of La Leche League International." *Gender and Society* 15 (1):130–51.

———. 2002. *The Paradox of Natural Mothering*. Philadelphia: Temple University Press.

Braun, Virginia, and Victoria Clarke. 2006. "Using Thematic Analysis in Psychology." *Qualitative Research in Psychology* 3 (2): 77–101.

Charmaz, Kathy. 2002. "Qualitative Interviewing and Grounded Theory Analysis." In *Handbook of Interview Research: Context and Method*, ed. Jaber F. Gubrium and James. A. Holstein, 675–94. Thousand Oaks, CA: Sage.

Foucault, Michel. 1995. *Discipline and Punish: The Birth of the Prison*. Trans. Alan Sheridan. New York: Vintage Books.

Galson, Steven K. 2008. "Practice Applications from the Surgeon General: Mothers and Children Benefit from Breastfeeding." *Journal of the American Dietetic Association* 108 (7): 1106.

Korosec, Thomas. 2003. "When Does a Snapshot of a Mother Breast-Feeding Her Child Become Kiddie Porn? Ask the Richardson Police." *Dallas Observer*, April 17.

McKenna, James. 1996. "Babies Need Their Mothers Beside Them." *World Health* 49 (2): 14–15.

Naples, Nancy. 1998. Grassroots Warriors: Activist Mothering, Community Work, and the War on Poverty. New York: Routledge.

Reich, Jennifer A. 2005. *Fixing Families: Parents, Power, and the Child Welfare System*. New York: Routledge.

———. 2010. "From Maternal Love to Toxic Exposure: State Interpretations of Breastfeeding Mothers in the Child Welfare System." In *Giving Breastmilk: Body Ethics and Contemporary Breastfeeding Practice*, ed. Rhonda Shaw and Alison Bartlett, 163–74. Toronto: Demeter Press.

Solomon, Nancy M. 2002. "Breastfeeding in Public Is a Basic Civil Right." *WEnews*, August 7. *womensenews.org/story/reproductive-health/020807/ breastfeeding-in-public-basic-civil-right*.

United Nations Children's Fund (UNICEF). 2009. *Statistics by Area / Child Nutrition: Breastfeeding*. New York: Division of Communication, UNICEF.

11

"It's Hard to Say"

Moving Beyond the Mystery of Female Genital Pain

Christine Labuski

It's red. It's raw. I get these little cuts. It itches. It's irritated. It feels like sandpaper, like someone poured acid on me, like ground glass. It's stabbing. Knifelike. It feels like you're taking a knife to me. It's going to hurt. I want to pull my knees in. It's really sensitive. It feels like a razor cut. Like a wire of pain. I just tense up. It itches so much I just want to tear my skin apart. It's like there's a wall in there. A wall of pain. It's that one spot. It feels like someone hit me with a sledgehammer in my crotch. It burns. Like someone put lighter fluid up there and lit a match. Like I'm sitting in fire.[1]

Dr. Robichaud: So, tell me what's been going on.
Deirdre: It hurts.
Dr. Robichaud: Where?
Deirdre: Down there.[2]

On a Friday evening in August 2009, I sat down to watch a special episode of the ABC news program *20/20* entitled "Medical Mysteries." A friend had alerted me about the show because she'd heard that it was going to feature vulvar pain, a condition I had been researching for most of a decade. Though I have a background as a women's health clinician, I study vulvar pain as an anthropologist, attending to the ways that culture shapes the emergence and the experience of symptoms. A major challenge associated with vulvar pain is that linguistic and social norms discourage most women, including symptomatic ones, from spending too much time "down there." These tacit prohibitions can be so stifling that women's private experiences of their genitalia are sometimes filled with an even greater sense of apprehension than are their public ones (Kaysen 2001; Reinholtz and Muehlenhard 1995). In the "Medical Mysteries" episode, ABC News adhered to this evasive storyline by repeatedly referring to the subject of their investigation with the nonspecific and gender-neutral phrase "sexual pain." Throughout the segment—interviews with symptomatic patients, visits to specialist clinicians and researchers, and concluding tips for the viewer—the producers refrained from uttering the word *vulva*, undercutting both their educational and journalistic efforts. The real "mystery," it seemed, was how a woman with this pain would be any more able to describe it—to anyone—than she might have been before the show aired.

Though rarely discussed, vulvar pain is fairly common. Estimated U.S. prevalence rates range from 15 to 18 percent among adult women, and a growing body of medical literature attests to the relative urgency of this condition (Goetsch 1991; Harlow and Stewart 2003, 2005; Harlow, Wise, and Stewart 2001; Leclair and Jensen 2005). Marked by such discomforts as an inability to tolerate vaginal-penile intercourse, wear pants comfortably, and sit down for longer than a few hours (Bachmann et al. 2006; Harlow and Stewart 2003), chronic vulvar pain is simultaneously characterized by an "absence of visible pathology or a specific, clinically identifiable disorder" (Goldstein and Burrows 2008). Nonexperts, who make up the bulk of providers consulted by these patients, and who can number up to five before the woman is referred to a specialty clinic, vacillate between furrowing their brows with incomprehension and prescribing ineffective (or inappropriate) medications and procedures. Expert clinicians, in contrast, spend a great deal of time guiding symptomatic women through a complex algorithm of treatment strategies—including antidepressants, surgery, and sex therapy—none of which has been proven to eliminate or "cure" vulvar pain.[3]

Because there is scant clinical evidence, women with genital pain have been historically misunderstood, often being told that they are just "too uptight" about sex. Many therefore come to rely on the external validation that mass media (such as a national news program) can provide.[4] But in late September, about a month after I had seen the *20/20* episode, I came upon an online support group that seemed to reveal a slightly more complex picture. Though many members were grateful simply that the show had aired—evidence of the "any press is good press" philosophy that peppers the vulvar pain support literature—one woman's voice instantly reminded me of the consternation that had colored my own experience of watching the segment. Frustrated by the producers' linguistic evasions, she poignantly observed the paradox through which vulvar pain patients live their disease: "I was VERY disappointed with the *20/20* segment. The words 'vulvodynia' and 'vulvar vestibulitis' were not mentioned once, even though the narrator kept mentioning how difficult it was for women to get a diagnosis. The word 'diagnosis' was used over and over, and yet they never actually said what the three women profiled in the segment were diagnosed WITH!"

Genital Dis-ease

How does one learn about—save recover from—symptoms that are located in a body part whose name is both unknown and unspoken? To answer this question, I conducted research among vulvar pain patients and found that their symptoms shed light on a broader cultural distaste toward female genitalia. In seeking relief, women often find that social constraints circumscribe their narratives, compounding their biological disease with a cultural one. I call this latter condition *female genital dis-ease* and I argue that, because it is socially produced and sustained, it afflicts many more women than those diagnosed with a pain condition. This cultural dis-ease mires female genitalia in discourses of pollution and renders suspect women who go public with the specifics of their genital bodies. For women with vulvar pain, this situation is exacerbated by the mismatch between the intensity of their symptoms and the normal appearance of their genitalia.

Because of the relative obscurity of this condition, specialty clinics in the United States are few; the majority are attached to university-affiliated medical centers in densely populated urban areas. I carried out my fieldwork in a state-of-the-art women's health center in a large research and teaching hospital in the northwestern part of the country. In thirteen months, I spent between twenty and twenty-five hours a week talking with and observing the patients, clinicians, and staff whose work and lives revolve around this "mysterious" condition. And though, as this chapter demonstrates, specialty providers are attuned to the unique medical needs of this population, they remain largely inattentive to the ways culture conditions female genital shame.

Seeking relief for genital pain is hard work, and the epigraphs for this chapter exemplify two major and contrasting facets of this experience: the amplified pain that many afflicted women felt and easily vocalized, and the awkward and hesitant sentences that demonstrate a different kind of "genital discomfort." But encounters with the specialty clinic can bring about a peculiar brand of bodily resistance. That is, by simply showing up for their appointments, symptomatic women refuse to keep quiet about their genitalia. Indeed, through learning, naming, touching, and eventually reconfiguring their genital bodies, these women challenged the cultural sanctions that discourage explicit encounters with their genitalia.

Though these patients' resistance was at times complicated by their complicity with social norms, their ongoing—if perhaps more muted—confrontations with hegemonic genital discourse has important implications for gendered and sexual relations in the contemporary United States. Their stories provide ethnographic evidence of a bodily plight in which ideologies about sex, gender, and genitalia crystallize. These narratives also demonstrate, however, that this dilemma can be transformative, and that symptomatic women's varying degrees of frustration (e.g., that of the support group member quoted earlier) can lead to a female bodily awareness that fully incorporates the vulva.

Most Women Don't Peek

A more accurate way to describe the "clinic" where I worked is as a block of appointments. That is, on one half-day a week, the Center for Women's Health dedicates itself to the evaluation of chronic and unexplained vulvar pain. The patients—most of whom have waited three to six months for an appointment—are evaluated by two female OB/GYN physicians named Dr. Robichaud and Dr. Erlich. Both doctors maintain busy practices during the rest of the week but they preserve this one morning for a set of patients that require a particular degree of attention. Indeed, all "clinic" staff members are so aware of the challenges facing these women that new patients are given hour-long appointments.

The women who came to the clinic during my fieldwork ranged in age from ten to eighty-two. They complained of pain that was dull, constant, aching, throbbing, knifelike, intractable, erratic, and almost always penetratively prohibitive.[5] They had learned to live with the severity of their symptoms for, on average, five to seven years. Such "diagnostic delays" (Duarte-Franco and Franco 2004, 7) routinely occur because most physicians—including gynecologists—are inadequately educated about vulvar pain and lack the skills to make an efficient diagnosis. Though many women feel comfortable reporting pain in the vague and "sexual" terms evident in shows like *20/20*, they rely on their provider to elicit the clinical detail that corresponds to a diagnosis and set of treatment options. In the "*absence of visible pathology or a specific, clinically identifiable disorder*" (Goldstein and Burrows 2008, 5; emphasis mine), however, many nonexpert clinicians proclaim the woman "fine," leaving her symptoms intact and unexplained.

Drs. Erlich and Robichaud knew that many of their patients had had several of these unproductive exchanges with other clinicians. Their response was to provide new patients with a variety of vocabulary terms, diagrams, and vulvar-specific questions around which patients could generate a coherent narrative. And when prompted by these experts, most patients were able to provide eloquent and abundantly detailed descriptions of what it was like to live with genital pain: the woefully ineffective treatment regimens they had thus far endured; the vulnerability of their intimate relationships; the feelings of "craziness" around friends and partners who had no medical or cultural context for their symptoms; and the remarkable efficacy of a bag of frozen peas for cooling down a burning vulva.

Clinic patients also expressed how difficult it was to "talk about" their symptoms, a situation that can tragically compound a disease that will likely worsen if ignored. But it is worth examining the precise ways that women "ignore" their symptoms. In addition to the tacit set of rules through which patients like Barbara understand that the act of "peek[ing]" at her genitalia is transgressive, women also learn to leave well enough alone by health care providers who do not fully invest in the well-being of their patients' vulvas. Transcripts from Sheila's (a nurse) and Debra's first visits to the clinic evince the varying levels of dismissal encountered by symptomatic women.

> SHEILA: My gyney said that I was just tensed up. He put me on Zoloft. He was more concerned about how it would affect my husband. So I didn't go back.
> DR. ROBICHAUD: Well, I can't blame you there.
> SHEILA: So I thought I was crazy. That's why I didn't go back to the doctor for years.

> RESIDENT: What have you tried?
> DEBRA: *Counseling*. To see if it had something to do with the abortion. I had been raped. I went to see my OB, and she said, "Well you have lube. So you're OK." So I figured it must be mental.

As with other gynecological conditions, the medical understanding of vulvar pain is bound up with a set of cultural assumptions that both physicians and patients have about the female body, sex, and sexuality, many of which have historically led to the marginalization of women's concerns (Kapsalis 1997; Maines 1999). But unlike participating in a consultation for contraception, an abortion, or even a "designer vagina" (Green 2005), narrating vulvar pain requires that a woman and her provider be comfortable discussing an area of her "sexual" body in a way that is not circumscribed by its procreative or heterosexual meanings. And this facet of the vulva is the root of our collective cultural dis-ease and the key to vulvar pain's transformative potential. In other words, when women imagine and symbolize female genitalia outside of heteronormativity and invest in them for themselves (e.g., to be able to sit down or wear jeans), they have an opportunity to reconfigure their sexual bodies on their own terms. A genital imaginary that foregrounds the vulva can include—though not be defined by—the vagina's penetrative/reproductive capacities; women seeking relief for vulvar pain may therefore have much to offer nonafflicted women whose experience with "vaginal" sexuality is disappointing or contradictory (Potts 2002; Wade, Kremer, and Brown 2005).

Encounters with specialty clinicians, fellow sufferers, and their own genital bodies allow symptomatic women to develop new ways of coping with their symptoms. In the following transcript excerpts, we see the beginnings of this transformation in the quiet but persistent efforts of Sheila and Molly to learn and do more for their vulvas than they have thus far been encouraged to do.

> SHEILA: My next question is whether there's anything that gets rid of it.
> DR. ROBICHAUD: Yeah!!
> SHEILA: You know, I don't remember ever learning about this is in [nursing] school. Do they teach this?
> DR. ROBICHAUD: No, not even in some medical schools. That's why you've been to four different gynecologists.[6]

> DR. ROBICHAUD: What questions do you have for me?
> MOLLY: [*Says they have all been answered so far.*] There have [always] been a lot of questions, but no actions taken.
> DR. ROBICHAUD: You're ready to move on.
> MOLLY: Yeah! [She begins to cry again.]
> DR. ROBICHAUD: [*Reiterates the 15 percent prevalence rate.*] It's common, it's out there, but it's not being talked about.

Before finding their way to Dr. Robichaud, both Sheila and Molly had been inadequately cared for by other clinicians, forcing them to layer their physiological alienation with a cultural one: sexually/genitally "shutting down" in the ways that many women with vulvar pain told me they did. But with the embodied knowledge that something was wrong, Sheila and Molly refused the narrative through which their genitalia are often ignored. Rather, by taking up space in vulvar clinic's waiting and exam rooms, their "pain-filled" (Jackson 1994) bodies asserted that this "mysterious" pain was a material—and for them, compelling—reality.

Nothing to Say about Such Things

> DR. ERLICH: I can show you with a mirror now.
> CLAIR: I think I have an idea.

A cultural preference for "vulvar-free" conversations means that many afflicted women must renegotiate the terms of their personal relationships, and a piece of Peggy's transcript illustrates how these narrative constraints can extend even to patients' loved ones. During Peggy's first appointment at the clinic, Dr. Erlich, who was pursuing an interest in familiar patterns of vulvar pain, asked Peggy whether the sister she had mentioned was also symptomatic. With a hint of a sarcastic smile, Peggy replied, "No. She's perfect and she shrivels if I talk to her about this." But her sister's intolerance was evident during the remainder of the visit. When asked to describe the pain at its worst—"What did it feel like? Where did it hurt? Could you say?"—Peggy was silent for a notable length of time. Eight years of quietly endured pain, four months of which were spent waiting for this appointment, had taken their toll, turning Peggy's pain—which in her words felt "like ground glass"—into a part of her life story that even her family had difficulty hearing.

In coping with their symptoms, women must cultivate a unique set of affective, cognitive, and psychomotor skills; one could liken the pace and content of this learning to that acquired by clinicians-in-training (Ross 1984). That is, to recover, women with vulvar pain need to gain expertise in a variety of realms unfamiliar to the routines of their daily lives. These include, but are not limited to, vocabulary terms, a working knowledge of their anatomy, behavioral techniques (such as medication application), and enhanced sexual communication with their partner(s). While none of these, when considered independently, constitutes a particularly subversive act, the gradual and continued deployment of this *set* of skills transgresses the boundaries of social decorum.

Vulvar shame is acute and deeply embodied; "overcoming" it often occurs in fits and starts. Vulvar dis-ease presents symptomatic women with a dilemma: tolerate the embarrassment or continue to live with the pain and sexual despair. Ophelia, who at twenty-seven had not had sex with her husband for three-and-a-half of the four years they were married, told me that she went as far as wearing dark glasses in order to tell her brother-in-law (who was visiting from out of town) about her impending surgery. All too aware of the paltry education he would likely receive regarding vulvar pain (he was in medical school at the time), she felt obligated to fill in the blanks. Ophelia could have easily avoided what she knew would be an uncomfortable conversation by eliding the vulvar-specific details of her surgery; her ability to tell the truth is a striking example of how patients risk social sanctions by learning to "say the word." Ophelia's peculiar solution to her problem, however, reflects the ways that genital dis-ease can compromise such acts of resistance: in addition to wearing sunglasses, she told her story from the front seat of the car—facing straight ahead—while the future physician listened from the back.

"Talking about it," then, is one of the most important ways that symptomatic women trouble the cultural attitudes through which their genitalia are often ignored. To do this, the woman must be comfortable not only with the form of her message but also with its content—that is, the actual words she needs to locate and describe her pain. Epitomized by the "down there" exchange in the epigraph involving Deirdre, articulating the relevant anatomical terms does not always come easily. An anecdote from my professional past illustrates the pervasiveness of this limited vocabulary. Several years ago, I learned to perform forensic exams on sexual-assault survivors. The week-long training, which was filled with and led by other (all female) nurses, included a language exercise in which we were asked to name the terms we used for female and male genitalia, as children and as adults. To a person, the childhood terms that participants shared were derogatory ("my stink"), geographical ("down there"), or—most often—missing ("I can't think of anything," or "I don't remember any"), and none was anatomically descriptive. Adult terms were too narrow ("vagina"), also nonexistent ("I don't really use any . . . it bothers me"; "I find all those terms for females insulting"), and infused with the same evasive tone as the mysterious and "sexual" pain investigated by *20/20*.

For Foucault (1990, 4), statements like these bear the "characteristic features [of] repression," an embodied social practice distinct from legal or formally institutional prohibitions. Repression, he says, "operate[s] as a sentence to disappear, but also an injunction to silence, an affirmation of nonexistence, and, by implication, an admission that there [is] nothing to say about such things, nothing to see, and nothing to know" (4). As children, clinic patients were undoubtedly raised with injunctions about female genitalia; as parents, many likely perpetuate the belief that "there is nothing to say about such things" in their own families. Moreover, as women with vulvar symptoms, they are cared for by well-intentioned nurses whose abilities to be genitally inclusive are hampered by the "cultural attitudes about women and their bodies [that] are not checked at the hospital door" (Kapsalis 1997, 63; see also Gremillion 2003). More important, physicians are not exempt from this awkwardness and one of the second-year rotating residents in the clinic—a woman who would begin her own gynecological practice in a few short months—told me one morning that she was "still getting used to saying the word *vulva*."

With purposeful practice, however, both residents and patients learn to include the vulva in their interactions at the clinic. Specialists like Drs. Robichaud and Erlich use every opportunity to counter genitally evasive tendencies with words, behaviors, and attitudes that make present what has been absent for far too long. When Joan, for example, said that she had been referred for a "vaginal" exam, Dr. Robichaud gently corrected her: "You don't have a vaginal problem, you have a vulvar problem. That's like saying an arm instead of a leg." And in the following exchange, we see one of the residents enlisting Mickey—who was still struggling with "saying the words"—into the clinic's alternative discourse by providing her with a larger-than-life (8½ × 11–inch) diagram through which she could connect to her own vulva.

> RESIDENT: Where is the pain?
> MICKEY: Well, you know, it's hard to say . . . I have to point.
> RESIDENT: Do you want to? I have a picture. [She takes out the large drawing of the vulva that the clinicians use in the patient's record.] This is the opening of the vagina.
> MICKEY: It feels like it was up at the top here. [They then use the drawing together to describe and delineate her symptom pattern.]

Ideally, recovering patients learn to confront their genital bodies with a neutral or positive attitude, and to respect the limits established by their pain. Though many patients describe years of complete sexual "shutting down," some report having engaged in painful intercourse to avoid disappointing their partners. Indeed, Judith told Dr. Erlich that rather than communicating directly with her husband about the extent of her pain, she "would find herself [in her words] 'always jockeying with my partner—trying not to let him know . . . trying to maintain my own flow.' She is demonstrating with her body what this looks like, by shifting her pelvis on the chair, etc." (Labuski, unpublished field notes). Though the clinic physicians routinely supply patients with topical anesthetics to make vaginal-penile intercourse more tolerable (Zolnoun, Hartmann, and Steege 2003), patients get even "better" when, rather than shifting their pelvises to accommodate their partner's pleasure, they reconfigure their relationships through needs and desires that are specific to their vulvas. Getting "the lay of the land," as one patient described the discovery of her own anatomy, is a first step in cultivating a sexuality that attends to vulvar sensation; making that sensation a priority is a shift that offers even those without genital pain an opportunity to challenge the notion of a sexually extraneous vulva (Braun, Gavey, and McPhillips 2003).

How Does Your Vulva Feel?

DR. ROBICHAUD: Can you see inside your vagina?
SHEILA: Yeah, but . . . [*She is scowling.*] Well, that's interesting.
DR. ROBICHAUD: What?
SHEILA: Well, I've never seen this before.
DR. ROBICHAUD: Pretty cool huh? [She then does a culture while patient
    continues looking. She is smiling.]
SHEILA: I'm almost fifty years old and I've never seen this before!

Vulvar pain illuminates a set of heterosexual norms through which both women and men prioritize penetration over sensation (Holland et al. 1998; Potts 2002). Though even some symptomatic women—pain notwithstanding—find pleasure in the act of vaginal penetration, the sexual scripts with which most women learn about their genitalia do not have a role for their vulvas. This usually means that, until they begin to hurt and pose an obstacle to "normal" penetration, labia and vulvas are as absented from erotic behavior as they are from cultural discourse. In treatment for pain, however, this formula becomes unstable; couples working with physical therapists develop and eventually incorporate behaviors grounded in the concept of vulvar sensation. Elsewhere (Labuski forthcoming) I argue that these behaviors constitute a type of subversion to a routine heterosexual order that often eclipses female pleasure. Here I suggest that it is the second major brand of resistance in which these patients engage.

To demonstrate the kind of "genital reconfiguration" made possible by increased vulvar attention, I conclude with the story of Libby who, at the time of her diagnosis, described her six-year marriage as "unconsummated." When I met her, Libby was planning to have excisional surgery, followed by a course of physical therapy sessions, both of which she hoped would allow her to eventually engage in penetrative coitus with her husband, David.[7] Notably, Libby told me that she and David had always wished for a way to simply "learn more about sex." What she meant by this was that since she and David were both virgins at the time of their marriage, they had often wondered about how "naturally" the ability to both please and be pleased came to most people. This aspect of their story is critical because it was during Libby's post-surgical physical therapy sessions that she and David were provided with just such a set of "instructions." Because they were centered on Libby's recovery, however, they focused as much—if not more—on her vulvar sensation as they did on the act of penetration. Guided by a physical therapist who understood that vulvar pain recovery required affective, relational, and biomedical strategies, Libby and David developed a sexual repertoire marked by—and oriented to—the question, "How does your vulva feel?" rather than "Was he able to penetrate your vagina?"

This question can be made available to all women whose experiences with "normal" heterosexuality marginalize their nonpenetrable genitalia, including the regularity with which Wade and colleagues (2005, 117) found the clitoral orgasm to be an "incidental" event in many straight couples' sexual routines. When Shirley, for example, responded to Dr. Robichaud's question about whether she used vibrators by saying, "No. Absolutely not. No toys, nothing. It's the real thing or nothing," she demonstrates a kind of "shutting down" that may not be in the best interest of many women, including symptomatic ones. In contrast, when Libby and David engage in penetrative acts, they do so with their fingers, her therapeutic dilators, a vibrator, or David's penis—all of which offer both of them an alternately configured sexuality, one that is not strictly defined by a heteronormative order.

The benefits of this vulvar-centered sex and sexuality need not be limited to women diagnosed with a pain condition. Indeed, for scholars and activists who theorize sexual difference, the vulva offers a site of female identity that does not conform to a model of complementarity or inversion (Irigaray 1985a, 1985b). This is a model of female sexuality that can include transwomen and others whose vulvas have been deemed variously "problematic": intersexed individuals, women with cut or otherwise altered labia, transmen who retain their biological genitalia, vulvar cancer patients, and women whose vulvas have been disfigured or lost through exposure to disease or disease-related treatments (Fausto-Sterling 1993; Karkazis 2008). This is a model around which individuals whose bodies bear the brunt of disparaging genital discourses can generate alternative and resistant narratives about the site and source of female sexual pleasure. This is a model that directly rebukes the erasures through which mainstream media and institutional medicine would have women come to know their genital bodies; a model that shifts the focus of the "mystery" from a clinically perplexing pain condition to a culturally pervasive disdain for female sexual anatomy.

A Lasting Refusal

Alongside the women I came to know at the clinic, I fully acknowledge the bodily reality of vulvar pain. My feminist and anthropological analysis, however, is not limited to the confines of clinical disease. Rather, a critical engagement with female genitalia in their cultural context—that is, with other possible causes of discomfort—brings forth a world of associations, memories, discourses, events, and experiences, all of which can be taken up and into a body that is in constant physical dialogue with its cultural milieu. "The sickness of the patient," Victor Turner (1967) argues in his analysis of Ndembu healing practices, "is a sign that 'something is rotten' in the corporate group" (32). Turner's strongly worded assertion can help us to de-emphasize

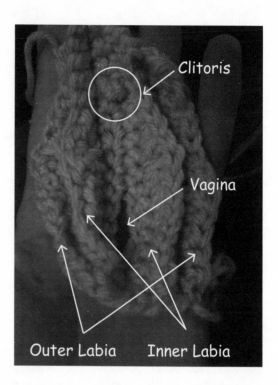

Clitoris

Vagina

Outer Labia   Inner Labia

Just one example of what can happen when women (and men) retell the cultural "story" regarding the female sexual body. Properly labeled, anatomically accurate, and held in a woman's hand, this reimagined vulva can be a source of information, amusement, or tactile pleasure rather than one of gender-specific shame. (Photograph courtesy of Heather Ann Kaldeway.)

the individuality of afflicted bodies and to attend to the ways that diseases are culturally conditioned.

In her phenomenological study of medical practice, *Presence in the Flesh*, Katherine Young (1997) argues that pathologists who perform autopsies locate personhood in a female corpse by draping her genitalia: "By shielding the corpse's most . . . private parts . . . the pathologists find personhood even [when those parts are] discorporated, dissevered, and dispersed about the room" (126). I suggest that a cultural dissection of vulvar pain can do the opposite. That is, by taking the discursive "drape sheets" off these genitalia, we can locate personhood in vulvas by safely and respectfully exposing (us to) them—by making present what polite society renders absent at virtually every turn. By remaining attentive to the transgression, confusion, and disorder evoked by vulvar pain, we can reimagine female genitalia in terms more animated than those currently available.

The emotional and cultural barriers to "talking about" one's vulva are imposing, and many symptomatic women would prefer to return to "normal," that is, to never have to think about their vulvas again. Through the concept of female genital dis-ease, however, a wide variety of afflicted individuals can come together through a more genitally inclusive cultural dialogue. The lives of many people stand to benefit from the recuperative efforts of symptomatic women; it is fitting, therefore, that we find common purpose in dismantling the verbal and cultural norms that degrade female genitalia. Such a collective challenge can fortify the courageous efforts of women with genital pain, build on the quieter (and context-specific) resistance enabled by their symptoms, and generate a lasting refusal to remain mystified by our own sexual anatomies.

NOTES

1. Each of these phrases was uttered by a woman with vulvar pain. I gathered them from two primary sources: medical interviews with physicians in the clinic, and one-on-one interviews with me (which usually took place outside the clinic). I have strung them together in this epigraph so that the reader can have the broadest possible sense of how these patients describe their symptoms.
2. Both names are pseudonyms, as are the remainder of the names in the chapter.
3. See Bachmann et al. 2006 and Haefner et al. 2005 for recent and thorough overviews of treatment strategies. See especially Goldstein and Burrows 2008 for a discussion of the evolving trends in nomenclature for these conditions.
4. In addition to the *20/20* episode, the television shows *Sex and the City* and *Private Practice* have featured vulvar pain in their storylines, both of which received positive feedback in the newsletter of the National Vulvodynia Association, the largest existing support network for these patients (*www.nva.org*). The *New York Times* ran a feature story by the health correspondent Jane Brody (January 29, 2008), and a growing number of women's magazines and blogs have written about various aspects of vulvar pain conditions.
5. The vast majority of women diagnosed with these conditions are heterosexual, a demographic reality that remains largely unexplored. See Labuski forthcoming for a larger discussion of this issue.
6. A situation that remains typical. In late 2008, a colleague told me that after she described my work to her husband, he told her that his class at Dartmouth Medical School had been taught about vulvar pain and he stressed how rare he knew that to be. Approximately one month later, a colleague at the University of Texas Medical Branch invited me to design a curricular module for their medical students, because they were currently not receiving any dedicated training in vulvar pain conditions.
7. Libby's surgery was a *vestibulectomy*, in which approximately one square millimeter of tissue is excised from the area between a woman's vaginal and anal openings; it is recommended only for women whose pain can be localized to a specific area of the vulva and can be reversed successfully with topical anesthesia. See Goetsch 1996 for a description of the procedure; see Goldstein and Burrows 2008 for a larger discussion of surgical candidates.

REFERENCES

Bachmann, Gloria A., Raymond Rosen, Vivian W. Pinn, Wulf H. Utian, Charletta Ayers, Rosemary Basson, Yitzchak M. Binik, et al. 2006. "Vulvodynia: A State-of-the-Art Consensus on Definitions, Diagnosis, and Management." *Journal of Reproductive Medicine* 51 (6): 447–56.

Braun, Virginia, Nicola Gavey, and Kathryn McPhillips. 2003. "The 'Fair Deal'? Unpacking Accounts of Reciprocity in Heterosex." *Sexualities* 6 (2): 237–61.

Duarte-Franco, Eliane, and Eduardo Franco. 2004. "Other Gynecologic Cancers: Endometrial, Ovarian, Vulvar, and Vaginal Cancer." *BMC Women's Health* 4 (Suppl. 1): S1–S14.

Fausto-Sterling, Anne. 1993. "The Five Sexes: Why Male and Female Are Not Enough." *The Sciences* 33 (2): 20–24.

Foucault, Michel. 1990. *The History of Sexuality*. Vol. 1, *An Introduction*, trans. Robert Hurley. New York: Vintage.

Goetsch, Martha F. 1991. "Vulvar Vestibulitis: Prevalence and Historic Features in a General Gynecologic Practice." Pt. 1. *American Journal of Obstetrics and Gynecology* 164 (6): 1609–14.

———. 1996. "Simplified Surgical Revision of the Vulvar Vestibule for Vulvar Vestibulitis." *American Journal of Obstetrics and Gynecology* 174 (6): 1701–5.

Goldstein, Andrew T., and Lara Burrows. 2008. "Vulvodynia." *Journal of Sexual Medicine* 5 (1): 5–15.

Green, Fiona J. 2005. "From Clitoridectomies to 'Designer Vaginas': The Medical Construction of Heteronormative Female Bodies and Sexuality through Female Genital 'Cutting.'" *Sexualities, Evolution and Gender* 7 (2): 153–87.

Gremillion, Helen. 2003. *Feeding Anorexia: Gender and Power at a Treatment Center*. Durham, NC: Duke University Press.

Haefner, Hope K., Michael E. Collins, Gordon D. Davis, Libby Edwards, David C. Foster, Elizabeth (Dee) Heaton Hartmann, Raymond H. Kaufman, et al. 2005. "The Vulvodynia Guideline." *Journal of Lower Genital Tract Disease* 9 (1): 40–51.

Harlow, Bernard L., and Elizabeth Gunther Stewart. 2003. "A Population-Based Assessment of Chronic Unexplained Vulvar Pain: Have We Underestimated the Prevalence of Vulvodynia?" *Journal of the American Medical Women's Association* 58 (2): 82–88.

———. 2005. "Adult-Onset Vulvodynia in Relation to Childhood Violence Victimization." *American Journal of Epidemiology* 161 (9): 871–80.

Harlow, Bernard L., L. Wise, and Elizabeth Gunther Stewart. 2001. "Prevalence and Predictors of Chronic Genital Discomfort." *American Journal of Obstetrics and Gynecology* 185 (3): 545–50.

Holland, Janet, Caroline Ramazanaglu, Sue Sharpe, and Rachel Thomson. 1998. *The Male in the Head: Young People, Heterosexuality, and Power*. London: Tufnell Press.

Irigaray, Luce. 1985a. *The Speculum of the Other Woman*, trans. Gillian C. Gill. Ithaca, NY: Cornell University Press.

———. 1985b. *This Sex Which Is Not One*, trans. Catherine Porter. Ithaca, NY: Cornell University Press.

Jackson, Jean. 1994. "Chronic Pain and the Tension between the Body as Subject and Object." In *Embodiment and Experience: The Existential Ground of Culture and Self*, ed. Thomas J. Csordas, 201–28. Cambridge: Cambridge University Press.

Kapsalis, Terri. 1997. *Public Privates: Performing Gynecology from Both Ends of the Speculum*. Durham, NC: Duke University Press.

Karkazis, Katrina. 2008. *Fixing Sex: Intersex, Medical Authority, and Lived Experience*. Durham, NC: Duke University Press.

Kaysen, Susanna. 2001. *The Camera My Mother Gave Me*. New York: Alfred A. Knopf.

Labuski, Christine. Forthcoming. "Out of the Comfort Zone: Why Vulvar Reluctance Is a Feminist Issue." *Feminist Studies*.

Leclair, Catherine, and Jeffrey Jensen. 2005. A Systematic Approach to Vulvodynia. *Current Women's Health Reviews* 1 (3): 209–16.

Maines, Rachel P. 1999. *The Technology of Orgasm: "Hysteria," the Vibrator, and Women's Sexual Satisfaction*. Baltimore: Johns Hopkins University Press.

Potts, Annie. 2002. *The Science/Fiction of Sex: Feminist Deconstruction and the Vocabularies of Heterosex*. London: Routledge.

Reinholtz, Rhonda K., and Charlene L. Muehlenhard. 1995. "Genital Perceptions and Sexual Activity in a College Population." *Journal of Sex Research* 32 (2): 155–65.

Ross, M. W. 1984. "Designing Sexual Medicine Courses: A Model." *Medical Education* 18:24–30.

Turner, Victor. 1967. *The Forest of Symbols: Aspects of Ndembu Ritual.* Ithaca, NY: Cornell University Press.

Wade, Lisa D., Emily C. Kremer, and Jessica Brown. 2005. "The Incidental Orgasm: The Presence of Clitoral Knowledge and the Absence of Orgasm for Women." *Women and Health* 42 (1): 117–38.

Young, Katherine. 1997. *Presence in the Flesh: The Body in Medicine.* Cambridge, MA: Harvard University Press.

Zolnoun, Denniz A., Katherine E. Hartmann, and John F. Steege. 2003. "Overnight 5 Percent Lidocaine Ointment for Treatment of Vulvar Vestibulitis." *Obstetrics and Gynecology* 102 (1): 84–87.

12

"What I Had to Do to Survive"

Self-Injurers' Bodily Emotion Work

Margaret Leaf and Douglas P. Schrock

> I can picture myself perfectly sitting at my desk in my bedroom with the glass in my hand. I didn't even know it was called self-injuring. I just knew it made me feel better. It made me feel happy for some strange reason. The anticipation as I held the glass over my skin was so exciting that it was almost unbearable. Then before I knew it there was a fresh scratch. And I was delighted when I saw the blood appear.

Our bodies may be the material that enables symbolic interaction (Mead 1934) and the experience of emotionality (Cooley 1902). But as Kate, a twenty-one-year-old self-injurer, suggests in the preceding quotation, we can also strategically employ them to suppress and evoke feelings.[1] In this chapter, we examine how self-injurers suppress distress and evoke authenticity and self-efficacy. As one interviewee put it, "This is what I had to do to survive in my eyes." We also show how self-injurers' emotional troubles derived largely from the precariousness of their everyday lives and how self-injury often unintentionally nourished the very emotional dilemmas they were trying to escape. In other words, rather than resisting or trying to change the social conditions causing them trouble, they blamed themselves and took it out on their bodies, which temporarily made them feel better.

Adler and Adler (2005, 345–46) define self-injury as the "deliberate, non-suicidal destruction of one's own body tissue," which can involve a range of behaviors including "self-cutting, burning, branding, scratching, biting, banging, hair-pulling, and bone-breaking." Psychologists dominate the study of self-injury, and many argue with each other over what alleged mental illness causes people to self-injure (see, e.g., Andover et al. 2005; Lochner et al. 2005). Adler and Adler, however, move research on self-injury beyond the purview of abnormal psychology by examining how self-injurers rationalize and carry out their actions, contributing to sociological theory on, and social-psychological understandings of, deviance. In this chapter we build on their work by showing how self-injurers can deepen our understanding of emotion work.

Hochschild (1979) defines emotion work as the "deliberate act of trying to change in degree or quality an emotion or feeling" (561). She points out that people do emotion work both to suppress undesired emotions and to evoke desired emotions, and that emotion work may be expressive (controlling outward expression), cognitive (changing the way one thinks about a situation), or bodily (changing an embodied practice). Hochschild names two examples of bodily emotion work: trying to breathe slower or relaxing muscles when trying not to shake. Similarly, Thoits (1989) suggests that people can manipulate bodily experiences to do emotion work, giving the examples of drug and alcohol use, deep breathing, and exercising. While the study of emotion work has flourished over the past thirty years, most research has neglected bodily emotion work and instead focused on how people do expressive or cognitive emotion work.[2]

Methods

We learned about self-injury by interviewing fifteen current or former self-injurers about their experiences. Interviewees approached us after hearing about the project from mutual friends, flyers posted around campus, announcements on online message boards, and canvassing in college classrooms. Thirteen of the interviewees were women and two were men, and they ranged in age from eighteen to thirty-three. All but two were white, and their educational attainment ranged from less than a high school diploma to a Ph.D.

Interviews lasted between one and four hours. During that time, the interviewees talked about their feelings and experiences with family, school, and work, as well as with self-injury. We assume that interviewees' descriptions and interpretations of their experiences are the closest we can come to accessing the "lived actualities" of their world (Smith 1987, 176). By coding interview transcripts for similarities and differences and brainstorming about the emerging analyses, we determined that framing self-injury as emotion work best encapsulated their experiences.

Self-Injury as Bodily Emotion Work

Although interviewees traveled different pathways to self-injury, most said they did not remember exactly why they first did it. For instance, when Kate was helping her mother pick up the pieces of a broken glass, she pocketed a shard "for no reason" and later used it to scratch her arm. Echoing others, she said it gave her a "rush" and made her "feel better." Only a few interviewees said that they had planned their first self-injury, which they linked to suicide. In the midst of suicidal thoughts, two said they ultimately decided that they did not want to die and turned to self-injury instead. Monica said of the first time she engaged in self-injury, "I thought of it as a rehearsal" for suicide.

Regardless of why they began, interviewees found that self-injury initially alleviated distress, evoked authenticity, and elevated self-efficacy. Self-injury was thus a form of bodily emotion work that made them feel better about themselves. But as they came to depend on cutting, it often backfired and evoked the negative emotions they were trying to escape.

Alleviating Distress

Adolescence and young adulthood are rife with physiological transformations (e.g., puberty) and social transitions (e.g., changing schools, shifting orientation from family to peers) that young people often experience as distressful. Distress refers to a mix of feelings, such as anxiety, loneliness, fear, shame, and anger (see Mirowsky and Ross 1995). Like the self-injurers Adler and Adler (2005, 352) interviewed, our interviewees cited the "mundane [problems] of ordinary adolescent life" as causing such distress. These problems included teasing and bullying at school, academic pressures, arguments with family and friends, and body image issues.

Others' policing of their non-ideal bodies, along with their own interpretations, evoked undesired emotions. Lauren recalled, "At primary school I was picked on and called a pig and never really had any friends." Dawn said, "I used to wear *really* big clothes. I felt like I needed to cover myself. I didn't like my body." Kate revealed that since she was "old enough to be body conscious," she has not liked her "chubby" body. Emily, in contrast, had "hang-ups" about her "skinny" body since high school when she was called names such as "skeleton," "ugly," and "freak."

Most interviewees also attributed their distress to familial disagreements or academic pressures. Amanda, a new college student, explained:

> The big thing for me was always my grades, which—partly because I'm always busy—are usually less than perfect, especially in high school. They just weren't straight A's. And that was a problem for [my mother]. And, so it was kind of, nothing was ever good enough. And then she'd take it to that means *she* wasn't good enough. And I'd internalize that: "I can't even make my mother feel like she's doing a good job as a mother."

Amanda thus viewed her distress as rooted in her failure to live up to her own and her parents' expectations for her to be a good student and daughter. Overall, interviewees' distress did not appear to stem from psychological dysfunction. Instead it appeared to derive in large part from their everyday lives and the larger culture. Some were teased because their bodies did not live up to impossible-to-reach gendered cultural ideals. Some were distressed by their inability to live up to high standards for academic achievement.

Like yoga or tai-chi practitioners (see Szabo et al. 1998), self-injurers used the body as a tool to alleviate distress and evoke tranquility. Gwen said, "I guess I just felt like there was just so much—there was just so much inside of me and I felt like I could not express it. . . . But [self-injury] was kind of like letting it out." After injuring themselves, interviewees were no longer overwhelmed with distress and could relax. Describing their cutting, Kate said, "[It was] the only way to clear my head and let me get some sleep," and Christine said, "It's what put me to sleep at night." Pam said she would "sometimes get kind of sleepy" after cutting herself.

Self-injurers' evocation of physical pain helped suppress their emotional pain, at least temporarily. Kate described the physical pain of cutting as inducing a trancelike state: "Before [cutting] there are all these thoughts about what a bad person I am. I feel angry, sad, stressed, upset and a thousand other things all at once. Then when I'm cutting . . . I feel almost nothing but the pain. It sends me into a sort of trance that lasts a few minutes. Then afterwards I feel peaceful." Amanda explained that self-injury could mitigate distress because the experience of physical pain demanded the self's attention: "[Cutting] is a complete distraction from anything else going on in your brain. Because physically your body is going to go to what it feels is most pressing . . . so then all the other problems really just feel insignificant for a while."

Interviewees also described the sight of blood on the skin as coinciding with a sense of release. For Pam, the "beading up" of blood was a "cue that that was enough." Amanda recalled that a "cleansing moment of clarity" would come to her "right after it started bleeding." And, like Pam, a scratch or cut would not "count" unless it bled. Like most interviewees, Pam and Amanda defined such do-it-yourself bloodletting as a kind of climax.

Interviewees said they often focused their attention on the physical bleeding, which further enabled them to temporarily escape their emotional pain. As Emily explained:

> The blood always [provided] a certain comfort . . . I would focus on it and watch it. It took my mind away from the world for a while. Seeing the blood would be like reality coming back for a while, and I would often cry [then] remain totally silent, numbed and still. I can't remember ever thinking about what had made me cut after I had done so, it seemed further away somehow. I'd be there, bleeding, and that would be it.

For Emily, focusing on the blood during self-injury alleviated distress and released tension. Some respondents, like Christine, shifted their cognitive focus from their emotions to their bleeding bodies: "Well—I just, I felt calm watching it. Like, watching it coagulate, watching it dry, it was just very calming to watch it. And it always made me think it was very beautiful, in some odd sense." Like some people's experience of other forms of art, their bodywork engulfed self-injurers' attention and made the turmoil of everyday life seem of a different world.

Overall, interviewees revealed that family life, academic pressures, and peer judgment caused emotional difficulties. But they sought personal rather than collective solutions to their troubles. Interviewees grew up in a culture that emphasizes individualistic and therapeutic understandings and solutions to social problems (Bellah et al. 1985). In addition to creating conditions for distress, such ideology shaped how they experienced self-injury. Many of the interviewees came to define their self-injury as cathartic, which suggests they used a cultural discourse of emotions to make sense of their experiences.

Evoking Authenticity

Our culture increasingly valorizes feeling "real" and "genuine." As Vannini (2006, 237) points out, "When individuals feel congruent with their values, goals, emotions, and meanings, they experience a positive emotion (authenticity)." People often label such feelings as evidence that they are being their "true selves." Adolescents and young adults often question whether their attitudes, personalities, and feelings are authentic and search for their so-called true selves.

Our interviewees described feeling "fake," "numb," "removed," or "unreal." Others felt their lives were "surreal" or just not "real enough," or they said that "consciousness is just a dream." They said that such feelings were especially sharp when they began self-injuring. At the time of her first self-injury at age thirteen, Pam remembered feeling alone and unreal at home as well as at school.

> I felt, like, not really real. I just felt so fake. Nobody really knew me. Even my own parents didn't know me. . . . It was around the time of my birthday and my parents gave me a bunch of gifts that, like, anybody who knew me would not have given me. . . . So I felt kind of like ghostlike and kind of unreal. And I was just really upset and I just wanted to do something that would change it.

Echoing others, Pam further explained that self-injury made her feel "much more in the world" and not "in the middle of a dead zone anymore." Cutting herself thus helped her feel like an authentically embodied subject rather than others' wrongly defined object.

While most respondents' feelings of inauthenticity emerged when others failed to affirm their emotions or identities, a traumatic event sometimes played a role. For Gwen that event was finding her boyfriend's body hanging lifeless from a noose. She said:

> I learned not to show emotion, . . . I kind of trained my mind—like, if anything started creeping up in my mind, just don't feel it, you know? So it kind of affected the cutting in the sense that when I felt like I *didn't* feel, or like nothing's really real, and I just kind of feel like I'm out of myself just, like, watching everything happen, then I want to bring myself to some place physical.

In response to her boyfriend's suicide, Gwen began to deal with her shock and grief by training herself to keep her emotions at bay. But distancing herself from the emotional experience led to a feeling of inauthenticity similar to, though far more intense than, what flight attendants often experience (Hochschild 1983). By creating self-inflicted physical wounds, Gwen, like other interviewees, felt as though she was healing other-inflicted emotional wounds.

Seeing and feeling themselves bleed, bruise, or scar made interviewees' pain more tangible and "real." Amanda said, "There was something about the blood. Like, it was, I was always just like, 'Hey, wow, that's really beautiful.' And I could see it. And it was like I could see into my self sort of. I could see, like, seeing it physically made me feel more real emotionally." Focusing on the blood and feelings of physical pain thus helped self-injurers evoke feelings of authenticity and alleviate distress.

Self-injurers often interpreted the scars left behind as bodily mementos of their emotional troubles. They saw such scars, which they usually hid from others, as a reminder of their true selves and the authenticity of their (perceived) damaged souls. Andrew compared his scarring to the story about "a guy who puts a notch on the bedpost for every woman he's slept with. The marks on myself [are] a way to visualize my frustration." Isabel preferred a different metaphor, referring to her scars as "maps to the places I have been." Monica's scars geographically represented a past abortion: "I now cut my stomach; right above where my pubic hair begins, [which] sort of fits the whole imagery of the abortion. I often feel like stabbing myself in my womb, as if to recall what happened. I like to see my scars there. [They are] a real sign that something terrible happened right there." As Monica explained later in the interview, the "scars show that my pain is *that* real and *that* bad." For Monica and others, the physical markings and scars of self-injury proved the authenticity of their emotional pain. Touching and examining the scars were like opening the lock to one's diary to review one's biography and authenticate the self.

While the larger culture markets feeling authentic to young people, the institutions in which they must spend their time—such as school and family—often constrain freedom of expression. In addition, interviewees often did not feel comfortable expressing the emotions they were feeling to others and others often did not validate who they believed themselves to be. As a result, they felt particularly inauthentic. As a form of bodily emotion work, however, self-injury helped interviewees feel more genuine and real.

Elevating Self-Efficacy

Gecas (1989) defines self-efficacy as feeling effective, competent, and in control of one's situation. Adolescents and young adults are usually embedded in institutions that constrain freedom and autonomy, and they generally lack resources that can be cashed in for efficacious feelings (Lewis, Ross, and Mirowsky 1999). Our interviewees revealed that peer relations, educational experiences, and family dynamics all contributed to their feeling powerless.

Becky talked at length about the lack of control she felt as a child and adolescent. When her family moved, she said, she was "at the bottom of the social ladder" at her new school and was constantly teased by her peers, who played tricks on her and called her names like "weirdo." Becky said she felt "hopeless, like nothing would ever get better." Echoing Becky and other interviewees, Christine also said she felt her life was especially "out of control," adding "[when] my stepmom and I got into an argument, or I found out that she was doing something behind my back. Or, at school, if someone said something about me and I found out about it later. Or if I didn't do well on a test or I didn't get something in on time." While interviewees clearly recognized that family disagreements, peer group dynamics, and educational evaluations and requirements had something to do with their lack of control over their lives, they drew on a therapeutic discourse to blame themselves. After Becky talked about being stigmatized at school, for example, she said, "I was angry at myself because I couldn't change my position." Others labeled feeling disempowered as evidence they were a "control freak," "immature," or "a high-anxiety person." Framing their lack of self-efficacy in individualist terms led them to search for personal solutions.

While they felt they had little objective control over their public lives, backstage they could temporarily reclaim authority over their corporeal selves in ways that felt empowering. For example, Becky, who felt "angry" and "hopeless" about her family and school life, said, "I couldn't punch my mom or the people teasing me, so I just, I did it to myself. . . . [Self-injury] really was a feeling of relief. Like, I could actually do something. Like I had power over something. Like, I could control something— which I really couldn't do when I was a teenager." Becky saw that she lacked control over her life, but self-injury allowed her to "do something" about it and elevated feel-ings of self-efficacy.

Interviewees most commonly revealed that two particular aspects of self-injury fostered a sense of control: carefully wielding their tools to control the severity of the injuries and the intensity of the pain. As Andrew put it, "I had all the control over it when I cut myself. It was my choice completely. How deep to cut, how long . . . It was something I had so much control over. I could control the pain. There was nothing else that I felt like I could control." Rachel similarly discussed controlling the pain and the severity of the injury—whether through the depth of the cut, the pressure of the blade, or the duration of the injury: "It makes me feel like I'm in control of the pain. Because usually when I'm doing it, I feel pain in some way—like emotional pain, I'm upset about something and it's painful. But when I'm doing it, I can control how much it hurts and how long it hurts." Rachel therefore viewed the physical pain of self-injury as easier to control than her emotional pain. Controlling the physical pain during self-injury made respondents feel more in control of their emotional pain and, by extension, their lives in general.

Self-injury also boosted self-efficacy in part because it involved negotiating the boundary between a nonfatal and a fatal injury. Interviewees often said they carefully chose how to cut to avoid serious injury. For example, in describing one episode of self-injury, Amanda recalled, "I actually cut my wrist that time. But I did it horizontally and I knew there was no way that thing was going to cut deep enough." In addition to their strategic choice of method, some interviewees discussed choosing locations to minimize severity. Even when they were feeling particularly out of control, interviewees usually directed their blades to geographically safe zones. Heather explained:

> I was about fifteen. I was fighting with my family and I couldn't stop crying, I wanted to break stuff and I felt guilty about what I had done—stolen money from them—so I got a knife and cut my arm. But I cut the front of my arm, that's where I've always done it. Never the back, I was afraid of hitting an important vein or something, so I never did it to kill myself, only because I was too overwhelmed.

Safely navigating the body through a dangerous mission evoked feelings of em-powerment.

As young people, the interviewees were constrained by institutional regulations and family authority structures and also were targeted by peers and other adults. At an age when they were supposed to be on the road to independence, they had little control over their lives and they blamed themselves for it. And while self-injury may appear to be an extreme form of emotion work, pragmatically speaking, it worked—at least temporarily.

Emotional Blowback

Strategies of emotion management, even if they appear to be "successful," can often have unintended consequences (Hochschild 1983). The primary unintended conse-quences of interviewees' bodily emotion work included decreasing emotional returns as well as increasing feelings of distress, inauthenticity, powerlessness, and shame. In other words, self-injury created a kind of "emotional blowback."

While self-injury could release distress, evoke feelings of authenticity, and foster self-efficacy, interviewees found that it was only temporarily effective. After her first cut, for example, Emily said, "I felt relief but it was very temporary." Dawn said that although self-injury allowed her to "forget about what my problem was [for] a while, something else would build up and upset me. So it . . . obviously wasn't a permanent solution." Similarly, Becky said that self-injury helped "get rid of my anger for while, until something else pissed me off."

Interviewees kept returning to self-injury, however, because they believed it was more effective than other methods. As Pam put it, "Anything I did just for the sole reason to get that effect, that relief, would fail. And because nothing is as good as cutting myself, I'd end up right back in the same situation." Echoing others, Amanda said, "I don't know if there's anything else that gives the same rush, the same control, the same feeling of power."

As interviewees continued using self-injury to cope with their emotions, however, they had decreasing emotional returns. To compensate, they increased the frequency and intensity of the bodily emotion work. After Pam first began cutting herself, she "found that the next time, a similar level of injury—like one little cut that bleeds—wasn't sufficient to get the same sort of result." Similarly, Dawn said, "When I first started doing it, I was probably doing it maybe once a week. And then it slowly got more and more until I was doing it every day. I got to the point where I think that I needed to do it to get through the day." Because cathartic experiences were more difficult to produce, many increased the frequency and severity of their self-injuries, even if only to survive another day.

As interviewees increasingly turned to and intensified their preferred method of bodily emotion work, they also increased the chances that others would find out about their self-injuries. People questioned and confronted them about their self-injury (especially if they noticed scars or bandages), evoking distress and, when they lied about it, inauthenticity. Echoing other self-injurers, Gwen indicated that when people inquired about her injuries, she knew they could "tell that [she was] just trying to make something up." Christine said her step mom "came running upstairs and basically attacked me, [yelling] 'Pull up your sleeves!'"

As interviewees increased their dependence on and the severity of self-injury to evoke desired feelings, they also increased the chances that something would go wrong. After Andrew "bought new razor blades," he said, "I didn't understand how sharp they were [and] I was frustrated about school and I broke down to the muscle." Like Andrew, Emily recalled trouble controlling the bleeding and sought parental help.

> I cut my leg maybe about four or five times, and it would *not* stop bleeding. It was just bleeding and bleeding. And I didn't know what to do. I actually told my mom—and that was after she had already known about it. I didn't even want to talk to her about it, because I was trying to stop it and I couldn't . . . I was doing it because I wanted to be in control, and . . . I was really out of control of the situation [and] it really scared me.

After Gwen's self-described "worst cut," she said, "I don't really remember much directly after I did this, because I was in shock and I was losing a lot of blood." She was discovered by her boyfriend, who took her to the hospital. She received twenty staples to close up the wound. "I got back to my apartment and I was like, holy shit! Blood everywhere!" she recalled.

Most interviewees recalled crossing the threshold into danger at least once. When they lost control over their bleeding, they also lost a sense of control over their lives, unraveling feelings of self-efficacy while evoking distress. And when others found out about their bodily emotion work, they also felt ashamed.

As their self-injury became more frequent and severe, and as others became more suspicious of it, problems in interviewees' lives only increased. When asked if she saw her self-injuring as a problem, Pam, who required medical treatment for some of her self-inflicted wounds, said, "I see it as a problem because of the consequences that I suffered from doing it. . . . It's a problem that makes you lose your job, makes you not be able to pay your bills, alienates you from your family because they're afraid that you're going to die."

Discussion

We have sought to better understand the experiences of those who injure themselves and explored how people use the body to shape their feelings. Although Hochschild's (1979) original theorizing on emotion included the notion of bodily emotion work, there has been little subsequent research or conceptual clarification. Whereas Hochschild (1979) discusses bodily emotion work as changing preexisting physical symptoms of undesired feelings to manage emotions (e.g., through deep breathing), we show how self-injurers create physical symptoms to manage emotions. While self-injury may seem extreme, bodily emotion work is quite common. Yoga and other forms of exercise, sexual activity with or without partners, as well as simple laughter can similarly change our feelings.

As young people, interviewees had little power over their lives. They were often the target of harassment, they were socially isolated, and they lacked economic and social resources that might have offered some emotional protection. As a result, they often felt overwhelmed with feelings of distress, inauthenticity, and powerlessness. To make sense of these feelings, they used an individualistic discourse and defined their feelings, rather than their social causes, as the problem and therefore sought personal solutions. They discovered that one strategy of bodily emotion work—self-injury—was particularly effective, enabling them to alleviate distress, evoke authenticity, and elevate self-efficacy. While this bodily emotion work induced immediate relief, its temporary nature led interviewees to increasingly rely on self-injury to manage emotions. As a result, however, they re-created the same emotional experiences and interpersonal tensions from which they were trying to escape.

How might one stop self-injury? According to S.A.F.E. (Self-Abuse Finally Ends) Alternatives, a leading self-injury treatment center, effective methods of treating self-injury include interpersonal therapy, voluntary institutionalization, a contractual agreement to stop self-injuring, and the development of alternative emotion work techniques (such as exercising or putting one's hand in a bowl of ice).[3] While we agree that it is important for self-injurers (and everyone) to find healthful ways to deal with their emotions, we fear that isolating, institutionalizing, and stigmatizing self-injurers as mentally ill likely increases their feelings of disempowerment, distress, and inauthenticity—feelings that could further drive self-injury underground.

Our interviewees who stopped injuring themselves believed that understanding and dealing with the social causes of their emotions was important. As Becky explained, "You're hurting yourself, for no really good reason. It makes you feel better, but unless you get rid of stuff that's making you feel crappy in the first place, it's not going to go away. Deal with that, and you won't want to mess yourself up anymore." By changing her social life and altering her reflexive sense of self, Pam said she stopped self-injuring in her late twenties.

> I think that there was a time, rather suddenly, where I figured a lot of things out. I figured a lot of why I was feeling that way to start with and how much it mattered to put a lot of things in perspective, from an adult perspective that didn't [create] a helpless, like, "I can't change this" feeling. And then I also met a lot of nice people in my life. I got a job and I kept it. And I met cool people. And I think that there are ways to feel a lot more real by just living your life [and] by being connected to other people.

Becky and Pam, echoing others, make several important points about quitting. It is important to come to an understanding of their emotional difficulties ("I figured out why I was feeling that way"), to address the source of those feelings ("Unless you get rid of the stuff that's making you feel crappy in the first place, it's not going away"), and to engage the social world and other people in ways that promote desired feelings ("[You can] feel more real by just living your life [and] connecting"). Quitting self-injuring, it seems, thus requires exploring the connections between emotions and social life, as well as developing a network of supportive others.

NOTES

1. All names are pseudonyms to protect interviewees' anonymity.
2. For example, while the review of emotions research in sociology in Turner and Stets 2006 mentions that emotion work may involve physical work, the authors do not cite any research that has investigated it.
3. "Safe Intensive," S.A.F.E. Alternatives: Self Abuse Finally Ends, *www.selfinjury.com/treatments/intensive/*, accessed January 15, 2011.

REFERENCES

Adler, Patricia A., and Peter Adler. 2005. "Self-Injurers as Loners: The Social Organization of Solitary Deviance." *Deviant Behavior* 26 (4): 345–78.

Andover, Margaret S., Carolyn M. Pepper, Karen A. Ryabchenko, Elizabeth G. Orrico, and Brandon E. Gibb. 2005. "Self-Mutilation and Symptoms of Depression, Anxiety, and Borderline Personality Disorder." *Suicide and Life-Threatening Behavior* 35 (5): 581–91.

Bellah, Robert N., Richard Madsen, William M. Sullivan, Ann Swidler, and Steven M. Tipton. 1985. *Habits of the Heart: Individualism and Commitment in American Life*. Berkeley: University of California Press.

Cooley, Charles H. 1902. *Human Nature and Social Order*. Piscataway, NJ: Transaction.

Gecas, Viktor. 1989. "The Social Psychology of Self-Efficacy." *Annual Review of Sociology* 15:291–316.

Hochschild, Arlie Russell. 1979. "Emotion Work, Feeling Rules, and Social Structure." *American Journal of Sociology* 85 (3): 551–75.

———. 1983. *The Managed Heart*. Berkeley: University of California Press.

Lewis, Susan K., Catherine E. Ross, and John Mirowsky. 1999. "Establishing a Sense of Personal Control in the Transition to Adulthood." *Social Forces* 77 (4): 1573–99.

Lochner, Christine, Sian M. J. Hemmings, Craig J. Kinnear, Dana J. H. Niehaus, Daniel G. Nel, Valerie A. Cofield, Johanna C. Moolman-Smook, Soraya Seedat, and Dan J. Stein. 2005. "Cluster Analysis of Obsessive-Compulsive Spectrum Disorders in Patients with Obsessive-Compulsive Disorder: Clinical and Genetic Correlates." *Comprehensive Psychiatry* 46 (1): 14–19.

Mead, George Herbert. 1934. *Mind, Self, and Society: From the Standpoint of a Social Behaviorist*. Chicago: University of Chicago Press.

Mirowsky, John, and Catherine E. Ross. 1995. *Social Causes of Psychological Distress*. New York: Aldine de Gruyter.

Smith, Dorothy. 1987. "Institutional Ethnography: A Feminist Research Strategy." In *The Everyday World as Problematic: A Feminist Sociology*, 151–80. Boston: Northeastern University Press.

Szabo, Attila, Andrea Mesko, Arcangelo Caputo, and Eamonn T. Gill. 1998. "Examination of Exercise-Induced Feeling States in Four Models of Exercise." *International Journal of Sport Psychology* 29 (4): 376–90.

Thoits, Peggy A. 1989. "The Sociology of Emotions." *Annual Review of Sociology* 15:317–42.

Turner, Jonathan H., and Jan E. Stets. 2006. "Sociological Theories of Human Emotions." *Annual Review of Sociology* 32:22–52.

Vannini, Phillip. 2006. "Dead Poets' Society: Teaching, Publish-or-Perish, and Professors' Experiences of Authenticity." *Symbolic Interaction* 29 (2): 235–57.

Intersex?

Not My Problem

Esther Morris Leidolf

My life changed completely when I was thirteen and was sent home from camp with abdominal pain. A pelvic exam revealed an imperforate hymen prohibiting the flow of menstrual fluid. I had surgery—my first of many—to open my hymen so I could menstruate. During the surgery, they found vaginal agenesis with a slight vaginal "dimple," and no detectable uterus. I had secondary sex characteristics—body hair and breasts—so they guessed I had ovaries . . . somewhere.

I was diagnosed with "congenital absence of vagina" and labeled with "sexual dysfunction." The doctors talked to my parents about vaginal reconstruction so I could have a "normal" sex life. I was suddenly and shamefully different. I went from selling Girl Scout cookies to correcting my *sexual dysfunction* in one afternoon. My abdominal pain was overlooked and the focus became creating my vagina ASAP. Yet all I cared about was the loss of fertility and my dream of having children.

I spent the next few years going to (male) specialists who ordered tests to confirm my gender; and curious doctors and their interns who probed me with multiple instruments in multiple holes at multiple times. My chromosomes were counted and discussed in front of me as if I were not there: "Got to run that test again just to make sure." They spoke about me but never to me. They examined my breasts, labia, clitoris, and vaginal dimple with blind eyes.

My doctors subscribed to a narrow version of "normal" and I wasn't it. Never once was I asked what I wanted, what I felt. I was too young to know I had rights—to ask questions or slow the process down. I had major doubts about what was happening, but I was not yet capable of asking the fundamental question: Whose struggle is this? Mine or my doctors? Frightened in a cloth hospital gown, I did what I was told, which ended my relationship with my body. Like an android on an assembly line, I felt my body was less and less my own. There was so much focus on the woman I should be that I lost all knowledge of the girl that I was.

Once I was officially determined female, my reconstruction was arranged. In 1972 I had my second and third surgeries. I was fifteen and a half. That summer I took a "trip" for three weeks to avoid explaining why I had to go to the hospital. I spent my recovery in the maternity ward. For seventeen days it was just me and my mom, and a lovely nurse named Donna, who protected me from night-shift professionals trying to satisfy their curiosity as I slept.

Esther Leidolf, the thirteen-year-old
I was not allowed to be. (Photograph
courtesy of author's family collection.)

Two weeks later I had the mold and stitches removed—my third surgery. My introduction to vaginal penetration was postoperative therapy to keep my vagina functional (read: big enough for a penis). I was told to insert a vaginal dilator every night to stretch the scar tissue, but nobody told me how.

The problem was solved, for everyone but me.

Their "surgical success" left me with unanswered questions: Why was my gender challenged in the first place and then confirmed as though it were something I didn't already know? Why was my body taken away and rearranged like a sexual action figure by men with knives? The pressing need to feminize my body actually neutered my soul; all the fuss just reinforced my despair. Inside this anomaly, I felt terribly wrong because I didn't really care that I was born without a vagina.

My anger resurfaced when I started having sex. After all that trouble I discovered that a penis would respond to anything. I felt abused in the most intangible way . . . like a victim of arrogance and assumption . . . an instant survivor. My doctors said I would never meet another woman like me, so I alienated myself from peers; and No! I don't have a tampon! Like the hunchback in the bell tower, I found a place to hide when normality failed me. Denying my depression, I began to understand that normal was merely a concept for people who couldn't cope with physical diversity. Even my "corrective" vaginal surgeries will never change the fact that I was born with vaginal agenesis.

When I was a teenager, the meaning of my vagina was so ingrained I didn't think to question the assumption that I should get one. I was told that my skin-graft vagina would make me a normal woman. In 2000 my sister sent me an article and I learned about Mayer-Rokitansky-Kuster-Hauser syndrome (MRKH) for the very first time. I got my medical records from each of my doctors and there it was: Mayer-Rokitansky-Kuster-Hauser syndrome. In over thirty years of medical visits, none of my doctors mentioned the actual diagnosis, or the other symptoms of my syndrome. Apparently, vaginal dysfunction was all my condition meant to them, and all they thought I needed to know.

Guided by a possible diagnosis, I researched MRKH and discovered many associated symptoms. The connection to my disabilities left me numb. If only I had known . . . Reading about MRKH made it painfully clear that my experience was not simply about one "abnormal" body. Nonconsensual cosmetic surgeries are so much broader than unusual medical conditions and people we think we will never know. This is about the power society has to force us to be other than we were born to be. Women are bombarded with artificially enhanced caricatures of the female body and encouraged to aspire to them. According to the American Society of Aesthetic Plastic Surgery, breast implants for teenage women eighteen and younger has risen nearly 500 percent from 1997 to 2007. Why?

I want people to understand that the concept of *normal* that we aim for is imaginary. People don't fail to meet the definition of "normal" gender, but the definitions fail to meet the people. Emotional and sexual counseling would have enabled me to decide whether and when I wanted surgery. But being born without a vagina was not my problem. Having to get one, without my consent, that was the real problem.

Visit *www.MRKH.org* or *www.IntersexCollective.org.*

LIVING RESISTANCE

Doula-Assisted Childbirth

Helping Her Birth Her Way

Angela Horn

Birth in the United States is a medical event. But it hasn't always been that way.

At the turn of the twentieth century, only a small percentage of women gave birth in hospitals. Today, nearly all women birth in the hospital and, while there, they are unlikely to experience a natural birth (Rooks 1997). For instance, over 75 percent of women in the United States give birth with epidural medication (Declercq et al. 2006), one in four labors is induced (Zhang, Joseph, and Kramer 2010), and one in three women has her baby by cesarean surgery (Menacker and Hamilton 2010)—one of the most commonly performed surgeries on women. This means that all but a very few women begin motherhood with stitches, postbirth pain, and in many cases disorientation and anxiety stemming from their overmedicated births. The standard medicalized birth does not bode well for babies either. Despite advanced technologies and the exorbitant funds pumped into maternal healthcare, the United States ranks a dismal forty-fifth in infant mortality (CIA 2010). This means that for every one thousand babies born, six will die in the first year (MacDorman and Matthews 2008).

I am a doula, a woman who provides expectant families with educational and informational support and aids in the relief of labor discomfort, typically through massage and labor-facilitating positions. The most challenging clients I work with are those who birth simply and naturally, that is, in contrast to accepted medical norms. After all, allowing labor to start naturally and eschewing pain medication are now considered "alternative" practices. And birthing at home or in freestanding birth centers is uncommon.

In my work, women tell me about their experiences with (what is now considered) conventional obstetrics. Often providers are supportive of a woman's choices to birth her way, but near her due date, things begin to shift. Doctors often withdraw support for the mother's wish to wait for labor to begin spontaneously once the due date passes. Even though the best evidence shows that the normal length of pregnancy in a first-time mother is forty-one weeks plus one day (Mittendorf et al. 1990), many providers induce labor at forty weeks if the woman has not begun labor. What's the problem with that? Well, induction is not risk-free: induced labors often require the use of medication to stimulate contractions or soften the cervix, and the resulting contractions are often longer and more painful and more often end in cesarean surgery— a major operation that itself increases the risk to mother and baby.

Provider disapproval surfaces at other times, too. When it is suspected that a woman is carrying a "large baby," induction or elective cesarean or both often follow. Ultrasound, however, is not an accurate way to predict fetal size; sonographers and physicians I have worked with indicate that estimations can be off by up to two pounds! Yet, in the final weeks of pregnancy, many providers suggest an ultrasound to check the baby's position and size.

In my practice, I witness countless situations in which women, desiring to birth as naturally as possible, encounter resistance from their care provider and sometimes even family and friends. Women are repeatedly reminded of potential health risks, reinforcing fears (often unfounded) about complications and undermining confidence. In some ways, anxieties are not unexpected. Birthing in a hospital, flat on the back (supine), with fetal monitoring and epidural anesthesia to numb the body from just under the breasts down is practically the only birth we hear about in America. But there are other birth stories and there can be more.

As a certified doula, my role is to help women who want a different birthing experience to actually have one. But it is also my responsibility to preserve a woman's faith and trust in her care provider. This means I must walk a very fine line. When a woman is being pressured into an intervention she may not need, I have to squelch my desire to scream, "You are being lied to! You are being duped!" Instead, I provide her with evidence-based information, help her formulate questions, and if she wants, role-play ways she can advocate for herself.

I recently worked with two clients who were being pressured into scheduled cesarean births because their providers suspected large babies. In both cases I educated the women and their partners about current practice guidelines that advise against induction of labor or cesarean for a suspected large baby, reliable rates of complications from a large baby, and how to prevent those complications—many of which are, ironically, the consequence of common obstetrical practices. For instance, birthing in the supine position contributes to malpositioning of the baby and narrowing of the mother's pelvis. In contrast, birthing in a squatting position can increase the pelvic opening by up to 28 percent (Blackburn 2007), allowing optimal dimensions for the passage of large babies. In other words, when a big baby is suspected, women should be encouraged to get up and squat, not lie down on an operating table.

One of these couples felt that they could not live with themselves if they attempted a vaginal birth and their baby was injured, even though the statistical incidence of shoulder dystocia is less than 2 percent (Gherman and Gonik 2008). The other couple's strong faith allowed them to take the small risk. With the first couple, I reflected back to the mother her views of the risks, letting her know that I understood her dilemma and that I supported her decision. With the second, we focused a lot on the couple's strong faith. I reminded her of her belief that God created her body in his image, perfectly designed to birth the baby. We also talked about her providers in this perfect design and that they come not from a place of trust but rather, a place of fear—fear of complications that can lead to injury to mother or baby, situations in which they are often blamed and sued. In the end, one woman chose a cesarean; the other chose to let labor begin on its own and had a vaginal birth. The eventual outcome was two happy couples and the births of two large, healthy babies. And while their births differed dramatically, both mothers claimed ownership over the way they brought their children into the world.

The twenty-first-century birthing scene is not friendly to providers, mothers, or babies. In this current medical climate with the threat of litigation hanging over care providers' heads, physicians and midwives tend to "over treat." They are sued over the cesareans that they do not perform, not the ones they do. Sadly, the threat of a lawsuit over an injured baby trumps evidence-based birth practices and takes labor out of the hands of expectant women.

When parents want something different for their families, they are faced with fear mongering. Some women are accused of intent to harm or kill their baby, simply because they question convention and trust that a low-tech birth can be a safe birth, even a safer birth.

My work enters here, where women want and deserve an empowering birthing experience that affirms women's potential to birth her way with the support of those she trusts, beginning her life as a mother feeling confident and supported. But I am a big believer that we cannot actually empower another; rather, we strive to foster the self-reflection and self-advocacy necessary for individuals to empower themselves. My mission, then, is to supply the education, information, and nonjudgmental support that helps expectant families discover their voices and find their power.

REFERENCES

Blackburn, Susan Tucker. 2007. *Maternal, Fetal, and Neonatal Physiology: A Clinical Perspective*. St. Louis: Saunders Elsevier.

Central Intelligence Agency (CIA). 2010. "Infant Mortality Rates." *The World Factbook. www.cia.gov/library/publications/the-world-factbook/rankorder/2091rank.html*.

Declercq, Eugene R., Carol Sakata, Maureen P. Corry, and Sandra Applebaum. 2006. *Listening to Mothers II: Report of the Second National U.S. Survey of Women's Childbearing Experiences*. New York: Childbirth Connection.

Gherman, Robert B., and Bernard Gonik. 2008. "Shoulder Dystocia." *The Global Library of Women's Medicine*. ISSN: 1756-2228; DOI 10.3843/GLOWM.10137.

MacDorman, Marian, and T. J. Matthews. 2008. "Recent Trends in Infant Mortality in the United States." *NCHS Data Brief* 9. Hyattsville, MD: National Center for Health Statistics.

Menacker, Fay, and Brady E. Hamilton. 2010. "Recent Trends in Cesarean Delivery in the United States." *NCHS Data Brief* 35. Hyattsville, MD: National Center for Health Statistics.

Mittendorf, Robert, Michelle A. Williams, Catherine S. Berkey, and Paul F. Cotter. 1990. "The Length of Uncomplicated Human Gestation." *Obstetrics and Gynecology* 75 (6): 929–32.

Rooks, Judith Pence. 1997. *Midwifery and Childbirth in America*. Philadelphia: Temple University Press.

Zhang, Xun, K. S. Joseph, and Michael S. Kramer. 2010. "Decreased Term and Postterm Birthweight in the United States: Impact of Labor Induction." *American Journal of Obstetrics and Gynecology* 203 (2): 124.e1–e7.

PART IV

Negotiating Boundaries and Meanings

13

The Politics of the Stall

Transgender and Genderqueer Workers Negotiating "the Bathroom Question"

Catherine Connell

On the promotional poster for the 2005 film *Transamerica*, a transwoman stands frozen between two bathroom doors. The symbol for Women and the outline of a stick figure in a dress marks one door. The corresponding Men symbol and a stick figure in pants marks the other. The poster is representative of the major theme of the film, which is one transwoman's journey (literal and figurative) from man to woman. The film itself does not address the question raised by the promotional poster—which bathroom a transperson should and could use—yet this is a significant concern for transmen, transwomen, and genderqueers alike.[1] "The bathroom question," as it is often referred to by transpeople, is one with symbolic and material consequences. For some trans- and gender-nonconforming people, choice of bathroom is fraught with anxiety, ambivalence, and anticipated harassment.

Though bathrooms are typically naturalized as apolitical spaces of bodily necessity, the lived experience of transgender workers suggests otherwise. The experiences of transgender workers show that workplace bathrooms, in particular, are sites of symbolic power and privilege. How a workplace answers "the bathroom question" for transgender and genderqueer workers affects these workers' senses of authenticity in their chosen gender, feelings of community and acceptance, and perceptions of the success of workplace integration.

In this chapter I ask, How do workplaces respond to "the bathroom question"? Further, how do transpeople respond to, negotiate, and resist these policies? I explore these negotiations and assert that they reveal an often-unexplored dimension of workplace inequality. Specifically, I argue that the spatial organization of bathrooms contributes to the gendered organization of work (Acker 1990) in a manner that perpetuates gender and sexuality privilege. As such, it is important that feminist sociological research explore the mechanisms of this spatial system of privilege and its implications for the possibilities of gender equality at work. Bathrooms, I argue, are an unexpected but important site of intervention that workplaces must address to further gender equality on the job.

Previous Studies

Even though the socializing power of bathrooms is rarely recognized in contemporary sociological literature, bathrooms have played pivotal roles in some of the groundbreaking research in gender and sexuality. For example, Laud Humphreys's (1970) research on the "tearoom trade" dramatically changed the way sociologists conceive of the relationship between sexual identity and behavior. Humphreys found that men used public bathrooms as a site of anonymous same-sex sexual encounters—including many men publicly identified as straight. This research challenged the assumed relationship between sexual identity and sexual behavior, using bathrooms as an unlikely but significant site of empirical investigation.

Erving Goffman (1963), who is credited with establishing performative sociological theories of gender that dominate the sociology of gender today, also considered bathrooms in his work, identifying them as a significant component of the system of folk beliefs that maintain the belief in the naturalness and inevitability of gender (1977). Judith Lorber (1993) also pinpointed bathrooms as a piece of the institutional gender system that upholds the (false) binary between men and women. The role that bathrooms play in these foundational texts begs a closer look at the gendered spatial organization of bathrooms.

Theoretical claims about trans- and gender-nonconforming people have suggested that they hold the potential to upset the taken-for-granted quality of the gender binary. Judith Butler (1990) was among the first to consider the transgressive possibilities of cross-gender performance. In her analysis of drag, Butler asserts that, "in imitating gender, drag implicitly reveals the imitative structure of gender itself—as well as its contingency" (137). In her more recent work, Butler (2004) extends this claim to include transpeople, who, by openly transitioning from one gender to another, similarly challenge the belief that gender and sex are inevitably connected. Similarly, theorists such as Kate Bornstein (1995) and Sandy Stone (1991) have argued that transgender experiences are key to dismantling the binary gender system that upholds gendered inequalities.

Recent research on transgender individuals offers some empirical support for these claims that transpeople have the potential to challenge naturalized gender arrangements. For example, Kristin Schilt's (2006) analysis of transmen at work finds that as "gender outsiders–within," they have unique insights into the structural advantages that accrue to men. Elsewhere, I have argued that transmen and transwomen attempt to subvert the gender binary in their workplace interactions and develop a feminist consciousness through the process of gender transition (Connell 2010). Outside the context of work, Raine Dozier (2005) finds that transmen challenge the assumed relationship between sex, gender, and sexual identity through their intimate relationships. Taken together, these theories and empirical studies suggest that the experiences of transpeople are important to address when considering the implications of our binary gender system. In this chapter, I specifically consider how their experiences challenge the naturalized gender assumptions that uphold the spatial organization of bathrooms.

Finally, this research also contributes to feminist studies of gender and work by extending previous claims about the discriminatory impact of the spatial organization of workplaces. Investigations of the disadvantages faced by women at work have pointed to the informal networking opportunities extended only to members of the "boys club"; these studies suggest that homosocial fraternization among men at work creates a network of opportunity that is unavailable to women (Bird 1996; Kanter 1977; Martin 2003; Pierce 1995; Roth 2006; Williams 1995). In this group of studies, relationships developed in the locker room, the golf course, the strip club, and other "men only" spaces preclude true equal opportunity in the workplace. While previous work has focused on the effects on *ciswomen*, or non-trans-identified women, this chapter considers how access to the gendered space of the bathroom might also contribute to interactional processes of discrimination for transpeople as well.

Methods

This examination of transpeople and workplace bathroom policies comes from a larger research project that involved asking transpeople about their experiences of the workplace. From these interviews, unanticipated findings emerged concerning the issue of on-the-job bathroom use. This chapter focuses on these findings and their implications for gender and work. The data presented here come from nineteen in-depth interviews with transpeople conducted between 2005 and 2006. I interviewed a range of trans-identified people, including eleven transwomen, six transmen, and two genderqueers. Most of the transpeople in this research were "out" as transgender in their workplaces (thirteen out of the eighteen employed participants). Of these, all but one had been employed at the onset of their transition and, as such, had to engage in either a formal or informal "transition plan" with their workplaces. All of the interviews were conducted in person and they usually lasted about one to two hours; each interview was tape recorded and transcribed. In the semi-structured interviews, research participants were asked to outline their work histories from their first jobs to their current employment situations. If they transitioned or came out on the job, we discussed that process (if not, we discussed how they came to the decision not to disclose at work). From there, we talked about interactions with supervisors, coworkers, and clients. Finally, I asked them whether their relationships to their work and their feelings about their work environments have changed since their coming out and, if so, in what ways.

As these interviews progressed, it became clear that the way workplaces negotiated and adapted to the bathroom preferences of trans workers produced anxiety, confusion, and, at times, distress and disadvantage for many of my research participants. What emerged from their narratives is the possibility that bathrooms are overlooked sites of power and privilege. All of the several different ways workplaces answered "the bathroom question" had symbolic and material consequences for the transgender workers who were affected by these policy decisions.

Findings

How Do Workplaces Respond to "the Bathroom Question"?

The participants in this study described a range of workplace responses, from hospitable to hostile, to their bathroom preferences. According to the transpeople I interviewed, workplace responses to "the bathroom question" were generally one of three kinds, each of which had different outcomes for trans workers. First, workplaces can support a transperson's choice of bathroom; this was the most commonly mentioned outcome of bathroom negotiations in my interviews. For those who were able to receive such support, workplace tensions about trans bathroom preferences seemed to be kept to a minimum. For example, Carolina's company, an engineering firm, encouraged her transition from the men's to the women's bathrooms.[2] Her human resources department's "diversity officer" was instrumental in smoothing the way for her bathroom transition. Carolina explained, "I had [Human Resources], the HR rep on my side, and the diversity person on my side. They basically said, 'It's not against the law, there's no reason why she shouldn't be using the female bathroom. It doesn't make any sense to have her go to the male bathroom.'" When some coworkers initially resisted this move, Carolina's HR department made sure to communicate her transition and bathroom preferences to other workers and to demonstrate support for her process. With such open communication and firm institutional support, Carolina did not experience any subsequent conflict over her choice of restroom. Carolina's experience suggests that occupational location might mediate the kinds of resources available for a favorable bathroom transition. As a relatively class-privileged worker—an engineer employed by a firm with the resources to have a dedicated diversity officer—Carolina was able to leverage these class-based resources in her favor as she transitioned at work.

The second and fairly common strategy for resolving the bathroom dilemma was through permanent segregation. In these cases, companies asked trans workers to use a single-stall bathroom, separate from the men's and women's bathrooms that other workers used. While some transpeople felt more comfortable using a more private bathroom, the transpeople I spoke with often found this solution stigmatizing, uncomfortable, and impractical. For example, when Laura, a call center supervisor, transitioned, she began using the women's restroom. But, Laura said, "there was a complaint made, so they took one [bathroom] upstairs and made it private . . . officially, it was for nursing mothers, but that was my designated area." While she was initially amenable to this arrangement, she explained, it quickly became burdensome.

> You know, I'm a manager, working ten or eleven hours a day, and when I have to go to the bathroom, I've got to go. . . . [My office] was downstairs in the back corner, and if I came up [to the single-stall bathroom] and it was locked—because we did have a lot of nursing mothers using it—I was screwed. I couldn't wait twenty more minutes. It got to the point where if I needed to use the bathroom, I left the building and had to drive to another location.

For Laura, separate bathroom space was impractical for her busy work schedule. For Laura and others, bathroom segregation was inefficient and inconvenient for their workdays.

The third solution workplaces implemented for "the bathroom question" was to use a transperson's birth-assigned sex as a determinant of bathroom option, regardless of gender identity. While this strategy was the least common in my sample, it had severe consequences for those who faced it. Jackie, who worked as a service representative in several customer-support call centers, endured this policy at several jobs. For Jackie, being forced to use the men's bathroom was unacceptably humiliating and frightening. She described her subsequent workplace interactions as "Isolation. Isolation. Girls are afraid of me, guys don't want to talk to me." The policy in her customer service job was, "You've got the boy bits, you're using the boy's restroom." Afraid of harassment and uncomfortable being reminded of her birth-assigned sex, Jackie refused to use the men's bathroom in three different workplaces. As a result, she was fired from two of these jobs and isolated to a male-only night shift at the third, which in essence segregated her to a single-user (women's) bathroom. Using birth-assigned sex as a bathroom criterion was, according to interviewees, uncomfortable, embarrassing, and disrespectful of a transperson's chosen gender identity.

What Is the Effect of Workplace Bathroom Negotiations on Trans Workers?

GENDER NONCONFORMITY AND THE THREAT OF DANGER

Conflict over bathroom choice operated differently for transwomen, on the whole, than for transmen and genderqueers. The location of the conflict (the women's restroom), however, and the source of the conflict (the specter of women's victimization) was almost always the same. This pattern is illustrative of the organization of gendered space and its consequences, for those who transgress it and for those who do not.

Several of the transmen in my study mentioned the hostile treatment they received in bathrooms before they transitioned. For example, when we talked about "the bathroom question," Mark, a bus driver, remarked, "It's kind of weird, because when I was a teenager, I would get run out of women's restrooms. When I was a young adult and in bars, I would continually have bartenders ask me to leave because women were complaining about a man in the restroom." Mark, who did not transition until his midthirties, experienced a good deal of harassment and exclusion by virtue of his gendernonconforming appearance when living as a woman. John, a genderqueer-identified retail worker who used women's restrooms at work also received complaints about his presence in the women's room.[3] While working as a sales associate in a national bookstore chain, John encountered "bathroom conflict." "There were a couple of instances," he said, "where a woman asked me to leave the bathroom, and another instance where a woman wouldn't speak to me, opened the door, then left." Though his boss told him that he would support his use of the bathroom of his choice, customers continued to complain about John's presence in the women's bathroom. As a genderqueer and gender-ambiguous person, John felt safer and more comfortable in the women's restroom than in the men's—yet his fellow bathroom patrons did not feel the same way.

While transmen in my sample tended to experience more of a bathroom conflict before transition (or, for genderqueer individuals, during their presentation of gender ambiguity), transwomen encountered more problems after they began the transition. As with transmen, most of these conflicts occurred in the women's restroom. Katie, a project manager for a software company, told me, "I dread the encounters in the bathroom. . . . I have seen some people look uncomfortable—especially mothers—who hold their little children closer." Katie and others expressed sadness and dismay at the alarm they incited in women when they entered women's bathrooms. Katie interpreted the motivating factor for this alarm as fear of predation. The appearance of a "man in woman's clothing" in the bathroom made women, especially mothers with young children, fearful of attack, according to Katie's interpretation.

Of the transwomen who experienced bathroom conflicts at work, Jackie had the most dramatic story. As previously mentioned, Jackie was fired from two customer service jobs for refusing to use the men's restroom. At one job, she explained, she was fired within four hours of starting the job when a coworker complained about her presence in the bathroom.

> JACKIE: They actually told me I was being fired for sexual harassment.
> INTERVIEWER: What was the story?
> JACKIE: Their story was: I used the wrong restroom. Bathroom politics is the number one killer for me . . . I mean, I'm not going in the men's restroom, and I mean, it's not like I'm a threat or anything. The argument that I gave them was, "I'm [a woman]. I'm no threat to anyone. And is this—how's this impacting my work for you?"

In response to her protests, Jackie's supervisor told her, "Women just don't feel safe around you for some reason." At another job, she was fired after four months when coworkers again complained about her use of the women's restroom. This time, Jackie went to the Equal Opportunity Employment Commission (EEOC) to file a complaint of wrongful termination. But, she said, she was turned away from filing a complaint after repeatedly being told, "We can't help you" by her EEOC representative.

The common link between the predominant experiences of bathroom conflict experienced by transmen, genderqueers, and transwomen was the perception that women felt threatened by their presence in a bathroom space. Conversely, the transmen in my sample who used the men's room spoke of their own fear of violence entering this male space, rather than fears on the part of other men. These trends suggest that much of the conflict transpeople experience with regard to bathrooms hinges on the operation of violence against women.

In a patriarchal society that is in part maintained by the threat and actualization of men's violence against women, it is logical that women might fear a masculine-appearing person in a space coded as protected from men's predatory gazes and actions as women expose bodies and bodily functions. Simultaneously, transmen who are raised as women in the same sexist (and homophobic) culture have reason to fear men's bathrooms as well. Additionally, there is a very real history of violence against transpeople and suspected gender transgressors that further shapes the fears of transwomen and transmen alike (Namaste 2000). At least 137 transpeople were murdered in 2009 alone in suspected hate crimes.[4] This history of violence is important because it identifies the operating principle that maintains bathroom conflict for transpeople beyond individual or circumstantial dynamics—the oppression of women and gender transgressors. In this way (and many others), transpeople have a stake in feminist change, regardless of gender identity. Illuminating the structural inequalities that underlie individual negotiations of "the bathroom question" bring this area of common interest to light.

ANXIETY AND HEALTH

Another pressing consequence of bathroom conflict for transpeople is a detrimental effect on their health and well-being. For those who have experienced or anticipate bathroom harassment, avoiding this space altogether might seem like the best, however inadequate, option. Kyle, a probation officer who openly transitioned in his workplace, explained, "I'm uncomfortable [using the men's room] because I'm afraid they're going to be thinking I'm looking at them or something like that. . . . It was easier for me to drive home and use the restroom than go through the mindfuck of going in the bathroom every day." Rather than use the bathroom in his workplace, Kyle tried to avoid relieving himself during work hours. When the need was too great, he would surreptitiously drive home to use his own bathroom out of fear of potential bathroom harassment.

Cory, an office assistant, worked in a building where he identified himself as a man to some and as a woman to others (he was in the process of transition and had a gender-ambiguous presentation). This situation made his choice of bathroom even trickier. When asked how he negotiated this dilemma, he responded, "It depends on the day, especially on how well I can pass that day. . . . Either way, I'll freak people out. . . . I find the one where there's no one there." This process entailed checking multiple bathrooms on multiple floors, each time risking being "caught" making a transgressive bathroom choice by coworkers. Kyle concurred, "[When I can't wait to drive home], I strategically learned to use the bathroom at certain times, and keep track of people and know when they're going in, that kind of thing. I still kind of hesitate when I get to the door."

For transpeople like Kyle and Cory, avoiding or sneaking into the bathroom were daily considerations. Such surreptitiousness can take its toll on one's physical and mental health. While none of my participants directly discussed the physical health implications of this inconvenience, medical research shows that withholding urination can be detrimental to urinary tract health. For example, primary and secondary school teachers suffer from a higher prevalence of lower urinary tract infections because of limited bathroom breaks in their workday (Masfety et al. 2006; Liao et al. 2007). Accordingly, bathroom conflicts are not just an interactional nuisance; they can have serious health consequences for transpeople. These health consequences should be recognized as legitimate considerations in workplace negotiations of bathroom use by transpeople.

RESISTING UNSATISFACTORY POLICY DECISIONS

While company policy decisions do go a long way in determining "the bathroom question," I found that transpeople themselves took an active role in negotiating this conflict, often through resistance to official decisions. It is crucial to recognize this subversion and its role in shaping gendered workplace interactions. This resistance represents a form of everyday activism that has the potential to challenge their co-worker's ideas about gender as well as the gendered divisions of workplace spaces.

Like others, Kurt found it stigmatizing to use a single-stall bathroom at his job in construction material distribution. Although he was asked to use a designated private bathroom after he transitioned on the job, he resisted and used the men's bathroom instead. When asked why, he said, "Because I want to be accepted, I just want to be—there's no reason to go to a separate one." This form of quiet resistance did little to challenge coworkers and workplace policy, but it did protect his feelings of gendered authenticity, the feelings of sincerity and legitimacy of transgender identity and expression, in a workplace that he felt did not recognize and support his gender identity. In this way, his decisions are an important source of resistance that deserve acknowledgment.

Laura, a call center supervisor, also rebelled against her workplace's suggestion that she use the nursing mother's bathroom. She explained:

> I was happy to [use the nursing mothers room], but when it's got someone in there who's going to be in there twenty minutes, don't expect me to stand here and dance in the hallway. And so after a while—and I don't know how long it was—but I let it go until about the third time, and that's when I went in and said, "Y'all do what you want to do, but I'm not doing this anymore. Somebody else has the issue, tell them to go use it. There's nine bathrooms in here, and I work in this back corner so they can go to the other bathroom if it bothers them." And that was the end of that.

By openly refusing her workplace's decision to relegate her to segregated bathroom space, Laura challenged the idea that employers are the sole arbiters of spatial decision making. She also reversed the idea that the comfort of fellow employees should be the primary concern in these decision-making processes. Instead, Laura claimed access to the bathrooms that would allow her to feel comfortable and experience a less interrupted workday. As a result, her workplace changed the bathroom policy and allowed Laura (and, presumably, future trans employees) access to the bathroom of their choice.

Stories like those of Kurt and Laura show signs of creativity and adaptation by transpeople, with affirming consequences in feelings of authenticity, acceptance, and comfort at work. For this reason, it is important to highlight these moments of resistance to show how transpeople play an active role in negotiating the terms of gendered space at work. Yet it is not enough to rely on individual strategies of compromise or refusal. As Jackie's multiple firings poignantly suggest, these strategies can backfire, leaving trans workers vulnerable to harassment and job termination. In particular, these strategies might be contingent upon occupational culture (for example, how "flexible" a workplace is with its policies) and the trans employee's location in the organizational hierarchy (notably, Laura had considerably more workplace clout as a tenured supervisor than did Jackie, a floor representative). Such factors might greatly affect the power of the individual worker to successfully resist workplace mandates. Accordingly, it is crucial to interrogate not just the actions of individuals but also the gendered hierarchies that structural arrangements of work maintain.

Discussion and Conclusion

According to the lived experience of the transpeople interviewed for this research, bathrooms have significant representational power. For these workers, negotiation of "the bathroom question" can affect their senses of authenticity, community, and acceptance. The symbolic meaning of bathrooms for these individuals demonstrates the power of bathroom interactions for shaping gendered workplace experience. While the spatial organization of bathrooms is often considered "natural," I have argued here that the organization of bathroom space is socially constructed and contestable, as the transpeople in this research indicate through their resistance to workplace bathroom policies and arrangements. How organizations address "the bathroom question" can support transpeople's chosen identities and imbue them with a greater sense of gender authenticity or it can refute their agency as gendered citizens.

At the same time that I want to highlight how "the bathroom question" affects the workplace experiences of individual transpeople, I would also argue that it carries an even greater significance. Trans- and gender-nonconforming people disrupt the taken-for-granted quality of the division of the social spaces of bathrooms through gender transition or transgressive appearance. As such, their experiences are key to challenging what Goffman (1963) refers to as "folk practices" that maintain the gender status quo. These experiences suggest that the bathroom responses offered by most of these transpeople's workplaces promoted a hierarchy of legitimacy and acceptance wherein gender-conforming, heterosexual cismen and ciswomen (or non-trans-identified people) accrue privilege. Their concerns and their spatial freedoms were privileged while the concerns and locations of others were marginalized.

Feminist researchers have long claimed that women's workplace progress suffers from gendered exclusionary practices at work (Bird 1996; Kanter 1977; Martin 2003; Pierce 1995; Roth 2006; Williams 1995). When we consider the experiences of trans- and gender-nonconforming people, we expand our understanding of the implications of gendered space to include discrimination and disadvantage against gender-nonconforming individuals. Work organizations that rigidly enforce the organization of private space in ways such as those described earlier perpetuate sexist, homophobic, and transphobic hierarchies.

Although the organization of bathrooms is undoubtedly problematic for transpeople, and, I argue, all people disadvantaged by our sex/gender/sexuality system, it is difficult to recommend a viable solution. As this research demonstrates, there are several possible bathroom arrangements for an individual undergoing gender transition at work. These arrangements have unequal implications for trans workers, who can feel either included or isolated by their workplace's decisions about bathrooms. These feelings are mitigated, in part, by worker status and gender presentation; more class-privileged trans workers and those who appeared more gender-normative often experienced more positive bathroom transitions.

While solutions to "the bathroom question" should be evaluated according to the context and preferences of individual trans workers, the participants in this project tended to favor a shared unisex bathroom system over other possibilities. Accordingly, this chapter recommends a movement to gender-nonspecific bathrooms as a way of supporting trans and gender-nonconforming workers. Such an arrangement has the added promise of challenging gender-segregated space in the workplace, which has the potential of renegotiating gender arrangements more generally. Workplaces could look to the spatial organization of institutions in other countries, some of which already use nongendered bathroom spaces.

Such a massive reorganization would require significant time, money, and most importantly, cultural validation. This is not simply a matter of raising awareness and ignoring the prejudices of individual workers. In a culture of violence against women, women possess a valid fear of integrating bathroom spaces. Overhauling bathrooms in a way that would not disadvantage women would require significant social and material change. While this solution is discouraging for the immediate project of trans-inclusive bathrooms, it underscores the importance of joining trans and feminist activists to achieve their common interests of gender equality. Promoting nongendered bathrooms is both a trans and a feminist activist project. Such a system would avoid forcing gender-variant workers into a false binary, and at the same time challenge other workers to confront their taken-for-granted ideas about gender and private spaces.

NOTES

1. The term *transwoman* is generally used to refer to someone designated "male" at birth who identifies as a woman, and, *transman* is generally used to refer to someone designated "female" at birth who identifies as a man. *Genderqueer* usually refers to someone who identifies as neither man nor woman but as belonging to the undefined space between these two gender categories. I use the term *transpeople* here to refer to the spectrum of trans-identified people, including transwomen, transmen, and genderqueers.
2. All names of participants in this chapter are pseudonyms, used to protect the confidentiality of respondents.
3. I use the gendered pronouns *he* and *his* when referring to John, in accordance with his stated pronoun preferences.
4. Transgender Day of Remembrance, "2009," International Transgender Day of Remembrance, *www.transgenderdor.org/?page_id=555*, accessed May 1, 2010.

REFERENCES

Acker, Joan. 1990. "Hierarchies, Jobs, Bodies: A Theory of Gendered Organizations." *Gender and Society* 4 (2): 139–58.

Bird, Sharon R. 1996. "Welcome to the Men's Club: Homosociality and the Maintenance of Hegemonic Masculinity." *Gender and Society* 10 (2): 120–32.

Bornstein, Kate. 1995. *Gender Outlaw: On Men, Women, and the Rest of Us*. New York: Random House.

Butler, Judith. 1990. *Gender Trouble: Feminism and the Subversion of Identity*. New York: Routledge.

———. 2004. *Undoing Gender*. New York: Routledge.

Connell, Catherine. 2010. "Doing, Undoing, or Redoing Gender? Learning from Transpeople." *Gender and Society* 24 (1): 31–55.

Dozier, Raine. 2005. "Beards, Breasts, and Bodies: Doing Sex in the Gendered World." *Gender and Society* 19 (3): 297–316.

Goffman, Erving. 1963. *Stigma: Notes on the Management of Spoiled Identity*. Englewood Cliffs, NJ: Prentice-Hall.

———. 1977. "The Arrangement between the Sexes." *Theory and Society* 4:301–31.

Humphreys, Laud. 1970. *Tearoom Trade: Impersonal Sex in Public Places*. New Brunswick, NJ: Aldine Transaction.

Kanter, Rosabeth M. 1977. *Men and Women of the Corporation*. New York: Basic Books.

Liao, Yuan-Mei, Molly Dougherty, Paul Biemer, Alice Boyington, Chin-Tai Liao, Mary Palmer, and Mary Lynn. 2007. "Prevalence of Lower Urinary Tract Symptoms among

Female Elementary School Teachers in Taipei." *International Urogynecology Journal* 18 (10): 1151–61.

Lorber, Judith. 1993. "Believing Is Seeing: Biology as Ideology." *Gender and Society* 7 (4): 568–81.

Martin, Patricia Yancey. 2003. "'Said and Done' versus 'Saying and Doing': Gendering Practices, Practicing Gender at Work." *Gender and Society* 17 (3): 342–66.

Masfety, Viviane, Christine Dedieu, Carmen Seidel, Elena Nerriere, and Christine Chee. 2006. "Do Teachers Have More Health Problems? Results from a French Cross-Sectional Survey." *BMC Public Health* 6 (1): 101.

Namaste, Viviane. 2000. *Invisible Lives: The Erasure of Transsexual and Transgender People*. Chicago: University of Chicago Press.

Pierce, Jennifer. 1995. *Gender Trials: Emotional Lives in Contemporary Law Firms*. Berkeley: University of California Press.

Roth, Louise Marie. 2006. *Selling Women Short: Gender and Money on Wall Street*. Princeton, NJ: Princeton University Press.

Schilt, Kristin. 2006. "Just One of the Guys? How Transmen Make Gender Visible at Work." *Gender and Society* 20 (4): 465–90.

Stone, Sandy. 1991. "The "Empire" Strikes Back: A Posttranssexual Manifesto." In *Body Guards: The Cultural Politics of Gender Ambiguity*, ed. Julia Epstein and Kristina Straub, 280–304. New York: Routledge.

Williams, Christine L. 1995. *Still a Man's World*. Berkeley: University of California Press.

14

The Everyday Resistance
of Vegetarianism
Samantha Kwan and Louise Marie Roth

> Tell me what you eat, and I will tell you who you are.
>   Jean Anthelme Brillat-Savarin

Are we really what we eat? What is the relationship between the things we consume and the politics we practice? For example, while vegetarianism may be connected to obvious ethical considerations such as animal cruelty, what is its relationship to seemingly unrelated systems of power such as gender conformity and consumerism? Addressing this question raises new ideas about how individuals embody ideologies and how the body can be a site of everyday resistance.

Symbolic Boundaries, the Profane, and Embodied Protest

In voluntarist market societies, individuals use symbolic boundaries to present themselves and judge the trustworthiness and character of others (Swidler 2001). Consumption, whether of food, music, or clothing, demarcates symbolic boundaries and consequently plays a central role in creating distinctions between groups (Bourdieu 1984; Bryson 1996; Griswold 2004; Lamont 1992; Lamont and Fournier 1992). For example, individuals use food consumption to draw moral and social boundaries, as observed in the rejection of eating as a sensual pleasure, the vilification of body fat as signifying a lack of control, and the exaltation of food denial as a virtue (Bordo 1993; Guthman 2003).

Some identities, such as vegetarian, virgin, and atheist, are based on what a person does not do rather than what he or she does. These identities express a moral stance and embody a symbolic boundary by opposing a conventional practice. They are also unconventional identities, so that "not doing" certain socially significant actions can be used to create an unconventional self (Mullaney 2001). Because the consumption of meat is customary, except in relatively small spiritual communities, its rejection in favor of a vegetarian diet is socially significant (Beardsworth and Keil 1992). Secular vegetarians are usually "converts" from a previous meat-eating status, and so their vegetarian identity typically results from conscious reflection about and rejection of customary dietary habits (Beardsworth and Keil 1992).

Because of the source of their vegetarian identity, vegetarians may reflect on and question what many individuals take for granted. Within this worldview, meat consumption may take on important symbolic meanings because, through a process of "incorporation," food has both physiological and symbolic effects; that is, individuals absorb nutrients, vitamins, and minerals into their bloodstreams, but they also assimilate the food's symbolic properties (Fischler 1988). Thus, a vegetarian lifestyle may be part of an ongoing protest against meat's symbolic properties. In this way, it is a "negative cult" based on rites of abstinence (Durkheim [1912] 1995). Negative cults establish moral boundaries by defining certain acts as sacred or profane. Accordingly, ethical vegetarians often think that meat "contaminates" vegetarian food (Rozin, Markwith, and Stoess 1997). Here, meat represents the symbolically impure, dangerous, or profane (Douglas 1966; Durkheim [1912] 1995), the abuse of animals and the environment, and hierarchy in human civilizations (Eder 1996; Twigg 1983).

Building on these theoretical insights, this chapter focuses on secular vegetarians. We argue that this population sets a symbolic cultural boundary that distinguishes them from mainstream society and, in doing so, embody a form of everyday resistance to mainstream Western cultural hegemony—the systemic power that is embedded in culture and institutions and is produced and reproduced in everyday interactions (Ewick and Silbey 2003; Foucault 1978; Gramsci 1971). Resistance to hegemony occurs when subordinated individuals make conscious efforts to challenge power relations that are taken as established facts. Relatively powerless individuals use everyday acts of resistance to protect their interests and identities within power structures that subordinate them (Ewick and Silbey 2003; Scott 1990). For example, counter-hegemonic discourses or "hidden transcripts" are the language that oppressed people use behind the scenes to resist domination and to subvert the legitimacy of the status quo (Scott 1990). Similarly, protest groups use "repertoires of contention," sets of tactics and strategies that they develop to produce strategic acts of resistance (Taylor and Van Dyke 2004; Tilly 1995).

While scholars have analyzed small acts of resistance using language, narratives, "repertoires of contention," or "counter-hegemonic discourse" (Ewick and Silbey 2003; Scott 1990; Tilly 1995), the ways that subordinated groups resist hegemony through bodily practices have yet to be fully explored. Resistance can be literally embodied through practices that establish symbolic boundaries between the bodies of those who hold social power and those who resist or negate it (Eder 1996). Food consumption can serve this exact purpose. We argue that vegetarianism is a bodily practice that some women use to resist taken-for-granted aspects of Western culture. As such, it constitutes a form of counter-hegemonic embodiment.

We define *counter-hegemonic embodiment* as active resistance against institutional power through resistant bodily practices and abstention from normalizing bodily practices. Systems of power such as male dominance, hetero/sexism, and racism encourage bodily discipline in the service of conformity and normalization (Foucault 1977, 1978). Individuals who abstain from these forms of bodily discipline symbolically reject these forms of institutional power. Their bodily practices do more than symbolize resistance to the status quo—they actually embody it. Counter-hegemonic embodiment thus resembles repertoires of contention because both are "learned, shared, and acted out through a relatively deliberate process of choice" (Tilly 1995, 42). They both also make claims on other people's interests that primarily challenge those who subscribe to the dominant politics. Yet they are different; counter-hegemonic embodiment does not work through organized collective action but instead writes protest directly on the individual body.

Methods and Sample

We conducted a qualitative study involving in-depth interviews with eighty-five women in a medium-size city in the southwestern United States.[1] The interviews were designed to capture women's appearance-related practices, or beauty work, including food consumption. We used a purposive snowball sample because we were interested in exploring variation in beauty work at the intersections of race, ethnicity, and sexual orientation. This "theoretical sampling" yielded the comparison groups that we desired (Glaser and Strauss 1967). Semi-structured interviews lasted an average of one hour and allowed respondents to elaborate about their experiences, feelings, and interpretations. We asked respondents extensive questions about eating habits, including reasons for eating the way they did. Analysis of these data revealed many women's reasons for avoiding meat along with a connection between political ideologies and vegetarianism that had not been previously theorized. Because the study was designed to examine women's beauty work practices, it does not permit us to determine whether similar processes are evident among vegetarian men.

The average age of the entire sample was 27.6 (ranging from 22 to 35), with a mean household income of approximately thirty-two thousand dollars. Fifty-six respondents (66 percent) identified as white, fourteen (17 percent) as Latina, and fifteen (17 percent) as non-Hispanic minorities (black, South and East Asian, and multiracial). These women were fairly well educated; about 70 percent had a bachelor's degree or higher. Additionally, fifty (59 percent) of the women identified as heterosexual, fifteen (18 percent) as bisexual, and twenty (20 percent) as lesbian. In the entire sample, seventeen women were strict vegetarians who ate no meat or meat products and fifteen claimed to be vegetarian but made exceptions for fish or, more rarely, poultry. We refer to this group as "vegetarian-identified" because they self-identified as vegetarians. For the purposes of our analysis, we often group together strict vegetarians and vegetarian-identified women and compare them to nonvegetarians, though we acknowledge that some vegetarians would dislike being grouped with pesco-vegetarians and occasional meat eaters.

In sum, in our sample, thirty-two women (38 percent) were vegetarian or vegetarian-identified. In comparison, a 2006 Vegetarian Resource Group survey (Stahler 2006) indicates that 2.3 percent of the U.S. population are vegetarian (individuals who never eat meat, poultry, fish, or seafood), with 3 percent of women and 2 percent of men being vegetarian. In national samples, many vegetarians do not eat meat for religious-cultural reasons (and thus may have never consumed meat). All of the vegetarians in our sample, however, had converted to vegetarianism from a previous meat-eating status, thereby permitting the development of a grounded theory of secular vegetarianism.

Findings

Vegetarianism and Gender Nonconformity

We uncovered a compelling relationship between vegetarianism and gender non-conformity, concerns for animal welfare and the environment, and other critical social perspectives. First, the majority of women in our sample who identified as vegetarians also identified as feminists. It is noteworthy that the interviews also revealed a strong relationship between, on the one hand, sexual orientation and, on the other, vegetarian identity. Nearly two-thirds of the vegetarians identified as lesbian or bisexual.

For many vegetarian respondents, the exposure to feminist ideas led to critical reflection on power relations. This exposure typically occurred in college, coinciding at times with their conversion to a vegetarian-identified status. For example, Celeste is a married, heterosexual, white woman, a strict vegetarian, and a self-professed feminist.[2] She felt unattractive as a child because she aspired to feminine ideals but felt that she did not measure up to the portrayals of women in fairy tales and the mass media. She even lived in a conventional sorority in college but became relaxed about her appearance after she was exposed to feminist theory. Here, Celeste's feminist orientation is evident:

> I'm not particularly interested with appearing attractive and that's fine with me. I've gotten older and probably more radical as a feminist. I am at this point in my life not really an object of the male gaze and I like that. It's like you can fly under radar a little bit. You know what I mean. Especially working too with—I don't work with battered women as so much as I work for them—and just seeing how many women suffer at men's hands and so whether men take notice of me favorably doesn't matter diddly-squat to me right now.

Celeste and her partner converted from being "big meat-eaters" to being vegetarians. When asked why they became vegetarians, Celeste, like most respondents, cited multiple factors, including a critical reflection of hegemonic practices. "It was," she said, "a combination of factors. We started educating ourselves about factory farming. You know, from the perspective of causing suffering to other beings, as well as health." Celeste's criticism of patriarchal social relations thus came hand in hand with her rejection of other hegemonic practices, such as agribusiness.

Many of the vegetarian women offered a feminist critique of mainstream cultural images of beauty as unhealthy or oppressive or both. In reference to conformist beauty ideals, Angela, a white heterosexual vegetarian, said, "I just realized that it was part of playing into this whole society thing of how women are depicted and how women have to be dressed up all the time and always presentable. And I just decided that that wasn't something I wanted to play into." According to the vegetarian respondents who identified as feminist, women should resist the imperatives of popular culture as much as possible and recognize that they exist to support capitalist greed and not women's self-esteem. Angela's decision to opt out of the beauty imperative was another way to embody resistance to this objectionable culture.

Gender nonconformity among vegetarian respondents is not only evident through the sustained feminist critique of patriarchal relations. It is evident also in the previously noted high rate of vegetarianism among sexual minorities, along with unconventional childhood gender expressions among heterosexual vegetarian respondents. Specifically, over a third of the heterosexual vegetarian respondents described themselves as "tomboys," as having an unconventional gender expression, or as not feeling "feminine" or "fit[ting] in" during childhood and adolescence. For example, Zoe, a vegetarian-identified white lesbian, said she was a tomboy as a child and that she felt most comfortable wearing baseball caps. She described herself as fashion-challenged throughout her childhood and often rebuffed her mother's attempt to get her to wear feminine clothing or braid her hair. Here she discusses how she felt she did not fit in with her peers and was oblivious to social norms:

> I felt like I had no way to fit in. Whatever I tried, I didn't really get it right. . . .
> I remember getting hair under my arms and just being stoked about it. More
> excited than anything else. You know, the first day of school I get to show it off.
> I wore a pink muscle to school with my baseball hat. And just massive social
> rejection. Everyone already knew that was not the thing to do except me. I had no
> clue.

In comparison, many nonvegetarians did not consciously identify with feminist politics and were more likely to consume mainstream media. For example, Marisol, a Latina homemaker who was not a vegetarian, described why she liked *Cosmopolitan* and *Glamour* magazines: "They show how to feel good about yourself. What to do to keep—to try new ideas to keep your husband happy and new clothing that could probably help or diets that could help. I've tried all kinds of diets, let me tell you." Very dissatisfied with her weight, and living in a traditional working-class Mexican family, Marisol largely accepted cultural ideals of beauty and the messages about how to attain them. Other nonvegetarian women also consumed these media more frequently than nonvegetarians, even if they did not accept their messages wholesale. In fact, while few women were fully accepting of mainstream cultural messages about women and appearance, nonvegetarians were less likely than vegetarians to articulate a sustained rejection of these messages or to abstain from bodily discipline that was designed to attain mainstream beauty ideals. Alternately, feminist denunciations of portrayals of women's bodies accompanied vegetarianism, in what some have described as "feminist vegetarianism."[3]

The connection between feminism and vegetarianism is well recognized in the existing literature. Carol J. Adams (1990, 1998) views vegetarianism as an essential feminist practice and draws an analogy between the oppression of women and animal exploitation, concluding that women, like animals, are caught in a cycle of objectification, fragmentation, and consumption. Additionally, Adams (1998) suggests a more general parallel between eating meat and oppressive constructions of masculinity, whereby "'meat' is claimed as 'real food for real people'" (68) and is also equated with the masculine. Josephine Donovan's (1990) work has explored extensively the relationship between feminism and vegetarianism, arguing that animal rights, while aptly building on the work of the natural rights and utilitarian philosophers, must also be grounded in a cultural feminist ethic—one that stems from women's relational culture of caring.

In contrast to these claims about the symbiosis between feminism and vegetarianism, however, our vegetarian feminist respondents did not make an explicit connection between feminism and vegetarianism. Rather, they seemed to embrace a larger package of counter-hegemonic ideologies and practices, implicitly supporting and embodying beliefs that reject systems of power and hierarchy such as male dominance.

Animal Welfare and Environmentalism

Along with their feminist orientation, our vegetarian respondents expressed an obvious concern for the welfare of animals. Wendy, a white lesbian and organic foods consumer, provided an explanation that was typical of vegetarian respondents: "It started out as a compassion thing [and] the main reason is still compassion and animal rights." For decades a discourse of animal rights and welfare has defined vegetarianism as a way to protest the oppression of animals (Midgley 1983; Regan 1983; Singer 1976; Tester 1991). A majority of both the strict vegetarian and the vegetarian-identified women interviewed articulated the centrality of animal welfare in their decision to avoid meat consumption, mentioning the inhumane treatment of animals, animal rights, and a love of animals. While vegetarian respondents often mentioned the health benefits of vegetarianism, many adopted this vegetarian lifestyle to protest the unjust treatment of animals in industrial societies through factory farming, inhumane housing and slaughtering conditions, and hormone injections. As Elsa, a Latina who was vegetarian-identified, bluntly stated, "Just the abuse of animals and the hormones freaks me out!"

Scholars have found that one of the strongest predictors of vegetarianism is the belief that it is beneficial to the environment (Beardsworth and Keil 1992; Gossard and York 2003; Kalof et al. 1999). Many vegetarians object to the environmentally harmful practices of agribusiness that pollute the air and lead to the destruction of the rainforest (Beardsworth and Keil 1992). These positions were also voiced by our vegetarian respondents who indicated that, alongside animal rights, environmentalism was a primary reason for food meat avoidance. As Jaimie, a white vegetarian-identified lesbian, said, "I think it's better for the environment. I think the lower you eat on the food chain the better it is." Similarly, when asked about her reasons for being a vegetarian, Josee, a white lesbian, responded, "I guess social reasons as far as how much energy it takes to make meat instead of like grain." As others have discussed, livestock require more water and cropland than would be used to produce an equivalent amount of plant-based food for human consumption, so that less harm would be done to the environment and fewer people would go hungry if animals were not farmed for their meat (Lappé et al. 1998; Lappé and Lappé 2002; Shiva 2000).

A Critical Worldview

Moral protest among vegetarian respondents extended beyond resistance to gender conformity and the oppression of animals and the environment. In our sample, vegetarians were committed to similar reflection in many other aspects of their lives, including their jobs (e.g., several worked in social services) and other consumption patterns (e.g., consuming only "not animal tested," "cruelty-free" products, and "eating organic"). We coded respondents for their anticonsumerist, anticonformist, or antiwar views, including those who described themselves as "punk," "radical," or "alternative," or who strongly criticized popular culture.

A majority of vegetarian participants adopted what we label a "critical worldview." For example, Naomi, a strict-vegetarian white lesbian with multiple tattoos and piercings, talked extensively about her activism and critical perspective. Regarding what she thought her appearance said about her, she replied, "I do think it says a lot about personal politics, which is probably the main reason that I have the appearance that I do. [It's] the emphasis on my personal politics—just like the whole punk rock thing of radical activism. It's not always practiced but it's certainly preached by punk rockers. And rejection of mainstream culture and norms." Naomi grew up surrounded by what she called "the granola aesthetic," which she rejected in favor of punk. She infused her personal politics into her outward appearance, repeatedly referring to the punk rock aesthetic and activism. In fact, Naomi's personal politics pervaded her life as well as her appearance and was apparent in her rationale for being a vegetarian. Exemplifying the many reasons for her vegetarianism, along with overlapping political ideologies, Naomi said, "The vegetarian thing is kind of complicated, because it's a lot of different factors. It's partly because I don't really like meat, but also a lot of the ethical reasons, plus environmental concerns, and animal rights concerns, and also health."

Similarly, Brandy, a white bisexual vegetarian, grew up as a tomboy. After she experienced power conflicts and control issues with her mother's romantic partners, she became reflective about the oppression of women and capitalist oppression. She expressed concern about the use of sweatshop labor to produce clothing and described shopping at secondhand stores as a strategy to opt out of the consumerist imperative: "I think that we can use old things instead of always buying everything new. And all that sweatshop labor, like in developing countries, that's an issue for me, and you cannot find anything that is not made by like some struggling Asian or Malaysian culture. It's frightening." Brandy rejected global capitalism and the exploitation of human labor and challenged the morality of industrial practices. She also reflected on her bodily practices, leading her to reject forms of bodily discipline that required mass-marketed and synthetically produced products, mass-produced clothing, or the products of mass-scale farming. When asked why she is a vegetarian and eats organic foods, she said, "Mostly for animal rights and justice issues. Factory farming, agricultural practices, all that I'd say. I guess it's also a spiritual thing, spiritual reasons. . . . I'm not really comfortable taking the life of an animal, or the life of anything. I mean, I even release roaches outside. The only things that I really kill are mosquitoes."

In sum, the rejection of meat accompanies the eschewing of a whole host of hegemonic practices and institutions, including consumerism, conservatism, and the culture of killing and exploitation that they represent, as well as sexism and heteronormative beauty imperatives. This connection between vegetarianism and the rejection of these systems of power is consistent with previous findings that individuals who hold more traditional values are less likely to be vegetarian than others (Dietz et al. 1995) and that vegetarianism underwrites a set of oppositional political, aesthetic, and moral perceptions (Twigg 1983).

The idea that one can embody a moral resistance identity by avoiding meat and the exploitation that it symbolizes may also explain why some respondents who occasionally eat fish and free-range chicken were vegetarian-identified. It may also explain why a small number of nonvegetarians said that they were not vegetarian but discussed at length their minimal meat consumption or the fact that they were "almost" vegetarian. The desire to identify as vegetarian suggests that respondents deem meat avoidance a moral and laudable stance, defined in opposition to oppressive hegemonic institutions and practices.

Discussion and Conclusion

In this chapter we explore the link between secular vegetarianism and the rejection of less obvious systems of power. Like Ross Haenfler's (2006) Straight Edge hardcore punk youth who practice various forms of "not doings," such as refraining from casual sex, alcohol, tobacco, and (since the late 1990s) the consumption of all animal products, our vegetarian respondents practice a host of counter-hegemonic ideologies that fit into a coherent moral and political worldview. As others have found, important forms of everyday resistance exist that are often unrecognizable and undetectable within the systems of power that they resist (Ewick and Silbey 2003; Scott 1990). By embracing vegetarianism, vegetarian respondents embodied resistance to perceived injustice, even though their vegetarianism was individual and largely invisible; still they embody an awareness of how power infuses social relationships and institutions.

The rejection of meat, including its symbolic meaning, may be a result of a process of critical reflection on the status quo, particularly by respondents who felt that they did not fit in with normative prescriptions, including those about their bodies. Exposure to critical ideas particularly during college may have encouraged further reflection on conventional norms and practices. For women who were vegetarians or vegetarian-identified, the rejection of the status quo was then literally embodied in their rejection of meat and other normalizing bodily practices.

This critical reflection may explain in part the high numbers of vegetarians identified as lesbian, bisexual, or gender nonconformists. This prevalence may be a result of a reflection process stemming from not fitting in, along with socialization in peer networks that directly or indirectly encourage reflection on the status quo. Lesbian and bisexual women must, for example, reflect on what is taken for granted in sexuality that may make them more likely to reflect on other taken-for-granted aspects of life. As such, sexual minorities may be more likely to reject a status quo that rejects them, and, for some, this rejection extends to the rejection of dominant food practice such as meat consumption. Their dietary choice is thus grounded in the experience of nonconformity and "otherness." This mechanism of extension merits further exploration; while we observe that certain resistant identities cohere, it is not clear why rejection of one hegemonic discourse leads to the rejection of another, such as vegetarianism, that is then literally embodied. Further analysis should also flesh out the temporal order of the rejection of mainstream discourses.

While the rejection of conventional practices can be seen as a form of self-policing and discipline, this policing departs from the self-regulation that takes place in the name of compliance and the creation of docile bodies (Foucault 1977). To the contrary, the conversion to secular vegetarianism encapsulates resistance to a variety of mainstream practices and belief systems. Self-discipline here thus embodies a negation of social power, inequality, and hierarchy (Eder 1996), expressing one's moral and political position and constructing a symbolic boundary that defines a person's moral character (Bourdieu 1984; Griswold 2004; Lamont and Fournier 1992). Furthermore, because resistance entails a self-conscious awareness of the ways that social interactions are infused with power and the subsequent rejection of the status quo, this reflection may be essential to the emergence of vegetarianism as counter-hegemonic embodiment (Ewick and Silbey 2003). Not everyone who reflects on and rejects, say, gender norms, male dominance, or consumerism becomes a vegetarian, but our data suggest that these ideologies and practices do tend to cohere.

The relationship between moral-political beliefs and food consumption practices is somewhat unsurprising because of the importance of food in everyday life. Food consumption is a social and symbolic event; families' togetherness rituals are almost always food centered, and what people eat is highly influenced by their culture (DeVault 1991; Gabbacia 1998; Gans 1979). Socialization through food consumption also profoundly affects the appearance, health, and functionality of the body, which is inextricably linked to identity (Grosz 1994). Moreover, as food production and distribution become increasingly global, the symbolic dimensions of food take on even greater meaning and importance. In this new political-economic climate, it is possible that organizations too adopt a "not doing" identity through their approach to food processes. How might, say, local farmers, cooperatives, or restaurants resist global hegemonic forces through everyday resistance? Indeed, embodied protest through food consumption practices calls for continued exploration in individual lives and on a broader organizational level.

NOTES

1. Mary Nell Trautner, Rebecca Sager, and Rachael Neal assisted with data collection. We list the authors in alphabetical order to represent equal contribution.
2. All names are pseudonyms.
3. While we observed a relationship between feminism and vegetarianism, the existence of omnivorous feminists and feminists who practice and advocate responsible meat consumption reveals that these two ideologies do not always come together. Some feminists have even argued that ethical vegetarianism discriminates against women, infants, and other cultures by presuming a male physiological norm (see George 1994).

REFERENCES

Adams, Carol J. 1990. *The Sexual Politics of Meat: A Feminist-Vegetarian Critical Theory*. New York: Continuum.

_____. 1998. "Eating Animals." In *Eating Culture*, ed. Ron Scapp and Brian Seitz, 60–75. New York: State University of New York Press.

Beardsworth, Alan, and Teresa Keil. 1992. "The Vegetarian Option: Varieties, Conversions, Motives, and Careers." *Sociological Review* 40 (2): 253–93.

Bordo, Susan. 1993. *Unbearable Weight: Feminism, Western Culture, and the Body*. Berkeley: University of California Press.

Bourdieu, Pierre. 1984. *Distinction: A Social Critique of the Judgement of Taste*. Trans. Richard Nice. Cambridge, MA: Harvard University Press.

Bryson, Bethany. 1996. "'Anything but Heavy Metal': Symbolic Exclusion and Musical Dislikes." *American Sociological Review* 61 (5): 884–99.

DeVault, Marjorie L. 1991. *Feeding the Family: The Social Organization of Caring as Gendered Work*. Chicago: University of Chicago Press.

Dietz, Thomas, Anne Stirling Frisch, Linda Kalof, Paul C. Stern, and Gregory A. Guagnano. 1995. "Values and Vegetarianism: An Exploratory Analysis." *Rural Sociology* 60 (3): 533–42.

Donovan, Josephine. 1990. "Animal Rights and Feminist Theory." *Signs* 15 (2): 350–75.

Douglas, Mary. 1966. *Purity and Danger: An Analysis of Concepts of Pollution and Taboo*. Boston: Routledge and Kegan Paul.

Durkheim, Emile. (1912) 1995. *The Elementary Forms of Religious Life*. Trans. and with an introd. by Karen E. Fields. New York: Free Press.

Eder, Klaus. 1996. *The Social Construction of Nature: A Sociology of Ecological Enlightenment*. London: Sage.

Ewick, Patricia, and Susan Silbey. 2003. "Narrating Social Structure: Stories of Resistance to Legal Authority." *American Journal of Sociology* 108 (6): 1328–72.

Fischler, Claude. 1988. "Food, Self, and Identity." *Social Science Information* 27 (2): 275–92.

Foucault, Michel. 1977. *Discipline and Punish: The Birth of the Prison*. New York: Random House.

———. 1978. *History of Sexuality*. Vol. 1, *An Introduction*. New York: Pantheon Books.

Gabbacia, Donna R. 1998. *We Are What We Eat: Ethnic Food and the Making of Americans*. Cambridge, MA: Harvard University Press.

Gans, Herbert. 1979. "Symbolic Ethnicity: The Future of Ethnic Groups and Cultures in America." *Ethnic and Racial Studies* 2 (1): 1–20.

George, Kathryn Paxton. 1994. "Should Feminists Be Vegetarians?" *Signs* 19 (2): 405–34.

Glaser, Barney G., and Anselm L. Strauss. 1967. *The Discovery of Grounded Theory: Strategies for Qualitative Research*. Chicago: Aldine.

Gossard, Marcia Hill, and Richard York. 2003. "Social Structural Influences on Meat Consumption." *Human Ecology Review* 10 (1): 1–9.

Gramsci, Antonio. 1971. *Selections from the Prison Notebooks*. Ed. and trans. Quintin Hoare and Geoffrey Nowell-Smith. New York: International.

Griswold, Wendy. 2004. *Cultures and Societies in a Changing World*, 2nd ed. Thousand Oaks, CA: Pine Forge Press.

Grosz, Elizabeth. 1994. *Volatile Bodies: Toward a Corporeal Feminism*. Bloomington: Indiana University Press.

Guthman, Julie. 2003. "Fast Food / Organic Food: Reflexive Tastes and the Making of 'Yuppie Chow.'" *Social and Cultural Geography* 4 (1): 45–58.

Haenfler, Ross. 2006. *Straight Edge: Clean-Living Youth, Hardcore Punk, and Social Change*. New Brunswick, NJ: Rutgers University Press.

Kalof, Linda, Thomas Dietz, Paul C. Stern, and Gregory A. Guagnano. 1999. "Social Psychological and Structural Influences on Vegetarian Beliefs." *Rural Sociology* 64 (3): 500–11.

Lamont, Michèle. 1992. *Money, Morals, and Manners: The Culture of the French and the American Upper-Middle Class*. Chicago: University of Chicago Press.

Lamont, Michèle, and Marcel Fournier. 1992. *Cultivating Differences: Symbolic Boundaries and the Making of Inequality*. Chicago: University of Chicago Press.

Lappé, Frances Moore, Joseph Collins, Peter Rosset, and the Institute for Food and Development Policy. 1998. *World Hunger: Twelve Myths*. 2nd ed. New York: Grove Press.

Lappé, Frances Moore, and Anna Lappé. 2002. *Hope's Edge: The Next Diet for a Small Planet*. New York: Penguin Putnam.

Midgley, Mary. 1983. *Animals and Why They Matter*. Harmondsworth, UK: Penguin.

Mullaney, Jamie. 2001. "Like a Virgin: Temptation, Resistance, and the Construction of Identities Based on 'Not Doings.'" *Qualitative Sociology* 24 (1): 2–24.

Regan, Tom. 1983. *The Case for Animal Rights.* Berkeley: University of California Press.

Rozin, Paul, Maureen Markwith, and Caryn Stoess. 1997. "Moralization and Becoming a Vegetarian: The Transformation of Preferences into Values and the Recruitment of Disgust." *Psychological Science* 8 (2): 67–83.

Scott, James C. 1990. *Domination and the Arts of Resistance: Hidden Transcripts.* New Haven, CT: Yale University Press.

Shiva, Vandana. 2000. *Stolen Harvest.* Cambridge, MA: South End Press.

Singer, Peter. 1976. *Animal Liberation.* New York: Avon.

Stahler, Charles. 2006. "How Many Adults Are Vegetarian?" *Vegetarian Journal,* 4 (December 20), *www.vrg.org/journal/vj2006issue4/vj2006issue4poll.htm.*

Swidler, Ann. 2001. *Talk of Love: How Culture Matters.* Chicago: University of Chicago Press.

Taylor, Verta, and Nella Van Dyke. 2004. "'Get Up, Stand Up': Tactical Repertoires of Social Movements." In *The Blackwell Companion to Social Movements,* ed. David A. Snow, Sarah A. Soule, and Hanspeter Kriesi, 262–93. Malden, MA: Blackwell.

Tester, Keith. 1991. *Animals and Society: The Humanity of Animal Rights.* London: Routledge.

Tilly, Charles. 1995. *Popular Contention in Great Britain.* Cambridge, MA: Harvard University Press.

Twigg, Julia. 1983. "Vegetarianism and the Meanings of Meat." In *The Sociology of Food and Eating: Essays on the Sociological Significance of Food,* ed. Anne Murcott, 18–30. Aldershot, Hants, UK: Gower.

15

Menopausal and Misbehaving

When Women "Flash" in Front of Others

Heather E. Dillaway

Most of the time, the closest we come to seeing menopause in mainstream culture is in movies like *Calendar Girls*, a British comedy about a group of middle-aged women who decide to pose naked for a calendar, or *Something's Gotta Give*, a romantic comedy about midlife relationships. These movies include many jokes and innuendos but few direct references to menopause. Unless we are lucky enough to view the episode of the *Golden Girls* where Blanche laments being menopausal, or to enjoy *Menopause, the Musical*, a live comedy show about "the Change," we are not forced to acknowledge menopause as an everyday experience.

Menopause is the cessation of menstruation, which most women experience in their late forties or early fifties. Biomedical researchers have suggested that it is a "deficiency disease" and a time of negative change (Lyons and Griffin 2003). Feminist scholars, alternatively, suggest that menopause is a broad, biosocial transition with many bodily signs and symptoms that increasing numbers of women see as positive or neutral (Dillaway 2005; Lyons and Griffin 2003; Voda 1992). From a feminist perspective, women may view menopause as ushering in a good life stage, better and more carefree than the one before it, because it represents relief from the burdens of pregnancy, menstruation, and contraception. Nonetheless, feminist researchers have avoided in-depth empirical explorations of the bodily experience of menopause, as well as women's potential apprehensions and frustrations about this reproductive transition (Dillaway 2005; Koeske 1983).[1] Menopause as a bodily experience can be simultaneously positive, negative, or mixed in meaning, in different everyday contexts. Because some bodily signs of menopause can be very visible, we must think about how women experience their menopausal bodies in front of others.

One of the most commonly cited signs of menopause in the United States is the hot flash (or hot "flush" in Canadian or British terminology) (Ayers, Forshaw, and Hunter 2010; Kronenberg 1990). Approximately 70 percent of women in Europe and North America report this "vasomotor" symptom (Ayers, Forshaw, and Hunter 2010).[2] A sudden change in body temperature causes this sensation and the intensity and frequency of this bodily change varies from woman to woman (Kronenberg 1990). While biomedical studies describe the physiology of hot flashes, we do not know what individual women actually feel when hot flashes occur or how they affect their everyday lives. Because hot flashes can challenge norms about beauty and bodily control and alert others to women's menopausal status before women themselves are ready to disclose it, I use this chapter to explore women's narratives about how they negotiate hot flashes in front of others. I highlight whether, how, when, where, and around whom women might hide or embrace hot flashes and, ultimately, accommodate or resist cultural norms.

In the United States, the contemporary standard for female beauty dictates youth, whiteness, slenderness or thinness, and "no noticeable physical imperfections or disabilities" (Zones 2000, 91). In addition, visible alterations to appearance are "negative" or "deviant" because individuals (especially women) are supposed to be in control of their physical bodies at all times (K. A. Martin 2003; Zones 2000). Susan Wendell (1996, 93–94) suggests that, as a culture, we believe "it is possible [to] have the bodies we want" and to prevent, mask, or postpone bodily change, illness, disability, aging, and death. Presumably, one's loss of bodily control can be prevented if one only tries hard enough, as evidenced by our cultural obsessions with diet and exercise programs, symptom relief medications, anti-aging products, and self-help literature (Calasanti 2005; Dworkin and Wachs 2009; Lyons and Griffin 2003; Wendell 1996). As a result, a body that randomly leaks (e.g., sweats) or changes color (e.g., becomes red or flushed) will be seen as "uncontrollable," "disruptive," and "misbehaving" (Epstein 1995; E. Martin 1992; K. A. Martin 2003; Wendell 1996). Individuals experiencing these bodily changes may try to "assimilate in order to avoid unwanted attention or to attract desired attention" (Zones 2000, 87).

Theorizing the actions that women take in the face of gendered cultural norms and social structures, Kandiyoti (1988, 274) suggests, "Women strategize within a set of concrete constraints. . . . Different forms of patriarchy present women with distinct 'rules of the game' and call for different strategies to maximize security and optimize life options with varying potential for active or passive resistance in the face of oppression." Thus, as women learn about and interact with gendered cultural norms, they choose varied "strategies of action" that represent both "accommodation" of and "resistance" to those norms (Swidler 1986; Weitz 2001). Individual women adhere to cultural norms without questioning them because they have no access to an alternative discourse (e.g., girls learn to hide menstruation from others but might not comprehend why they are doing so) (Lyons and Griffin 2003; E. Martin 1992; Swidler 1986). Once realizing the power of cultural norms, however, some women make very conscious decisions to accommodate these norms because of the social rewards garnered by this behavior (e.g., a woman wears makeup to a job interview to increase her acceptability as a job candidate); thus, accommodation of cultural norms allows one to come closer to reaching life goals (Swidler 1986; Weitz 2001). Others might not purposely choose to resist social norms but may do so because of their life circumstances (e.g., a nursing mother feeds her child in public out of necessity). Finally, women might call on their own positions of power to actively resist cultural norms (e.g., a teacher informs female students about how to assess their own fertility and contraceptive options) or use their own bodies as platforms for their resistance (e.g., a woman engages in extensive tattooing, menstrual activism, or home birth).

Agency is "the ability of human beings to create viable lives even when they are constrained by social forces" (Baca Zinn and Eitzen 1999, 469). While terms like *agency* imply conscious resistance in the face of oppressive cultural norms and social structures, agency also includes less transformative survival strategies (what Hollander and Einwohner [2004] define as unintentional, "everyday" or "externally-defined" resistance). There are forms of agency or "strategies of action" that most women engage in that do not eliminate oppressive cultural norms and social structures but, rather, help women deal daily with norms and structures (and their bodies) (Swidler 1986). Komter (1989, 203) reminds us that a "strategy" is simply a "conscious or unconscious way of self-expression (verbal or nonverbal) in order to achieve what one wants or to prevent what one does not want." Strategies could range from unconscious accommodation to conscious resistance of cultural norms as women "bargain with patriarchy" in everyday contexts (Kandiyoti 1988).

Methods

Between 2001 and 2008, I interviewed ninety-eight midwestern women, aged thirty-eight to sixty-three, who self-identified as "menopausal" or "in menopause." Half of the sample identified as European American and white (fifty women or 51 percent). Most women of color were self-reportedly African American or black (thirty-five women or 36 percent). Almost two-thirds (fifty-four women or 55 percent) had earned an undergraduate degree, and many (twenty-four women or 30 percent) held a graduate or professional degree. Of those reporting incomes, one-third (twenty-five women or 32 percent) reported personal incomes greater than fifty thousand dollars; thirty-seven (50 percent) reported family incomes greater than seventy thousand dollars. Finally, ninety-three interviewees (95 percent) identified as heterosexual. Thus my findings primarily characterize the thoughts and experiences of European American or African American, middle-class, heterosexual women.[3]

I used an inductive, phenomenological approach throughout data collection, coding, and analysis in that I attempted to allow women to explain their lived experiences of menopause in their own words. Interview data analyzed here come from women's descriptions of menopause at the beginning of their interviews and from answers to questions such as, "Tell me about your symptoms," "Who do you talk to about menopause?" "Does menopause ever come up at home or at work?" and questions about body image.[4]

Findings

Even though I did not ask women directly about whether, when, or where they experienced hot flashes, they eagerly volunteered this information. About one-third of the women in this study discussed having hot flashes at work, about half discussed having them around family or friends, and about one-fifth discussed having them around strangers in other public spaces.[5] Interviewees characterized hot flashes more negatively than other potential signs or symptoms of menopause (such as irregular bleeding, vaginal dryness, and mood swings) because of their visibility. Since women in my study often could not prevent hot flashes from occurring, they reported strategies for dealing with them in front of others. Collectively, women's strategies represent a continuum of accommodation and resistance to cultural norms. Four themes emerged: the first two involve women's strategies of accommodation and the second two illustrate strategies of resistance.

Trying to Hide: "I'd Just Not Give Onto It"

Hot flash conversations often arose in interviews when women had a story to tell about trying to hide this bodily sign or symptom from others. Women tried to hide hot flashes, for instance, if they occurred in certain paid work settings.

> I didn't want these broken out sweats, hot flashes, these all-out sweats. I'd sit in meetings and wonder if everyone could tell . . . whether I was beet red, an all-male meeting or something, and so I think that's the issue. . . . There are so many societal, well, like men especially, I think, um, I mean, men don't get periods, let's face it. (Julia, European American)[6]

> I [am] the hot flash queen. . . . My biggest thing [I worried about is] if you could tell by looking at me [that I am having a hot flash]. . . . That was important because I manage people and, if there's an uncomfortable situation and . . . I'm put on the spot or I'm asked a question that . . . I know they don't like the answer to . . . I [want] to make sure [a hot flash isn't] showing. (Elaine, European American)

Julia and Elaine worked in managerial or administrative positions, with mostly male coworkers and bosses. Julia expected male coworkers not to understand hot flashes (or menopause more generally) because of a lack of personal connection to the experience. Elaine worried about whether the visibility of hot flashes might undermine her professional credibility in front of coworkers (especially men) and detailed how she labored to uphold gender norms about "appropriate" business clothing and youthful appearance as well, so that her image and personal power could be sustained in the paid work setting.

It is tempting to explain Julia's and Elaine's reluctance to acknowledge hot flashes at work as a result of the fact that they work in predominantly male-dominated atmospheres that do not allow for an understanding of women's changing bodies or reproductive experiences. Women are not supposed to be in these environments, and, therefore, women's primary job may be to appear similar to men (Acker 1990; Pierce 1995). Nonetheless, interviewees employed in female-dominated work settings also told stories about trying to hide hot flashes, suggesting that demographics alone do not determine whether women will attempt to hide flashing bodies within paid work settings.

> [When I had hot flashes at work], *I would just not give onto it.* . . . There's a lot of sort of unwritten rules in this office. . . . There is this sort of rule that you don't spend a lot of time sort of chatting and, . . . you know, we've alluded to . . . hot flashes or this or that, but . . . it's just not in the nature of the office really to talk about personal things. (Sharon, European American)

Despite an almost all-female office setting, Sharon (an administrative assistant) explains that talking about or acknowledging hot flashes in her office setting (a large room filled with rows and rows of gray cubicles, almost all filled by women) would be equivalent to "chatting" about personal issues. Therefore, attempts to hide hot flashes ("*not give onto it*") can be enforced structurally by office rules (and not always by the presence of men); women employed in service-sector jobs (especially those paid by the hour) are supposed to be thinking only of work tasks while they are "on the clock." Sharon was also constrained by the lack of closeness among her and her coworkers, and this lack of closeness, too, is a feature of office policy, since workers like her are supposed to operate as if they were solitary (and not working in rooms full of similarly aged, similarly gendered bodies).

Some interviewees discussed trying to hide hot flashes in order to avoid embarrassing interactions with coworkers about their changing bodies. Stephanie (European American) noted that hot flashes "weren't debilitating as much as they were embarrassing," because coworkers (in a small sales company) commented and laughed. Thus, the physical sensation of hot flashes bothered Stephanie less than their visibility. The same was true for, Donna (European American), who said she quickly went to the doctor after her coworkers (all administrative assistants just like her) started teasing her about her afternoon hot flashes: "[My] coworkers would say, 'Donna, you got a fever? Your face is red.' . . . One lady said I was probably having a power surge, and they all laughed . . . I remember that so clearly, you're embarrassed, and you're all just beet red."

When women talked about hot flashes at work, trying to hide them was usually the strategy of choice so that interviewees could conform to office norms and keep gendered bodily processes (and a lack of bodily control) private. As a general strategy, trying to hide hot flashes represents accommodation of cultural norms, because women assessed the weight of cultural norms within paid work settings and decided it was safer and more comfortable to conform.

Whether women were able to hide their flashing bodies in paid work settings is debatable. Some women in this study intimated that they were not able to hide hot flashes (because of obvious sweating or red, flushed skin) and highlighted coworkers' comments to confirm their inability to mask bodily changes. Others with milder hot flashes assumed they succeeded in hiding or controlling them but did not always report confirmation that their attempts had worked. Nonetheless, the widely reported attempts to hide hot flashes speak to women's reluctance to acknowledge their menopausal bodies in paid work settings and a perceived unacceptability of changing bodies in certain social spaces.

Acquiescing to Others' Definitions: "We're Part to Blame"

Sometimes others noticed women's hot flashes and defined them negatively. Some women gradually acquiesced to these definitions rather than offering any sustained resistance. For instance, within family settings, male partners especially, but also children at times, became exasperated with women's "uncontrollable" bodies. Several women in this study reported that male partners chose to sleep in a different bedroom while women experienced hot flashes. Jane (European American) said that her husband and sons would joke in her presence about her "out-of-control" flashing body. Women who described these situations did not report contradicting the meanings of menopause or women's bodies that were cemented in these moments. In fact, Jane reported laughing with her husband and sons, and others reported apologizing to their partners for their annoying symptoms (e.g., "I'm sorry, honey, I'll be fine in a minute" [Deborah, European American]). Lenora (African American) also relayed her daughters' frustrations with her for turning off the heat in the house (because of her hot flashes) and "not caring how cold they got." While Lenora did adjust the temperature to suit her own bodily needs at times, she and others in this study reported that it was difficult to ignore their children's complaints and needs. As "good" mothers, menopausal women found it important to prioritize their children's needs and sacrifice their own.[7]

Some interviewees were aware of their ability to resist and re-create the meanings of menopause within family conversations but did not take the opportunity to do so. Explaining that she herself had to get used to being menopausal, Chris (European American) said, "I think *we're part to blame* . . . because they're hearing us saying, 'What the heck is going on?'" The reaffirmation of menopause as an abnormal process that produces misbehaving bodies occurs in these interactions; some women found it easier to consent to others' frustrations and try to minimize others' contact with hot flashes, rather than resist them. Acquiescing to others' definitions, then, could be a strategy of conscious accommodation after women realize how others react to their flashing bodies.[8]

Accepting Visibility: "I'm Having a Hot Flash" and "There's Nothing I Can Do"

Depending on the severity of women's symptoms and the organization of their daily lives, however, interviewees like Lynn (African American) sometimes had no choice but to publicly confront hot flashes. In her words:

> I'll be at the counter waiting on people, and I feel it coming and have to stop and go to the bathroom or something. . . . People are standing there looking at you. I've had . . . times [when] a couple of my bosses said, "You can't just walk away like that." I'm like, "I have to go do something. *I'm having a hot flash.*" . . . I've had some that really understand, some older bosses that have . . . gone through menopause themselves, and I have some younger bosses that don't really know and [think it is] an excuse to leave the floor for a minute. . . . *There's nothing I can do.* . . . It's a medical condition that I have to deal with. . . . I can't stand here like this. Standing selling candy in a fudge shop, with water dripping down my face.

Because Lynn was not allowed to take many breaks from serving customers, she was forced to deal with her often severe hot flashes in front of customers and bosses. Both the intensity of her symptoms and the nature of her paid work compromised Lynn's ability to mask her changing body while in public settings. Lynn also described flashing while riding a public bus—another situation out of her control because she did not own a car.

> [When] riding on the bus and having to crack my windows a little bit, . . . I'll see younger kids sometimes kind of snickering. . . . I sweat really bad and it will be like just pouring. That's why I got that little fan to carry with me. If I can get something to just fan with for a few minutes until they go away, then I'm OK. But it's embarrassing to be some place . . . and all of a sudden you're all wet, people think, "What the heck is wrong with that woman?"

Women with greater economic stability than Lynn (e.g., Donna and Stephanie) sometimes tried to find a medical solution to alleviate bothersome hot flashes and ease public interactions. Lynn did not have health insurance and could not resort to medically prescribed forms of relief (nor did she express wanting medical treatment). Her only choice was to decide how to deal with flashing in front of others. Because Lynn's hot flashes were so noticeable to others, her negotiations with hot flashes were akin to an "unwitting" or unintentional resistance to social norms (Hollander and Einwohner 2004).[9] The visibility of Lynn's hot flashes, and her attempts to deal with them in front of others, resulted in an unintentional public acknowledgment of menopause and recognition that bodies can be uncontrollable at times. Lynn acted indifferently or exasperatedly when describing experiences of flashing in front of others, however, because her body resisted cultural norms before she wanted to. Therefore, these were not comfortable or purposeful cases of resistance.

In some instances, women gradually became accustomed to dealing with how their bodies disclose their true selves before they are ready to do so. Annette (African American) suggested that menopausal women get to the point where they cannot care anymore about hiding hot flashes and a visible lack of bodily control.

> ANNETTE: People notice it because they are looking right at you. They are probably saying, "What the heck is going on?" [*Laughter.*] . . . *After a while*, you don't pay any attention to it. And sometimes you just say, "I'm having a hot flash."
> HD: Yeah.
> ANNETTE: You know, people look at you and [that's] OK. [You say to them,] "You are going to have one, too, if you [*laughs*], if you get to that point, you'll have one too." So, that part doesn't bother me [anymore].

In this instance, flashing in front of others can become more active resistance as women gain experience in responding to others' reactions to their flashing bodies and come to terms with the fact that there is "*nothing [they] can do.*" Annette clarifies, though, that women's first instincts may be to try to hide the signs of menopause, acquiesce to others' definitions of their bodies, and blend in as much as possible. Annette explained that women who decide to accept the visibility of hot flashes are often those who realize how much energy it takes to hide them or those who find their own way of dealing with (and no longer caring about) others' reactions. "After a while," individuals can move from a strategy of accommodation to a strategy of resistance (or from passive to active resistance) when flashing in front of others.

Joking and Teaching: "We're Doing the Power Surges" and "Thermostat Wars"

Some interviewees reported resisting a bit more purposely in brief, people-specific, and setting-specific moments. When interviewees were around other menopausal coworkers, or students or younger female coworkers whom they could teach about menopause, for instance, flashing in front of others seemed less forbidden. As Gail and Brenda explained:

I have several coworkers who are about the same age. And *we're doing the power surges* and the senior moments, and we all, we can joke about it. I've never seen us joke with a male about it, you know, it's just amongst the women. And . . . there's a certain camaraderie with [younger women] as well. . . . I don't tend to exchange a lot of personal things with students, but a [female] student might come up and say, "I'm sorry if I was rude today, I'm just really kind of PMS-y," . . . and I might say "That's OK, I have hot flashes." . . . But outside of that [situation] . . . I don't discuss it. (Gail, European American)

Sometimes when I'm teaching, . . . I have to take my jacket off. I turn flush and the students will say, "You OK?" [I say,] "No, I'm fine. Give me about ten minutes or so." . . . And I make light of it and tell them, . . . "You guys, your moms might be going through the same thing." (Brenda, African American)

Gail and Brenda identified certain situations (same-age, same-gender, all-menopausal, safe spaces), moments (sharing female reproduction-related physical symptoms with a younger woman), and identities (mothers and teachers) in which they realized that it was safe to acknowledge and embrace their hot flashes. Sharon, who talked about getting in trouble for "chatting" if she announced her hot flashes at work, described having "*thermostat wars*" with her daughter, "in a joking way." Sharon also talked about how much fun it was to be going through menopause at the same time her daughter was going through puberty, reveling in the connections between their life stages and changing bodies. In each of these joking or teaching moments, the relationships that these women held with others in a specific setting appeared critical in determining whether flashing would be acknowledged positively and become a public conversation. If women embraced a teaching or mothering role (a position of power, in the face of subordinates) or felt equal to other individuals in their environment, they were willing to reconceptualize hot flashes (and menopause) as a point of connection and as a positive, normal phenomenon. The safety of these situations did seem to be related to the fact that men were not present in these situations because, without men present, women could be in charge of defining their flashing bodies. For a brief moment, their bodies are no longer "misbehaving" but, rather, acting normally for their life stage. Gail explained later in her interview that, as soon as another person (of a different age, gender, or occupational position) walked into the room or the hot flash subsided, these moments usually ended.

Discussion and Conclusion

The physical sensation of a hot flash is only one part of a woman's experience of this symptom. An equally important part of her experience is whether and how others might see a hot flash and, therefore, how she feels she must handle its visibility. Bodily signs and symptoms can be quite normal and natural but, within the context of gendered cultural norms about beauty and bodily control, a hot flash that everyone can see may feel abnormal, disruptive, and negative. Comments about the uncontrollability of their bodies often accompanied interviewees' comments about hot flashes, such as "I never know what my body will do next" (Brenda). And even though she felt fairly comfortable flashing in front of others, Kara (European American) still said that "symptoms are always negative." In most women's accounts of dealing with hot flashes, the idea surfaced that menopause is a personal problem and not a normal, nearly universal female experience. Lyons and Griffin (2003) and E. Martin (1992) suggest that biomedical discourses urge women to define menopausal signs and symptoms in this way, and that women lack widespread access to alternative discourses. Dominant cultural ideas about women's beauty, disability, illness, and aging also suggest that any type of bodily change is the direct result of individual failure to control the physical body (Calasanti 2005; Dworkin and Wachs 2009; Epstein 1995; K. A. Martin 2003; Wendell 1996). What women do in response to their flashing bodies, then, is telling about the power of cultural norms and the lack of alternative discourses and clear paths for resistance.

Ultimately, interviewees' strategies for dealing with flashing in front of others fall along a continuum of accommodation and resistance. On one end of this continuum, women report trying to hide hot flashes and acquiescing to others' definitions of their flashing bodies. On the other end, women publicly acknowledge hot flashes and openly converse with others about these signs or symptoms. But whether they accommodate or resist, women act in subtle ways to (1) carve out their own (gendered) position within workplaces, other public spaces, and family relationships in the midst of hot flashes; (2) facilitate an easier life for themselves; (3) brace themselves against others' reactions to hot flashes and face the fact that their bodies are transgressing norms; and (4) engage in continual assessments of whether they are in safe spaces with safe people so that they know whether they can talk or act openly. In these ways interviewees locate themselves and their bodies in a given moment and setting and strategize about flashing in front of others.

In this study, most women's reactions to flashing in front of others can be seen as nontransformative acts of agency or accommodation of cultural norms, in that they are responding, reacting, and acting on their own behalf but not offering direct resistance to cultural norms. Nonetheless, hiding hot flashes is hard work, to which women end up having to be very committed. Doing the work to hide hot flashes (e.g., dressing in layers, drinking and eating certain ways, managing stressors that might trigger a hot flash, seeking medical treatment) takes considerable time and effort—extra gendered work surrounding women's midlife stage. The extra relationship and interactional work that parallels the visibility of hot flashes is also a responsibility of menopausal women. Whether they choose a strategy of accommodation or one of resistance, women are engaging in choices and assessments that involve important decisions about the benefits and costs of their actions, in the face of oppressive cultural norms and social structures (Kandiyoti 1988; Komter 1989). Women also choose different strategies or multiple strategies (since these strategies are not mutually exclusive and could be combined) at different times, depending on their understandings of the norms and the power relationships within a setting, the potential effects of their accommodation or resistance within that setting, their goals within that setting, and the severity of their hot flashes (Kandiyoti 1988; Swidler 1986). The "bargains" that women must make with patriarchy are varied, and women might choose to accommodate in one moment and resist in the next.

Documenting our incomplete knowledge of bodily signs and symptoms and how they are defined and experienced is critical, if we seek to understand women's menopause experiences more completely. An effort to listen to women's narratives about flashing bodies combines the feminist tradition of studying gendered social contexts with the study of the (potentially negative, frustrating, annoying, and sometimes uncontrollable) physical body. In such an effort, we do not allow biomedical researchers to be the only ones who discuss bodily signs and symptoms—we join in on the conversation. In the light of my findings, additional exploration of women's hot flash experiences is needed. Expanding feminist research on menopausal signs and symptoms may eventually help more women know that their flashing bodies are not misbehaving or "out of control"—rather, they are acting normally. Researchers can take the ideas proposed in this chapter and explore interactions that individuals have when experiencing any bodily sign or symptom, for we have a lot more to learn about bodily signs and symptoms themselves, especially those visible to others.

NOTES

1. Until recently, feminist researchers have devoted their energies to refuting biomedical perspectives and recasting menopause as positive, rather than developing their own comprehensive understanding of this bodily experience.
2. Even though this reproductive transition affects nearly every woman in some way, the prevalence of hot flashes and experience of menopause in general varies considerably between cultures and countries. For example, hot flashes are not so widely reported in India, Japan, and China (Ayers, Forshaw, and Hunter 2010; Dillaway et al. 2008). Differences in symptom reporting may result from varied diets and levels of exercise, availability of medical treatment, and wide-ranging attitudes toward hot flashes, menopause, and aging.
3. I identify women's race locations within the findings section of this chapter, because race represents a major form of difference among women in my study. While I do not have major race-based findings to report about women's experiences of dealing with hot flashes in front of others, African American women and European American women in this study did report different attitudes about menopause at times, and therefore women's race locations are important to track (Dillaway et al. 2008).
4. Additional information about research methods and a greater discussion of women's bodily experiences of menopause can be found in Dillaway (2005, 2008); and Dillaway et al. (2008).
5. These numbers would likely have been higher if I had asked direct questions about how they dealt with hot flashes.
6. To uphold confidentiality, all names reported in this chapter are pseudonyms.
7. See Dillaway (2006) for a further discussion of motherhood during menopause.
8. Whether these interviewees should be resisting rather than accommodating, once they acknowledge the possibility of resistance, is a question we could ask here. Perhaps women alone are the ones who are capable of resisting and re-creating the meanings of menopause, but participating in active resistance may be risky or undesirable, depending on women's everyday contexts, social locations, life goals, the potential effects of their resistance in a particular setting, and their current bodily experiences (Kandiyoti 1988; Swidler 1986). Komter (1989) suggests that the "invisible inequalities" built into the institution of the family also make it difficult for women to actively resist their partners' definitions of situations, and therefore women may feel that it is safer to acquiesce to others' (often men's) definitions of their hot flashes. Good mothering ideology also

reinforces women's attention to others' (i.e., children's) needs (Dillaway 2006). To truly understand why women choose strategies of accommodation over resistance, then, we must analyze the gendered power relationships and gendered ideologies that exist in any setting.

9. Lynn's perception of her situation is important here because there is no way to tell whether the "kids" on the bus were actually laughing at her. The situation she describes could be one within which she felt others' gazes on her hot flashes even if they were not really paying attention to her. Menopausal women may feel as if others are noticing their hot flashes even when they are not, and they may strategize about how to deal with their hot flashes because of their perception rather than any real evidence that others care about their hot flashes.

REFERENCES

Acker, Joan. 1990. "Hierarchies, Jobs, Bodies: A Theory of Gendered Organizations." *Gender and Society* 4 (2): 139–58.

Ayers, Beverly, Mark Forshaw, and Myra S. Hunter. 2010. "The Impact of Attitudes Towards the Menopause on Women's Symptom Experience: A Systematic Review." *Maturitas* 65 (1): 28–36.

Baca Zinn, Maxine, and D. Stanley Eitzen. 1999. *Diversity in Families*. 5th ed. New York: HarperCollins College.

Calasanti, Toni. 2005. "Ageism, Gravity, and Gender: Experiences of Aging Bodies." *Generations* 29 (3): 8–12.

Dillaway, Heather E. 2005. "(Un)Changing Menopausal Bodies: How Women Think and Act in the Face of a Reproductive Transition and Gendered Beauty Ideals." *Sex Roles* 53 (1/2): 1–17.

———. 2006. "Good Mothers Never Wane: Motherwork at Menopause." *Journal of Women and Aging* 18 (2): 41–53.

———. 2008. "'Why Can't You Control This?' Women's Characterizations of Intimate Partner Interactions about Menopause." *Journal of Women and Aging* 20 (1/2): 47–64.

Dillaway, Heather E., Mary Byrnes, Sara Miller, and Sonica Rehan. 2008. "Talking among Us: How Women from Different Racial Ethnic Groups Define and Discuss Menopause." *Healthcare for Women International* 29 (7): 766–81.

Dworkin, Shari L., and Faye Linda Wachs. 2009. *Body Panic: Gender, Health, and the Selling of Fitness*. New York: New York University Press.

Epstein, Julia. 1995. *Altered Conditions*. New York: Routledge.

Hollander, Jocelyn A., and Rachel L. Einwohner. 2004. "Conceptualizing Resistance." *Sociological Forum* 19 (4): 533–54.

Kandiyoti, Deniz. 1988. "Bargaining with Patriarchy." *Gender and Society* 2 (3): 274–90.

Koeske, Randi Daimon. 1983. "Lifting the Curse of Menstruation: Toward a Feminist Perspective on the Menstrual Cycle." *Women and Health* 8 (2/3): 1–15.

Komter, Aafke. 1989. "Hidden Power in Marriage." *Gender and Society* 3 (2): 187–216.

Kronenberg, Fredi. 1990. "Hot Flashes: Epidemiology and Physiology." *Annals of the New York Academy of Science* 592 (1): 52–86.

Lyons, Antonia C., and Christine Griffin. 2003. "Managing Menopause: A Qualitative Analysis of Self-Help Literature for Women at Midlife." *Social Science and Medicine* 56 (8): 1629–42.

Martin, Emily. 1992. *The Woman in the Body: A Cultural Analysis of Reproduction*, 2nd ed. Boston: Beacon Press.

Martin, Karin A. 2003. "Giving Birth like a Girl." *Gender and Society* 17 (1): 54–72.

Pierce, Jennifer L. 1995. *Gender Trials: Emotional Lives in Contemporary Law Firms*. Berkeley: University of California Press.

Swidler, Ann. 1986. "Culture in Action: Symbols and Strategies." *American Sociological Review* 51 (2): 273–86.

Voda, Ann M. 1992. "Menopause: A Normal View." *Clinical Obstetrics and Gynecology* 35 (4): 923–33.

Weitz, Rose. 2001. "Women and Their Hair: Seeking Power through Resistance and Accommodation." *Gender and Society* 15 (5): 667–86.

Wendell, Susan. 1996. *The Rejected Body: Feminist Philosophical Reflections on Disability*. New York: Routledge.

Zones, Jane Sprague. 2000. "Beauty Myths and Realities and Their Impacts on Women's Health." In *Gender through the Prism of Difference*, ed. Maxine Baca Zinn, Pierrette Hondagneu-Sotelo, and Michael A. Messner, 87–103. Boston: Allyn and Bacon.

16

The Transformation of Bodily Practices among Religious Defectors

Lynn Davidman

Sima rebelled by resisting and transforming the bodily practices of Ultra-Orthodox (Haredi) norms for women's attire.[1] She explained:

> For me, putting on pants was the equivalent of taking off your *kipa* [the skullcap worn by observant Jewish men], or stopping to put on *tefillin* [leather boxes containing Torah passages worn by male Orthodox Jews] for boys. It was like the, the most. And really when I went with pants for the first time, first of all, I felt . . . I felt lots of things. First, I felt like I was sort of naked, like I was really exposed. But on the other hand I was very, very happy.

Religions are inscribed on the bodies of their members. Religious communities require members to engage in a variety of bodily practices—rituals performed by and enacted on the body—that create, maintain, and display membership in the group. As children are socialized into a religious community, they come to embody the group's rituals and corporeal rites by internalizing its norms, beliefs, practices, and values. Within strict, enclave religious communities, such as some Muslim and Haredi Jewish groups,[2] numerous rituals and laws involve bodily practices that occupy members throughout the day and are central to the display, presentation, and ongoing construction of religious identity.

But what happens when those who grew up in an enclave community defect from their religious group?[3] Studies of conversion (e.g., Greil 1977; Greil and Rudy 1984) have documented the ways converts take on new bodily practices to establish, mark, and perform membership in their new religious communities. Is there a similar process in shedding religion? There are few recent studies on defection and little attention has been paid to the processes through which the exiting is accomplished, including changing bodily practices and, for example, among Haredi Jews, divesting oneself of the bodily markers of Haredi identity.

Religion and the Body

Students of religion have intermittently analyzed the role of the body in religious rituals, often focusing on how particular social groups set themselves apart by cultivating distinctive bodily practices (Bartkowski 2005, 11; Kanter 1972). In *Born Again Bodies: Flesh and Spirit in American Christianity*, R. Marie Griffith (2004) shows the ways women in evangelical Christian groups practice strict diet and exercise routines to shape female bodies that are ideally suited for servants of Christ. Carol Laderman (1994) outlines the belief of many Malay cultures that certain foods have the power to upset bodily harmony and balance. The Shakers, whose celibate way of life Meredith B. McGuire (2008), Rosabeth Moss Kanter (1972), and others have studied, had prescribed routines guiding members' physical practices and routines of everyday life, including the exact order for getting out of bed and dressing each morning. Regulations concerning diet, comportment, appropriate dress, and other rituals of embodiment are central to building and maintaining commitment in utopian communities; relinquishing individual freedom is often visually performed by adopting and conforming to the rules of behavior of the group (Kanter 1972). Within the frame of commitment mechanisms, bodily practices aid in forging tight communal bonds (see, e.g., Davidman 1990; Warner 1997) even as they establish strong boundaries between members and outsiders.

Rituals involving the body, however, such as those illustrated so powerfully in Saba Mahmood's (2005) study of the women's Mosque Movement in Cairo, are more than just symbolic commitment mechanisms. The repetition of quotidian bodily practices also contributes to the constitution and cultivation of long-term religious beliefs and identities within religious communities. These embodied practices built a particular type of ethical orientation and were central in shaping religious identities. Religious representations of selves not only symbolize pious individuals, they also perform the work of creating them. Mahmood's analysis helps shed light on Haredi Jewish life, where cosmic significance resides in the precise performance of every detail of daily life and repeated observance of commandments is viewed as a means of building belief (Fader 2006).

In discussing strictly controlled religious enclaves, social theorists such as Bryan S. Turner (1984) and Anthony Giddens (1991) have described these communities as "traditional" or "pre-modern" in their organization of bodily life, in that they appeal to transcendent authorities to reinforce the groups' regimes of bodily discipline. Haredi Jewish lives are built on a fundamental belief in a transcendent being whose commandments are practiced and guarded within enclave communities that seek to maintain a sacred canopy binding and shielding group members from the influence of the outside world. The group's narrative is created, perpetuated, maintained, and reinforced by members' continuous performance of the countless rituals that repeatedly reproduce their way of life.

To comprehend the significance of changing long-held bodily practices, it is important to understand that a person's bodily behavior is deeply tied to his or her ontological security (Giddens 1991; Turner 1984, 1992). One can, however, become "disembodied" (Giddens 1991), if and when one begins to feel a significant distance between bodily routine and self-identity, such as when defectors continue to perform daily religious practices when they no longer believe in the doctrine associated with them. This situation creates anxiety and anomie. As Giddens (1991, 59) explains: "It expresses existential anxieties impinging directly upon self-identity." These existential anxieties are a key feature of the narratives of Haredi defectors. Respondents explained that they resolved these feelings of dissociation by changing their bodily practices. These physical transformations, as described by all respondents, were a crucial means of both disinscribing their Haredi bodily markers and learning and performing the bodily practices of the new groups they enter; they constitute an important means of negotiating a new, ontologically secure, non-Haredi identity.

Methods

This chapter is part of a larger project that analyzes the narratives told by people who grew up Orthodox and later left their religious communities. Its goal is to explore, analyze, and compare narratives of defection and illuminate how they systematically differ along several axes: whether the informant was an Israeli or an American; a woman or a man (enclave groups have deeply structured gender norms); and brought up modern Orthodox or Haredi. I left respondents free to define "leaving Orthodoxy" for themselves, allowing my definition to evolve from the ground up (Glaser and Strauss 1967). Thus, respondents ranged from those who have continued certain traditional practices to those who have become entirely secular. Most narrated their transformation as a process of biographical disruption (see Becker 1997; Bury 1982; Davidman 2000) that they continually attempted to repair.

I began this research in the summer of 2003 and have since continued my conversations with defectors. In the United States, I located my respondents by word of mouth; snowball sampling; advertisements in Providence, Rhode Island, and Boston, Massachusetts, newspapers; an ad in the *Village Voice*; and postings on the website H-Judaic, an Internet listserve for people interested in Jewish studies and Jewish life. Several of the Israeli respondents were located through the H-Judaic website, a few by word of mouth, and half through Hillel, an organization whose sole purpose is to help Haredim leave Orthodoxy. In the United States, I carried on these conversations in English, whereas in Israel nearly all of them were in Hebrew. I did not ask questions in a set order but used an interview guide to ensure that a certain set of issues was addressed in each interview. The interviews lasted between two and six hours; generally they were completed in three.

The data for this chapter are drawn from a subset of my sample, comprising twenty-five former Haredim in the United States and Israel. Of the respondents, fourteen were living in the United States at the time of the interview and eleven were living in Israel. The sample includes twelve men and thirteen women. The majority of the American ex-Haredim had defected from Hasidic communities, while half of the Israelis described themselves as having grown up in non-Hasidic (Litvak) Haredi enclaves.

Haredi Bodily Life

The intense and wide-ranging religious laws guide all aspects of day-to-day existence; they shape all bodily practices as they are performed throughout the day, including morning rising, washing, eating, treatment of hair, ritual purity of the body, sexuality, dress, sleeping, and many others. Bodily practices—or performances—which produce and reproduce their relationship with God, also are essential in creating, maintaining, and performing a Haredi identity.

Orthodox Jews follow strict dietary practices that include never mixing meat with milk, eating only meats and fowl that are deemed kosher and are slaughtered in a ritually approved way, avoiding all shellfish, and waiting a number of hours after eating meat before having any dairy. Haredim are distinguishable from outsiders—and each other—by dress. Haredi women, who are expected to be "modest" at all times, cover their heads with wigs, hats, or "snoods" and wear clothes that cover their bodies— long skirts, blouses that cover their collarbones and have long sleeves, and high socks or stockings. Among other details of their dress code, men wear white shirts and black slacks and, depending on which group they belong to, perhaps a long black coat or a fur hat or both.

Bodily Practices and the Negotiation of a New Identity

Many respondents told stories of breaking a Haredi bodily practice as they tested what it might be like to live outside of the community and its laws. Their resistance to Haredi life was a form of embodied resistance when they secretly violated one of the rules and taboos for appropriate behavior and self-presentation. These acts were private, although they might have taken place in a public place where the defector was anonymous. Erving Goffman's (1959, 112) delineations of "backstage" and "frontstage" performances illuminate this process of experimentation. Individuals went backstage, to a place where they were unseen by their family and community, to engage in rule-breaking activities that would reveal their rebellion in their frontstage community lives.

After incipient rebels found that God did not strike them down for their violations of community norms and laws, many said they were emboldened and continued, slowly and privately, to experiment with transgressing God's other commandments. Their narratives illustrated how backstage experiments with bodily practices became the initial steps in their eventual defection, allowing them to "try on" a different life before revealing it publicly. Defectors' very awareness that they could find backstage locations where they could experiment with forbidden bodily practices reveals that for them, the sacred canopy was beginning to unravel.

"Private" Experiments

As Goffman (1959) points out, the performance of identity and the contours of social interaction are deeply linked to bodily comportment. Does "normal" bodily behavior depend on the social context? "Passing," then, refers to the individual's manipulation of bodily practices in accordance with varying social norms. Early in their processes of leaving, many respondents experimented with alternative identities by "passing" between non-Orthodox and Haredi worlds, following their distinct norms for comportment. Interviewees' narratives of their experiments with passing between the Haredi world and the larger U.S. society reveal that these ventures amounted to embodied resistance to the community's guidelines and boundaries. In these situations, they said, they could experiment with crafting a new self designed for the world outside the enclave.

For example, Leah, a forty-two-year-old American ex-Hasid, became frustrated with the Haredi life, particularly women's roles in it, at a young age. She had cognitive, social, and emotional questions that, in her teenage years, led her to "privately" violate Sabbath and the dress code together.

> It just became claustrophobic and I could not stand it anymore. I just hated, you know . . . the countdown, and when Shabbos started. I did really bad things . . . like, I lived in Boro Park (an Ultra-Orthodox section of Brooklyn), and on the edge of Boro Park there were these bars. And at some point, I just needed to go to a bar . . . [to] feel like an international adventuress or something . . . like in the movies [which she had snuck out to see]. Bette Davis or something. That is who I was: Lauren Bacall or Katharine Hepburn. And they would walk into a bar and say, "Give me a drink." And so I was trying to be a woman of assertion. I could just do that and I don't care if anyone says anything to me. I would tuck some money into a pocket and I would sneak out of my house on a Friday night with pants under my skirt, remove my skirt as I approached the bar. . . . Luckily no one ever talked to me because I would have been so dumbfounded. And after I had my drink and paid for it, I left the bar, put my skirt back on, and returned to my house, crept into bed and went to sleep.

Leah was too young to fully make the transition out of her community. But to ease her feelings of confinement, she experimented with the outside world by passing back and forth between secular places and her Haredi family and community. Her exposure to Hollywood films contributed to her knowledge of ideals alien to members of her enclave and allowed her to present an alternative self in the outside world. Although she maintained the appearance of an obedient young Haredi woman inside the community boundaries, her experimentation with costume changes was an act of rebellion that could effect and reveal her defection.

Yair, an Israeli ex-Hasid, explained that taking off his *kipa*, a form of embodied resistance, allowed him to gradually negotiate a path away from the Satmar Hasidic community. When Yair first removed his *kipa*, he made sure to do so away from community eyes and judgment. He remarked, "Now I am taking off my *kipa*. That was a question. It was like, at what distance from my house can I take it off?" As he grew more comfortable in his process of exiting a Haredi life, he increasingly shortened the distance from home where he could walk without his *kipa*. Yair's ever-changing negotiations and calculations of the proper distance between himself and the outer boundaries of the community are reflected in his narration of behavioral changes. His narratives, like those of most of the others, made clear how he negotiated all stages of defection and the ways in which he "passed" by privately manipulating a visible but readily changeable symbol of religious life.

"Keeping up appearances" within the Haredi community took its toll; the defectors' narratives revealed the high level of discomfort they experienced as they tried to simultaneously preserve and perform their habitual selves and their emerging new selves. They described experiences of cognitive dissonance when they, as one Israeli interviewee cited the folk saying, tried "to dance with the same 'tush' at two weddings." For that woman, living and presenting herself as two distinctly embodied beings became increasingly difficult. It was clear when we met that, despite living outside of Haredi codes and practices for the past decade, she was still troubled and somewhat ambivalent about her choices.

Ezra, who plainly stated he found it impossible to keep trying to live in two worlds, provided a perfect articulation of cognitive dissonance. During the years leading up to Ezra's "coming out" publicly as non-Haredi, he had internal questions and misgivings about the life and community of origin. As long as he kept these to himself, his continued self-presentation as a member of a Haredi community produced a sense of distress and emotional tumult that could be remedied only by the translation of his ideological rejection into action.

> You have to conform, and this was blending in with my being increasingly uncomfortable with not only Judaism on the intellectual level but on the level of daily practice. At that point, it was becoming just too painful to keep continuing, keep putting on the *tefillin* everyday when I was just not believing. I just . . . I had decided for myself I was just completely atheist. Then what am I doing here? What am I pretending? And it's really painful. I can't do this anymore. I can't continue doing this, but it would be very hard for me to stop being Orthodox being with all my friends and relatives and family. It's just almost impossible.

In another vivid example, Moti described how the process of passing between two worlds led him, like Leah and Yair, to defect from Haredi life, creating new identities and bodily routines that were consistent with his emerging sense of self as a non-Haredi individual. Moti recounted how, when he was no longer comfortable with his symbolic and embodied representation of himself as Haredi, he effected changes in his self-presentation, such as hiding his curls. In Moti's early adolescence, his introduction to the practices of passing revealed that he could manipulate his appearance and others' views of him simply by showing or hiding his *peyos* (curly sidelocks). This bodily practice became, for him, a means of passing between social identities.

His friends made clear, however, that he could not disappear without affect. After Moti hid his curls, in a place forbidden to all Haredim, his friends, as he recounted, questioned his Jewishness.

> I was like fifteen years old, I and two or three other [Satmar Hasidic] guys went to like clubs, dancing clubs. I was never really into dancing clubs because we still had the curls. And I mean I always hung out with a lot of my friends, but they had their curls down. So I didn't like the idea of goin' to a club and people like starin'

at us. Instead of starin' at the girls dancing they were starin' at us. So whenever I went outside the Satmar village [in Monroe, New York] I just put my curls over my ears. I tried to hide it. And a lot of my friends started to make fun of me like, "Oh, now you're not Jewish. I don't even see that you're Jewish because I don't see your curls." I'm like, "Listen, I'm gonna try to hide it because I don't want people starin' at me instead of looking at the crowd."

Moti's story gave a clear indication of the centrality of bodily practices to the maintenance of Haredi identity. Haredim generally discount the authentic Jewishness of all but Orthodox Jews. Seeing Moti without his *peyos*, powerfully visual symbolic markers of his religious identity, his friends doubted his Jewishness. By hiding his curls, Moti was able to pass as secular, easing the social discomfort of standing out as Orthodox in a secular club. The response of his friends is even more telling, because their teasing indicates that one might step in or out of Jewish identity by simply manipulating facial hair. When Moti decided to leave Orthodoxy definitively, cutting off his *peyos* dramatically removed him from the Haredi framework.

Several interviewees said their initial forays and experiments into the larger society involved tasting *trayfe*, nonkosher food. Rachel's narrative of her "first time" emphasized how she protected her face—her frontstage—in the community by going to a somewhat distant shopping mall where, unseen by her coreligionists (she was not yet sure about God) she could be a "regular person" and enjoy a bacon, lettuce, and tomato sandwich. She chose to break fundamental codes of law and behavior she had grown up with at a place some distance from her own world, where she sought anonymity, rather than lose her familial and social connections so early in her process of questioning. Actions like hers were a constitutive step in breaking away from Haredi bodily practices and defying the validity of laws formerly governing their lives. Rachel marked the beginning of her experimentation by eating bacon, a heavily weighted symbolic representation of the essence of *treyfe*, nonkosher, an infraction so serious she protected her identity in the Haredi world by taking her "sins" outside it.

> I went to this shopping center that was like, I would never have gone to in a million years, and I very furtively ordered a bacon, lettuce, and tomato sandwich and was waiting to be . . . you know, the lightning to strike me or something, and, of course, the lightning didn't. God, like bacon, it's got to be the worst, and I mean . . . it was just a coffee shop in a very, you know, a poor neighborhood type shopping center way so nobody would see me, and I was like trembling the whole time, but I managed to . . . you know, I survived it and that was like the start of the rebellion at that point.

For Rachel, simply eating the sandwich was fraught with cosmic implications. She was poised at a tipping point, rebellious enough to transgress a dietary law central to her Haredi identity, which was still asserting its presence through her fear of immediate and fatal divine retribution. Lightning did not strike, and her first experiment with bodily contravention of Haredi norms was successful, encouraging and enabling future transgressions in her ongoing process of defection. The community's norms and its representations of God's will were so strongly imbued that even in breaking the rules Rachel sought to maintain her frontstage appearance as an upstanding member of her community.

These narratives reveal that those in the process of defection felt turmoil about terms of the social separation that might result from publicly breaking community norms and experimenting with new physical practices. For Leah, Ezra, and Moti, the process of exiting involved a variety of attempts to pass and the realization that they could not, at least in their physical practices, comfortably remain between two worlds forever. Practically speaking, a man cannot be bearded according to community norms and shaven according to a personal desire at the same time. Defectors' narratives underline a key point: private experimentation cannot be a long-term strategy for those who want to leave the Haredi world. To reduce cognitive dissonance and construct a coherent narrative of self, in which identities coincided with bodily routines, defectors eventually transformed backstage to frontstage, and the non-Haredi embodied selves that were first privately performed became their regular public personas.

Coming Out, Newly Inscribed

The emotional and existential difficulties involved in passing led to a key moment in the narratives of defection—a singular public act or display of disincription that marked respondents as outsiders to their native communities. Just as, for Haredim, the continuous cultivation of daily practices involving food, facial hair, and clothing creates, maintains, and displays their identities as members of their enclave community, the repetition of new bodily practices, first experimented with in private, eventually leads to changes in their embodied identities that allow them to accomplish public defection.

Aliza, an American woman who grew up in the highly strict and segregated Satmar Hasidic community, described the first time she wore pants in public—a woman's form of embodied resistance—as a moment of great internal and external transformation. As seen in other narratives, for Aliza, breaking the clothing or hair norms of the community was an emotional moment that allowed her to publicly proclaim her individuation from the Haredi enclave. Describing her first experience of buying pants, a garment she had been taught since birth was forbidden for women, she expressed anxiety about the very public nature of her transgression.

> The first time that . . . the first time I put on a pair of pants . . . that was one thing I didn't do right away, I waited . . . it was this store that was right near the subway station, so I walked in and picked up the first pair of pants I saw; black velvet, very simple. Held it against me, it looked like it fit. I wasn't gonna try it on; I bought it. Was too scared to try it on, but I bought it and I took it home.

When asked why it was so difficult to buy and wear pants, she explained that the sheer visibility of changing her mode of dress made it into a large statement: "You were making it clear to everyone else what you were doing. It wasn't just for me . . . it was how people would see you, so it was more about change in the way that people would look at you. And it was a blatant separation from the community, so it was very obvious."

When Aliza wore these pants daily, she publicly engaged in a bodily practice that had been taboo. Pants, for Aliza, were a major symbolic representation of her movement away from the ideological and behavioral norms of her religious community. Thus, changing her mode of dress translated Aliza's cognitive objections into a concrete, public symbol of defection. The Haredi clothing norms are imbued with religious and community significance, and Aliza's description of her transgression illustrated the same conflicting emotions that many other respondents reported: the consolidation of individualized, personal identity brought feelings of liberation, but this gain implied the loss of one's group identity, which was often accompanied by feelings of bereavement and isolation. Respondents' narratives richly described their deep fears that by engaging in embodied resistance to the strict laws of enclave Orthodoxy, they would lose everything they had ever had.

Those growing up in these communities are so deeply imbued with its laws and practices that even after they have been gone from the community for several years, they might still feel the tug of their former bodily practices. For example, Shlomo explained that years after he had stopped wearing his *yarmulke* (*kipa*) he still was occasionally haunted by the loss of his religious identity and his terrible guilt about his defection.

> I'm sometimes walking in the hospital, and I'm like are you doing anything wrong now? You're not wearing a *yarmulke*, kind of not wearing [the Haredi garb].
> So yeah, I will catch myself; sometimes it's sort of this fear. It's like I'm doing something wrong. I'm in the wrong, and I'm behaving not badly, but that there's an impending sort of judgment in it. But then I say "Oh," I let it pass and . . . I know that I've got to deal with it. So yeah, I do feel sometimes a level of . . . it's not guilt in terms of you're doing something wrong from heaven, but it's guilt in leaving tradition, this loss of this identity.

That Shlomo continued to "work against" these negative feelings, and that he still noticed the lack of a *yarmulke* in his daily life, reveals the power that foundational bodily practices continued to exert even when defectors no longer identify as Haredim. The feelings of impending judgment, guilt, and loss were continual reminders that the cessation of key Haredi bodily practices both symbolized and enacted a loss of Haredi identity. He did not view his deviation from the Haredi law concerning headgear as constituting something "wrong from heaven" but rather a loss of community, which he expressed by referring to "tradition" and "this [Orthodox] identity."

Conclusions

Interviews with people who have left the Haredi Jewish community reveal that tightly knit, face-to-face religious enclave communities such as this, which exert power over the beliefs and ideologies of their members, also exert power over the very details of their embodiment. In my book *Tradition in a Rootless World: Women Turn to Orthodox Judaism* (Davidman 1991), I analyze how Jewish women who choose to become Orthodox go through the exacting and demanding process of marking this religion on their bodies. They change what they eat, how they dress, and their very bodily comportment. Thus, bodies can be a primary site on which religious communities embed their rules and practices, as well as a key instrument of defection.

When people think of exiting strictly religious communities, often they assume that a loss of faith—a cognitive change—is more central to religious defection than any other factor. Judaism, however, is not so much a "faith tradition" as one of behaviors and practices. In the process of Haredi socialization, children internalize their community's norms, beliefs, and practices; this patterned way of life becomes embedded in their very beings. Young Haredim grew up with the certainty that God, their community, and their families have set out a precise system governing all aspects of their behavior and comportment for every moment of their lives. They come to "know" their community's precise prescriptions for how to live minute by minute, day by day, month by month—following a lunar calendar—right through their lives. Even after death Haredim enact hundreds of bodily practices that bring the period of mourning and its sensibility into being.

To the degree that their bodies are important sites of religious socialization in the Haredi world, embodied resistance is a powerful way to enact a rebellion against the Haredi life. The enclave communities in which Haredim live is alive with "police" (Haredi community members) who observe others' lives and press them into compliance if they stray. What better way for the defectors to thumb their noses at all the authorities than by brazenly presenting a body that is markedly non-Haredi, such as with a beard shaved off or a blouse with a regular V neck? When defectors expose their newly inscribed bodies and their newly acquired behavioral repertoire, they establish, in that moment of public revelation, that they have left the community's way of life. Not a single word need be said; their physical, embodied presence is all people need to confirm the rumors of a member's leaving.

Haredi exit narratives illustrate the degree to which the body is key in transforming and resisting religious commitments. Although a defector's changes in his or her bodily practice might seem insignificant to people outside the enclave, the obscurity of these practices makes them particularly suited for illustrating the power of the body as a mechanism of protest. Within the Haredi world, the seemingly smallest infraction brings swift and immediate sanctions. In a small space, every move acquires greater significance. Embodied resistance is a potent form of protest against all kinds of social norms, not only religious. Just as bodily rituals signal group membership, the abandonment of bodily rituals can signify resistance or defection.

NOTES

1. All names are pseudonyms.
2. The term *Ultra-Orthodox* is eschewed by Haredim (the plural word for Haredi Jews) because of the implication that their interpretations of Jewish law and practice are "ultra," or extra, in comparison with other Orthodox Jews.
3. I use the term *defection* in contrast to *disaffiliation*, which denotes leaving a religious group one has joined later in life (Davidman and Greil 2007).

REFERENCES

Bartkowski, John P. 2005. "Faithfully Embodied: Religious Identity and the Body." *disClosure* 14:8–37.

Becker, Gaylene. 1997. *Disrupted Lives: How People Create Meaning in a Chaotic World*. Berkeley: University of California Press.

Bury, Michael. 1982. "Chronic Illness as Biographical Disruption: Towards an Integrated Perspective." *Sociology of Health and Illness* 4 (2): 167–82.

Davidman, Lynn. 1990. "Women's Search for Family and Roots: A Jewish Religious Solution to a Modern Dilemma." In *In Gods We Trust*, ed. Thomas Robbins and Dick Anthony, 385–407. New Brunswick, NJ: Transaction.

———. 1991. *Tradition in a Rootless World: Women Turn to Orthodox Judaism*. Berkeley: University of California Press.

———. 2000. *Motherloss*. Berkeley: University of California Press.

Davidman, Lynn, and Arthur L. Greil. 2007. "Characters in Search of a Script: The Exit Narratives of Formerly Ultra-Orthodox Jews." *Journal for the Scientific Study of Religion* 46 (2): 201–16.

Fader, Alaya. 2006. "Learning Faith: Language Socialization in a Hasidic Community." *Language in Society* 35 (2): 205–29.

Giddens, Anthony. 1991. *Modernity and Self-Identity: Self and Society in the Late Modern Age*. Stanford, CA: Stanford University Press.

Glaser, Barney G., and Anselm L. Strauss. 1967. *The Discovery of Grounded Theory: Strategies for Qualitative Research*. Chicago: Aldine.

Goffman, Erving. 1959. *The Presentation of Self in Everyday Life*. New York: Doubleday.

Greil, Arthur L. 1977. "Previous Dispositions and Conversion to the Perspective of Social and Religious Movements." *Sociological Analysis* 38 (2): 115–25.

Greil, Arthur L., and David Rudy. 1984. "What Have We Learned from Process Models of Conversion?" *Sociological Focus* 17:305–23.

Griffith, R. Marie. 2004. *Born Again Bodies: Flesh and Spirit in American Christianity*. Berkeley: University of California Press.

Kanter, Rosabeth Moss. 1972. *Commitment and Community: Communes and Utopias in Sociological Perspective*. Boston: Harvard University Press.

Laderman, Carol. 1994. "The Embodiment of Symbols and the Acculturation of the Anthropologist." In *Embodiment and Experience: The Existential Ground of Culture and Self*, ed. Thomas J. Csordas, 183–97. Cambridge: Cambridge University Press.

Mahmood, Saba. 2005. *Politics of Piety: The Islamic Revival and the Feminist Subject*. Princeton, NJ: Princeton University Press.

McGuire, Meredith B. 2008. *Lived Religion: Faith and Practice in Everyday Life*. Oxford: Oxford University Press.

Turner, Bryan S. 1984. *The Body and Society: Explorations in Social Theory*. Oxford: Blackwell.

———. 1992. *Regulating Bodies: Essays in Medical Sociology*. London: Routledge.

Warner, R. Stephen. 1997. "Religion, Boundaries, and Bridges." 1996 Paul Hanly Furfey Lecture. *Sociology of Religion* 58 (3): 217–38.

Crossing the Menstrual Line

David Linton

It all began with Prince Charles. In 1993 "Camillagate," sparked by a surreptitiously recorded telephone conversation between the prince and his lover, Camilla Parker-Bowles, hit the international press. The two were heard engaging in sex talk, which included Charles's gushing, "I'll just live in your trousers or something. It would be much easier!" These words led to banter about Charles's becoming a tampon and other absurd fantasies. I was struck by the randiness of their exchange and the surprising inclusion of tampons in their phone sex. It led me to think about how women and men handle the presence of the period in their sex lives, so I turned to the classic works—Alfred Kinsey's two volumes on human sexual behavior—to find out what the pioneer sex researcher had found. To my amazement I discovered that Kinsey had skipped the topic entirely. Its absence inspired me to investigate further.

So I owe it to the Prince of Wales and Dr. Kinsey for turning me into a menstrual scholar and activist.

Though Charles has been roundly ridiculed and misrepresented for his tampon talk, I came to view him as an unwilling menstrual hero, a man who, at least in his private life, is not put off by the menstrual stereotypes.[1] There are other menstrual heroes, most notably Jesus. In the book of Luke (8:43), a woman "had had a flow of blood for twelve years and could not be healed." Today she would probably be diagnosed with menorrhagia or Von Willbrand disease, a rare blood-clotting disorder, but then, she would have been viewed as a perpetual menstruator, eternally unclean, contaminating, and forbidden to have contact with any man. In the story, the woman sneaked up behind Jesus to touch the hem of his garment in the hope of being healed. When Jesus sensed the contact, his disciple Peter, knowing that Leviticus decreed that, if the woman touched him, Jesus would have to go away and be cleansed, tried to deny her access. But then Jesus did what I have come to view as one of the most radical acts of his life. He accepted the touch and defied the taboo, telling the woman she was healed, and then turned to his other business.

Unfortunately, this act of sexual liberality has not been passed on as effectively as Jesus's many other admirable traits. And that fact testifies to the overwhelming power of the menstrual taboo, a set of tacit prohibitions that apply not only to women but to men, too. The menstrual cycle is commonly perceived as "women's business," a topic women should keep quiet about and men should avoid altogether. And men comply, rarely expressing interest in menstruation, except to gauge sexual availability or assess whether a woman is "PMS-ing."

When a man appears "excessively" curious about menstrual matters (which means curious at all) he crosses the menstrual line. Eyebrows are raised, questions are asked ("Why are *you* interested in the period?"), which imply that the man harbors an unseemly fascination or, worse yet, some sort of kinky, fetishistic fascination with a topic he should have learned to ignore.

I've been crisscrossing that line for years.

Though the Prince Charles story raised my curiosity, I don't recall ever having the "ewwwww" response at the mention of menstrual blood, being put off by the sight of blood on my penis during sex, or shopping uncomfortably for menstrual products. And I don't recall ever having dismissed a woman's behavior or feelings because she was getting her period. But it wasn't until I began researching and teaching menstrual studies that I can say I became a menstrual activist, someone committed to resisting the menstrual status quo.

Eight years later, I've accumulated a full range of puzzled, skeptical, suspicious, distrustful, hostile, appreciative, bemused, and sometimes encouraging responses to my work. Each reaction, I've learned, presents an opportunity to think about the meanings of menstrual embodiment and what it takes to resist menstrual stigma.

Admittedly, my position as a man, a straight man, has its advantages. And my status as a professor of communication studies helps, too. Though people rarely say this directly, I sense that once they get over their initial surprise at my interest, they really listen to what I am saying. I don't have an obvious ax to grind, after all, since I don't menstruate. And people don't typically see my fascination through a heteronormative lens as they might if they assumed I am gay (read: "Oh! I get it. No wonder he's interested in feminine things!") This set of privileges has helped me pry the period out of the closet.

The most powerful menstrual activism occurs in the classroom, in a course I designed and teach called the Social Construction of Menstruation. In the first session, I ask the students (mostly women but always a few men as well) what kinds of reactions they got when they told people they were taking this class (and the unexpected gender of the instructor). They respond with stories of incredulity or they reveal their own reluctance to utter a word to anyone. It is clear that the very act of signing up for the course is transgressive, and talking about it even more so. I want to support my students as they take these risks, so I tell them my own "menstrual history." The idea is that everyone has a menstrual history in the social and cultural sense, not only those who menstruate. These menstrual histories are constructed through what I call "menstrual transactions"—the encounters we have with one another that shape our attitudes toward the menstrual cycle. Every menstrual transaction reveals something telling about our cultural attitudes and our deeply embedded notions about gender and the body. As I help students ponder menstruation—hidden, forbidden, yet strangely ubiquitous—we enhance our understanding of how gender works. Our shared journey across the menstrual line leads us into new and exciting territory—an expansive place where honest talk and deep exploration make social change happen.

NOTE

1. I have written elsewhere about the press coverage; see David Linton, "Camillagate: Prince Charles and the Tampon Scandal," *Sex Roles* 54, no. 5/6 (March 2006): 347–51.

LIVING RESISTANCE

Myself, Covered

Beverly Yuen Thompson

"Would you just *look* at that guy with all those tattoos on his arm? Why would he do that?" my father growled, scowling at the man seated across the restaurant. I stared into my bowl of oatmeal, waiting for the moment to pass. I was careful not to pull self-consciously on the sleeves of my shirt, aware that it might give me away. It was, after all, difficult to justify wearing long sleeves in the middle of summer, every summer, for more than a decade. Luckily, my eighty-something father didn't seem to notice. But just in case, I had a list of excuses ready: sun protection, stylistic preference, acclimatization to the humidity of my adopted hometown three thousand miles southeast.

Aside from my father, I'd describe Spokane as having a very tattoo-friendly culture. That context fostered my early love of tattooing as an art form, along with my close friendship with Charissa Vaunderbroad, a local tattoo artist. When we were both nineteen, she tattooed an armband on my upper arm. With this third tattoo, however, I quickly discovered a deep conflict. While I loved the medium for personal expression, I did not love the attention, or, more accurately, the hostility that my tattoos often invoked, especially from older people. So I began my practice of hiding my tattoos, more and more as they encroached on my "public" skin. I chose to hide my tattoos from my father—for good reason. He knew of my friendship with Charissa and each time she was mentioned, he would unleash a torrent of angry verbal insults about the low status of tattooing, concluding with the damning question, "*You* haven't gotten any more tattoos, *have you?*"

I eventually told my father about my first two tattoos, but the third tattoo crossed the line of my father's grudging tolerance. From then on, I hid all my tattoos from him.

A new tattoo effectively sealed off the possibility of disclosure to my father. When I tattooed my Chinese zodiac sign—a snake—in a visible place on my arm, I knew I had crossed another line. My father harbors a hysterical, nearly phobic hatred of snakes; even the sight of the reptile on television provokes him to grab the remote control and zoom to another channel. Aware that my father could not endure even a televised snake, I knew he was incapable of casually glancing at his daughter's snake-decorated arm. I chose to hide the tattoo from my father. Even though my Chinese astrological sign is central to my self-understanding, concealment is necessary to preserve our otherwise close relationship.

Ironically, the bond of our shared profession (we are both academics) became the basis of my full backpiece tattoo. It depicts Saraswati, the Hindu goddess of book knowledge; a caricature of me reading stacks of books for graduate school; and a

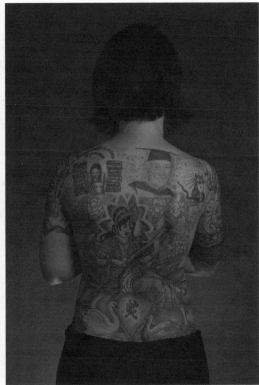

Beverly Yuen Thompson. (Photograph courtesy of Matt Crawford.)

portrait of my father in his academic regalia. Even more ironically, the location of the tattoo threatens to peek out of my shirt collar, thus requiring great vigilance about my clothing during my semiannual visits. I call it my "redemption tattoo" reasoning that, if my father were ever to find out about my heavily inked state, I could at least point to his portrait as proof of my desire to honor, not denigrate, him.

Later, when I moved to Manhattan to attend graduate school, I immediately felt unwelcome. As I walked around Chinatown during the sticky days of midsummer, angry glares pierced my tattooed skin. I could feel the onlookers' revulsion, so reminiscent of my father's own reactions. I had moved into a family member's apartment in a neighborhood full of long-term residents. As a mixed-race Chinese and Anglo American, heavily tattooed twenty-two-year-old, I was different. I spoke only English, entertained white people, and blared punk rock music. Many Chinese people perceived the tattoos that covered my body as deviance, as the worst possible outcome of Americanization. The reactions I experienced in Chinatown—social rejection and ostracism—were dramatically different than those in Spokane.

Luckily and curiously, Chinese hostility toward tattooing practices did not flow from my mother, who unconditionally accepted me. She was the exception. Her sister, however, expressed the quintessential negative reaction that I came to expect and dread from Chinese people. My aunt voiced discontent for all forms of body decoration, even threatening to revoke my cousin's financial support when she got her tongue pierced. Undeterred, my cousin enlisted me to find a tattoo artist. Thrilled by her interest in things her mother deemed illicit and I deemed beautiful, I spontaneously got a tattoo along with her, Chinese kanji symbols. This was risky; if her mother found out, surely our relationship would be in jeopardy. Unhindered, my cousin continued to get tattoos related to her heritage; at the same time, she continued to hide them from her mother. I understood why.

I became heavily tattooed because of my love of this particular art form. But my appreciation for the decorated body is fraught with heavy social sanctions from others around me: my father, my Chinese community, and my elders. My heavily tattooed status intertwines with my other identities: young, female, tattooed, professional, bisexual, and mixed race—each adds a layer of complexity to how others perceive me. While some treat me with hostility, others express acceptance, most notably, my Chinese mother. Once I asked for her impressions of my heavily tattooed state. She embraced me and simply said, "I don't really like it, but you're my daughter and I love you no matter what."

Afterword

Barbara Katz Rothman

What would it be like to be in a different body—for an hour, a day, a year, a lifetime? How much does the body you are (are in?) shape your life, your experiences? Some people play at this, create online personas, act "as if" in another body—but that will give you everything but the embodied experience.

We have astonishingly varied bodies—all so remarkably the same, all so equally remarkably different. Human beings range routinely from under seven pounds to over three hundred pounds and from about twenty inches tall to almost seven feet, and they have skin and hair in a well-remarked variety of colors and textures. As adults, we have all moved from somewhere near the smallest body size to somewhere closer to the largest. Other kinds of human variation remain forever foreign to some, ordinary to others: What does it feel like to have wind blowing through your long fine hair? Wind blowing through a tight bush of hair? Across a bald head? Some of those features we can play with—shave the head as one of the contributors did. Some we cannot—only a small minority of humans can ever feel the wind through long straight hair.

There are other differences we hardly know how to think about: What does a food taste like on another's tongue? How do colors look through other eyes—or what would it be like never to have seen color at all? To be "color blind"? To be totally blind? A few hours with a blindfold—an exercise designed to raise awareness of the experience of blindness—cannot answer that.

The world of scholarship has a long history of almost disembodied thought, acting as though scholars were pure minds, engaging with each other in bodiless worlds. Only recently are we confronting the body—its limitations, its lived experience, its consequences—and turning our attention to how people, embodied people, step in and out of their experience to confront the body.

This book focuses on not just the body but the body as a site of resistance, on the ways that people—sometimes in anger and sometimes in play, sometimes in community and sometimes all alone—make use of the body as a way of resisting social expectations.

Gender weaves its way through every one of these pieces—sometimes as its central theme, sometimes less so, but never absent. Is this showing some strange essentialism of gender, its place as an orienting point for confrontation with and through the body? Or is the prominence of gender in this book just a limitation of the state of scholarship, so heavily and recently influenced by feminist critiques of a male-assumed body? My phrasing of the question implies my answer: Feminist scholarship, I would argue, has in the past four decades forced an academic confrontation with the body.

In calling the past four decades "relatively recent," I bring to the fore another universal, perhaps essentializing body difference, that of age. A person in her sixties, as I am, can think of four decades of feminist scholarship as "relatively recent." A person in her twenties or younger, as so many readers of this volume are likely to be, might not see it that way. The pieces in this volume that do deal with age, do that too through the lens of gender, looking at menopause and at the members of the Red Hat Society's play with sexuality and aging.

Race is sometimes used as an essentializing body difference, but it is far harder to do that: the "race differences" are so often rather random—hair type defining race in one culture, nose shape in another, skin color in yet others. In the piece on body hair, for example, so deeply focused on gender, race/ethnic differences come through a very odd and (again in the context of a sixty-plus-year life span) relatively recent American lens in which "Latin American" women are a race group, contrasted with "white" women. Locate the project in a different community or moment, and "white" women would include fair-skinned, light-haired Irish women and dark-skinned, black-haired Greek women, and the awareness and presence of body hair would be strikingly different.

So what do we learn from this? That there are no universals? That it makes no sense to essentialize the body? Sure, of course. But more profoundly, I think, we learn that people are so very clever in their uses of the tools that are available to us. And the body is, whatever else it is, our tool. We work it, with some success, with some failure, with some joy and some agony, we negotiate the world in the bodies we have or can make for ourselves. The body is our universal tool; the body is our essential presence in the world. If we are political, we must be political through our bodies. If we are angry, happy, engaged, disengaged, organizing or isolating ourselves, we do it through our bodies.

It's time then, more than time, for this book and the ones that will follow, for academics to rise up, stretch, wriggle to a more comfortable position, rub our overfocused eyes, and look—not just out, not just around, but also inward and downward—at the hands that write the treatise, with fingers that are manicured or not, bejeweled or not; at the face and body at the podium, dressed and made-up according to whatever are the standards of the moment. And when we do look around, we need to look at the bodies seated in classrooms and seminars all around us. It is time to look at all this, and think about the body, as the editors and contributors of this book are doing. It is time and more than time for scholars to see how those bodies are being used as tools of the people who are those bodies, people who are in those bodies, people who own and are owned by those bodies. Only then can we move to a new scholarship of "the body," a scholarship that deals with our own and each other's bodies.

Classroom Resources

1. The Specter of Excess: Race, Class, and Gender in Women's Body Hair Narratives

Discussion Questions
1. Michel Foucault has said that power is tolerable only on the condition that it remain invisible. How might this statement apply to the enforcement of shaving norms? How might hair relate to power?
2. Does the hairless norm for women symbolize the sexualization of youth? Is the shaved vulva a symbol of a prepubescent girl? Why is it considered "sexy" and what does its being so say about hegemonic masculinity?
3. What social penalties are in place for those who violate shaving norms? What experiences have you had personally with this? Why do individuals who are otherwise politically rebellious and progressive feel the need to maintain the status quo with their shaving practices? What does their doing so say about the social construction of body norms?

Class Assignments and Exercises
1. Offer students extra credit for rejecting the cultural norm of shaving for one semester, despite their current shaving status. For most women, this would involve not shaving for ten to twelve weeks. For most men, it would involve shaving for ten to twelve weeks. Ask students to keep a log of their experiences and to write a one- to two-page reflection paper guided by the following questions: What did you feel emotionally while rejecting the cultural norm of shaving? What was this experience like? In what way did this experience affect your health, sexuality, and feelings about your own body? Did anything change behaviorally? What about internally? What kind of external feedback, if any, did you receive? What did that feel like? How has this experience allowed you to reflect on the social construction of bodily norms, particularly as they relate to sexuality?
2. Ask students to interview at least five friends and family members about their body hair practices, ensuring that they interview at least one woman and one man. Students should ask interviewees about their body hair practices, probing for how race, class, gender, and sexual identity factor into their decisions. Students should then write a reaction paper detailing their reactions to these conversations; their friends' and family's reactions; and the race, class, gender, and sexual identity implications of body hair practices.
3. Show students a variety of images of women who have body hair. Discuss their initial reaction to these images—disgust, empowerment, and so on—and confront myths surrounding dirty and unhygienic discourses about women's body hair. Break students

into small groups and ask them to discuss the following questions: How are these images unusual? Does shaving imply agreement with society's regulation of women's bodies? How else can the body be politicized? Does race, sexual orientation, and socioeconomic class affect how people view women's body hair? Why do women feel pressured to conform to body norms and how or why might they resist these norms?

Films

Juggling Gender (1992)—27 minutes

A film that explores the life of Jennifer Miller, a self-described "bearded lady" who grows facial hair naturally and purposefully does not shave to challenge expectations about gender and performance. The film examines people's reactions to Miller and features Miller's narratives about violating the norms of facial hair. Directed by Tami Gold.

Fuck Off, I'm a Hairy Woman (2007)—56 minutes

The British director of this film that explores body image and contrasting stereotypes about women's body hair conducts an experiment in which she grows out her body hair for six months. The film takes up questions about what it means to grow body hair in a culture that demands hairlessness as a fundamental standard of beauty for Western women. Directed by Shazia Mirza.

Why We Wax (2007)—19 minutes

A short, humorous documentary that explores modern culture's preoccupation with hair removal and why women remove pubic hair. Film website: *www.whywewax.com/*. Directed by Kimberly Wetherell and Amy Axelson.

Web Resources

www.thefword.org.uk/features/2007/05/a_hairy_dilemma

Features one woman's discussion of hair removal as a feminist issue. Emma Chaplin is a writer and counselor.

www.theladyfinger.com/2009/03/body-hair-and-gender-binary.html

A blog post featuring a feminist reflecting on why she chooses not to shave. The blog includes a discussion of internalized definitions of women's beauty and the perspective that growing out body hair is a step in breaking down gender binaries.

www.straightdope.com/columns/read/625/who-decided-women-should-shave-their-legs-and-underarms

A Q&A about the historical origins of women shaving their underarms, legs, and pubic hair, including marketing campaigns targeting women as early as 1915 and early razor advertisements in the 1920s.

2. "Is That Any Way to Treat a Lady?": The Dominatrix's Dungeon

Discussion Questions

1. Why has the intersection of BDSM (bondage, discipline, sadism, and masochism) and gender been an issue of concern for feminists? Consider both sides of the major feminist debate about BDSM, including the merits and drawbacks of each side.
2. Describe some ways in which pro-dommes "wear" traditional femininity on their bodies. How are these performances contradictions, that is, acts of both gender complicity and subversion?

3. Summarize Butler's argument about the "parodic recontextualization" of gender on the body. How do pro-dommes and their clients "parodically recontextualize" gender in their cross-dressing scenes?

Class Assignments and Exercises

1. Hold an in-class viewing of the episode "Love Hurts" of the television show *House M.D.* (2004 [season 1, episode 20]). In the episode, a patient arrives at the hospital with injuries inflicted by a professional dominatrix. Have each student write a short essay reacting to the episode, using this chapter as a context. Does the chapter challenge, refute, or affirm any of the claims about professional erotic dominance this television show makes?
2. Hold an in-class viewing of the episode "La Douleur Exquise!" of the television show *Sex and the City* (1999 [season 2, episode 12]). In this episode, the protagonist, Carrie Bradshaw, begins to think about her relationship with her lover, "Mr. Big," in terms of sadism and masochism. Engage the class in a discussion about the episode, in the context of this chapter. What does "La Douleur Exquise!" reveal about the ways in which BDSM reflects gendered relationships in larger society? Have students assess the argument the episode makes about erotic sadism and masochism as components of more "traditional" erotic encounters outside of the dominatrix's dungeon.
3. Divide the class into two groups: one group to defend and one group to critique female-dominated BDSM from a feminist perspective. Have the groups confer for ten minutes and then present their arguments. Have them confer once more and then respond to the other side's arguments. Conclude with an open discussion.

Films

Secretary (2002)—1 hour, 44 minutes
>   A film about an S&M relationship that develops between a young woman, who has just been released from a mental hospital, and her boss at a law firm. The man becomes the "dominant" partner and the woman becomes the "submissive" partner in their relationship. Directed by Steven Shainberg.

9½ Weeks (1986)—1 hour, 52 minutes
>   A film that explores the dynamics of a violent sexual relationship between a Wall Street businessman and an art gallery owner. Directed by Adrian Lyne.

The Notorious Bettie Page (2005)—1 hour, 31 minutes
>   A biographical film that follows the life and career of the 1950s pinup and bondage model Bettie Page. Directed by Mary Harron.

Web Resources

sm-feminist.blogspot.com/
>   A blog of a self-identified pro-S&M feminist that includes comments from those who agree and those who disagree with the blogger's politics.

www.bettiepage.com/
>   The official Bettie Page website, featuring an extensive photo gallery, including her controversial bondage photographs.

www.maxfisch.com/
>   A portal to an index of dominatrix websites listed by U.S. city.

3. "Cruisin' for a Bruisin'": Women's Flat Track Roller Derby

Discussion Questions
1. How would the most recent revival of roller derby have been different if it had remained strictly an occupation for women? Would "professionalizing" the sport change it in any significant ways?
2. How do other women's sports compare with flat track roller derby? Reflect on your own experiences with rugby, soccer, tennis, basketball, cheerleading, and other sports. Where else in women's sports do we see the potential for embodied resistance?
3. Is it important to have both a cultural and physical space in sports for transgressive, marginalized, or "othered" bodies? Why or why not?

Class Assignments and Exercises
1. Place students in small groups. Assign each group to a derby-related website or allow students to select a derby-related website of their choice. Instruct each group to analyze the contents of their chosen site. Each group should then present their "findings" to the class. What did they discover about gender, sport, and body? Several possible websites beyond the three recommended in "Web Resources" include *www.deviantderby.com*, *www.fracturemag.com*, *www.gothamgirlsrollerderby.com*, *www.bayareaderbygirls.com*, and *www.derbynewsnetwork.com*.
2. Plan an in-class screening of one of the three recommended films. Use the film as a lead-in to a discussion about this chapter. Ask students to reflect on the portrayals of embodied resistance in the film and in the chapter. In what ways are the portrayals similar; in what ways are they different?
3. Ask your local roller derby league for the names of skaters who might be willing to speak in your class. Have students prepare "interview questions" for the skaters who agree. Or, consider taking your class to a roller derby bout. Have students write up field notes from the evening, paying special attention to the meanings about gender, body, and sport.

Films
Whip It (2009)—1 hour, 51 minutes
    A film about Bliss Cavender, a girl who grows tired of her small-town Texas life and finds excitement after joining a roller derby team. Based on the novel *Whip It* by Shauna Cross, a former Los Angeles Derby Doll. Directed by Drew Barrymore.
Hell on Wheels: The Birth of All-Girl Roller Derby (2008)—1 hour, 30 minutes
    A documentary that explores the roots of the modern roller derby revival that began in Austin, Texas. Directed by Bob Ray and produced by Werner Campbell.
Blood on the Flat Track: The Rise of the Rat City Rollergirls (2007)—1 hour, 35 minutes
    A documentary about Seattle's premiere all-women's flat track derby league, the Rat City Rollergirls, and their first two seasons. The film focuses on the individual players and the relationships between teammates. Directed by Lainy Bagwell and Lacey Leavitt.

Web Resources
www.wftda.com/
    The official website of the Women's Flat Track Derby Association, the international governing body of women's flat track roller derby. Includes roller derby rules, tips, and information about tournaments and rankings.

www.bigderbygirls.blogspot.com/
> A blog dedicated to challenging misconceptions about female athletes of size. Maintained by rollergirl Cindy Lop-Her, whose early entries discuss how derby has helped her become comfortable with her body. Features the "Campaign for Real Booty," which displays photos of larger derby girls to celebrate the larger physique.

www.derbyhurts.ning.com/
> A website, described as the "online home for the injured and fallen," where injured derby skaters can communicate with one another and share stories, photos, and advice. Maintained by skater Raven Von Kaos.

4. Becoming a Female-to-Male Transgender (FTM) in South Korea

Discussion Questions

1. What are some situations in which sex-specific ID cards might prove problematic for South Korean transgender individuals? What are the consequences of having sex identification on national ID cards? Are there similar scenarios for transgender individuals in the United States? Discuss the benefits and the drawbacks of these ID cards.
2. Should there be government-imposed guidelines for legal sex reassignment? If yes, what should these guidelines include? What are the potential consequences of these guidelines? Are there cases in which the government should not allow legal sex reassignment? If so, why?
3. Think of an occasion or a context in which you had difficulty or hesitated to use a gender-specific pronoun (such as *he* or *she*). Why did this hesitation arise and how did you respond to the situation? Did it make you uncomfortable and, if so, why? What would you do in a situation in which you were not sure about a person's gender?

Class Assignments and Exercises

1. As a class, watch the film *Transamerica* and consider the role of medical institutions in the transgender transitioning process. Discuss the following questions in groups: What role do psychologists play in the transition? Do family members need to be notified or consulted when a person makes a decision to transition? At what age do you think an individual should be able to make the decision to transition without parental consent? To what extent should aspects of the transition, such as hormonal therapy and surgery, be covered by health insurance?
2. Ask students to think about their experiences with gender and sexuality during middle school and high school and to describe the ways in which gender and sexuality were formally or informally regulated. What kind of sexuality and gender behavior were considered "normal" or "popular" in the peer culture? Were there school regulations concerning non-normative gender behavior or homosexuality? Then ask students to write a brief policy recommendation for a high school that addresses how teachers and administrators should handle gender nonconformity. Include a list of any rules they believe should be implemented in the school and a list of any specific rights they believe students should have in the area of gender expression.
3. Have students undertake a short survey of transgender people's rights in various countries. Students should choose several countries that grant legal recognition for

transgender people and briefly describe when and through what process the country granted legal recognition of transpeople. They should compare the rights that are available in each country (e.g., support for sex reassignment surgery, laws prohibiting discrimination based on gender identity, rights concerning legal sex reassignment). Students could also look at countries that do not recognize transgender people's rights and compare these societies to those of countries that do. After completing this research, students should present their findings to the class.

Films

Transgeneration (2005)—4 hours, 32 minutes

An eight-part documentary series that depicts the everyday lives of four transgender college students in the United States. The film features Raci (an MTF first-year college student and an immigrant from the Philippines and TJ (an FTM graduate student from Cyprus) as they deal with issues of ethnicity, social class, and family in the process of transitioning. Directed by Jeremy Simmons.

Transamerica (2005)—1 hour, 43 minutes

One week before her sex reassignment surgery, Bree, a transgender woman previously called Stanley, receives a telephone call from seventeen-year-old Toby, who claims that Stanley is his biological father. Before undergoing her surgery, Bree takes a journey across the United States with her son. Directed by Duncan Tucker.

Beautiful Boxer (2003)—1 hour 58 minutes

This film tells the story of Thailand's famous transgender kickboxer Parinya Charoenphol, who enters Muaythai boxing to save enough money to pursue a sex reassignment surgery. The film follows her life story from her childhood to her stunning career as a kickboxer, defying the normative constructions of femininity and masculinity. Directed by Ekachai Uekrongtham.

Web Resources

www.ftmi.org/

FTM International is the largest international female-to-male organization. The organization publishes a FTM newsletter and provides information for family members, and information about legal rights and about attaining medical care.

web.hku.hk/~sjwinter/TransgenderASIA/

The Transgender ASIA Research Centre brings together researchers and medical and legal experts to promote an understanding of transpeople in Asia. The website features news updates on issues affecting the transgender community and a directory of research conducted by members of the organization.

alp.org/

The Audre Lorde Project is a lesbian, gay, bisexual, two-spirit, trans, and gender nonconforming people of color community-organizing center that focuses on New York City. Since 1994, the website has provided information about their positions on issues affecting the community, helpful websites for the community, and an events calendar.

5. "Give Me a Boa and Some Bling!": Red Hat Society Members Commanding Visibility in the Public Sphere

Discussion Questions

1. The authors of this chapter argue that the social construction of aging implies that one should approach the "maintenance" of aging with some degree of acceptance of the inevitable, even humor. Why do you think the majority of women in this society feel it is psychologically more difficult to age "gracefully" than, say, women of fifty years ago? What avenues does the Red Hat Society (RHS) provide for women to age "gracefully"?

2. Visualize yourself at fifty, sixty-five, and eighty-five. What will life be like for you? What will you care about? Will you be old? Why or why not? Discuss what visualizing yourself as an older person is like. What will you most look forward to? What will you most fear?

3. Think of an older woman that you know either personally or through books, movies, television, or other media who is a positive role model for older women. What about this woman makes her a good role model? How is this woman's behavior and appearance a reflection of the themes raised in the chapter?

Class Assignments and Exercises

1. Go to the RHS website (*www.redhatsociety.com/*) and find an RHS group in your area. Contact that chapter's queen mother and arrange for students to attend a meeting. Observe and interact with the group. After the meeting, ask students to write an analysis exploring concepts raised in the chapter. For example, how do RHS members resist aging stereotypes for older women? Alternatively, invite RHS members to class for a panel discussion about their involvement in the RHS. Ask students to prepare questions to ask members about their aging experiences.

2. Ask students to interview a family member or friend who is an RHS member. Have them ask her about her experience participating in the RHS. Does she consider herself an "old lady"? Does she think about her participation as resisting stereotypes? What personal benefits does she get out of participating? How do her responses help you understand the role of the RHS in the lives of older women? Or, ask students to interview an older relative of friend who is not a member. Have them ask her about her experience with getting older and her thoughts about stereotypes and the role of the RHS in challenging them. Does she consider herself an "old lady"? What does she think about the RHS? Does she think it is important to resist stereotypes of older women? How do her responses help you to understand the role of the RHS in the lives of older women? Is participating in the RHS the only way to combat stereotypes of older women?

3. Have students read and discuss excerpts from one or more of the books the following list. Have them also write an analysis of the work(s) based on the ideas raised in this chapter.

    Cooper, Sue Ellen. 2004. *The Red Hat Society: Fun and Friendship after Fifty*. New York: Warner. (ISBN-10 0446679763; ISBN-13 978-0446679763)

    Cooper, Sue Ellen. 2005. *The Red Hat Society's Laugh Lines: Stories of Inspiration and Hattitude*. New York: Grand Central. (ISBN 0446695114)

    Smith, Haywood. 2005. *The Red Hat Club*. New York: St. Martin's. (ISBN 0312349548)

    Sutherland, Regina Hale. 2006. *The Red Hat Society's Acting Their Age*. New York: Warner Vision Books. (ISBN 0446616745)

Films

The Remarkable Red Hat Society (2007)—55 minutes

A documentary detailing the origins and evolution of the RHS from a small group in California to an international sensation. The film also explores the various ways women participate in the group, including sisters, coworkers, mothers, and daughters. Directed by Fredric Cohen.

Raging Grannies (2009)—30 minutes

An award-winning documentary that follows the activities of the Raging Grannies Action League from the San Francisco Bay Area Peninsula. These elderly women dress in outrageous outfits and protest against various forms of social injustice. Directed by Pam Walton.

Still Doing It: The Intimate Lives of Women over Sixty—54 minutes

A documentary that explores the sex and love lives of nine older women ages sixty-seven to eighty-seven. These women offer frank accounts of their sex lives and demonstrate the diversity of sexual experiences older women can experience. Directed by Deirdre Fishel.

Web Resources

www.redhatsociety.com/

The official website for the RHS, with information about how the organization started, what they aim to do, how to join, special discounts for members, weekly broadcasts, and photographs of gatherings.

www.redhatsociety.com/partners/musical/index.html

A website for the musical comedy *Hats!* inspired by the experiences and philosophies of the RHS. It features press coverage, biographies of composers, and song clips from the musical.

www.bluethongsociety.com/

The official website for the Blue Thong Society, an organization of women of all ages who "fight frump" and aim to be fabulous while being philanthropic. Features membership information, the story of how they started, and photo galleries.

6. Fat. Hairy. Sexy: Contesting Standards of Beauty and Sexuality in the Gay Community

Discussion Questions

1. Individuals are drawn to big men's and bear groups mainly to fulfill their social and sexual desires. How and why do these groups also produce activity that can be defined as protest?

2. How do big men, bears, and chasers challenge cultural codes within the gay male community? Within the queer community? Within U.S. culture as a whole?

3. In what ways do big men, bears, and chasers embody resistance similarly? In what ways do these three groups embody resistance differently?

Class Assignments and Exercises

1. Have students watch television for half an hour, noting endorsements of the thin ideal, for example, the prevalence and characterization of thin and fat people in shows and commercials and advertisements for diets, "low fat" foods, and other weight-loss

products. Students should bring their notes to class for discussion, thinking about how these depictions affect how we think about gender, sexuality, and physical attractiveness.

2. Ask students to surf the Internet for mainstream gay-male-targeted media, for example, *out.com* and *gay.com*. What kind of body image ideal is being endorsed here? What kinds of bodies are displayed as sexual and sexy? What kinds of bodies are excluded? Have students write a short reflection paper on their observations.

3. Have students go to *BiggerCity.com*, click on "Profiles," and then use the drop box labeled "I'm seeking" to select (1) bears and (2) chubs. From the pictures, what major similarities and differences do they observe between these two groups? Given the similarity and overlap between these two identities, what might lead someone to choose one or the other? Discuss these issues in small groups.

Films

Bear Run (2008)—52 minutes

A documentary that profiles three bear-identified men and talks about how they came out, dealt with body image, and found connection and affirmation in the bear community. The film provides a window into the bear culture's values and rituals. Film website: *www.bearrunthemovie.com/*. Directed by Dan Hunt.

Bear Nation (2010)—1 hour, 22 minutes

Directed by a bear-identified filmmaker, the film features interviews with people at bear conventions nationwide and discusses issues about body image and the dominant gay community. Film website: *bearnationmovie.com/*. Directed by Malcolm Ingram.

Web Resources

www.biggercity.com/aboutus/default.aspx

Launched in 1999, Biggercity is an online community that has since grown to become the largest online site for large gay men and their admirers. It functions as a social networking site where big men and their admirers who might not otherwise have met find connections.

www.bosf.org/index.html

Founded in 1994, Bears of San Francisco (BOSF) has become one of the largest and most active bear organizations. The website features an events schedule, newsletters, and information about the organization. Every year BOSF hosts International Bear Rendezvous, one of the most popular annual bear events.

www.queertheory.com/academics/scholars/names/scholars_wright_les.htm

Provides information about the scholar Les Wright, editor of two books on the bear community. The site features Wright's two books, *Bear Book* and *Bear Book II*, which discuss from an insider's perspective the origins and trajectory of the community.

7. Belly Dancing Mommas: Challenging Cultural Discourses of Maternity

Discussion Questions

1. What expectations are placed on pregnant women and new mothers today? What do you think of these expectations? Are they reasonable or unreasonable? Why do you think so?

2. How are expectations about pregnancy communicated to women? How are they

enforced? Do you agree with the author that belly dancing challenges these expectations? Why or why not?

3. What is your opinion of belly dance as a form of recreation for Western women? Do you see problems with this practice? Why or why not? Do you think women who belly dance are helping or hurting feminism? Why or why not?

Class Assignments and Exercises

1. Ask students to spend a few hours in a setting where pregnant women are readily visible, such as a park, a fair, a mall, or stores catering to children or pregnant women. Note how the women are dressed and how they behave. Do their appearances and behavior conform with or challenge the cultural discourses of maternity outlined in this chapter?

2. Have students interview two women—someone who is or has been pregnant and someone who has never been pregnant. Have them ask questions similar to those asked in the chapter: What are some stereotypes about pregnancy and early motherhood? What expectations or rules does society place on pregnant women's appearance, behavior, and activities? On new mothers? Have students compare their interviews with those by other students and with the narratives in this chapter.

3. Break students into teams, with at least one woman in each team who is willing to "play" being pregnant. Devise a way of making her appear pregnant (e.g., stuffing the midsection of her clothes) and modestly clothed (e.g., full shirts, longer shorts, skirts, or pants). Position her in public settings, with other team members in locations where they are able to view her and others' responses to her. Note baseline observations: How do people react to a presumably pregnant and modest woman? Change her dress, however possible, in ways that seem more or less modest and note reactions. Change her presumed activities, however possible, in ways that seem less appropriate; for example, have her hold a cigarette, enter a bar, exercise vigorously, or eat junk food, and observe reactions from bystanders.

Films

Dance to the Great Mother (2008)—38 minutes

A performance by American belly dancer Delilah during her third trimester of pregnancy. Through dance, she expresses the joy and mystery of the arrival of new life through the female body. The film also includes an interview with Delilah about her performance and, more generally, about belly dancing. Directed by Delilah Flynn.

Belly Dancing During Pregnancy (1997)—1 hour, 30 minutes

A German-based film that provides information about the history and benefits of belly dance during pregnancy. The film includes interviews with a historian and physiotherapist and an instructional portion for conditioning and childbirth preparation. Directed by Gaby Oeftering.

Prenatal Belly Dance (2006)—35 minutes

A dance and workout video for expectant mothers, geared toward pre- and postnatal fitness, comfort, and stress reduction. The instruction is aimed at beginners and nondancers. Directed by Naia.

Web Resources

www.bellydanceforbirth.com/

Provides information about the benefits of belly dancing during and after pregnancy and about Bellydanceforbirth, a curriculum created by Maha Al Musa, a professional belly dancer and doula of Middle Eastern descent.

www.youtube.com/watch?v=XkVBmJBWKAA/

A 1994 video of the professional belly dancer Lynette Harris of Gilded Serpent. In this video, Lynette performs at a show with one of her snakes when she is thirty-eight weeks pregnant.

www.youtube.com/HOTmilkLingerie/?has_verified=1#p/u/2/D9KO-Oq_SZU

An advertisement for Hot Milk Lingerie, a maker of maternity lingerie. Depicts a woman performing a seductive dance for her partner. She dances clumsily because of her pregnancy, which is revealed only at the end of the commercial.

8. "It's Important to Show Your Colors": Counter-Heteronormativity in a Metropolitan Community Church

Discussion Questions

1. What is heteronormativity? How do members of Shepherd Church engage in counter-heteronormative embodiment? While the authors offer a particular example of oppositional embodiment, what are other ways individuals and groups strategically employ their bodies to resist or challenge heteronormativity?

2. Why are our bodies central to the practice of religion? How do people use bodies to give meaning to who they are as social and religious beings?

3. In what ways do you and your friends reproduce or challenge heteronormativity? Why do you think it is difficult for some people to challenge it? If heteronormativity were completely dismantled, how would our embodied selves be different?

Class Assignments and Exercises

1. Place students into small groups and ask them to develop their own religious group based on three moral rules. Ask them to consider the following: How would you encourage new converts to use their bodies to mark who belongs or not? How would your groups' embodied practices reflect your new religion's moral foundations? Groups should then present their "new religion" to the rest of the class.

2. Have students sketch a picture of a "religious" person and of a "nonreligious" person. Pass the sketches around in small groups. Within the groups, have them answer the following questions: (1) What characteristics do the "religious" people have? (2) What characteristics do the "nonreligious" people have? (3) What might the responses to the first two questions tell us about how religious identities are embodied?

3. Put students in small groups and have them develop their own religious ritual. Use the following questions as a guideline: How would people use their bodies to perform the ritual in congregational services or activities? How would these bodily endeavors demonstrate particular religious beliefs, values, and meanings to those who witnessed or participated in the ritual? How does the ritual begin or end and who decides or signals these details to the other participants and how do they do it? What might this exercise tell us about the importance of the body for marking membership in a particular religious culture? Groups should then present their "religious ritual" to the rest of the class.

Films

For the Bible Tells Me So (2007)—1 hour, 35 minutes

A documentary that explores how some Christian groups have used scriptures to deny human rights to gay and lesbian people around the world. The film features interviews with Protestant and Jewish theologians and five Christian families, each with a gay or lesbian child. Directed by Daniel G. Karslake.

Prayers for Bobby (2009)—1 hour, 30 minutes

A film chronicling the story of a young gay man and his mother, Mary, who struggles to reconcile religious teaching with homosexuality. After losing her son to suicide, Mary seeks answers about homosexuality and religion and, in doing so, becomes an advocate for gay rights and Christian tolerance. Directed by Russell Mulcahy.

A Jihad for Love (2007)—1 hour, 21 minutes

A documentary directed by a Muslim gay filmmaker that explores the struggles of homosexual Muslims in twelve countries. The film examines how they reconcile their sexuality with their religion and Islamic law, which defines homosexuality as an act punishable by death. Directed by Parvez Sharma.

Web Resources

www.mccchurch.org/

The official website of the United Fellowship of Metropolitan Community Churches. The site offers an expansive overview of denominational and congregational plans, programs, activities, and theological interpretations promoted by the membership.

www.religioustolerance.org/

Represents a conglomeration of religious interest groups and perspectives on a wide variety of social issues. It includes a section on homosexuality and bisexuality with essays from a wide variety of theological perspectives.

www.chirhopress.com/

Chi Rho Press publishes books and resources about spiritual and religious concerns of lesbian, gay, bisexual, and transgender people. The site contains summaries of their books and links to other spiritual websites pertaining to the LGBT community.

9. Anorexia as a Choice: Constructing a New Community of Health and Beauty through Pro-Ana Websites

Discussion Questions

1. In what ways is pro-ana resistance similar to or different from other forms of resistance discussed in this book? Are there limits to this type of resistance?

2. Freedom of speech is a fundamental right in the United States, but people's first reaction to pro-ana websites is often a desire to shut them down. Indeed, the site providers have shut down many pro-ana websites. Discuss the importance of freedom of speech in contrast to people's desire to avoid promoting anorexia.

3. Discuss the representations of women in the media compared with women in the real world. In what ways are the women on television and in film (not just models but also police officers, doctors, and homemakers) different from the women we encounter in real life? Discuss recent ad campaigns that seem to advocate greater acceptance of women in various sizes, such as Nike's "Big Butts, Thunder Thighs, and Tomboy

Knees" or Dove's Campaign for Real Bodies. Do these campaigns represent a truly new perspective? Do they depict women who are actually "normal" or "big"?

Class Assignments and Exercises

1. As an in-class exercise, have students work in small groups to conduct a content analysis of magazine advertisements, looking for themes of body image and gender. Each group will work with one magazine, flipping through the entire magazine and paying attention to the advertisements. Who is portrayed in these ads? Approximately what percentage of the entire magazine's ads contains men? What percentage contains women? What types of products are being advertised? How is sex and sexuality portrayed in these advertisements? What body sizes are most common in the ads? Are there any outliers? Ask each group to choose one advertisement they feel is representative of the overall pattern found in the magazine. After answering these questions as a group, have each group present their results to the entire class.

2. Have students explore websites devoted to the fat acceptance movement (such as Fat!So? at *www.fatso.com/*). Compare the different forms of resistance related to health, beauty, body image, and size. In what ways is resistance in the fat-acceptance movement similar to, and different from, pro-ana resistance?

3. Arrange for an in-class screening of Jean Kilbourne's *Killing Us Softly 4*. Ask students to write a short reflection paper that compares the different perspectives on media influence. Which is more powerful, media or individuals?

Films

Killing Us Softly 4 (1999)—45 minutes
Part of the *Killing Us Softly* series, a film featuring Jean Kilbourne, who analyzes print and television advertisements and discusses the destructive gender stereotypes they create. Directed by Sut Jhally.

Dying to Be Thin (2000)—1 hour
A NOVA documentary narrated by Susan Sarandon that covers anorexia nervosa and bulimia. The film explores cultural pressure for thinness, why some people develop eating disorders, and the role of psychotherapy for recovery. Film website: *www.pbs.org/wgbh/nova/thin/*. Directed by Larkin McPhee.

Thin (2006)—1 hour, 42 minutes
A film that features four women who struggle with anorexia at Renfrew Treatment Center. The film follows the women for six months and highlights the complexity of eating disorders. Directed by Lauren Greenfield.

Web Resources

www.something-fishy.org/
A website organized to raise awareness of what eating disorders are and how to recognize them. The site provides resources for those recovering from eating disorders, and their family members.

famine.brokensanity.org/
A comprehensive website examining many of the features of pro–eating disorder websites, including discussions of the dangers of eating disorders. The site includes health consequences of "tips and tricks" anorexics use and a comparison of "photo-shopped" bone pictures with the original images.

webiteback.com/
> A website devoted to those who formerly visited (and sometimes created) pro-ana websites. Its goal is recovery by attempting to provide the same support that young women found on pro-ana websites.

10. Public Mothers and Private Practices: Breastfeeding as Transgression

Discussion Questions
1. What do you perceive to be the norms for breastfeeding? Do you feel they are appropriate or should they be challenged?
2. Is there an age when a child is too old to breastfeed? Does your opinion change according to the country he or she lives in or what other access to food or water might exist? What should be the responses in such situations? That is, how should these expectations of acceptability be enforced?
3. What is one activity you do every day in public that is important to you? Smoke? Drink coffee? Drink alcohol? Ride a bike? Run? What would you do if you received negative reactions in public to this act? How would you change your behavior?

Class Assignments and Exercises
1. Have students examine the laws regarding protection for breastfeeding mothers. (The La Leche League website, *www.llli.org*, described under "Web Resources," includes a map.) Some laws protect women in public, some simply exempt them from criminal prosecution, and some provide job protection and assurance of a space to pump breast milk or feed babies. Discuss the following in small groups: Do you think these laws are necessary? Are they fair? What additional laws or changes to existing laws would you want to see passed?
2. Ask students to look at media images from magazines from various genres. What are the differences in how breasts are seen or represented? Are breasts sexualized? How are these images different than images of breastfeeding? Do they see images or information that supports breastfeeding? How do these images reflect and reinforce cultural notions about breasts? Have students write a short reflection paper addressing these questions.
3. Newborn babies nurse every two to three hours (measured from the start of one feeding to the start of the next) for thirty to forty minutes each time. Older babies nurse every three to four hours for twenty to thirty minutes each time. In thinking about a mother's schedule, which might include paid employment, volunteer work, picking up and dropping children off at school or care, going out to dinner, taking children to the park or mall, running errands, or visiting with friends, how do students imagine breastfeeding would fit into her day? What ways do they see to do this without nursing in public? How do the demands of breastfeeding complement or collide with other social expectations of women? Have students write a short reflection paper addressing these questions.

Films
Away We Go (2009)—1 hour, 38 minutes
> A film about an expectant couple who take a transcontinental trip to meet old friends and relatives to decide where they would like to raise their child. They meet up with

an old friend who makes them feel uncomfortable when she breastfeeds her toddler in public and reveals her other personal quirks. Directed by Sam Mendes.

20/20: Extreme Breastfeeding: How Old Is Too Old? (2008)—video clips

A news report exploring how long mothers should breastfeed their children. Features interviews with parents and children about their experiences with breastfeeding past infancy and an interview with the anthropologist Katherine Dettwyler, who has written commentaries on extended breastfeeding. (Originally aired November 9, 2008.) Web clip available at: *www.youtube.com/watch?v=qRqGXS6RmKs* or *abcnews.go.com/video/ playerIndex?id=6427971.*

Breasts: A Documentary (1996)—50 minutes

A film featuring twenty-two girls and women, ranging in age from eleven to eighty-four, who talk about their breasts. Subjects covered include adolescence, bras, commercial images of women's figures, plastic surgery, breasts as power tools and as objects of pleasure, and cancer. Directed by Meema Spadola.

Web Resources

www.007b.com/breastfeeding_movies.php

The 007 Breasts website promotes breastfeeding. It features a list of breastfeeding scenes in movies, information about the breastfeeding taboo, and information about breastfeeding in public.

www.llli.org/

Started by seven women, La Leche League International is an organization that provides information and support to breastfeeding mothers worldwide. The site includes mother-to-mother forums, question-and-answer pages, and education about breastfeeding.

www.cdc.gov/breastfeeding/

The Centers for Disease Control and Prevention provide information, resources, overview of research, and professional recommendations about breastfeeding.

11. "It's Hard to Say": Moving Beyond the Mystery of Female Genital Pain

Discussion Questions

1. Why is the word *vulva* so uniformly absent from popular conversation? What is its relationship to the word (and idea of a) *cunt*? What effect do you think this linguistic absence has on a woman's ability to fully understand her body? How is the word *vagina* different and how do these differences matter? Does the regular use of any of these three words constitute an act of resistance? Of complicity?

2. What does the author mean by "heteronormativity"? What is the relationship she posits between a straight-oriented social order and the way vulvar pain is experienced by symptomatic women? How might vulvar pain be treated—both socially and clinically—in a "queer"-oriented society? Can a person identify as heterosexual and still resist hegemonic sexual norms?

3. What is the role of popular and social media in strengthening and resisting social conventions? Does a news program like *20/20* have the power (or responsibility) to change public attitudes toward a condition like vulvar pain? What are the pros and cons of media that "play it safe" by using words such as *sexual* rather than *vulvar*? Should we look to other media sources for words and images that challenge the norm? What

are some of these so-called alternative media sources and what qualities make them alternative?

Class Assignments and Exercises

1. In small groups and taking the author's concerns into account, ask students to redesign the *20/20* segment about female genital pain. Have students imagine that they are the woman who posted her complaints on the social networking site: What information would they want to know? Would they be happy if the word *sexual* is simply replaced with the word *vulvar*? Would the author be happy? What new information would have to be contained in the episode in order to treat vulvar pain as both a cultural and a biomedical condition? Ask students to be specific, including images, concepts, and language. Have students outline and present this redesigned segment to the class.

2. Have students think about an embarrassing situation from their past. Then ask them, using a journal-entry format, to describe the experience of that embarrassment. What were some of the tactics they used to avoid discussing the situation? Did the situation, or their response to it, alienate them from friends or family? Was their embarrassment related to a set of social conventions that were difficult to challenge? Did they challenge them? What factors influenced their embarrassment and their ability to overcome it (if they were able to)? Without being specific about the details of their situation (unless they want to), have students discuss how they coped with it with their classmates.

3. Conduct the exercise described in the chapter. Have students write down the words they used as a child and the words they use now to describe male and female genitalia. Then present these lists to the class for discussion.

Films

Dangerous When Wet (1998)—62 minutes
> An ironic and humorous tale of a woman's first orgasm, and her difficulty in finding a language to describe the experience. Directed by Diane Bender.

The Powder Room: What Women Talk About When Men Aren't Around (1996)—50 minutes
> Documentary footage by the National Film Board of Canada from women's "private" spaces, including high school bathrooms, New York nightclubs, and senior citizens' powder rooms. A rare look into what women talk about when relatively uninhibited. Directed by Ann Kennard. Produced by Michael Allder.

Passion and Power: The Technology of Orgasm (2008)—74 minutes
> A documentary about vibrators, emphasizing their political, social, and subversive histories. Directed by Wendy Slick and Emiko Omori.

Web Resources

contexts.org/sexuality/
> A blog about sexuality and society that explores the relationships between social institutions, cultural practices, sexual health, and sexual policy. Maintained by sociologists, the site includes regular posts, an extensive resource guide, and an ongoing list of critical writing assignments that link policy, society, and sexuality.

nsrc.sfsu.edu/
> Run by the Sexuality Studies department at San Francisco State University, the National Sexuality Resource Center provides information, opinion, news analysis, and a host of links to and resources on a wide range of topics related to sex and sexuality.

www.ohsu.edu/xd/health/services/women/services/gynecology-and-obstetrics/services/vulvar-health-program/index.cfm

The website for the vulvar specialty clinic where the author conducted fieldwork. Provides resources for clinicians and patients and links to Oregon Health and Science University's Center for Women's Health, the larger center within which the clinic operates.

12. "What I Had to Do to Survive": Self-Injurers' Bodily Emotion Work

Discussion Questions

1. What were the causes of interviewees' emotional troubles? What led them to use self-injury to cope with them and what consequences did it have?
2. Have you ever known someone who engaged in self-injury in ways that had a negative effect on his or her life? How did people respond to this person? Now that you have read this chapter, how do you think people should act toward people who self-injure?
3. This chapter shows how the body can be used to shape emotional experience, a process that is called bodily emotion work. Can you think of other forms of bodily emotion work that have positive or negative consequences for one's life?

Class Assignments and Exercises

1. Ask students to think of a time in their lives when they felt overwhelmed with feelings of distress and then write a short reflection paper about their experience. What did they think about these feelings? Where did they come from? What did they do to manage or alleviate these feelings? Did these strategies work?
2. Have students read a story or watch a film clip about self-injury. How do others define this behavior? How does the self-injurer describe her or his actions? Is he or she even given a chance to speak on the subject? What does the coverage suggest about social attitudes toward self-injury? Do the students agree or disagree with these suggestions? Why?
3. If students are having trouble understanding why someone would ever engage in self-injury, have them close their eyes and think about something they are worried or stressed about, paying attention to how the stress flows through their body. Then have students hold an ice cube in their hands as it melts. How does the experience of their body and emotions change?

Films

Thirteen (2003)—1 hour, 40 minutes
   Thirteen-year-old Tracy befriends a popular girl who introduces her to drug and alcohol abuse, self-injury, and sexual experimentation. These new behaviors wreak havoc on her relationships with her family and old friends. An autobiographical film based on cowriter Nikki Reed's life. Directed by Catherine Hardwicke.
Girl, Interrupted (1999)—2 hours, 7 minutes
   A film following a teenager's eighteen-month stay at a mental institution where she meets several women with personality disorders who engage in self-harm. The film focuses on the women's diagnoses and how they cope with being in the institution. Adapted from Susanna Kaysen's memoirs. Directed by James Mangold.
In My Skin (2002)—1 hour, 33 minutes
   After an accident leaves a business woman with deep gashes on her legs, she becomes

preoccupied with her skin and addicted to cutting herself. The film features graphic scenes of self-injury. Directed by Marina De Van.

Web Resources
www.selfinjury.com/
Offers information about treatment and resources for self-injurers, their friends and families, and schools and therapists who work with them.
www.selfinjury.org/
Offers information and resources for National Self-Injury Awareness Day, a grass-roots movement seeking to educate and inform the larger population about self-injury issues.
www.firstsigns.org.uk/
A website that serves as an online community providing support resources and information for people facing self-injury issues.

13. The Politics of the Stall: Transgender and Genderqueer Workers Negotiating "the Bathroom Question"

Discussion Questions
1. How do bathroom policies affect the larger experience of work for transpeople? Of workplace opportunities? Workplace relationships? Workplace satisfaction? How do these workers' experiences illustrate social anxiety around gender transgression?
2. What does this chapter tell us about the social construction of gender? Are there other forms of "bathroom politics" that maintain inequality by race, gender, class, or sexuality?
3. What criteria do you think workplaces should use to determine bathroom policies for trans workers? Do you agree with the policy conclusions drawn by this chapter? Why or why not? What other changes might you suggest?

Class Assignments and Exercises
1. Have students draw up a list of the "pros" and "cons" of moving to unisex-only bathrooms based on the arguments of this chapter and their own concerns and observations. Using this pro/con list, ask them to write a one-paragraph policy recommendation for workplaces and present their suggestions to the class.
2. Have students record their own experiences of bathroom transgression through an experiment. Ask them to briefly walk into the "wrong" bathroom for their gender presentation and record the responses to their presence in this space. Include their own feelings about transgressing in this public space. Alternately, students can conduct a brief field observation outside a unisex bathroom. If there are unisex stalls on campus, in their workplace, or in other spaces they frequent, ask them to sit outside the bathroom and observe the norms of bathroom behavior in this space. For example, do two or more people enter the bathroom at the same time, or do people always form a line outside the door? Do men ask women to use the bathroom before them, or to use the bathroom privately? If the unisex bathroom is next to traditional "women's" and "men's" rooms, compare the frequency of use of the unisex bathroom and the single-gender bathrooms. Who uses a unisex bathroom rather than a single-gender bathroom? What conclusions about gender and gendered space do they draw from these observations?
3. Arrange for students to watch the film *Cruel and Unusual* to consider other ways that gendered institutional arrangements might discriminate against and disadvantage

transpeople. Discuss in groups the following questions: What are the key issues facing transwomen in prison? How is the spatial organization of prisons similar to those of bathrooms? What are the consequences of these divisions? How might the United States. rearrange prisons to avoid cruel and unusual punishment against transwomen?

Films
Normal (2003)—1 hour, 50 minutes

After being married for twenty-five years, a midwestern man decides to reveal to his family and friends that he wants to undergo a sex-change operation. The film shows his coworkers and church members' intolerance. But his wife begins to understand him and supports his decision. Directed by Jane Anderson and based on her play *Looking for Normal*.

Southern Comfort (2001)—1 hour, 30 minutes

A documentary about a transgender man in the Deep South who is dying from cancer in his female reproductive organs. It details his relationship with his girlfriend, his social community, and the dynamics between him and his family. Directed by Kate Davis.

Cruel and Unusual (2006)—1 hour, 10 minutes

A documentary that follows five transgender women incarcerated in men's prisons across the United States The women discuss their experiences of being denied medical and psychological treatment and how they were victimized by rape and violence. Directed by Janet Baus, Dan Hunt, and Reid Williams.

Web Resources
www.thetaskforce.org/

Founded in 1974, the National Gay and Lesbian Task Force Action Fund works toward complete equality by building the grassroots political power of the lesbian, gay, bisexual, and transgender (LGBT) community. The site features their positions on issues, fact sheets, and reports on issues affecting the LGBT community.

www.outandequal.org/

Out and Equal Workplace Advocates champions safe and equitable workplaces for LGBT employees. They are the largest national nonprofit organization working toward workplace equality for the LGBT community.

www.nclrights.org/site/PageServer?pagename=issue_employment

The National Center for Lesbian Rights is a national legal organization committed to advancing the civil and human rights of LGBT people and their families through litigation, public policy advocacy, and public education.

14. The Everyday Resistance of Vegetarianism

Discussion Questions
1. Aside from adopting vegetarianism, how do individuals turn to food consumption to protest hegemonic structures? Also, what are other means of protesting these structures through "not doing" the norm? Are these effective forms of protest and resistance?
2. How do individuals use food to do identity work and to distinguish themselves from others? Consider the man who criticizes his coworker for eating Velveeta and American cheese, indicating that he prefers imported Camembert. Or consider the woman who,

on a first date, refuses to order the salad entrée, choosing instead the twelve-ounce T-bone steak.

3. Does vegetarianism have special meaning for women, racial and ethnic minorities, individuals who identify as GLBTQ (gay, lesbian, bisexual, transgender, and queer), and other minorities? Why or why not? How do political ideologies cluster? Do similar ideologies always come in "political packages" producing coherent identities? If vegetarianism is associated with resisting hegemonic structures, how might one explain the secular vegetarian practices of individuals who do not resist dominant ideologies?

Class Assignments and Exercises

1. Ask students to interview a secular vegetarian. In these interviews, encourage students to explore in-depth why this individual converted to vegetarianism, along with any related issues of political identity and resistance. Discuss as a class the findings of these interviews.
2. Ask students to write a journal entry about the foods they eat, beginning with a list of the foods they consumed in twenty-four hours. They should then address: Why did they eat these foods? Was there a political consciousness to their food consumption? Why or why not?
3. If there is a vegetarian restaurant in the city, ask students to conduct a participation observation study by eating at this restaurant (preferably during peak hours) and documenting their observations, addressing, among other questions: Who is here? What are they wearing? What is on the menu? What is the décor in the restaurant?

Films

Meat the Truth (2008)—1 hour, 13 minutes

Examines scientific information on climate change and livestock farming. Directed by Karen Soeters and Gertjan Zwanikken.

Food Inc. (2008)—1 hour, 34 minutes

Demonstrates how America's food supply is controlled by a few corporations that prioritize profit over consumer health, farmer livelihood, and the safety of food workers. Directed by Robert Kenner.

Truth or Dairy (1994)—23 minutes

"A vegan is as an old hippy who wears sandals, eats nothing but lentils and lives on his own, probably in a hut," right? A film that explores the truths behind the myths of veganism. Directed by Benjamin Zephaniah.

Web Resources

www.vrg.org/

A website about vegetarianism and related issues of health, environment, and ethics.

www.themeatrix.com/

A website about sustainable food and problems with factory farming.

www.foodispower.org/

The website of the Food Empowerment Project, which attempts to build, for communities of color and low-income communities, access to healthful fruits and vegetables, along with alternatives to meat and dairy products.

15. Menopausal and Misbehaving:
When Women "Flash" in Front of Others

Discussion Questions

1. Do you know anyone who is menopausal? If not or if so, how do you know (i.e., what has signified her menopausal status to you)? Discuss the visibility of menopause within your experience. How visible has this reproductive transition been to you, and why?

2. This chapter implies that bodily symptoms are always negative, at least when occurring in front of (or visible to) others. Do you agree? Why or why not? Do you think men and women experience bodily signs or symptoms, to some degree, negatively?

3. Think about ways in which you try every day to mask, control, embrace, highlight, or fight for your body. Select one of these ways and describe a situation in which you did this. Is this an example of accommodation or resistance or both, and why? What made you do this? Have you always done this? Do you think you will always do this? Why or why not? (And why did you use this particular example?)

Classroom Assignments and Exercises

1. Even though this chapter is about menopausal women's experiences with hot flashes, it is really an exploration of individuals' experiences with bodily signs and symptoms. Ask students to think about their experience of bodily signs and symptoms. Ask them to: (1) Define and discuss a time when or situation within which their body or someone else's body did something in public that it was not supposed to do. (2) Describe at least one cultural norm that was broken by this "misbehaving" body. (Be sure to have students define the norm before describing how it was broken.) (3) Explain the outcome of the situation, by highlighting how they or the person experiencing the misbehaving body acted, as well as how others reacted. (4) Decide whether accommodation or resistance to cultural norms (or both) took place. Have students discuss these issues in a personal reflection paper or in small groups.

2. Encourage students to think about another bodily sign or symptom besides hot flashes (e.g., pain, acne, loss or growth of bodily hair, burping, farting, sweating related to athletic activity, weight gain or loss, bleeding, coughing, slurred speech, stuttering). Ask them to complete a literature review on this symptom to determine: (1) why this sign or symptom occurs physiologically, (2) how or whether it might be treated medically, and (3) whether it is normally occurring (and even representative of "health") or whether it is seen as a representation of sickness. Finally, have students assess attitudes about this sign or symptom and do an in-class presentation on their final draft.

3. Have students select a cultural norm that they think affects bodily experience (e.g., a beauty norm, a norm about bodily control, an age-based norm, a racial norm, a norm about motherhood, a norm about sickness) and write a paper about resistance and this cultural norm. In this paper they should: (1) define and discuss the norm, highlighting its possible origins and history (as well as whether and how it has changed), (2) outline the effect of this norm on individuals' bodily experiences, (3) describe historical resistance to this norm, and (4) discuss whether resistance to this norm is widespread and how this norm has affected their own bodily experiences.

Films

"End of the Curse," *Golden Girls* (1986 [Season 2, Episode 1])—30 minutes

In this episode of *Golden Girls*, Blanche is horrified when she thinks she is pregnant and learns that she is actually going through menopause. Her roommates try to convince her that menopause is not a big deal. Directed by Terry Hughes.

Streetcar Named Perspire (2007)—7 minutes

A short animated film that portrays the "rollercoaster ride" of menopause and depicts its signs and symptoms. Directed by Joanna Priestley.

Calendar Girls (2003)—1 hour, 48 minutes

A British comedy about a group of middle-aged women who decide to pose naked for a calendar, in honor of the husband of one of them. While not explicitly about menopause, this movie highlights women's perceptions and experiences of their aging physical bodies. Directed by Nigel Cole.

Web Resources

menstruationresearch.org/

The Society for Menstrual Cycle Research is made up of academic researchers, health care providers, policy makers, health activists, artists, and students who are interested in the role of the menstrual cycle in women's health and well-being. The site provides links to helpful resources, information for instructors, and an excellent blog called re:Cycling that focuses on women's health news.

www.minniepauz.com/

The website Minnie Pauz, "The Rebel with the Pauz," offers information about menopause with a humorous slant and provides an entertaining forum for women who are going through menopause. The site also includes cartoons, videos, a blog, a book club, a newsletter, and medical information about menopause.

www.menopause.org/

The official website for the North American Menopause Society, an interdisciplinary nonprofit organization that works to improve women's lives through an understanding of menopause. The site offers information about menopause for consumers and practitioners.

16. The Transformation of Bodily Practices among Religious Defectors

Discussion Questions

1. What bodily practices do your religious or cultural traditions prescribe? How do you feel about them? Is observing these bodily practices necessary to be considered part of this religious or cultural group?

2. Have you ever resisted these bodily practices that are part of your religious or cultural traditions? What happened? How did resisting them make you feel? How did others react?

3. Is something resistance when no one knows that a norm is being challenged? Reflect on Rachel's experience of consuming a bacon, lettuce, and tomato sandwich in a shopping center where nobody knows her. Is this resistance? Why or why not?

Class Assignments and Exercises

1. Have students make a collage of pictures that they think represents the bodily practices that other people expect of them. Students should then explain to the class what these pictures represent and compare their collages to those made by other students. How are they similar? How are they different?

2. Ask students to choose a religious or cultural group that is different from their own and learn about the bodily practices of this group. They should gather information by reading about these groups and, if feasible, by talking to group members. They should then write a short reflection paper about this new group, their bodily practices, and how group members might embody resistance.

3. Ask students to write a short reflection paper about their bodily practices. Use the following questions as a guideline: What is significant about these practices? Why do you observe them? What would happen if you decided to change or stop performing these bodily practices?

Films

A Life Apart: Hasidism in America (1998)—1 hour, 30 minutes

> This PBS documentary explores the history, daily life, and beliefs of contemporary Hasidic Jews in New York City. It features interviews with members of the community and commentary by scholars. Film website: *www.pbs.org/alifeapart/*. Directed by Menachem Daum and Oren Rudavsky.

The Chosen (1981)—1 hour, 48 minutes

> A film about the love and friendship of two Jewish boys in 1940s Brooklyn. Danny is Hassidic and Reuven is a Zionist, but they are drawn together through a common interest in baseball. Based on a novel by Chaim Potok. Directed by Jeremy Kagan.

Trembling before G-d (2001)—1 hour, 24 minutes

> This documentary is about gay Hasidic and Orthodox Jews and how they reconcile their sexuality with their religion. Film website: *www.filmsthatchangetheworld.com/site/*. Directed by Sandi Simcha DuBowski.

Web Resources

www.hasidicstories.com/

> This website features a collection of Hasidic stories from various rabbis and authorities on Hasidic narratives. The site also includes articles on the background of Hasidic stories and articles about Hasidic storytelling.

www.orthogays.org/

> This website provides information for gay Orthodox Jews on how they can be both gay and religiously observant Jews. The site features an extensive FAQ section and quotations from rabbis who have spoken out about gay Orthodox Jews.

www.myjewishlearning.com/

> This site provides an introduction to Judaism and information about Jewish beliefs, rituals, cuisine, and music. It also has extensive sections on Jewish holidays, texts, history, and ethics.

Contributors

Catherine Bergart has been writing professionally for over twenty-five years. Her personal essays have been published in the *New York Times*, *Marie Claire*, and a variety of literary journals, including *Bellevue Literary Review*, *mrbellersneighborhood.com*, and *Gander Press Review*. One of her pieces was listed as a Notable Essay in *The Best American Essays*. She has been married for fourteen years to Ed, a man who happens to be quadriplegic.

Samantha Binford is a sophomore and an Honor's College student at the University of Houston majoring in biology with a minor in Spanish. She is actively involved in several organizations on campus and hopes to pursue a career in the medical field.

Hanne Blank is a writer and historian whose books include the first edition (Emeryville, CA: Greenery Press, 2000) and updated second edition (Berkeley: Ten Speed Press, 2011) of *Big Big Love: A Sourcebook on Sex for People of Size and Those Who Love Them*; *Virgin: The Untouched History* (New York: Bloomsbury, 2007); and *Straight: A History of Heterosexuality* (Boston: Beacon Press, forthcoming). Former Scholar of the Institute at the Institute for Teaching and Research on Women, Towson University, she lives in Baltimore, Maryland.

Chris Bobel is an associate professor of women's studies at the University of Massachusetts, Boston, where she teaches gender and the body, feminist research methods, and feminist theory. She is the author of *The Paradox of Natural Mothering* (Philadelphia: Temple University Press, 2001) and *New Blood: Third Wave Feminism and the Politics of Menstruation* (New Brunswick, NJ: Rutgers University Press, 2010).

Elizabeth Cherry is an assistant professor of sociology at Manhattanville College, where she teaches social movements, youth subcultures, and environmental sociology. Her research centers on cultural analyses of social movements and social movement analyses of contentious subcultures. Her work on veganism as a cultural movement was published in *Social Movement Studies*, and her research on animal rights activists' strategies for changing cultural structures recently appeared in *Sociological Forum*.

Hae Yeon Choo is an assistant professor of sociology at the University of Toronto. Her research engages the issues of gender/sexuality, citizenship, and migration, and her work has been published in *Gender and Society* and *Sociological Theory*. She has translated the work of Judith Butler and Patricia Hill Collins into Korean.

Catherine Connell is an assistant professor of sociology at Boston University. She received her Ph.D. from the University of Texas at Austin in May 2010. She received the 2009 ASA Sally Hacker Award and the 2009 Sociologists for Women in Society Cheryl Allyn Miller Award for her master's thesis research on transgender employees. She has published articles on transgender employment issues in *Gender and Society* and *Gender, Work, and Organization*. Her more recent work examines the employment experiences of gay and lesbian teachers in Texas and California.

Sara L. Crawley is an associate professor of sociology at the University of South Florida, where she teaches sociology and women's studies on topics of social and feminist theory, gender, sexualities, and bodies. A big fan of autoethnography, she is the author of several articles on heteronormativity, sexualities, embodiment, and pedagogy, as well as the coauthor (with Lara J. Foley and Constance L. Shehan) of *Gendering Bodies*, part of the Gender Lens Series (Lanham, MD: Rowman and Littlefield, 2008).

Lynn Davidman is the Robert M. Beren Distinguished Professor of Modern Jewish Studies and a professor of sociology at the University of Kansas. Her first book, *Tradition in a Rootless World: Women Turn to Orthodoxy* (Berkeley: University of California Press, 1990), won a national book award and has become a classic in the field. Her other books include *Motherloss* (Berkeley: University of California Press, 2000) and *Feminist Perspectives on Jewish Studies*, edited with Shelly Tenenbaum (New Haven, CT: Yale University Press, 1996). She is currently completing a book on religious defection, *Tears in the Sacred Canopy: On Leaving Orthodox Judaism*.

Denise A. Delgado received a B.A. in women's studies and psychology from Arizona State University. She is currently a Ph.D. student in The Ohio State University's women's studies program, and her research focuses on Latina and African American representation in popular culture and the politics of passing.

Heather E. Dillaway is an associate professor and director of graduate studies in sociology at Wayne State University. Her broad research interests lie within the study of women's health and structural inequalities (age, gender, race, class, and sexuality). Her primary research project focuses on women's experiences of menopause and midlife. Her most recent work is published in *Journal of Women and Aging, Journal of Family Issues, Healthcare for Women International, Women and Health*, and *Journal of Applied Gerontology*.

Breanne Fahs is an assistant professor of women's studies at Arizona State University. She has a Ph.D. in women's studies and clinical psychology from the University of Michigan (2006) and currently holds a faculty appointment at Arizona State University while also working as a private practice clinical psychologist in Avondale, Arizona. She has published articles on women's sexuality, the politicizing effects of divorce, and radical feminist histories in several journals, including *Feminist Studies, Frontiers, Journal of Divorce and Remarriage*, and *Sexualities*.

Angela Horn is a certified birth doula, founder of Birth Renaissance, and central coordinator for Desert Doula Birth and Postpartum Services in Tucson, Arizona. In practice for more than ten years, she has served over one hundred families in their birth journeys. She has assisted with home births, unmedicated and medicated hospital births, inductions/augmentations, vaginal birth after cesarean, and emergency and unplanned cesarean sections. She is a proud mother of three and has been married for sixteen years.

Barbara Katz Rothman is a professor of sociology at the City University of New York. She holds visiting professorships in the International Midwifery Preparation Program at Ryerson University in Toronto, the Charité Hospital and Medical School in Berlin, and the University of Plymouth in the United Kingdom. Her books include *In Labor: Women and Power in the Birthplace* (New York: W. W. Norton, 1991), *The Tentative Pregnancy: Prenatal Diagnosis and the Future of Motherhood* (New York: Viking, 1986), *Recreating Motherhood* (New Brunswick, NJ: Rutgers University Press, 2000), *The Book of Life* (Boston: Beacon Press, 2001), *Weaving a Family: Untangling Race and Adoption* (Boston: Beacon Press, 2005), and, with Wendy Simonds and Bari Meltzer Norman, *Laboring On: Birth in Transition in the United States* (New York: Routledge, 2007).

Noa Logan Klein, Ph.D., is currently a lecturer in the Department of Sociology at the University of California, Santa Barbara and is working on a book entitled *Loving Touch: Therapeutic Massage, the Socialization of the Body, and the Healing of U.S. Culture.*

Samantha Kwan is an assistant professor of sociology and a women's studies faculty affiliate at the University of Houston, where she teaches the sociology of the body, the sociology of gender, and research methods. She conducts research in the areas of gender, body, health, and culture, focusing on how cultural and social structures shape women's physical and emotional well-being. Her most recent work appears in *Feminist Formations, Sociological Inquiry, Teaching Sociology,* and *Qualitative Health Research.*

Christine Labuski is a visiting professor in the Department of Anthropology at the University of Arkansas. She teaches and conducts research on female sexuality, sexual difference, and the role of culture in shaping the physical body. Her most recent article "Out of the Comfort Zone: Why Vulvar Reluctance is a Feminist Issue" was recently published in *Feminist Studies.*

Margaret Leaf is a research analyst in Madison, Wisconsin. She received her M.S. from Florida State University in 2006. Her thesis on self-injurers won the 2006 Blumer Award from the Society for the Study of Symbolic Interaction.

Esther Morris Leidolf is a medical sociologist who founded the MRKH Organization (*www.mrkh.org*) to increase awareness and share resources for women with Mayer-Rokitansky-Kuster-Hauser syndrome. Her writing has appeared in *Sojourner, Our Bodies Ourselves* (2005 and 2011 editions), *Journal of Gay and Lesbian Psychotherapy, Journal of Homosexuality, Broadside,* and *The New Internationalist.* She has appeared on GenderVision (*www.gendervision.org*) and speaks regularly at colleges and universities in the Boston area. She cofounded the Intersex Collective (*www.intersexcollective.org*) and cofacilitates for MRKH conferences at Children's Hospital, Boston.

Danielle J. Lindemann received her Ph.D. in sociology from Columbia University in

May 2010. She has published work on topics ranging from sex-toy legislation in the United States to arguments against pornography in Atlanta, Georgia. She is currently a postdoctoral research scholar at Columbia's Institute for Social and Economic Research and Policy. She is working on a book about the interactions between professional dominatrices and their clients in New York City and San Francisco.

David Linton is professor of communication arts at Marymount Manhattan College in New York City. His previous scholarship has included studies of the media environment of Elizabethan England and Shakespeare's plays, the reading behavior of the Virgin Mary as depicted in paintings and sculpture, film criticism, media education, and the history of the Luddite movement. He has published several essays on the social construction of menstruation and teaches an interdisciplinary course on the subject. He is currently completing a book titled *MENstruation: A New Perspective on the Period*.

Annette Lynch is a professor at the University of Northern Iowa. Her research interests include the cultural construction and transformation of gender through dress and the use of dress to manage stigmatized identity. She is the author of three books published by Berg (Oxford): *Dress, Gender, and Cultural Change: Asian American and African American Rites of Passage* (1999); *Changing Fashion: A Critical Introduction to Trend Analysis and Meaning* (2007); and *Porn Chic: Exploring the Contours of Raunch Eroticism* (2011).

Lydia K. Manning is a doctoral candidate in the social gerontology program at Miami University, Oxford, Ohio. She holds a master of gerontological studies degree from Miami University. She is passionate about improving the lives of older adults. Her research interests include exploring spirituality within the context of gender and age.

Angela M. Moe is an associate professor of sociology and a gender and women's studies affiliate at Western Michigan University, where she teaches courses on gender, justice, family, and research methods. Her lines of research involve women, victimization, and justice, as well as gender, the body, performance, and healing. Her most recent work appears in *Violence against Women, Affilia,* and *Women and Criminal Justice.*

Tari Youngjung Na is a member of the Policy Committee and Sexuality Politics Committee of the New Progressive Party in South Korea. Since undertaking her research on female-to-male transgenders in 2006, she has engaged in transgender and gender justice activism in South Korea and has participated in WIG, the Queer Cultural Theory Research Circle.

Natalie M. Peluso is an assistant professor of sociology at Concordia College in Moorhead, Minnesota. Her research and teaching interests include the sociology of gender, sexualities, and the body.

Nathaniel C. Pyle is a doctoral candidate in sociology at the University of California, Santa Barbara. His research interests are fat studies, queer communities, live music communities, and social movement studies. He lives in San Francisco with his partner, Michael Loewy, with whom he has written an article about fat gay men and their admirers published in *The Fat Studies Reader* (New York: New York University Press, 2009). He is a proud fat admirer and fat activist.

M. Elise Radina is an associate professor of family studies at Miami University in Oxford, Ohio. Her research focuses on perceived changes in family/relationship quality of life following breast cancer from the perspectives of multiple family members, changes in family life resulting from breast-cancer related lymphedema, the role of the Red Hat Society in the lives of older women, and the experiences of ethnically diverse families with regard to illness and care giving. Her work has been published in *Family Relations*, *Journal of Contemporary Ethnography*, *Sociological Perspectives*, and *Journal of Women and Aging*.

Jennifer A. Reich is an associate professor of sociology and criminology at the University of Denver. Her research explores the intersections between the state and family. She is the author of *Fixing Families: Parents, Power, and the Child Welfare System* (New York: Routledge, 2005) and several articles and book chapters about reproductive decision making, multiracial families, the child welfare system, service providers and evacuees from Hurricane Katrina, parents' decisions about vaccination, and qualitative methods.

Abigail Richardson is an assistant professor of sociology at Mesa State College in Grand Junction, Colorado, where she teaches social inequality, research methods, health and illness, and sociology of the body. Her research interests involve qualitative investigations of the body, health, and culture. Her current project focuses on the meanings and practices associated with healthy eating and dieting. Other current projects focus on conducting community-based research with undergraduate students.

Louise Marie Roth is an associate professor of sociology at the University of Arizona, where she teaches sociology of gender and families in society. She conducts research on gender, family, and organizations. Her recent publications include *Selling Women Short: Gender Inequality on Wall Street* (Princeton, NJ: Princeton University Press, 2006) and an article on the gender gap in religiosity in *American Sociological Review*. Her current research examines how health insurance, liability insurance, and malpractice law influence childbirth.

Douglas P. Schrock is an associate professor of sociology at Florida State University. His work focuses on how identity, emotion, and the body play a role in reproducing and challenging inequalities.

Marybeth C. Stalp is an associate professor of sociology at the University of Northern Iowa. She received her B.A. from Regis University, her M.A. from Southern Illinois University at Carbondale, and her Ph.D. from the University of Georgia. Her research centers on the intersections of gender, culture, and leisure; and she writes about women quilters, Red Hat Society members, and artists. She is currently the coeditor of the *Journal of Contemporary Ethnography*.

J. Edward Sumerau is a graduate student in the Department of Sociology at Florida State University. His research explores intersections of gender, sexuality, and religion.

Beverly Yuen Thompson is an assistant professor of sociology at Siena College in Albany, New York, where she teaches sociology of the family and sociological perspectives. She recently completed a documentary about women and tattooing entitled *Covered*.

Rose Weitz is a professor of women and gender studies at Arizona State University. She is the author of two monographs, *Life with AIDS* (New Brunswick, NJ: Rutgers University Press, 1991), and *Rapunzel's Daughters: What Women's Hair Tells Us about Women's Lives* (New York: Farrar, Straus, and Giroux, 2004), and, with Deborah A. Sullivan, the coauthor of *Labor Pains: Modern Midwives and Home Birth* (New Haven, CT: Yale University Press, 1988). She is also the editor of *The Politics of Women's Bodies: Appearance, Sexuality, and Behavior* (New York: Oxford University Press, 2010), now in its third edition. Her most recent article addresses midlife women's sexuality in film.

Index

Page numbers in bold refer to illustrations.